Here's what readers have loved

'Suc... ...losing hope.'
...Amazon customer

'So poignant it has left me speechless.'
Amazon customer

'As a reader this book takes you through a whole wide range of emotions. You also find yourself asking how could no-one have known of this poor, innocent child's existence.'
Sandra R

'What makes this book is her constant hope for a better life and, now she is free, to be able to help others. She certainly reminded me of the beauty of freedom and the privilege of being able to make choices.'
Calzean J

'What a brave young woman to have lived through this most cruel of times and then to re-live all the details which I am sure she would rather forget.'
Colette M

the girl in the shadows

MY LIFE IN A CULT

Held captive and
brainwashed for thirty years,
I never gave up hope.

KATY MORGAN-DAVIES

WITH KATE MOORE

CORGI BOOKS

TRANSWORLD PUBLISHERS
61–63 Uxbridge Road, London W5 5SA
www.penguin.co.uk

Transworld is part of the Penguin Random House group of companies
whose addresses can be found at global.penguinrandomhouse.com

Penguin
Random House
UK

First published as *Caged Bird* in Great Britain
in 2018 by Bantam Press
an imprint of Transworld Publishers
Corgi edition published as *The Girl in the Shadows* 2019

Copyright © Katy Morgan-Davies 2018

Katy Morgan-Davies has asserted her right under the Copyright,
Designs and Patents Act 1988 to be identified as the author of this work.

Every effort has been made to obtain the necessary permissions with
reference to copyright material, both illustrative and quoted. We apologize
for any omissions in this respect and will be pleased to make the
appropriate acknowledgements in any future edition.

A CIP catalogue record for this book
is available from the British Library.

ISBN 9780552174893

Typeset in 10.44/12.2pt Bembo by Jouve (UK), Milton Keynes.
Printed and bound in Great Britain by Clays Ltd, Elcograf S.p.A.

Penguin Random House is committed to a sustainable future
for our business, our readers and our planet. This book is made
from Forest Stewardship Council® certified paper.

FSC
www.fsc.org
MIX
Paper from
responsible sources
FSC® C018179

1 3 5 7 9 10 8 6 4 2

For you who have helped me find my wings.
You know who you are.

Author's Note

Although everything in this book is true, and much of it a matter of public record, I have changed some names, physical descriptions and locations so as to protect the anonymity of some of those involved. With Leanne and Cindy, this is a legal requirement given the nature of their evidence in court, but with others it is to respect their privacy, something that was never afforded to me.

Contents

From childhood's hour I have not been
As others were — I have not seen
As others saw — I could not bring
My passions from a common spring —
From the same source I have not taken
My sorrow — I could not awaken
My heart to joy at the same tone —
And all I lov'd — I lov'd alone.

'Alone', Edgar Allan Poe

Prologue

Cries were emanating from the baby's crib, but none of those gathered round it moved to comfort. They had eyes only for the single man among them.

With reverence, they stared at him, eyes shining not with happiness but awe. They trembled in his presence, bodies alert, ready to serve him better. Not a word crossed their lips: they waited instead for him to speak.

Still the child cried: disrespectful. Irritated, the man seized the cot and shook it roughly. Silence fell. He opened his mouth to fill the void.

'This child,' he began in his commanding voice, looking down into the cot, seeing far into the future, 'will be my worst enemy.'

Part One
Faith

1

I love Beloved Comrade Bala

I carefully finished shaping the curve of the 'a', my three-year-old hand clasped tightly around the pencil, and sat back on the cushion on my chair. These were the first words I had ever written.

Although, secretly, I was pleased with myself, I didn't glance up at the comrade teaching me for praise: the achievement wasn't mine, it was thanks to Comrade Bala, and it would be self-love to think otherwise.

Bala was the star of our lives; the only person in the world who could be praised. That was why the comrades were teaching me to write, so I could celebrate him using the written word. I would no more have written my own name – Prem Maopinduzi – on the paper than I would a swear word; the actions were comparable.

Writing was a way of life in our house – people wrote reports and rotas all the time, and comrades often had to write things down rather than saying them aloud, in case fascist agents were listening – so it was a thrill for me to learn, especially because I'd always loved words; I felt as if I'd been born reading. Yet Comrade Josie soon corrected the angle of my letters. My words sloped backwards, which meant I was backwards too. My handwriting had to be just like Bala's: anything else was a sign of revolt.

Beloved Comrade Bala's full name was Aravindan Balakrishnan; we also called him AB. He lived with me and six adult comrades – Josie, Sian, Aisha, Leanne, Cindy and Oh – leading our Communist Collective (CC) in south London, which at that time was called the Workers' Institute of Marxism Leninism Mao Zedong Thought. AB's wife, Comrade Chanda, and her disabled sister Shobha also shared our home, but as a small child I saw very little of them. Cindy and Leanne were marginal figures in my life too because they went

5

Outside to work, earning Big Units for AB's CC. The rest of us, me included, spent our time working for AB: our lives were dedicated to his service.

His standing could be gauged in our united deference to him. We stood up when he entered a room; always said 'hello' if we passed him in the corridor; offered him the first helping of whatever food was being served. We could not enter his room without knocking and awaiting a response, and were required to face him when in his presence, making continuous, unbroken eye contact as a sign of our respect. Comrade Bala was a *very* important man. He may have looked rather ordinary – 5 foot 3, black curly hair and brown skin, his dark eyes framed by thick square glasses – but that was an illusion.

Comrade Bala was the future leader of the world.

Presently, he was in a kind of exile, with just us comrades as acolytes, but his was the new world in the making. One day, when his covert leadership became Overt, he would overthrow all governments and assume his rightful role.

Every day I was told how lucky I was to be the first child of AB's new world. The comrades would exclaim how jealous they were because I had none of the disadvantages of the old world – such as family or friends. Unlike the comrades, I had no parents. I was told that, on 7 January 1983, I had 'jumped on to Comrade Bala's hand', and ever since then experienced the benefits of his sole influence. Although all members of the Collective participated in my 'controlled development', it was AB to whom I was promised; AB for whom I had to build a temple inside myself: my self *was* AB's. The nature of my upbringing was dubbed Project Prem: a blueprint for how all children would be raised in future.

Yet for all the advantages of my pioneering life – in fact, because of them – I was also in great danger.

'Comrade Prem!' I heard time and again, as a comrade hissed or shouted at me in alarm. 'Don't look out of the window!'

For if I looked out of the window, someone Outside might see me. The current governments, I was told, would stop at nothing to prevent AB from overthrowing them. The evil British Fascist State (BFS) was obsessed with finding him and preventing his leadership from becoming Overt, and kidnapping and killing me would strike a blow at the heart of AB's new world. So, in our terraced house on a tree-lined street in suburban south London, we operated in a constant state of war.

I was never allowed to be alone, for my own protection. Comrades accompanied me everywhere, taking turns to lie beside me in bed or stand guard in the bathroom as I went to the toilet. I could not set foot outside the house without a minder, even – or especially – to the back garden, for the neighbours living beside us were the very agents we feared most. What opportunity they had to snatch me! I was told that the Collective had once looked after another child, Eddie, whose destiny was in his name: Ed-DIE. He'd climbed over the wall in the garden, was taken by the ugly dirty white neighbours and killed. If I didn't want to meet the same fate, I was not to look over the wall or wave or talk to anyone Outside.

'Under no circumstances should anybody ever come into the house and breach the defences of the Collective.' This was perhaps the most sacrosanct of AB's many guidelines for how we should live – and it was taken seriously. The front door was rarely opened; comrades would shout through it instead and tell people to go away. I was warned not to go near the telephone, for fear enemies might send waves through it to harm me. If ever I happened to be close to the phone when a call came in, I was instantly hushed: a child's voice in the background would alert fascist agents to my presence; the Collective didn't want anybody to know I was in the house.

From birth, I knew I was something to be hidden. The comrades told me that was because I was so special and precious and lucky . . . but I didn't *feel* lucky.

I felt scared.

It was terrifying, knowing that everyone Outside was an enemy and the only people I could trust were the few comrades in the house. I had nightmares about the fascist agents surrounding us: faceless figures in black suits and hooded masks. When they lifted those masks in my dreams, they had the faces of our next-door neighbours.

Sometimes, those neighbours were shameless in revealing their monitoring of our lives: 'I haven't seen him for a while,' a neighbour once remarked to Comrade Sian of me – believing I was a boy from my masculine clothes and haircut – when to protect me the comrades had kept me indoors for several weeks. As time went on, AB decided the best method of protection would be to let me go out as infrequently as possible: the risk was simply too great.

Shut inside, I felt the enticement of the windows deeply. Though I knew it was dangerous, I was nevertheless drawn towards the natural light that poured through the net curtains. Despite my fear of Outside, I still wanted to see it. I think I had a natural curiosity, but I wasn't stupid. If I dared draw near to a window – keeping a close eye on whichever comrade was minding me, in case they spotted my transgression – I was always careful to avoid being seen by anyone Outside.

I had opportunity only to sneak peeks. But I was glad I did. To see all the people Outside walking past our house, on their way to destinations I could not imagine, in clothes that seemed so colourful compared to those worn in the house, seemed almost magical. There were Indian people like AB and Chanda, black people, and ugly dirty whites. Despite what I was told, I thought they *all* seemed nice. It was hard not to like the sight of people laughing and talking as they strolled along.

Laughing was banned in the CC. I was disappointed, because I had a natural sense of humour with a fondness for pranks, but I wasn't permitted to say silly things, fantasize or giggle. Talking was frowned upon generally: AB said if something was important, write it down and KQ (Keep Quiet). He'd hook a finger to his ear or shape his hands into binoculars to remind me fascist agents were always keeping tabs. Mealtimes were held in silence, 'no talking when eating'; we'd have to sit like statues round the table instead.

In contrast, Outside seemed . . . freer, somehow. People threw their heads back and roared with laughter or smiled easily at one another. Standing behind the net curtain, behind the safety of the glass, I felt a peculiar emotion, given all I'd been told.

I felt sad that I wasn't a part of it.

One day, when I was three, I watched a white family ambling along. They seemed so happy and their joy touched my heart. Unthinkingly, I shared my thoughts aloud: 'I like ugly dirty whites,' I announced.

'WHAT did you say?' AB's voice was loud and aggressive, and I felt my stomach clench, as it always did when he roared.

In a flash, he was across the room and beside me. He could move so suddenly; it always took me by surprise. I risked a look up at him and his face was dark, dark like a thundercloud.

Though the danger was Outside – or so I'd been told – I felt suddenly fearful . . . of *him*. For his eyes were ringed red and burned like black coals flaming with rage. Before I could speak, before I could move, his hand was upon me, beating his guidance into me with unstoppable force.

I cried out with the pain – but not with surprise. I'd been looking Outside; I'd said I liked ugly dirty whites, whom AB abhorred. My words had been a direct violation of AB's guidelines, which was the worst thing anyone could do. If ever I liked something he didn't, it was going against him – whether it was a person or a piece of fruit. (Once, I gagged on a raw persimmon and threw up; Comrade Sian was so horrified at my disrespect for AB's favourite fruit she fed my vomit back to me, telling me all the while how ungrateful I was.) 'AB knows everything,' I was told repeatedly. His opinion was always correct and you couldn't ever offer an opposing view. 'Two plus two equals four,' he would say contentedly, meaning his assessments were as irrefutable as arithmetic.

I cowered under his hands as he beat me black and blue. Though I was only three, I knew my age was no protection. I was no innocent. As Bala told me almost every week, I had fallen from grace when I was eighteen months old: he'd been holding me and I'd wanted to be put down, so I'd wriggled in his arms, flailing, and struck him as I did so. He hit me all over my body in return, to teach me 'don't ever show anger towards Bala'.

He wasn't being cruel, in beating me: he was being kind. It was for my own good. That's what the comrades told me: AB was saving me through beating me; hands-on medicine to make me well. As a little girl, I thought it necessary. 'Love is a practical thing,' AB pronounced – the beatings were a sign of how much he cared; my discoloured bruises marks of love. When he beat me, he called it a Good Struggle, as he battled against my internal negative forces to put me on the rightful path towards the ways of the new world.

Violence dominated my earliest memories – and not just against me. For my fellow comrades also had to follow AB's guidelines, and they often needed to be taught lessons too. I remember seeing Sian thrown down on to the sofa by the force of his blows; him pulling

Cindy towards him so hard that all the buttons pinged off her purple blouse; Oh's face squashed beneath his big black boot; thick trails of blood trickling from countless noses and ears over the years. The worst, for me, was seeing Comrade Aisha beaten, because she was a tiny woman, only 4 foot 8, and she seemed so defenceless. I remember flinching when Bala hit her, unable to watch.

Though I was told it was necessary, and no one else seemed alarmed, I found the violence terrifying. There would be horrific screaming and shouting and then the beatings would begin. I never intervened – what could I do? I used to hide away, try to make myself as invisible to the Collective as I was to the Outside. Once, one of the cult members intervened when AB was beating Sian, but he just flung her off and beat Sian ten times harder for her interference. After that, no one ever stepped in or spoke up for anyone else. We'd all just stand in a circle and watch.

In truth, the likelihood of a comrade leaping to another's defence was remote anyway because most of the beatings arose precisely because someone had reported. Everyone kept a hawk's eye on everyone else in case of any tiny transgression, and if one occurred the comrades would eagerly write down their colleague's misdemeanour or have a quiet word in AB's ear; sometimes somebody would haplessly share a secret and the information would go straight back to Bala. I saw a terrible jealousy between the women, a desire to prove that they were AB's most loyal follower, so each one was always trying to put the others down to get herself higher on his list of favourites.

To my unlearned eyes their behaviour seemed ugly, but AB seemed to think it noble. The truth was that everybody disliked everybody else, and everybody was scared of everybody else, and if ever two people happened to get along it was for the sole purpose of putting down a third. Yet if two comrades ever seemed the least bit friendly towards one another, AB would declare they were forming 'an anti-party clique' and abruptly issue punishment for not focusing solely on him. It was a house full of hate.

Whenever AB beat us, he would be frenzied, vile and violent. 'Twenty-one beats,' he might spit out, 'seventeen more to come.' Yet despite his sadistic pleasure, the understanding within the Collective was that *we* had pushed this gentle, good man to rage because we had done unspeakable things. The comrades, to my mind, seemed thankful to be hit; Aisha kept murmuring, 'Yes, yes, yes!' I only ever remember Oh talking back to him, unexpectedly defending herself against whichever charge had been brought: an absolute no-no because AB was judge, jury and executioner and no mercy would be given. Secretly, very secretly, I admired her for having an independent mind – but she was always crushed in the end.

Any transgression could incur a punishment. Making noise; being drowsy in the morning; praising another comrade if you liked her hair. One of the most difficult things about living in the Collective was that the rules could change instantly, so something that was allowed one day was anathema the next. It made me worried sick; there was no contentment or peace for a moment. If I'd been beaten wearing a particular outfit, I'd try to avoid wearing the same shirt and trousers again; I felt the clothes were cursed and I might be hurt if I wore them.

But despite my superstitious efforts, I was beaten all the time; sometimes with his hands, on other occasions with a ruler or the huge wooden broom that was used to sweep the patio. Every now and then, he even made me beat myself, taking hold of my little hand and forcing it brutally into my face. Yet the most humiliating punishment was when AB took off his slipper and hit me with it; a way of displaying his contempt for me. 'You're not worth the dirt on my shoe!' he would sneer. Or, another favourite: 'You can't qualify to eat the shit I dropped as a little kid!'

The beatings were painful – *so* painful. He'd hit me again and again on the same spot. He often beat me so hard his own hands would bruise. 'Look how you've hurt me!' he would cry. He would say how much it pained him to hurt somebody he loves.

Occasionally after a beating he would hug me to him and ask – gently now, the consummate teacher – 'Who causes the rift between us?'

From everything I'd been taught, even at three years old I knew the answer I must give: 'It's me. I caused the rift.'

It was always my fault; if I'd been a good person, this would never have happened. That knowledge was awful: it made me hate myself. With no one ever speaking up for me – with *everyone* I knew only ever agreeing with AB that I was bad – my wickedness was an incontrovertible fact, as much a part of me as my shadow.

Having been battered for saying I liked ugly dirty whites, I picked myself up off the floor gingerly. I was lucky, I reflected, that it was only a beating. For AB could kill us using a single pressure point or his death stare if he wanted. 'Do as I do if you want to live,' he would intone. 'Do what you want if you want to die.' Frequently, he threatened me: 'You will pay with your life.'

The power I perhaps feared most of all, however, was spontaneous human combustion (SHC). AB and Comrade Josie used to discuss it a lot: how it had happened to a few people and all that was left of them were a few buttons from their clothes, the rest had vanished without a trace. 'Wrong ideas can burn you to death!' promised AB – and I knew it was not hyperbole, for no transgressive thought was safe. I learned AB had the power of thought control, which meant both that he (and his invisible machines located all over the world) could read minds and that he could cause bad things to happen with a single thought.

AB's lessons were drummed into me daily. Over time, they started to take effect. One afternoon in the mid-1980s, I was permitted a rare trip out to the overgrown garden with Comrade Sian. AB deliberately let our garden become wild so that fascist agents would struggle to spy on us or gain access. On this day, I happened to glance up through the long grass to see that, shockingly, the ugly dirty white woman next door was brazenly waving to me from her window. She, too, rarely went out; she was disabled.

Comrade Sian had also spotted the woman's gesture. 'The bloody fascist state is trying to take you away!' she exclaimed in disgust. 'Don't wave to her!'

And I kept my hands by my side. I turned away from the woman in the wheelchair. Like the good soldier I was being trained to be, I obediently followed my leader.

2

'Comrade Prem, *no!*'

Comrade Sian took firm hold of my hands, which had been hopefully reaching for a cuddle, and pushed them roughly away from her. She was a white woman in her mid-thirties with long light-brown hair; I thought her very pretty, but her personality was nowhere near as beautiful as her face. Cold and disciplinarian, she was the person who most frequently reported me to AB, for the least infringement, and I despised her. Yet she was also lying beside me in my bed right now, in my tiny little box room, during the compulsory Collective-wide afternoon nap, and I yearned for some love and kindness. True to form, however, she had rejected me again.

I found the afternoon naps very difficult. Stuck in the house all day, with no opportunity to be active, I had unused energy zinging through my veins and the last thing I wanted or needed was to sleep.

I could have borne those naps if I had been allowed to cuddle the comrades who took turns to sleep beside me. But the comrades and I were banned from hugging or even touching: we had to lie like sculptures next to one another instead. I couldn't reach out a hand to stroke their hair, nor nuzzle gently into them. To do so would be to betray AB. If I became close to another, I was not focusing on him. So I was reprimanded if ever I said I liked someone else and was instructed to be hostile to them instead, while the comrades were ordered to report me for reaching out to them affectionately.

This included reporting things I'd done in my sleep. Comrade Josie was terribly worried one night when, fast asleep, I put my arms around her. It was such a shameful episode it was never spoken of aloud: Josie's written report was handed back to me along with AB's written guidance: 'Be self-critical! No laughing matter!', adding that I must destroy my weaker self if I wanted to stay alive. For months afterwards I kept wetting the bed in fear. If I couldn't even escape punishment for things I did in my sleep, what hope was there?

The comrades, too, would be at fault if they ever responded to my clumsy attempts to make friends. AB declared that any comrade conspiring with me against him would be thrown out of the house. Project Prem, he lectured, was about leaving the old-world encumbrances of friendship behind, to stand alone, the better to serve AB. Part of my training was to be denied any measure of companionship.

So, time and again, my hesitant overtures of friendship ended in failure and betrayal, either shot down by the comrade I was befriending or by another observing our growing closeness. Time and again, I was reassured by all the comrades that if such 'friendship' had continued, it would have been bad for me and my future. 'Don't be upset,' they would urge, as my bottom lip wobbled and I fought the need to cry. 'It's in your best interests.'

AB, in contrast, was permitted to touch me. Every morning and evening, I stood meekly before him. At the appointed time, he would embrace me, running his fingers slowly up and down my back. Sometimes, he would even give me a 'big smell', pursing his lips and pressing them to my cheek. (Later, I learned this was also called a kiss, but AB deemed kissing to be poisonous and never used the word to describe his own actions.)

I found his touch creepy, as though he was putting his stamp on me: *you're mine*. Given the amount of beatings I received at his hands, the supposed niceness felt contrived. It never felt like a hug from somebody who cared about me, but more like an exchange: payment for obeying him and being what he wanted me to be. Comrade Bala's love was always conditional.

I couldn't make sense of my feelings. Everybody else loved and worshipped him so much; why didn't I feel the same? I put it down to not knowing enough; to my 'infantile disorder', as AB called it, when he blamed my inability to follow him 100 per cent on my being a child.

Nevertheless, as AB was the only person who ever touched me, who pressed a warm hand to my equally warm, honey-coloured skin, some part of me liked his embraces. I was so starved of affection that as a child I was grateful even for Bala's creepy touch. Desperate for cuddles, at night I would hug my blankets to me, burying my face in them. Sometimes the sheer loneliness of my life would swamp me: a sob would rise up through my throat. Hurriedly, I'd stuff the quilt into my mouth – a friend indeed – and it would muffle my cries so they were not discernible to whoever was lying next to me. I was not allowed to cry in front of others.

I soon learned that inanimate objects were much more trustworthy than people. I used to feel so heartbroken every time a comrade betrayed me that in the end I learned not to put my trust in anybody. I didn't have much – AB gave me only educational toys; dolls were banned – but I did have some Lego, and I formed a real attachment to a little figure in a white suit, whom I named Maria Franklin. But one day Maria disappeared. Wherever I looked for that Lego figure, it was nowhere to be found.

The same thing happened to other objects to which I became attached. Aged three, I loved to cuddle a particular yellow blanket. But because I liked it, it was taken away. Bala kept it in the top cupboard in his room so I couldn't have it. He'd show it to me from time to time, and I'd feel so sad because I wanted to hug it, but that was not allowed.

My isolation was perhaps most apparent when I was sick. Illness was a sign of not listening to AB's guidelines; the view in the Collective was that you were bad if you were poorly, as though the rottenness inside was now on show. So I'd be chastised if I vomited or had a poorly tummy; if I'd been focusing on AB properly, such a thing would never have happened (despite the fact I sometimes found it was *because* I'd been focusing on AB, anticipating a beating, that my guts had clenched and I'd soiled myself in fear).

'*Think* yourself well and not ill,' AB would instruct. All I had to do was focus on him to get better: every disease was reversible with AB's help. The rules applied to everyone in the Collective; I would never have been permitted to go to the doctor anyway, because of the need to conceal me from Outside, but AB said 'NHS means Never Help Self' and that doctors (DR) were Death Restorationists: all part of the old world.

Sometimes, AB made allowances for the backwards, old-world needs of the comrades and permitted medicine to be taken. He himself never needed it; 'I never even go to the pharmacist,' he would boast. More often, however, he would declare that the illness needed to be beaten out of the person.

That was what happened in September 1987, when I was four. I'd been ill for a week, vomiting every morning. Bala was enraged at this continued disobedience and had been showering his 'practical love' upon me, but it hadn't made any difference. I heard him and Comrade Sian discussing me in hushed voices. My stomach turned over again: being beaten by Bala was only one of the punishments given for violating his guidelines, and my mind was churning about what they might do next.

Some of the penalties were more bearable than others. No food was one, but eventually mealtimes would resume and they did not let me starve. The one I feared most was when everybody walked out of the room and closed the door behind them, leaving me alone. I was *never* alone. I'd been told over and over about the life-threatening consequences of not having a comrade watching over me, so it was petrifying. AB made a point of reminding me of the danger: 'Go out of the room,' he'd say to everybody but me, 'and then the neighbour can come and take her away.'

I was so afraid that something bad would happen to me if I was on my own. I'd run to the door and struggle to get out, wanting – *needing* – to be reunited with them, but they'd stand on the other side and hold the handle to stop me. The more I cried, the longer they did it. In time, I learned that the best thing to do was pretend I was in agreement. From an early age, I adapted to become quite deceptive, just to survive.

I must never show what I am truly thinking; I must learn to hide my real feelings, as adeptly as the Collective keep me hidden from the world.

But there was no hiding from AB's mind-control machines. Any thought transgression was soon punished, for example by my becoming ill.

In AB's view, the worst punishment of all was when he refused to talk to me or see me. Yet I always felt a mixture of rejection and relief when that happened. Some anxiety, too – because I didn't know what else he might be plotting while he was silent, so the eerie quiet was pregnant with unknown horrors.

That was how I felt on that September day, queasy both with sickness and with fright, listening to AB and Comrade Sian on the other side of the door discuss how best to handle me. Unexpectedly, AB came into the room and said he would call 'them' if I didn't get well immediately.

I didn't know who 'them' was; I think, now, he may have meant an ambulance. But 'them', to me, meant fascist agents and I was horrified. It was the worst thing he could have said. When I saw Comrade Sian picking up the phone I hurriedly pasted a fake smile on to my pallid face to stop her calling.

I succeeded in holding them off – but still I didn't get well. So AB finally decided enough was enough. As I lay weakly on the floor on Sunday 20 September, with the acid tang of vomit still souring my mouth and nose, he dragged me through the house and hurled me into the hallway, near the front door. I lay curled in a ball; I had never seen AB so angry. Drawing back a foot, he booted me viciously in the head, then prepared to stamp on my face, nose-first. I quickly turned my face away; his bare foot trod on my cheek instead.

Yet it wasn't punishment enough. With a final, frenzied roar, AB seized me, threw open the front door – and threw me Outside.

I felt the shock as though I'd landed in icy waters, even though it was a balmy autumn day. AB slammed the front door in my face and I felt terror rising in me, just as a drowning victim feels her lungs fill with briny sea.

I was Outside. I was alone.

Anything could happen.

Although making noise and crying were both outlawed in the Collective, I screamed as loud as I could. Tears mixed with snot and vomit on my face as I sobbed and begged for mercy. I pounded my little fists on that hard green door, increasingly desperate, casting looks over my shoulder for fear a fascist agent might walk down the tree-lined street beyond the gate. I didn't *know* the Outside world; I barely spent time even in the garden. It was as though I'd been stranded on a hostile, unknown planet. And without a comrade to guard me, I *knew* an enemy agent could kidnap me at any minute. I *knew* I would die without AB – it was only a matter of time.

Weakly, I banged again on the door, whimpering now in terror and distress. They had to let me back in. *Please let me back in . . .*

Finally, like the good man he was, AB proved merciful. After what may have been only a few minutes, the green door opened and I was permitted into the warmth of the new world again. I was grateful to be back, subsumed within the protection of the Collective, so when the comrades next recited AB's Truths, I joined my voice to theirs, finding relief in the familiar refrain.

'AB is Nature, Nature is AB.'

17

For AB had power over all the world: the sun, the moon, the Earth, the stars. He could make a frost sweep a nation; a wildfire burn for days. Earthquakes were engineered by him as retribution for his enemies; explosions could be detonated at will or individuals doomed to death. 'ARA [Aravindan] is everywhere – Supernature,' AB explained in my lessons, drawing diagrams which showed him at the centre of all things.

The comrades and I continued to chorus: 'India is the World, and the World is India.'

AB came from Kerala, in India, so when the time came for it to be Overt, India would be the centre (as, covertly, it already was). 'Everything originates from AB's India,' I was told. 'If you think it doesn't, you are mindless.' AB would become enraged if he ever read lying propaganda that the first man came from Africa or rice sticks from China, or if the British Fascist State (BFS) claimed credit for any innovation. 'Comrade Bala said how the ugly dirty whites say that they have discovered everything . . . whereas it is AB's KER-ALA that has discovered everything,' I recorded neatly in my book.

'AB's Knowledge is the Truth, and the Truth is AB's Knowledge,' the comrades and I went on, our voices melding together until we spoke as one. 'AB's CRIS HELP is the Key, and the Key is AB's CRIS HELP.'

CRIS HELP meant Continued Revolution in Stages and Heavenly Eternal Life Programme: the name of the training AB was giving us to allow us to be part of his new world. The 'Eternal Life' was significant; something else I was taught about our leader.

AB was immortal. He had the power of eternal life.

He claimed that if we followed him properly, we too could have extended, even eternal life.

There was a final, fifth Truth – but it was a hidden one, something we had to KQ about. When we reached it in our litany, our voices would always fall away to silence. Nevertheless, our mouths still moved.

'AB is God, God is AB.'

3

Somewhat unusually, AB was modest about his divinity, perhaps because of the huge nature of the secret that we lived with a god. Though some of his followers wanted to pray overtly to him, as one might do in a traditional religion, he would dismiss such ideas.

'You look at me through the eyes of the old,' he would lecture the comrades. '*Practice* is prayer.'

This meant: carry out his instructions to the letter and never disagree with anything he said.

Perhaps because of AB's modest attitude, I had confusing, mixed feelings about his holiness. To me he seemed just like everybody else, but with the others all fervently believing, treating him with reverence and faith, I had to go along with it. *I don't understand because I am just a child*, I reasoned.

Comrade Sian was his most devout worshipper, completely servile to him. 'Beloved Comrade Bala is the STAR of our lives! We owe our lives to Comrade Bala' was the very first thing she taught me when I started my formal education in the Collective. She wrote it in huge Communist-red letters in my book, the colour we reserved for anything special.

I considered her to be rather like the sheepdog of the pack, snapping at the heels of the other women to keep them in line. I suspected her devotion to AB was the reason she was appointed to oversee my training; Comrade Sian was the woman who looked after me the most.

I would rather it had been any other comrade but her. Perhaps it was because they didn't have direct responsibility for me, but with the others I was a lot more successful at gaining a little leeway here and there – they'd occasionally allow me an unreported giggle if something funny happened or allow me to make a mistake. But Sian took her duty so seriously that the smallest indiscretion would be reported to AB without a first, let alone second chance. It was as though she poured all her energy into a pointed effort never to become close to the child in her charge.

She was often assisted by Comrade Josie, who was almost three years younger than Sian, also white, and wore her brown hair, when long, in a tight bun or a twisted plait. She looked the perfect stern lady; I can still remember the glare of her blue eyes. She used to stare, stare, stare at everything I did, as though she believed me to be untrustworthy and felt she had to maintain near-unblinking eye contact to ensure I obeyed AB. The intensity of her gaze unnerved me.

It was Josie and Sian who took charge of improving my reading and writing as I grew older. I read children's books from China, *Monkey Subdues the White-Bone Demon* and *Bright Red Star*. Both were about AB, I was told. ('*Mon*' means 'eldest son' in Malayalam, the language AB spoke in Kerala, and AB was the eldest son in his family, while 'key' meant the key person.) When I was four or five, Bala bought me a diary and instructed that it must be written in every day; I think perhaps it was intended to record my childhood for posterity, given the importance of Project Prem.

It was another tool with which to monitor me. Sian wrote it for me for the first couple of years, after which I took responsibility, always overseen by a comrade to ensure I didn't write anything off-message. It recorded every minute detail of my life: what I ate, how many times I went to the toilet, whether my shits were loose or hard. As I so rarely left the house, it did not always document what I did all day, which was essentially to sit at home and learn about Comrade Bala. But, as a devout follower, I would record all of AB's movements – where he went when *he* went Outside, what time he left the house, what he wore – and all the anniversaries of his great victories against the British Fascist State. Generously, he gave me a lock of his hair a few times, which I gravely pasted into the book.

My lessons were all focused around AB. I learned he came to Britain in 1963 and that the CC was set up in 1967, when he and Chanda became engaged; the other comrades had joined in dribs and drabs over the following decade. In August 1971, AB had scored a victory over the BFS when he avoided an assassination attempt in a London taxi; the BFS had sent a death ray to kill him via the meter, scheduled to hit when he leaned forward to pay – but, dashing their plans, AB's fellow passenger had paid the fare, so the ray intended for AB's head had hit AB's chest instead. You could still see the mark, a red blemish the size of a coin that looked rather like a large boil. I found the whole story petrifying – as if there wasn't enough to fear Outside!

I was also told the story of how Sian moved from being a Suspicious Doubtist to Bala's most devoted follower. Although it seemed impossible to imagine, she had once questioned AB's claims and requested proof. On 1 February 1976, when the Collective had lived at another address, Bala had fought a most heroic battle with the upstairs neighbours: fascist agents who were rowdy and always causing trouble for AB, just as the BFS had asked them to. After a night of raucous parties, Bala had brandished a meat cleaver at them. One of his targets had his hand upon the banister; Bala brought the blade down, attempting to sever his hand from the wrist, but the agent pulled his hand away just in time. Such was the force of the blow that the cleaver embedded itself in the banister.

Bala spent nearly two months in jail, framed by the fascist state for his political activities in battling with its agents. For Sian, it was the day she 'woke up' about the true nature of the fascist state in Britain. Imprisoning an innocent man for his political activities was something she had previously thought happened only in Third World countries. After that, when AB told her, 'Don't ask for proof, just have faith, believe in me, focus on *me*,' she did as directed.

That wasn't the only time the BFS unfairly imprisoned Bala. In 1974 he was admitted to St Albans Mental Hospital for two days, I believe for fighting with the police. He used to boast about it, gloating, 'They thought I was mad!' But it had all been part of AB's master plan: he wanted the experience of being incarcerated so that when he ruled the world, he would know all about the institutions of the fascist state from the inside. Then, in 1978, he was jailed for assaulting a policeman. He wore all of these experiences as badges of honour; they were evidence of both the persecution he faced at the hands of the BFS and his own valiant nature.

I also studied world history. AB's birthday was 16 July, making his conception day 16 October, and all great world events therefore happened around these two dates, because AB was the centre of everything. Whether it was the launch of Apollo 11 on 16 July 1969, taking Neil Armstrong to the Moon, or the test of the first atomic bomb on 16 July 1945 in the arid deserts of New Mexico, I was taught that everything was linked to AB. AB himself had been born in 1940, but of course his spirit had always been around.

Perhaps most importantly of all, I learned about Synchronizations: that events Outside were directly influenced by Bala and related to the goings-on within the CC. AB would frequently use his power over the natural world, which could be exercised by written or spoken word or thought, in retaliation for any manner of offences. I had to write out long lists of them all: 'This earthquake happened when the landlord called to ask us for our rent', 'Malaysian Prime Minister Abdul Razak died when AB said, "To hell with Razak!"', 'The Challenger space shuttle exploded when comrades went against AB'.

This last one really affected me when I learned of it – because I had been alive, three years old, when it had happened in 1986. All seven crew members had died in the disaster. It was Challenge-R, AB said – R short for Ara – and we comrades had been *challenging* him, vYing with him; thus the shape of the smoke being formed into a Y when the shuttle had exploded. I listened in horror as he drew the connections: this was proof.

It was sickening to think *our* going against AB had resulted in seven people's deaths. As I listened to the lesson, an acrid taste swelled uncomfortably in my mouth and I simply could not swallow it down. I felt as though something was staining me, deep inside.

Guilt.

For those deaths were on my head. Their blood was on my hands.

I took a very deep breath. I knew there was only one way to avoid such future devastation.

I must do better. I must be *a better person.*

I resolved to follow AB even more devoutly than before. But, this time, it was not to save my own skin from his beatings, but to protect all others from his wrath.

4

'Warm – it – up – a – bit-bit,' crooned Comrade Aisha in a singsong voice, moving her spoon, laden with ice cream, back and forth in time with the ditty. I loved it when she did this and opened my mouth wide, eyes smiling, already knowing what was coming next.

Smoothly, she popped the spoon into my mouth and the cold ice cream melted sweetly on to my hot tongue. Though, aged five, I was a little old to be fed, this was a secret routine Aisha and I had shared over the years, and I wouldn't have stopped it for the world.

If I had to pick a favourite comrade, Aisha was probably it. She was the eldest of the women, though four years younger than AB himself, in her early forties. Malaysian, she had short dark straight hair that hung like curtains around her face and heavy-rimmed glasses. Unusually, she didn't treat me as a little adult, but as a child, and I savoured the difference. Comrades Sian and Josie had never dealt with children before being appointed to work on Project Prem, whereas Aisha had lots of brothers and sisters, so she had more experience with youngsters. I think that was why, every now and then, she would treat me to some childish fun, seeming to know I yearned for it. I thought of her as a lucky mascot or a guardian angel.

In a way, though, as sweet as it was to share such scenes with Aisha, it always made her betrayal, when it inevitably came, that much harder to bear. I innocently commented to her one day that I liked the word 'Israel' better than the word 'Palestine'. I was making no political comment – I was five – I just enjoyed the hard hiss of the 'Is' and the smooth roll of the 'rael' as the word unravelled on my tongue.

I think Aisha mentioned the comment to Sian, who had instructed all comrades to share details of all I did, so of course it got through to Bala. He slapped me for being reactionary, then dragged me across the living room by my legs, from one side of the room to the other, my body seared by the dark-blue carpet with red flowers every step of the way. The stinging carpet burns served as a reminder that no one could be trusted.

Nonetheless, with only nine people populating my own little planet within the Collective, the comrades were the only people from whom I could learn. Comrade Oh – a small Malaysian woman of Chinese descent – was a role model of sorts, although not in the way Comrade Bala would have liked. She was a very capable individual, who often made decisions (such as whether to buy a new product in a shop) on her own initiative, without consulting Bala first. It seemed very daring. Whereas many of the comrades appeared rudderless without his direction, Oh could hold her own. She and Josie clashed all the time – Oh's strong personality made her rather blunt – and it was usually Oh who felt the sharp end of Bala's stick in retribution for the pair not working well together. There was supposed to be harmony within AB's CC Family (Pilot Unit).

I saw very little of Comrade Cindy, who was the Collective's most recent recruit, having been with them less than ten years. Occasionally she'd take a shift sleeping by my side, but she was out most of the time at work and seemed tired when she came home. Quiet in character, she also appeared deeply unhappy, though I did not know the reason why.

Then there was Leanne. Oh, Leanne. Because she worked, she wasn't around to report on me so much, which meant I felt friendlier towards her than the others. Yet unlike Cindy, who also worked but was often downcast, Leanne always managed to be pleasant, no matter how exhausted she was. She used to cut my hair – a severe crop, fit for a boy – and though I only really saw her at the weekends, when I did she would smile and be a bit cheeky.

Best of all was when she took the Saturday night shift sleeping beside me. The atmosphere was totally different to when Sian or Josie was on duty. Sometimes, Leanne would even whisper to me as we lay side by side, telling me stories about what had happened at work.

Strangely, unlike AB's every report about Outside, Leanne's stories never featured any fascist agents. She talked about her colleagues or an accident that had happened on the train. I loved those Saturday nights. She wouldn't cuddle me, of course, while her words weaved wondrous worlds for me, but if I was very lucky – and Leanne was feeling very rebellious – she would sometimes pat me on my leg, just once.

It was heaven.

She had the power to make other things fun too. I was given a pink bicycle with stabilizers and a wicker basket – then told, naturally, that it was only to be ridden inside. But Leanne cleared the hallway for me, popped a torch in the front basket and turned off all the lights. It was so exciting! I loved powering the pedals, seeing the beam of light flashing wildly on the walls, feeling empowered and thrilled as the movement took me . . . I spent almost all my time sitting down, so to wheel about on that bike felt like flying, even if the stunted length of the hallway didn't give me much room to manoeuvre. I couldn't help it: I giggled as I rode.

Sian and Josie soon put an end to that particular game. Stupidly, I enthused to Sian about Leanne's brilliant ideas, because I wanted Sian to be more like Leanne. Sacrilege. Leanne was promptly reported; we both were, for forming an anti-party clique. After that, Leanne didn't tell me stories so *much* any more . . . but she *did* still tell me stories.

There was something about Leanne that didn't quite fit with the rest of the group. Perhaps it was because she went Outside every day and was tainted by the old world – that was certainly what AB would have said.

It seemed the old world's influence was powerful. For on 23 April 1988, when I was five, Leanne suddenly made an unexpected announcement while we were all milling together in the living room that evening (I believe Cindy may have been at work).

'I'm going,' she said abruptly.

She meant it: she wanted to leave AB's CC.

I was shocked to my core. Only one person had ever left the Collective: Denise (now nicknamed Bad Dennis by the group), who'd been thrown out in 1984 for going against AB; at least, that's what the comrades said had happened. Such was the severity of her transgression, I'd been told Bad Dennis had died.

'Sit down,' AB spat in disgust when Leanne voiced what she wanted. When she didn't immediately obey him, he pushed her roughly into a chair.

But she got up out of it and began walking across the room.

'Hold her down!' he ordered sharply.

And like puppets on strings, some of the other comrades moved into action. There was a certainty to their movements, borne of strength in numbers. Like a pack of wolves, they grabbed Leanne and pinned her to the ground.

AB swiftly straddled Leanne as the others held her down for him. She struggled, but it was hopeless. As hard as he possibly could, AB punched Leanne's face with both his hands, over and over again.

I watched from the sidelines, trying to conceal my true feelings of horror and dismay.

'The fascists have got inside her!' AB declared in excitement. He was never one to back down from a fight with the BFS.

The other women held her more firmly at his words. If the fascists were inside *them*, I guess they'd have wanted the comrades to do the same.

Even as I watched, my eyes on stalks of unblinking terror, Leanne's pretty face, normally so full of light, began to turn black, the skin around her eyes shaded by the constant strike of Bala's blows. I felt sick, but I couldn't show it. I couldn't cry out, I couldn't help her: I could do nothing but watch.

It was the most chilling thing I had ever seen. Leanne was slammed to the ground while AB gloried in the punishment. The sound of his fist against her face; her wounded cries; the other comrades' hot, quick breaths . . . I found I couldn't bear it. A warm stream of urine trickled down my leg as I stood there, frightened as a rabbit by what I was seeing, my mind racing just as fast as my heart.

I knew, in my head, that this was for Leanne's own good. Why, then, was every atom in my body screaming that this was wrong?

I thought it must be because *I* was bad that I couldn't see the light. There was something wrong with me – there must be, when everyone else I knew believed this action to be correct. I had been told time and again that AB's practical love was a sign of his goodness: something beautiful to behold.

But try as I might, as I watched Leanne's face becoming bloody and bruised beneath AB's fists, to me it looked nothing but ugly.

'Even if it doesn't appear right to you, it *is* right,' the comrades always murmured. 'AB knows everything. Just have faith, Comrade Prem. There will come a time when you will understand why it is right.'

What is wrong with me? I worried. I should love AB more purely than anyone; I had been born into the Collective. But from an early age all I could remember was disliking him. As a very small child, before I knew better, I had once even said aloud, 'I don't like Comrade Bala.' I'd been punished, of course.

Why, I thought, *all this time later, can I still not bring myself to worship him with all my heart?*

I just had to be patient, I promised myself. I squeezed my eyes shut, unable to watch any more. One day I would learn.

5

I sang our revolutionary songs in praise of Bala even louder after that. It wasn't hard to remember the need for devotion as, for weeks afterwards, Leanne's face boasted bruises that warned of the dangers of going against AB. So violent had the beating been that she was forced to take several weeks off work. In my diary, AB's 'heroic struggle' against her was faithfully recorded. He talked of it often, proudly: 'Remember the time Leanne ran into my fist?'

We sang songs for AB every morning in the Collective: 'AB's Got the Whole World in His Hands', 'Shit on Britannia' and 'Death to England', 'Integrate with AB's Eternal Spirit'. We sang songs about destroying the old world and building the new world, songs about how 'uniquely resolute' AB was, songs in praise of AB's India. I did not get the chance to listen to any other music at that time, so in some ways it was fun.

I tried my hardest, too, to concentrate in Discussions. This was held morning and night, for hours at a time; Leanne and Cindy had to participate after work even if they were dead on their feet.

'Discussions' was a bit of a misnomer: it was a daily monologue from AB. We all stood in a circle (I was permitted, as a child, to sit) and kept our eyes glued to his face while he talked. If anyone looked down or was even caught blinking, he would shout at them or slap them. The women were often tired, as all the comrades kept to a punishing schedule of chores, and on occasion one of them would nod off where she stood as AB's monotonous voice droned on and on. After a few seconds, she'd jerk upright, disorientated, desperately hoping he hadn't noticed – but, at times, it was AB's stinging palm itself that had startled her awake.

There was no structure to the talks. AB discussed himself, current affairs, his plans for the new world. What I remember most clearly, however, and what happened most often, were his personal attacks on the women. He would denounce them repeatedly, for he believed they needed to tear up all sense of self and annihilate their personalities. He would denigrate their past experiences, mock their former joys, castigate them for the very things that had previously made them *them*.

'If it's a new world,' Aisha explained, 'you can't take the old with you.'

His teachings were that the women had to cut all ties to anything outside the Collective: it was the only way to prove their fealty. This extended to the women's families. Unlike me, who had no parents and was born on to AB's hand, each comrade had once had a mummy and daddy. It was an alien concept to me, but from the way AB described it, I wasn't missing out. Not for me the daily task of denouncing the family from which I'd come, which was what the other comrades had to do, writing vicious essays and publicly rejecting those they'd once loved. Sian, as ever, was hailed as a model student. A favoured anecdote was often cited: Sian's mother, Ceri, desperately seeking her daughter's whereabouts in the early 1980s, had finally tracked her to our home, only to be greeted by the curt message: 'Go away, I've got no mum.'

Self-criticism was encouraged too. We had to write down all the things that were wrong with us; Comrade Sian eagerly wrote mine for me when I was small. It could take up a *lot* of time – because there was an awful lot wrong with all of us.

'There is nobody as useless and stupid as those who come around me,' AB would say. According to Bala, the comrades' ineptitude was such that direct assistance from a deity was the only solution; that was why they had sought him out. 'I never invited any of you,' he would rant. 'Out of the goodness of my heart I am taking care of you, so remember how lucky you are.'

In Discussions they would slavishly agree. Aisha would say, 'Thank you, thank you' repeatedly if he spoke to her. Oh picked coyly at the front of her blouse. Comrade Josie used to gaze adoringly at him, as if she was truly seeing the divine apparition she believed him to be, and she would knit her brows together tightly, the better to drink in every drop of heavenly nectar dripping from his lips.

Though sometimes AB denounced the whole group, most attacks

were sharply personal. He always seemed to know exactly how to turn the screw. Josie came from a wealthy family, so AB falsely condemned them as genocidal war criminals who'd profited from the blood of innocents in unjust wars and occupations. Sian's father had committed suicide when she was seventeen – she'd been the last person to speak to him – so AB declared that *she* was the reason he'd blown his head off with a shotgun; and maligned her too for the madness that surely now ran through her veins. With Aisha, he'd remind her that deportation could be just a phone call away if she did not follow him properly.

With AB having taught the comrades that annihilating self was to their benefit, many were keen to help their colleagues achieve that empty interior: the zenith to which they aspired. So when AB went after an individual in Discussions, his was not the only voice that stabbed and slashed. Like a pack of hyenas, they would all come together to hunt their quarry. Not everybody joined in, but even when just one person did, it made it that much worse. Laughter ran round the circle like wildfire, licking fiercely into places that AB's own words may not have reached.

I hated it when it was my turn to be attacked. Bala used to haul me up from where I sat in the circle and insult and abuse me while the others watched or sometimes joined in. I developed a nervous giggle: a hugely unhelpful tic given I was beaten for laughing. But I just couldn't help it; it was a coping mechanism: *If I don't laugh, I'll cry* . . . I'd feel a bubble of giggles threatening to burst out of me and try to hold it back, like a burp – but it was just as unstoppable and just as uncouth. Out it would come: the obscene sound of a child laughing.

They'd take it in turns to have a go. I'd be picked to pieces, vultures feasting on the very meat of me. Perhaps the scariest thing of all was seeing the comrades, who could be sweet people sometimes, turn into these unadulterated monsters who would set upon me at a word from AB.

While it was happening, I tried not to think. I tried to pretend that it did not upset me. I knew I was not permitted to cry – and there was supposed to be nothing to cry about, after all, because this was only for my benefit – but in all honesty I would not give them the satisfaction of adding that misdemeanour to my charge sheet of crimes. I did not have much, but I did have my dignity, and I was determined to preserve it at all costs. Often, just to get through it, I'd stare at the carpet or the walls and I'd pretend they were a blank canvas – a canvas I was writing on with my eyes.

'Who cares about your feelings?' AB would sneer at me.

I'd fix my eyes upon the wall and slowly create my own secret words.

'You're the most disgraceful, stupid, idiotic person I've ever met . . .' he would continue.

Meanwhile, I'd luxuriate in the imaginary sentences I'd crafted, taking comfort from them, taking strength. *I made this sentence. I am still here. I haven't vanished beneath the pecks and scratches of their many beaks and talons.*

Perhaps worse than when I was the focus of Discussions, though, was when AB encouraged me to become a vulture myself. As far back as I can remember, I wanted to be outside it all and not be part, but Project Prem was dedicated to my learning new-world ways. I was to be a pioneer, a leading light showing others how it's done. My reticence was not good enough; AB used to call me 'weak-kneed' for not going after the other comrades all guns blazing. He wanted me to learn from him. He wanted me to be like him. The highest praise he and Sian ever gave me was when they called me 'Little AB'.

Though Bala was fair, at least, in ensuring that *every* comrade was attacked, that summer of 1988 Leanne was frequently the target of his rage, given her aborted attempt to leave the Collective in April. 'I never forgive and I never forget' was AB's motto. He thought forgiveness was for the weak.

Yet it seemed Leanne hadn't forgotten her forbidden hope, either, for on 22 July 1988 she once again tried to leave. She got as far as Southampton, from what I remember, but became disorientated: a fish out of water once permanently out in the old world without AB. She rang the Collective and returned.

'If you ever do that again,' AB shouted when he brought her home, 'you will *never* be allowed back into the fold.'

The pack of wolves was out in force for her. 'Traitor! Renegade!' they hissed and jeered.

Comrade Sian pulled me aside one day shortly after she'd returned.

'Tell Comrade Leanne she's betrayed AB!' she ordered. 'Tell her she's a vicious traitor!'

I felt uncomfortable; I didn't want to do it. Everyone else was already attacking her – wasn't that enough? Even though I knew I shouldn't like Leanne, I couldn't help the affection present in my heart. She told me bedtime stories. She made indoor bicycling fun. I didn't *want* to call her names. I didn't have any friends, but the closest I had ever come was the time I spent with her.

One day passed, and then another, and I thought I'd got away with not doing it. But Sian kept reminding me: 'Don't forget . . .' I knew she was watching; that AB was watching too.

I mulled over my dilemma. I thought of all the things that could happen if I went against AB. I thought of how Bala and Sian were trying to help me become a *better* person – not the bad child who always needed beating, but someone who could be a shining example to all.

So I found a quiet time, when the whole group wasn't around. Just one or two comrades were present as I reluctantly walked up to Leanne. She smiled at me, as always, and that made what I had to do ten times worse.

I spoke in a halting voice. I was supposed to tell her that *I* despised her, but I couldn't quite bring myself to claim the words.

'I was told to tell you you're a traitor.'

She did not look shocked that I'd said it; that I had denounced her too. Resigned, is how I remember it; as though she had almost expected it.

It was my destiny, after all.

6

Ring, ring! Ring, ring!

The telephone chimed in the back room and Comrade Sian went to answer it. It was somebody for Comrade Chanda, AB's wife.

Cautiously, in case anyone caught me, I tiptoed to stand behind the door of the back room, where I could eavesdrop on the conversation.

Please be someone asking to visit, I thought, *please be asking to visit . . .*

The only times I got to go Outside these days were when Chanda's relatives came to the house. Though they weren't fascist agents, for some reason AB didn't want them to know I existed either, so on those infrequent occasions when they came to see his wife he deemed it best to take me away from the house.

It was one of many inconsistencies of life in the Collective that Chanda and AB were allowed to maintain contact with their families. A two-tier system was in place and AB treated Chanda and Shobha better than the rest of us because they were his legitimate relatives (even though such a connection was supposedly old world). That's not to say he wouldn't put them in their place when needed, and they suffered the same humiliations and physical violence as the rest of us, but they were raised up as paragons of virtue and given special privileges. We had to be slavishly subservient to them: no one was allowed to disagree with anything Chanda said, no matter how outrageous or downright wrong.

I didn't know what I'd done to offend her, but I felt Chanda always looked at me as if she wished I was dead. She barely treated me like a fellow human, more like a bothersome fly. Even uttering my name seemed an affront: I was always just 'the kid'. I have memories of her slamming doors in my face or cold-shouldering me in the corridor; I felt as if a dark spell fell on any room she entered, when a peculiar mix of terror, nervousness and gloom settled deeply within me. I could almost feel her aversion to me emanating in noxious waves.

I wanted to like her, but – her distaste of me aside – she struck me as a rough and rather boorish woman. She often charged about the place, confident in her superior status.

It was fascinating watching Comrade Sian with her. Sian, who was top dog amongst the comrades as AB's foremost follower, was like a different woman with Chanda, always trying to please her. She used to make us all fall respectfully silent when Chanda walked past. Yet no matter what she did, as far as I could tell Chanda gave her only dirty looks that were deadly enough to fell a tree.

Chanda's little sister, Shobha, spent most of her time with Comrade Oh, who had been given the job of caring for her as Shobha had long been in a wheelchair. Though she was thirty-nine, Shobha struck me as rather childlike, which included the occasional tantrum. Both she and Chanda were fond of bossing the other women around, something I observed when I innocently said one day, 'Comrades Chanda and Shobha seem to complain all the time!'

Josie's face went the colour of puce. I knew that voicing such opinions was taboo, yet I had also always been told to be honest – what a contradiction this predicament presented! AB soon corrected the error of my ways and it wasn't long before I was sketching out another family tree of his glorious antecedents – something I did several times a year – featuring AB's mother, Amma, 'the best woman in the entire universe'.

I always found the discrepancies of life in the Collective jarring. Why was Chanda allowed to have visits from her family? Why were we told to be good to others . . . *unless* AB and Chanda didn't like them, at which point it was all-out war? Why did AB encourage us to observe AB's SOWETO day (Serving Others Without Ever Thinking Of Self) when he spent all day, every day, thinking of nothing *but* himself? Listening in Discussions, the slightest discrepancy had my ears pricking up, but everyone else seemed to overlook it. I think I may even have asked about it once or twice and was told that because AB was the centre, the rules did not apply.

Standing behind the door, struggling to work out from the one-sided conversation whether a trip Outside might be looming, Chanda's continued relationship with her family was one double standard I could only embrace. I had just turned six and my life was different from the one I had known even a short time ago when it came to time

Outside. When I was very, very small, I'd been allowed to play in the garden with a comrade every few days; I even went Out regularly in a car. But as though AB was gradually stuffing my opportunities for fresh air into an ever-narrowing funnel, the boundaries of what was permitted had grown tighter and tighter over time. In the previous autumn of 1988, I'd accidentally scratched my neck while playing with a stick in the garden; AB had been furious when he'd seen the graze, as though his own property had been damaged, and he beat me forty or fifty times for being careless. I think his greatest fear was that if something serious happened to me, it could lead to others becoming aware of my existence.

The threat from fascist agents was ever-present and increasing. We had moved from the house with the disabled neighbour, but now lived next door to something worse: an elderly couple with a grand-daughter. The girl was a little blonde child, perhaps a bit younger than me. Recently, she'd come up to the fence when I was Outside with Sian and Aisha and tried to talk to me through the wire.

I was transfixed by her. She was so small! My world was popu-lated by grown-ups, all long legs and looming faces – but this person was my height and with the same short legs and arms. She was an ugly dirty white girl, whereas my skin was lightly tan, but I saw in her more similarity to me than anyone else I'd ever met. I wasn't allowed to look in a mirror, so this child was the closest I got to see-ing someone like me.

Such was my interest in her, despite everything I'd been told I started moving towards the fence, excited by her presence and her sweet, high-pitched voice calling to me.

A hand was instantly clamped upon my shoulder. Sian and Aisha dragged me back into the house and warned me *never* to speak to her. There were lots of hushed whispers and then Sian sat me down with a sombre face, as though about to impart some dark informa-tion they'd decided I was finally mature enough to know.

'That little girl was a fascist agent, Comrade Prem,' she said, 'sent by her evil grandparents to try to lure you next door. And do you know what they were planning?'

I shook my head.

'They were planning to drink your blood and eat you in a satanic ritual sacrifice.'

After that, the garden didn't seem safe at all. I didn't go Outside for months and months at a stretch – that was why I was so keen to hear if a trip might be on the cards now. It was so boring, seeing the same four walls every single day. My daily routine was mind-numbingly familiar.

1. *See Beloved Comrade Bala / Discussions.*
2. *Singing.*
3. *Writing.*
4. *Food.*
5. *Afternoon nap.*
6. *Bathtime.*
7. *Study.*
8. *'Sum up' with Comrade Sian to debate if I'd been a good soldier for AB that day.*
9. *Food.*
10. *See Beloved Comrade Bala / Discussions.*

If something exciting *had* ever happened beyond that painfully regular rota – such as the landlord coming round to demand his rent or a plumber dropping by to fix a leaky tap – I would try to retrace my footsteps in the days that followed, recreating the scenes, wearing the same clothes, begging for the same food to be made, superstitiously hoping beyond hope that if I did, if I could make everything just as it had been, a thrilling event would happen again.

Comrade Bala still went out just as much as before. He would bring me things back to stick in my diary – his ticket from the London Transport Museum, his Travelcard, some flowers from the East Bridge over the Serpentine – but it wasn't the same as being able to go Outside myself. Sian told me to treasure these items with my life, and chastised me if I didn't fall over myself saying 'thank you' for them.

But I felt resentful, rather than grateful. It was a particularly glum time, that spring of 1989, because Aisha had been banned from looking after me a short while before; she'd been sleeping with me one night when I'd wet the bed, and AB had blamed her for it, for being too liberal with me. He'd beaten us both, then outlawed interaction between us.

That was why I was so desperate for Chanda's relatives to come – because I was bored and fed up and lonely. I was extra cautious as I held my breath and listened. AB didn't like me eavesdropping; he would say, 'Don't listen to telephone calls, trying to listen whether you're going out! If you don't go deep into AB's CC then you won't be going out at all!'

Yet for all his threats, *every* time the relatives came I would be whisked out of the house; it was the one thing about which I could be completely certain.

I let out a sigh of relief. Good news: they were coming. And I was off to London Zoo.

7

'Remember the rules,' Comrade Sian instructed as we stood in the hallway, on the verge of going Outside. 'Don't talk to other people. Stay close. Don't get separated. If you do, *don't* talk to the police. Don't keep looking around. Don't ogle. Just concentrate on Bala and you'll be fine.'

I nodded my head eagerly. I knew the rules; they were drummed into me every time I left the house. I wasn't frightened about going Outside – the comrades, and Bala himself, would be with me and I knew they would keep me safe. In many ways it was scarier being in the garden, with the certified fascist agents on either side of the fence, just waiting for their chance. Not everyone Outside was an agent, as I understood it, but the neighbours definitely were. That meant, on these trips further afield, I stood a chance of seeing someone nice.

I think that was what I was most excited about. Forget the benefits of fresh air to my lungs: a stranger's smile or kind eyes could keep me breathing for months. I liked those people who looked at me warmly, rather than with the guarded, hostile glares I received in the house. Being smiled at when I went out gave me such a feeling of immense joy that it lasted for days, even weeks. It counteracted what I was always told in the Collective: that I was a bad person whom everyone disliked. The only thing that made me uneasy about these interactions was when a stranger glanced at me and then asked in confusion: 'Are you a boy or a girl?'

Though not everyone was an agent, I had to remain vigilant at all times about ugly dirty white men. Comrade Sian in particular had a pathological hatred of them; perhaps because she was going out of her way to prove to Bala she was faithful by vehemently rejecting men of her own race. She and the others used to call all men, but white men in particular, 'elements', and their fury would rain down on me if ever I had the slightest interaction with them. Outside, they would deliberately ignore white men if they spoke to the group.

As we prepared to leave, there was a final check for the neighbours; we couldn't leave the house until the coast was clear. A nod was given. Then the front door swung wide and I felt my spirits soar as, inch by inch, Outside was revealed. And then the best moment of all: stepping over the threshold and into thin air.

It *was* like being on a different planet. Here, no solid walls blocked me in on all sides – there was distance on the horizon, roads running every which way, and everywhere you looked was another possibility. Different plants and flowers and hedges grew in gardens up and down the street, giving off fragrances and rustling noises quite alien to me. No ceilings curtailed my viewpoint: up, up and away stretched the blue or grey or drizzling sky – *different* every time, which was part of its beauty. I could have spent hours marvelling at it, savouring the sun on my face or the breeze that gently fingered my dark crew-cut hair, entranced by the ever-moving clouds and the changing vista.

I *could* have spent hours marvelling at it – but I felt a comrade push me from behind, sucking on her teeth at my dallying, and I hastily followed AB to the garden gate. With him walking in front of me, I couldn't really see where we were going; he was careful to keep me shielded so I never had a clear view of the street.

On any outing I made Outside, there were always at least three people with me. This group protection was not unusual for the Collective; all the comrades had to go out in pairs for their own safety, to preclude an attack from the fascist state. My trio of bodyguards used to walk all around me so I was in the middle. It made it hard to get a sense of things, and if I dared to look around as we walked along our suburban street, Comrade Sian would snap, 'Don't ogle!' I had to focus solely on the back of AB's anorak, all the way to the bus or Tube station, marching in time with the comrades' slow steps as though we were soldiers on parade.

But this was not a drill. I could feel the tension in the comrades surrounding me; they seemed on edge, charged by the responsibility of keeping me safe Outside. They planned the outing as a military operation: Travelcards were bought in advance and handed to the comrades before we even left the house. I never saw them use a ticket machine or have an exchange with the staff behind the counters; when we went on the Tube, we were through the barriers in seconds, the flow of our ever-moving mass of bodies, with me safely secreted at the centre, barely interrupted.

I thought public transport was extraordinary. I loved the trains the best; I decided I wanted to be a train driver when I grew up. Train drivers got to go to all sorts of different places. Imagine going to a different place every day! The idea of being in control, having responsibility, driving people to all those wonderful destinations, felt very grand to me. On public transport, there was a chance someone nice might sit near me, too, although on the bus AB always put me next to the window, blocking me in by taking the aisle seat. I would be so busy covertly watching the other passengers, hoping to catch their eye and receive a smile, that I had no time to look out of the windows. It was always AB who said, 'It's time to get off now,' and I would follow him meekly, with no understanding of where we were or where we'd been or what we might have passed along the way. Once off the bus, it was back to staring at AB's anorak as we walked the final stretch to our destination.

In some ways it was easier to focus on AB's jacket. Everything else was so colourful, so bright, so noisy, so *fast*! Even though what I saw were mere glimpses, I couldn't take it in: it was utterly overwhelming. In the house, *nothing* happened. Outside, events never seemed to stop. I couldn't identify the different noises: the squeals, shouts, beeps, roars, whirs and whines were a jagged soundscape without names or labels. I couldn't separate one from the other; I was just assaulted by this wave of sound.

It may have been overwhelming, but I *loved* it. I loved being Outside. Joyful – that was how I felt, walking down the street, going somewhere *new*. I never felt joyful in the house.

London Zoo was just one of the places AB took me to when Chanda's relatives came. The Science Museum and Commonwealth Institute were other favourites (AB always being careful to shepherd me away from any displays that pushed the false messages of the BFS), and we sometimes went to restaurants too. It was so exciting to be Out and sitting *somewhere else* rather than at the same old table at home. I don't recall ever looking at a menu and choosing what I wanted; food was chosen for me – and it tasted so good! I probably couldn't have coped with the choice anyway, with the stress of potentially selecting for myself something Bala didn't like. I was terrified when I favoured something he didn't, for fear of the retribution when he read my mind.

A strange thing happened when the comrades went Outside. As I watched them interacting with people – white men aside – they seemed . . . *friendly*. It was most peculiar. Though *I* was told not to talk to anybody, they would chat quite easily with the people we encountered; no trace of vulture or monster to be seen. You would never have known AB was the covert leader of the world, fighting a war with fascist agents. I guess that's what made him so good at it.

We had an amazing time at the zoo, seeing all the animals. For someone who never saw anything different, here was variety in spades. We went to the reptile house, where I was fascinated by the slide and slither of the snakes. My senses were assaulted every which way: the calls of the creatures, the stink of their pens, the diverse textures of their pelts and coats. Yet it wasn't just the animals I was watching. Everywhere I looked in London Zoo, families weaved their way in and out of the crowds: children running about; a boy hoisted high upon his father's shoulders; a daughter scooped up in her mother's arms. *Everybody seems so nice*, I remember thinking. *Why is there not that niceness in our house?*

I stared jealously as a woman embraced her child, affectionately ruffling his hair. The rationale behind the no-hugging rule had been explained countless times to me, but I still felt it as the cruellest of blows. *If only the comrades could hug me like that*, I thought, feeling melancholy in the certainty it would never be allowed. If ever I dared to express a longing for it, I was called ungrateful and selfish.

There was only one disappointment to the visit. I'd wanted to see the aviary, but we couldn't, for some reason. It may have been because I'd enthusiastically pointed out the condor I'd spotted in the brochure, impressed by its majesty, but was told I was bad for liking it because the bird had an affinity with the bald eagle of the USA, a country populated by genocidal war criminals.

I adored birds. Although I was still officially banned from looking out of the window at home, every now and then I'd catch glimpses of the wrens or sparrows flying here and there in the garden. There was something about them that felt so free.

41

The very worst part of any trip Outside was having to come home. I remember being castigated for saying, 'I'm upset to be back.' AB said it showed ingratitude and that if I carried on he would never take me Out again. Immediately, I would zip my mouth shut and hurry to get ready for bed.

That night in 1989, after the trip to London Zoo, I lay down in bed and closed my eyes.

Vroom!

Everything was rushing before my eyes, the darkness that was usually behind them when I shuttered my lids now filled with colour and life. Everything I'd seen that day was present: the cars and the train and the bus and the creatures and the sky and the food and the people . . . I could remember the wind of the Tube train arriving almost flattening my face, the sheer energy of it pressing into me. The roar of the traffic; the grunts of the animals. At home, the only thing I heard grunt or roar was Beloved AB.

I lay there so happily, my brain alive with memories, and imagined myself flying like those birds I'd seen Outside – going up, up and away from this house and zooming back to all the places I'd been. Whenever I went Out in the world, I always wanted to go back. I always wanted *more*.

I guess that's how Leanne felt, too. On 18 May 1989, she finally left for good. She didn't say she was leaving – she didn't say goodbye – she just went Out to work one day and when she was meant to come home, she didn't.

It was perhaps that same evening, in Discussions, that the words I'd been dreading were said. I'd feared it when she was absent, but now I knew: she was dead.

8

Life seemed even emptier than before. I felt really sad without Leanne; I missed her. Aisha was still banned from looking after me, so even the snatches of happiness I had sometimes found with my two favourite comrades were denied to me now. I grieved for Leanne. I wished I'd spent more time with her when she was alive.

AB didn't grieve. 'Good riddance to the traitor,' was what he said. He didn't even care that we had lost the income of her salary and now had to rely solely on Cindy; even before Leanne had gone, he'd declared 'rent strike' against the fascist state and was no longer paying any money to our landlord, whom he despised. Even at that age I remember thinking that it didn't seem fair to the landlord.

Someone else appeared to share my view because, a month after Leanne died, an envelope arrived at the house with her handwriting on: she'd sent a cheque to cover the rent; something AB ranted about in Discussions.

The world skewed on its axis as I heard him talk. So Leanne was *not* dead, after all, despite what Bala had said; despite the fact that she had so brazenly gone against him! I felt the relief at her survival wash through me, almost as pleasurable as the waves of sounds I heard Outside. I think AB must have deemed me too young or stupid to pick up on his contradictions, but I was super-sensitive to them, given this was my only way to learn about the world.

The more he talked about Leanne's 'death', however – because he did so time and again – the more I realized what he actually meant when he said she was dead. Though she was still alive in body she had lost what *mattered* to be alive: AB. Therefore, she was *worse* than dead.

There was a song we often sang in the mornings, 'Which Side Are You On?' At the end of it we would recite the list of AB's enemies. For years, Bad Dennis had received citation; now, Leanne joined her – but she was no longer Leanne. In transgression, she had been transfigured. AB declared to the group that we would call her Fartcolour from now on; a racist joke.

The rest of that year was taken up with denigrating Fartcolour. In the immediate aftermath of her departure, everyone except me was asked to write a report on how evil she was. Though I didn't want to write an essay like that, part of me was still sad not to have the chance to write my own report, simply because seeing all the comrades scribbling away made me hugely jealous.

I loved to write. Yet I never had an opportunity to write anything other than my lessons and my praise for Bala. I would have been ecstatic to be able to write down a made-up story on a piece of paper, but AB insisted that he didn't want any imaginary rubbish from me: I had to be real when I did anything, whether it was writing or playing. I'd once seen a woman with a baby Outside, pushing her child in a pushchair along the tree-lined street, and promptly pretended I was doing the same thing. That was nonsensical behaviour, according to AB, and immediately banned. I was not to do ISA (Imagining, Speculating, Assuming) because imagination of any kind was poisonous.

Ironically, the ban meant the only way I could indulge my love of writing was to use my imagination even more. I soon extended my canvases of the walls and floor that I'd discovered in Discussions. Now, when I lay in bed, I traced words and sentences on to the sheet with my finger in the dark. I loved it – my only form of expression – but my writings were as insubstantial as me, the shadow-child no one ever saw.

Though I could not write creatively, I was allowed to read. I inhaled the books I was given, the act of reading as essential to me as air. I was always craving to read more. That was why, when AB gave me the Puffin Reference *Atlas of the World* but instructed me not to read the blocks of text headed 'Did you know?', I could not resist temptation. I found it enthralling! I was particularly taken to learn that Junko Tabei of Japan was the first woman to climb Mount Everest. I liked the musicality of her name.

The inevitable happened. In the loo with Josie one day, I accidentally sang the words, 'Junko Tabei of Japan!' Josie interrogated me as to what I was talking about and I clammed up. At dinner she raised it with Sian. Guessing where I must have found it, Sian checked the

Puffin book and reported to Bala that I had been reading the prohibited text. He was furious and slapped me, then forbade me from going near that book again.

I was devastated. I yearned for knowledge. So much confused me about the world. My gender, for example. The disabled neighbour had thought I was a boy when she'd said to Comrade Sian, 'I haven't seen him for a while.' People Outside seemed uncertain which I was. I couldn't help but notice the differences between the comrades and AB; the women had rise-and-fall to their chests whereas Bala's was flat as a pancake . . . *as was mine*. I asked Comrade Sian about it once.

'Your chest is flat and you are like Bala,' she explained. 'You are special, because you are like him. And if you carry on being good, then you'll be like him for ever.'

Yet when the comrades talked about me, they always said 'she'; they didn't say 'he' or even 'it'. I held on to that 'she' as though it was a port in a storm. Because I didn't feel 'special' about all this, whatever Comrade Sian declared. I felt freaky. If I *was* a girl, why couldn't I *be* one?

For I was dressed in boy's clothes, hateful shirts and trousers, and my hair was always cut brutally short. I used to see little black girls Outside in colourful dresses, beautiful beads braided through their long hair, or Indian daughters with shiny ebony plaits swinging over their shoulders, and I'd think: *why can't I have that?* I wasn't allowed to choose my clothes; the comrades went Outside to shop for me and brought back shoes, shirts and trousers. Even my name, Prem, was androgynous, more usually given to boys. AB also said it sounded like 'sperm'; I didn't know what that was, exactly, but apparently it meant I was just like a boy.

I felt as if my identity was being taken away from me – but, of course, 'my' identity was never mine to have. I was Project Prem, my life dedicated to serve AB. What need had I of gender? It was as bad as a family; it would only hold me back.

If I had to pick a gender to be, however, if one had to choose clothes and haircuts to make one's way in the world, then boy was best. In AB's view, female energy was negative. I'm not sure he meant women were lesser than men, per se, but more that women were lesser than *him*. He was the only man in the Collective; the only man in my world. He was the yardstick by which everything

45

was measured. Yet AB valued that vaunted position. For that reason, although I was dressed as a boy, he didn't want me to be one, nor grow up to become a man. A man would be a rival to him. Far better was this opaque middle ground.

I wanted to be a girl. The comrades dressed in plain shirts and trousers too, but I longed to wear the clothes that Chanda and Shobha did; one of their privileges. They donned the most beautiful salwar kameez: knee-length dresses with trousers underneath. Made of silks and chiffons, they were crafted in bright colours, purples and rose-pinks; I thought them so graceful. Comrade Chanda wore her hair long, and sometimes even jewellery. I would beg to be allowed similar things but was told in no uncertain terms that I would never be permitted, and castigated for my 'jealousy'. AB told me not to MAC (Mimic, Ape, Copy) Chanda and declared I was a 'spoilt brat'.

Race was another sensitive subject – and another grey area for me. I knew being Indian was best of all, but as with my gender, I wasn't sure which race was mine. I had honey-coloured skin and dark-brown hair, but I wasn't as brown-skinned as Bala – no matter what Sian said. She was emphatic that I be 'little AB' in every way and claimed my hair was black as his, but when I pointed out – on a sunny day when the light brought out the brown – that it was much fairer, she flew into a rage.

Although Sian would not accept that I wasn't the same as AB, Bala himself gloried in keeping me separate. Because I was born in Britain, he said I was just as responsible for the crimes of the BFS as ugly dirty whites. I wanted to be part of his Indian family – with all the privileges I saw his wife receive. Given AB treated them with so much more affection, too, it was undoubtedly something to aspire to. But Bala kept saying hurtfully, 'You're British, you were born here, so you're not part.'

I hated the British aspect of my identity, hearing it maligned day after day. When Josie came into my bedroom one evening when I was standing behind the door and accidentally bashed into me, I was thrilled.

'Smash me all up!' I cried enthusiastically. 'I'm too European!'

I felt like nothing about me was right. I'd been born in the wrong place, my body had the wrong bits, my hair was the wrong colour . . . All I wanted was to belong, but it seemed beyond my reach.

In December 1989, AB made a decision that put me even further out of touch. The Collective had begun as a Maoist group, but in AB's opinion one Mao Zedong had been getting a little too big for his boots. Who was he to rival Bala, who was, after all, a god?

Suddenly, AB declared Mao to be the worst genocidal war criminal the world had ever seen. Denunciations of the man the comrades had previously celebrated now became a key part of the daily routine. I found the change mind-boggling: this was the complete *opposite* of everything AB had said before.

But – he now revealed – his previous praising of Mao over the formative decades of the Collective had been a test for his followers: to see whether they were truly loyal to AB or could be tempted to focus on his rivals.

The comrades had all failed dismally by worshipping Mao.

Despite the fact I hadn't been born throughout most of this 'test', I was not immune from AB's ire: my name was Prem Maopinduzi. The worshipping of false idols was clearly stitched into the very fabric of me. Abruptly, I was forced to change the spelling to 'Mapinduzi'.

An odd thing happened as I listened to AB rant against his former hero.

I feel sorry for Mao.

It was such a transgressive thought I was alarmed, on edge awaiting retribution. The sheer reach of AB's power was one of the hardest things I had to live with. He could read my mind *and* he would never die. I felt the tight grip of those pieces of knowledge as a noose around my neck. Tighter and tighter they held me, as day after day I made mistakes and feared for the consequences.

But there was one way to escape it, I realized over time. From within the mist of my confused thoughts, a truly transgressive one emerged.

The only place Bala can't follow me is if I die.

I was only six. But the thought was strangely sweet. I remembered the power of that Tube train travelling beneath the ground, the way it had roared into the station with such speed and sound. *If I jumped in front of that train*, I thought, *I would be free.*

I was so lonely and unhappy. There was no Aisha; no Leanne; no light in my life at all. Every day, when the post arrived through the letterbox with a swishing sound that signalled Outside, there was never any letter for me: the only person in the whole Collective who never received a single thing. When I thought about the Tube at night now, remembering its roar, I thought idly, *I'd love to just jump in front of that train . . .*

It was supposed to be a secret, but I was only six. On 3 January 1990, it all spilled out of me. Heart on sleeve, truth unvarnished, I haplessly declared: 'I don't care whether I'm alive or dead.'

9

Bala was dismissive.

'Mind hygiene and self-criticism are key,' he told me briskly. I had to surrender to him totally – *then* I would get life – otherwise I'd be trapped in the 'death field'. He nicknamed me 'dodo' to signify my slowness in following his guidelines. If I did not learn to follow, I'd soon be as obsolete as the bird. My emotions were irrelevant; worse, unhelpful for my training. He blamed my suicidal urges on my '40 per cent'.

Bala believed there were two types of 'input' I was gaining in the world. The lion's share was AB's Knowledge, CRIS HELP, which was my 'good' 60 per cent. But I also had 40 per cent of bad input, put there by what he now called 'Maozi waves': invisible negative energy released by AB's enemies as they attempted to programme me with their remote control. AB hated my 40 per cent, he told me time and again. He also told me that slowly, very slowly, I was winning my battle against the evil Maozi waves, but it would take years to overcome these internal enemy forces. Only in the year 2000, when I'd be turning seventeen, would I finally reach 100 per cent good. To an almost-seven-year-old, it seemed a lifetime away.

Yet this glory wasn't guaranteed – and there were plenty of chances for me to take a huge step back. I nearly lost 15 per cent in one day for admiring Cindy's shapely figure. Yet the biggest risk was my habit of not working nicely with the comrades. This was sacrilege, because AB had tasked them with my training.

'If I hear comrades struggling with you,' he told me, 'I will beat you and beat you and beat you until you are numb and can't move about.' He fixed me with his black eyes, which were steeled both with threat and disappointment behind his square glasses. 'You're becoming very out of hand,' he observed.

Perhaps my glum mood – or my 40 per cent – was prompting it, but I was becoming more vocal with the comrades as I grew older. There were times when I felt very irritable about their nit-picking and surveillance, as I was still watched round the clock, including in the bathroom. Even though I knew it was for my own protection, it also gave me nowhere to hide. I always felt I lived in the unforgiving glare of a spotlight. So, using the language I'd heard AB employ, I began to shout at them, barely understanding what I was saying and often simply saying it for effect.

'I want to smash Comrade Sian's head in!' I might yell. 'I want to kill Comrade Josie!'

I wouldn't have hurt anyone; sometimes I think I wanted to start a scene just to make my days a bit different. AB once told me off for putting the comrades down by saying they weren't brought up by him; I sneeringly called them 'second-class'.

'Never even heard of AB till they read the leaflet!' I jeered, not liking myself as I did it, but lashing out all the same. I was put down by everybody, *all* the time; perhaps I just wanted to feel a sliver of superiority.

The older I got, the more I wanted to spend time alone with AB. Until now, I had never really had any alone time with him. I saw him at Discussions, for our creepy daily hugs and when he was beating me, but that was pretty much it; he did not eat with us. I'd barely even had a conversation with him, just lectures from him at the end of which I'd say, 'Yes, Beloved Comrade Bala.' But I thought if we spent more time together, he might love me more. He only really saw me through the comrades' eyes and I hoped that if he and I could have our own relationship, he might just be a bit nicer to me.

So I was pleased when, in 1990, we did start to share a little more time.

'I WENT TO COMRADE A. BALA'S ROOM! THREE TIMES! AND SAT BESIDE HIM ON HIS MAT!' I wrote in my diary, encouraged by Sian to describe this privilege in the excitement of ALL CAPITAL LETTERS.

I started to notice something from this time alone with AB. He was much nicer when the others weren't around. I didn't understand it, I was just grateful for the occasional flash of blue sky in my grey world. For my desire to make my world turn black beneath the screeching wheels of a Tube train never went away, although some days were more bearable than others. I wore the emotions like a second skin beneath my masculine shirts and trousers. They were always there, but I learned to live with them, an emotional white noise I became skilled at tuning out.

It was a blue-sky day on 7 January 1990 when I finally turned seven. Six days before, AB had given me 1 per cent of my goodness back, in so doing deducting 1 per cent from my Superidiot percentage; I was now 61 per cent good and 39 per cent bad. I felt a real sense of achievement, commensurate with my new maturity.

My birthday was no different from any other day in the Collective; we sang songs for AB and he lectured. I did not go Out. There was no birthday cake – that was far too Western a tradition – but the comrades made an Indian sweet. Presents were not the norm. Birthdays were acknowledged, not celebrated, in the Collective; the exception to this rule was of course AB. His birth and conception days were the biggest festivities of the year.

I loved AB's big days. They were the two days in the year when you could be sure the atmosphere in the house would be happy because no one would dare cause a scene on such a special occasion. I would spend weeks making things for him – a summary of his life, which the comrades made into a 'book'; a handwritten anthology of all the lyrics to our revolutionary songs. The day before the event, the comrades would clean like whirling dervishes so the whole house would be sparkling from top to bottom, then they'd prepare a delicious feast of Keralan curry and Indian sweets. AB accepted it all with a benign, expectant smile.

The rest of the year, every day of it, our important work towards the new world continued. Around this time, AB revealed to me that when his leadership became Overt, I was to be his minister for children, leading his children's army. He unveiled the appointment as though he was bestowing a great honour upon me.

I couldn't say – although I thought it before I could stop myself – *I don't want to do that* . . . I wanted to drive those lovely trains, not fight a bloody war.

But that was not my destiny. So, when I was seven, rather than playing at being a train driver I began making multiple handwritten copies of a document Sian had created, 'Convince Oneself with the Following Affirmative Facts from 1964 with One's Positive Experience with

AB, the Uniquely Positive Natural Centre, While Using Self-Criticism to Struggle Against One's Negativity'. It was a chronicle of AB's life and activities and all Synchronizations since 1964, and I had to write it out, in full, at least three times. It took *all* year, even with me writing it every single day.

I also started to study other subjects: science, where I experimented with chemicals and viewed objects through a microscope; history, where I wrote a series of essays on 'Crimes of the Americans and British'; the natural world, where I charted the macro to the micro, Universe to Electrons, with AB topping and tailing the items on my list. I'd have liked to be given exams as part of my schooling, so I could feel a sense of progression and achievement – but such things were old world and too likely to lead to self-love. Always I had to remember it was thanks to AB I knew anything.

Just once a month, I was allowed to paint; something I really enjoyed. I struggled for subjects, however. If I painted a self-portrait, I'd be accused of fascist individualism; if I painted a picture of our house and all the comrades living in it, I wasn't focusing on AB. Occasionally, I painted pictures of our leader, and he also permitted me to recreate such scenes as 'Indian kids protesting against Rajiv Gandhi'.

Hardest for me was when I tried to sketch a landscape. My world was the house. Even though I'd been Outside, I found it hard to retain detailed memories of the few places I'd been, as though my brain had been overexposed and couldn't capture the images. As months always passed between each outing, I didn't go Out frequently enough to be able to pin the mental pictures into place; they'd be fresh when I arrived home, but bleed away over time.

Comrades Chanda and Shobha both painted, so I tried to copy what they'd done or model my artwork on the few pictures in the house. I painted colourful skies, reflections in the water, trees in the distance: things I'd rarely or never seen myself. It was ISA, in a way, but because Chanda and Shobha also liked to paint, the rule was bent as a privilege.

As ever, though, not *always*. That uncertainty was what made life hard. Once, I showed AB some flowers I had drawn and he scribbled over them, writing angrily: 'AB hates PM's 39%!' Several times, he destroyed things I had created, burning them, tearing them up or

stomping on them till they were dirty and torn. It was heart-breaking –
because I bonded with the things I made, having no other outlet for my
love. To have them destroyed was terrible, as though he was destroying
a part of me.

For AB, though, it was worth it – because we were fighting
a war.

And the other thing I learned in my lessons was who we were
fighting against.

AB revealed that there was a secret world government. One
might think each country had its own, but actually they were all
controlled by another body behind the scenes. Prime ministers and
presidents were puppets, front men, while the real power lay behind
the public thrones. AB called this organization the Shadow World
Government (SWG) and its primary work, every day, was to snoop
on him and analyse what he said. That was why we had to KQ: the
house was bugged, both video and audio. Occasionally, he would
say misleading things aloud to put their agents off the scent.

He was their nemesis, and their power players his arch-enemies.
David Rockefeller, Henry Kissinger, George Bush, Edward Heath,
Alec Douglas-Home, Deng Xiaoping . . . There were many. Though
Mao was dead, the 'Mao Clique' was another foe. AB had a pathological hatred of them all and denounced them as evil monsters and
genocidal war criminals. He taught me that they ate and burned
babies.

Knowing more about our enemy made me even more frightened
of the world beyond the window. At times I became hysterical with
fear about the neighbours, those baby-eating agents who were just a
stone's throw away. So intense was my terror that AB actually took
me Outside one afternoon to see the houses, to try to stop me being
quite so scared.

He took my fear as a slight. He wanted me to be vigilant and
never interact with the agents, but my anxiety was so extreme it
implied I didn't trust him and the Collective to protect me.

'As long as you follow me,' he promised, 'they can't touch you.'

As it turned out, it wasn't long before I got a chance to put that
to the test. On 2 May 1990, I was sitting on the toilet – with Comrade Josie looming over me, watching – when I heard a very unusual
sound.

There was a knock upon the front door of the house.

Not just a knock. This was a hammering. An intervention. Fists on wood. BANG BANG BANG!

And then: an authoritative shout.

'We know you're in there! Open up!'

10

The house – normally so staid, so quiet – was suddenly a riot of noise and activity. Cautiously, Josie and I tiptoed out of the bathroom. My heart was hammering – with both fear and excitement. This was something new . . .

'Open up the door please!' the strong voice called again.

'Break down the door *please*!' Bala hollered back. He sounded as if he was in his element: the revolutionary leader rising gloriously to the occasion. Taunting the men on the other side of the door, he relished the drama.

What's happening? I wondered, jumping in shock as the front door shook violently on its hinges once again, the pounding ten times louder than before. *The defences of the Collective have never been breached like this . . .*

In whispered conversations, an explanation emerged: the men were bailiffs, here to evict us from our home. 'Rent strike' had been going on more than a year; the fascist state had now come to torment Bala for his noble political stance.

Once I knew it wasn't the next-door neighbours, of whom I was petrified, I relaxed – and almost began to enjoy the drama too. My days were so dull; in all my seven years, nothing so exciting had *ever* happened.

For as long as I could remember, AB had lectured about this kind of battle with the BFS – now I got to see him in action. As I watched, breathless with the thrill of it, he stood valiantly firm throughout the next hour or so, point-blank refusing to open the door, no matter how many times the men demanded it, and jeering when the landlord begged him to comply.

Finally, with an enormous crashing sound, the green front door was broken in: an explosion of splintered wood and sound that let the Outside in.

In the eerie quiet of the aftermath, I peered curiously along the hallway and beyond the broken door. Several tall figures loomed there.

'Leave all your things!'

The order came from AB. I panicked – what about my Lego, my pink bicycle? But this was not the time to ask. With a fleeting backwards glance towards my bedroom, filled with familiar things, I followed the others into the front garden.

I blinked on the threshold, struck by the sudden brightness of light, so different to the gloom indoors. My eyes were out on stalks at the multitude of new faces surrounding me; the people were so *close* to me – the comrades never normally let me Out without me being secreted within that protective circle of bodies. This time, there'd been no time to prepare.

I didn't dare breathe a word to any of the men, but as I stumbled out into the sunshine I studied their expressions, as though they were on scientific slides beneath my microscope. There was one I was drawn to: a short black man with a friendly face. He turned out to be the landlord. He appeared a bit sad, as though he didn't really want to be doing this; somehow, it didn't fit with the ruthless portrait AB had painted. As I walked out of the house, his expression turned to shock.

I dropped my eyes to the ground before Sian could tell me not to ogle. So few people ever saw me that it was unsettling to see his face change the moment he laid eyes on me. Yet I suspected I knew why his expression had altered: because I wasn't supposed to be here; there wasn't supposed to be a child living in this house. I saw the same expression flit across his face when Comrade Shobha rolled out in her wheelchair, and when one comrade after another exited the house. AB was a fugitive from the fascist state, so as many of us as possible also had to stay under the radar. I think the landlord had had no idea we'd all been staying in the house.

When I next risked a glance up at him, he smiled at me broadly and I felt my spirits soar. But that was as nothing to what happened next. As I stood with the comrades in the garden, all of us mingled together with the bailiffs in the confusion of the day, one of the men – perhaps motivated by a touch of guilt at booting a young child out of her home – reached out a hand and casually ruffled my boy-short hair.

My heart almost stopped with pleasure. *That felt nice*, I thought happily. *I liked that.*

I wanted to feel that touch again, the strange yet comforting weight of another's hand on me – but Comrade Sian was already glaring, her eyes like daggers pinning me in my place.

She hissed in disgust to Bala: 'That man was touching her!' There was an ugliness to her tone, but that simple touch to me had been nothing but beautiful.

I would treasure the memory all my life.

Bala led us in victory to a new home in Streatham, London. It was a modest two-up, two-down terraced house on a quiet residential street. One of the first things the comrades did was hang net curtains in all the windows; it was a priority to keep me out of sight. Similarly, the garden was left to go to ruin, the grass eventually growing three or four feet high.

The new house was damp and attracted hundreds of insects – woodlice and centipedes – that made my skin crawl. Yet the Collective refused to do anything to rid the house of them, saying it was good to put up with the infestation so that, when AB's leadership became Overt, we could say we had shared 'weal and woe' with the people of the world. AB never replaced his spectacles, which were falling apart, for the same reason, instead sticking them together with tape, pieces of plastic and, once, even some bits of fried onion.

The dampness of the new house made the electrics dangerous. Several times comrades received shocks when switching on appliances; the plug of the iron once blew up in a shower of sparks, leaving a lingering smell of burnt plastic. The comrades explained to me that these things had happened because they hadn't been following AB properly, which left me fearful of touching any domestic appliance myself. I was one of his worst followers – what would vengeful electricity do to *me*?

AB told me not to worry about what had happened at our former home; ever since his enemies had committed the crime of evicting AB's CC, AB had unleashed 'ABSOLUTE BERSERK TERROR', he said. As the previous house had a *green* front door, AB had unleashed *green*house gases, causing global warming in retribution for the eviction. AB said they had walked '100 per cent into his trap'.

In fact, I wasn't worried – I was excited to be somewhere *new* – but I did miss my things. All our belongings, including the yellow blanket I had loved as a child, had been lost in the move. We had to start from scratch.

Refreshingly, however, that included the unexpected rewriting of some of the rules. I was now informed that I would be permitted to use the toilet on my own for the first time in my life – 'But, Comrade Prem,' AB instructed, 'you must always tell somebody when you are going to pee or shit.' On 22 June 1990 another gift was given: 'Comrade Prem,' AB said benevolently, 'you can put on and off the hot and cold water taps in the dirty white basin – *not* the bath.' Previously, this licence had been denied to me.

If I hadn't been fearful of self-love, I'd have been proud of my new responsibilities. Surrounded by adults and castigated for my 'infantile disorder', I felt a strong yearning to grow up and hated anything I felt was childish – such as the fact AB insisted I call my knickers 'nappies'. I wasn't yet allowed to bathe alone, though. Given my new liberty in the bathroom, I felt the presence of their ever-watching eyes more pointedly after that. I used to pull the shower curtain round me so my nude body wasn't completely at the mercy of their unblinking gaze.

It was something of a revelation, being allowed to go to the bath-room alone. At first, I was hesitant, the warnings of so many years still embedded in my brain, but with AB's permission given and no fascist agents swooping in, I began to enjoy the time on my own. Before, being alone had always been a punishment. Now, I experienced a different side to solitude.

The bathroom had a lino floor made up of squares. While I sat on the loo, adjusting to the sensation of *not* being watched, I used to stare at each one and imagine it was a sheet of paper I could write on with my eyes. Every now and then, I sang quietly to myself. Before long, I treasured being alone in the bathroom. I began staying longer than I needed to; I reported that I had constipation and required more time.

The slim chink of autonomy seemed to open up my mind in other ways, too. When I'd been watched *all* the time, every chang-ing expression on my face had been noted, just as cloud-spotters track the shifting landscape of the skies. I'd had to be careful not to think *too* much, just in case I had a Maozi-wave thought and the comrades identified it. Now, with no one monitoring me in the loo, I could finally let my mind wander.

I found I kept thinking about Chairman Mao. Perhaps this felt a safe place to start, because I was still confused by AB's about-turn on his former hero. Every day, I had to listen to long lectures about how terrible that 'prostitute' Mao was. I felt Mao was being picked on; I wanted to be there for him, in a way no one had ever been there for me. So I developed a crush. AB used to talk gleefully of how much pain Mao had been in before he'd died, debilitated by his motor neurone disease, and I would fantasize that I was looking after him, mopping his brow and bringing him trays of healthful food.

It was so nice, living in those fantasies. I was aware, of course, that it was wrong to like someone AB had denounced, but AB had also preached that we should be kind to people, so I hoped it wasn't *too* much of a transgression ... Perhaps I would only get a runny nose rather than a vomiting bug. I was enjoying myself so much that I concluded any resulting illness was worth it. I took pleasure in my small act of rebellion. Though I feared AB, I also felt a kind of righteous satisfaction in liking the very person he had singled out for attack.

I spent more and more time in my imaginary world. Perhaps for the first time in my life, I found I could be happy. In my mental cocoon, no one ever shouted and everyone was always smiling and nice. It was the safest place in the world. I would jump up and down in the bathroom, thrilled, knowing no one could get into that world with me.

But the cocoon proved fragile, spun by gossamer threads of fantasy that could be ripped asunder with a single report or beating. And the downside to our move to the Streatham house was all the beatings . . .

For the room I spent a lot of time in was directly above AB's study. The comrades kept telling me, 'Sit still, sit still,' but despite my aspirations to maturity I was still only seven years old: I *couldn't* sit still. Not when I'd already been sitting all morning; not when I had to lie down for two hours for my afternoon nap. Sometimes the sheer kinetic energy inside me felt impossible to contain. I would have this intense need to *run*. Just to use my arms and legs: to leap, to jump, to scamper. Banned from the garden, where else could I go? Sure enough – soon enough – AB would hear the sound of my footsteps above his head.

'SHUT UP!' he would bellow. But if I'd provoked him that far, he wouldn't hold back. Out came his fist or his palm or his ruler, and I'd be beaten fifty or sixty times for making noise.

'Isn't it easier to do as you're told?' he'd sigh wearily afterwards, pushing roughly on my head as I knelt subserviently before him. 'Remember that I am in the house and take that into consideration – *cherish* the rare privilege.'

Although Bala didn't care about the bruises that bloomed on my body – who was going to see them outside the Collective when I so rarely went Out? – *I* cared. Bala may have called them marks of love, but I considered them marks of shame. I'd pull down my shirt-sleeves to hide them; button my collar tight. They were an indelible sign of my evil nature and I hated the comrades seeing them: a visual and humiliating reminder of just how bad I'd been.

But the comrades didn't need bruises to remind them: they had AB. After a beating, the practice was that I would be shunned. Everybody would isolate me and make their disgust plain. It felt like the whole world hated me. I knew I was all alone. I was told that everyone, and everything, had turned against me.

One day after such a beating, I retreated to the bathroom, claiming I needed to relieve myself, but needing to do so only through tears. I sat down on the toilet, miserable to the soles of my feet that were not quite brown enough. Every time I was beaten, my happy cocoon was smashed into a million pieces and it took time to rebuild it, so I couldn't even comfort myself with thoughts of feeding Mao.

I took a deep breath. I couldn't stay in here any longer; it would start to look suspicious. To maintain the illusion of the necessity of my visit, I stood to flush the toilet, anticipating that the handle would jam because AB had said nothing would work for me now that I had dared to go against him.

But when I pressed the silver handle down, water roared and gurgled – and the toilet flushed!

'You're on my side!' I exclaimed, the shock of it almost bringing me to my knees again – this time in gratitude. I felt overwhelmed. Awkwardly, I bent down and wrapped my arms around the cool porcelain of the loo, squeezing hard. 'Thank you, Toilet, for being on my side.'

When I went to the sink, I turned the tap on in distant hope, but to my amazement it didn't stop working either. The stream of water sounded like a melody. I washed my hands, an endorsement I had no right to receive. I could not believe the tap had gone against AB.

So, before I left the bathroom, I bent my head to the sink and gave that tap a huge, affectionate kiss, my lips pressed against the cold metal.

This was someone I could trust.

'Thank you,' I whispered, 'for being my friend.'

11

The bathroom became even more special after that. The only draw-back of my new friends, Tap and Toilet, was that they couldn't talk to me. I used to hold back-and-forth conversations with myself instead.

Such was my isolation that, despite the rules, I continued to try to see what was going on Outside. Having moved away from the elderly couple who wanted to drink my blood, I felt a bit more con-fident. In the downstairs back room, there was a patio door that looked out on to the garden – and not just ours, but next door's too. An issue of much anxiety to the Collective was that the fence between the two properties had blown down; they worried that fas-cist agents would be able to see in. To their relief, however, the ugly dirty white man next door began building a new boundary: a wall made out of bricks. To their relief – and to my fascination.

I could only watch him when one of the more liberal comrades had care of me. If they'd caught me looking, they would have stopped me, but if I was careful I was able to snatch some time gaz-ing out of the door, which was also covered over by the usual net curtain.

He had a little mixer that went round and round, and I enjoyed seeing him layering up the crimson bricks, one by one. *I would* love *to do something like that*, I thought. *How nice it must be to work outside and do work where you have to use your body.*

I watched him day after day, always careful to keep to the shadows, knowing I must not be seen. Yet he must have felt the weight of my eyes. One afternoon, while I was staring at him enviously, he straightened up from the half-built wall and squinted in my direc-tion. Then he lifted his hand and waved.

My heart thudded in my chest. But unlike in our previous house, fear wasn't the overwhelming emotion – not fear of him, at least, more fear of how the Collective would respond. For his wave was accompanied by a friendly smile and that made me feel my usual joy at being smiled at by a stranger.

He hesitated after he waved, as though expecting some response from me. But I'd swiftly darted back into the shadows, my hand glued firmly to my side. I *couldn't* wave back.

Yet I felt an odd sense of having done something wrong as I moved away from him. *Was it rude of me not to respond?*

I was in a state of panic afterwards. *To tell or not to tell?* What if the man told on *me*; reported I'd been looking out the window? Was this AB testing me somehow? I knew I was meant to report straight away if anyone from Outside ever communicated with me.

Yet part of me didn't want to report, treasuring the gift of that wave and smile – the man had *seen* me, which made me feel a bit more solid in myself. Nevertheless, the years of training had taught me that such niceness could be a trick.

Confused by my feelings about it, in the end I told the comrades he'd waved. Luckily for me, they were so enraged at his behaviour that they didn't discipline me. I think they thought he had taken advantage of me standing near the window, so I was simply told to make sure he could never see me in future. I obeyed. If I ever saw him in the garden again, I moved away.

Perhaps the neighbour's audacity prompted another rule change that happened around this time. AB announced that things were getting 'more dangerous' as the time for the 'all-out lightning war' approached. It was never explicitly stated what would happen before AB's leadership of the world became Overt, but AB sometimes talked of 'a victorious war of annihilation to the finish'. The coming conflict sounded scary, but AB said all would be well as long as I followed him. Now, as a measure of added security, AB declared I could *never* go Outside without him – even to the garden. Before then, I had been able to leave the house with three comrades present, even if AB wasn't there. But the world was now too dangerous for him to entrust my safety to the comrades. I could only ever go Out with him.

It meant my rare outings became even more limited – because AB often didn't want to go Outside himself, preferring to stay at home, though we still went Out when Comrade Chanda's relatives came, which happened two or three times a year. When he did go Out, to the cinema or a museum, he rarely took me with him.

Once or twice, he took me to the corner shop, where I was entranced by the cashier and the musical ring of her till, though I had no understanding of the concept of money or how to use it. AB said that when it became Overt he would abolish money, so I had no need to learn.

It was so *dull* indoors. Every day was the same. When the clocks went forwards or backwards in the spring and autumn, it was a highlight of the year because it made for a *change*, a little lighter or darker in the evenings. In Streatham we still did the same daily singing and Discussions and I found I often had to stifle my yawns as AB lectured on and on; the other comrades seemed to find him charismatic, but I didn't. With my diary-writing overseen, even that task, which could have been enjoyable, was oppressive. I always wrote in the third person: 'Comrade Bala disciplined Comrade Prem for wanting to look at ugly dirty whites'; 'Comrade Bala denounced Comrade Prem as a superidiot and gave her ultra-ugly grade'; 'Comrade Bala made Comrade Prem go down on her knees. He said how can she criticise others if she doesn't criticise herself?'

Writing in the third person may have been intended to ward off fascist individualism, or came about because Comrade Sian had originally written the diary for me, but as I grew older I liked the distinction. 'Comrade Prem' almost became a different girl to *me*: the things in the diary, and the beatings and reports, happened to *her*, but *I* was the friend of Chairman Mao, who made him mashed potato. Over time I became two people: the comrade working for AB and a fantasist living in my cocoon. My active imagination made the beatings much easier to bear.

There was one new element to my studies that began in the Streatham house. Every day now, Sian, Bala and I put together *The New World*, a homemade newspaper for the Collective which everyone *had* to read. Five or six newspapers from Outside would be read by AB, he'd cut out particular articles of note, and then Sian and I would stick them down on a sheet of coloured A3 paper, laid out in columns like the Outside media. We were not permitted to read those parts of the newspapers that AB had not selected.

After Sian had given the finished A3 sheet back to AB, he would add his learned comments before *The New World* was circulated within the Collective, so that all the comrades could benefit from the wisdom of his insight. He would cross out '1997' in any mention of the scheduled Hong Kong handover, because the Overt would have happened by then so AB would be ruling it instead. He would declare that the upcoming 1992 Olympics would be the last to be held before the Overt. Repeatedly, he reminded us that we must not read his scribbled comments aloud because of fascist spies listening in; once, Aisha forgot, enthusiastically praising AB for some comment, and was beaten for her stupidity.

To begin with, I enjoyed helping AB with *The New World* – it was something different and, as I was always yearning to read more, I loved having a daily newspaper to pore over. But the more I learned of Outside from the articles, the more scared I became. Frankly, Outside sounded petrifying. *No wonder AB wants to build a new world . . .* I grasped the necessity of his plans, perhaps for the first time.

For I read about children being kidnapped; women being raped. (AB called this 'poking wasteholes' and told me sex was death.) Very quickly, I realized it was not just fascist agents I had to fear. Children were starving to death in their thousands; others brutally shot by death squads. The Gulf War was raging at that time and AB insisted on showing me nightmarish pictures of the grotesque burns suffered by Iraqi children in the Allied bombing; as well as, a bit later, images of Somalians dragging round the corpses of US soldiers.

I also discovered a lot more about the horrible reality of old-world families. AB chose articles that described how one man cooked and ate his wife; how newborn babies were abandoned in rubbish bins; how another man murdered all his relatives.

'See how you're protected from all of this?' AB would say benevolently. '*This* is why I do not want you to go Outside.'

And I *did* see. What a blessed relief it was to be a member of AB's CC! I felt thankful for his protection all over again; glad the glass was always between me and the world when I looked Outside.

Yet not *everything* was bad . . . One day in June 1991, I was sneaking peeks into the garden when I saw something unexpected. Vaguely, I could hear the laughter and chatter of several children in next door's garden; I couldn't see what was happening because of the brick wall, but it was clearly some special occasion. As I stared aimlessly Outside, several brightly coloured balloons bobbed up over the wall – and came into *our* garden!

I was entranced. I never saw anything colourful; I had never had a balloon. Now, *five* of them appeared before my eyes: green, yellow, blue, red and dirty white. They floated over the wall as though dancing in the wind, playfully bouncing against each other. On their sides was printed: HAPPY BIRTHDAY.

AB, as ever, was on his guard. As I cautiously watched from the window, he tore out of the house and ran towards the balloons, enraged at their infringement. I think he must have thought this was a ruse by the BFS. To my bitter disappointment, he burst every last one.

I yearned to see what was going on next door: *I* wasn't scared of the balloons; they had been so beautiful. The only way I could properly see into their garden was from Comrade Shobha's room, but as she was always sitting there in her wheelchair I knew I wouldn't get a chance. However, a few days later, while she was going to the loo, I snuck into her room and stared out at next door's garden.

It had changed. Set up on the neatly mown lawn was a beautiful bright-red slide. I realized the laughing children I'd heard must have been playing on it; it must have been a birthday party. I felt a twist of jealousy in my gut. Why couldn't I have such things?

I dared to ask Bala.

'I don't like the rubbish that goes on next door,' he said brusquely.

Yet I kept on talking.

'If you're so interested in the bright-red slide and all the rubbish games they do next door, you should join them!' he declared angrily.

I cringed in fear. I knew he didn't mean I could nip next door to use the slide and then come home again. This was AB: his world was black and white. 'Which Side Are You On?' we sang in the mornings; I couldn't like red slides *and* be part of the Collective. If I left to play on that slide, I'd be banished from the safety of his presence.

'If you go, you might have fun, but I would lock the door so you could never come back,' he hissed at me. 'You'll *never* be allowed back.'

I listened to his words in terror. I was eight years old and I *knew* about Outside now: I knew there were not just fascist agents out there, but child-killers and thugs. Even if I risked it, who could I turn to? I didn't know anybody outside the Collective; I had never spoken a single word to anyone not in the group. Where on earth would I go?

Sadly – because I really did like that slide – I acquiesced to AB's guidelines and gave up my dream of playing on it. Such things were not for me.

But a seed had been planted, nonetheless.

Were *some* things better Outside?

12

'Why is Gorbachev not dead yet?' I asked AB impatiently. Bala had been crowing about the downfall of the former leader of the Soviet Union in late August 1991; I couldn't understand why he didn't just kill him, given he was such an enemy and AB had the power.

'Ah,' said AB expansively, 'I have a programme for him – just like I have for you . . .'

That year, AB's programme for me required that I write down my dreams for him: although he could already read my mind, he demanded an account of all my waking *and* sleeping moments, so as better to train me. No stone was to be left unturned: he wanted control over every aspect of my life.

I couldn't really remember my dreams, only the nightmares, which were often about the scarred Iraqi children AB had shown me, or starving African children with worms in their bellies: what I thought might be my fate if I was ever abandoned by AB. With no genuine dream material at my disposal, I excitedly spied an unexpected opportunity – to write. It was the comrades who would oversee my work and *they* didn't have the power of thought control, so they wouldn't know that I was really making up stories!

I used to write pages and pages, delighting in the freedom to express myself. My 'dreams' often starred my friend, Mao, although I would write: 'Dreamt I was organizing a meeting to *denounce* Mao!' I liked that I got the chance to write his name and create something.

I was so happy, writing those 'dreams'. I felt less of a shadow-child when I could see words unravelling from the end of my pen. Afterwards, I'd stare almost in wonder at the page of writing: *I did that*. It was proof that I existed. Over time, I began reading my 'dreams' aloud to the comrades when we were together in the kitchen, whenever AB was not there.

I liked the kitchen. Food was one of the highlights of my life; a punctuation point amid the dreariness of the day. It was my one daily pleasure, and it gave me comfort on days when I was feeling miserable.

Comrade Josie was the best cook, though I could never openly praise her skills. She and the others made a lot of Indian food – liver masala, vegetable curry, stuffed sweet samosas and banana erussery. I relished the opportunity to help in the kitchen, where I would pick through the rice to remove debris or gather ingredients for a recipe. I wasn't taught to do any actual cooking, and was too terrified of the electrical appliances to use them, but nonetheless I much preferred the kitchen work to doing my studies about AB. Bala himself was in two minds about allowing me time in the kitchen – my work as his soldier was far more important. Sometimes he disallowed it as a punishment, but on the whole, to my relief, he permitted it.

It meant the kitchen and bathroom soon became my two favourite rooms in the house. As I grew a little older, I tried closing my bedroom door in the hope of a little more privacy, but AB disciplined me, reminding me that the Shadow World Government (SWG), led by David Rockefeller, would take me away and kill me if I did not allow the comrades to maintain their constant watch.

Then, to my horror, he started worrying again about allowing me privacy in the bathroom. It seemed he had noticed the ever-lengthening time I was spending in there and decided to put a stop to it. On 10 December 1991 he gave a strict guideline:

1-2 minutes for peeing.
3-5 minutes for shitting.

The comrades should report if I disobeyed.

I was devastated. Life became harder – not helped as 1991 turned into 1992 and AB became more violent than before, as though me turning nine meant I'd graduated into a new world of pain. He'd spit in my face and swear at me. 'If you carry on like this,' he'd yell, 'I will break your fucking finger.' He threatened to take a chair and beat me to a pulp; to smash my head in; to chop off my fingers if I bit my nails. Those suicidal feelings I'd had aged six buzzed up again, like a swarm of bees stinging me beneath my shirt.

Such was my desolation that I'd sometimes even speak back to

AB. When he gave me five 'beyond ultra-ugly' grades one day, I responded: 'I don't care.' If ever I talked back like this, I was always severely punished.

To my surprise, however, I no longer seemed to be the only person in the Collective feeling that way. Ever since we'd moved to Streatham, Comrade Cindy had been acting strangely. She used to stand far off in Discussions now, almost out of the circle, as though she couldn't bear to be near AB. She barely talked to anyone; if she did speak, she would snap. Once, there was a huge fight when she failed to greet AB on passing him in a corridor. For hours at a time now she would sit on the edge of her bed, face turned away, and silently draw line after line on a piece of paper. I didn't know what she was doing; her behaviour frightened me. Something wasn't right.

Too young to be able to figure out what was up with Cindy, I tried to lose myself in the happiness of writing 'dreams'. But in September 1992, AB wandered in one day while I was reading my 'dream' aloud.

He was furious. Outwardly, he said he was angry because the fascist state might be eavesdropping; inwardly, I wondered if it was *really* because he knew the story was made up. He pushed me roughly to my knees and I cried out; even more so when he slapped me and I felt the sting of his heavy palm. He went for Comrades Aisha and Sian too, for allowing me to read out what I'd written. It had not been expressly forbidden, but they were expected to have anticipated it was wrong.

Worse was still to come. Before I could stop him, he reached out a hand and grabbed the book I'd written my stories in. Without missing a beat, he tore it in two and then thoroughly shredded the pages.

I felt the pain deep inside, far worse than any beating. Each rip of the paper felt like he was ripping up my soul. Everything I wrote was sacred to me. Like Tap and Toilet, my words were my friends.

'You must all ask yourselves,' AB raged in Discussions, ' "Did AB ask me to do this? If not, *WHY* AM I DOING IT?" '

AB had not asked Comrade Cindy to make all those lines on her pieces of paper. That autumn, he finally started attacking her for her strange behaviour, whereas previously he had let it go. In hindsight, I think he was worried about money. Throughout 1992, whenever I requested something, I was told: 'No, there are no units to waste.'

But it seemed, despite the money worries, that Cindy's insubordination had become too much.

As always happened, we were asked to join in with the attacks. I did so too, denouncing Cindy, and much more happily than I had Leanne because Cindy never seemed upbeat, so it was hard to find anything pleasant to say about her. AB began picking on everything she did, escalating his violence against her. Later, he said this was a test: she had to show that no matter how hard on her he was, she wanted to stay in AB's CC, to prove herself a good person.

Cindy failed the test.

On 13 October 1992, she didn't come home from work. Like Fartcolour before her, she had left the Collective. 'Traitor Cindy got wiped out!' I wrote in my diary.

It was all part of AB's plan.

After Cindy left, with no one in the Collective working we really were poor. The Indian feasts dried up; we ate a lot of biscuits for breakfast. Two old tops of mine got stitched together to make a new one because we couldn't afford replacements. Everyone seemed stressed. AB developed a toothache soon after Cindy's banishment and blamed us – we were the ones creating it through our disobedience.

Dentists, like doctors, were part of the old world – so none of the comrades ever went, no matter the pain of their teeth. Consequently, they all had dreadful teeth, black and brown or simply missing. AB instructed they should let their rotten teeth fall out – because when they reached the age of a hundred, new ones would grow.

That winter, no matter what I did I could not get back in Bala's good books. Shobha was ill one day and I helped look after her, but I was beaten for building an anti-AB clique. Other transgressions were more familiar: I mentioned, a bit uncertainly, that I *thought* I looked more like a girl than a boy . . . AB promptly told me I was an 'ugly cadaver' and he didn't want to hear any more talk about girls; he wanted *people* for his Collective, not *men* and *women*. I was beaten 63 times; given 12 kicks. My diary charted every crime and punishment.

On 3 December 1992, AB beat me – again – for running above his room. It was a particularly bad beating, even by AB's new standards, and coming on top of all the other kicks and shoves and slaps

I'd received in the past few weeks it was too much for me to take. Increasingly, I'd felt it was *unfair*, what AB was doing in attacking me. 'I am very innocent!' I'd told him once. 'I don't know why I should work with you when you attack me when I am so innocent. I am very hurt and offended by the way you treat me.'

My reasoning always fell on deaf ears.

On 3 December, I limped away from AB after his latest beating. I may have looked defeated and compliant as I bowed my head and hobbled away, but inside I felt anything but. Rather than feeling sorry for myself, or believing that I was wicked and *deserved* to be hit, for once my overwhelming feeling was anger.

With the time limits now imposed on the bathroom, I could not retreat there to lick my wounds. With my cocoon blasted to bits by all the beatings, there was no relief to be found with my old friend Mao.

So – unusually – I let my anger grip me, rather than running away from it into a peaceful fantasy that calmed me down. I let it flood my mind, vine its way along every vein. Until now, my thought transgressions had been fairly minor – finding a friend in Mao, a man who had once been a friend of AB. But, in that moment, I tried to think of the most outrageous thing possible. I almost wanted AB to know I was angry. I'd already been punished and I felt I didn't care if he beat me again: what was one more bruise on top of all the rest?

So I racked my brains, trying to find the right words to give voice to all these feelings. How could I express the depth of my rage?

Trembling with fear, I closed my eyes and thought with all my might: *I HATE AB AND I LOVE DAVID ROCKEFELLER! I HOPE DAVID ROCKEFELLER FINDS AB AND PUTS HIS FOOT ON HIS FACE!*

I cowered afterwards, expecting my body to explode in a conflagration, for Spontaneous Human Combustion to engulf me in a searing heat . . .

Nothing.

A beat later, still alive, I opened my eyes gingerly, expecting to see fire and brimstone raining outside the window; for the ground beneath me to shudder and tear apart; for a lightning bolt to strike me dead . . .

Nothing.

I looked around me, waiting. But no disaster, natural or otherwise, befell me in those first few minutes after I'd made the curse.

When I next saw AB, I searched his face for any sign he'd heard me . . .

There was none.

In the days and weeks that followed, I didn't fall sick and nothing untoward happened at all. I could not comprehend or make sense of it. *AB is God, God is AB . . .*

But *still* nothing happened.

How can this be?

I think it was then that the realization struck me, with all the intensity of that lightning bolt that never came.

AB cannot read my mind. He does not have that power.

I felt on the brink of a brave new world.

Part Two
Insurrection

13

I sat quietly on the plastic chair, swinging my legs. Lambeth Housing Advice Centre was not particularly busy on 28 October 1993 but nonetheless the unfamiliar sounds – phones ringing, computer keys clicking, the officious voices of those in charge – swamped my ears until my head ached. With Comrade Cindy and her salary gone, we had lasted almost a year in the Streatham house without paying rent, but two days ago had been unceremoniously evicted and were currently staying at a guest house.

I was thrilled by the eviction. There were so many wonderful *new* things I was experiencing as a result – such as a hotel! I was captivated by the other residents, including several nice-looking African women who had children. As with the blonde girl at the fence when I was five, these small citizens confounded me. Comrade Sian had told them all I didn't speak any English so, to my disappointment, they ignored me. I had watched jealously as children from different families introduced themselves to each other and then scampered off to play. Even if Sian hadn't stopped me, I would have been at a loss as to how to do the same.

AB was spitting mad about the 'warlord criminal' landlord who had evicted us; the day before he'd unleashed wildfires over California in retribution. Though I despised the stinking landlord too, I also found it amusing watching AB fulminate about his enemy. Since that powerful December day the previous year, I'd formulated a nickname for our leader in my head: AB = Anger Burns. It was apt both for his constant rage and for the way his beatings burned me.

It was also sacrilege to have devised such a thing. Though AB was always seeing secret meanings in words and inventing acronyms – something he called 'AR Adiction' – the rest of us were banned from doing so. 'Don't do, "This means that and that means this!"' he would say petulantly when I tried to copy him, or to make up my own new words. '*I* am the natural centre – no one else!'

Yet despite my breaching of the guideline, no harm had come to me, so I merrily continued to use it. My mental cocoon had welcomed new allies alongside Mao, too – the most transgressive of whom was the British Prime Minister, John Major. Secretly, I considered him to be the greatest hero the world had ever seen or would ever see (aside from AB). More than in my mind, John Major was in my heart. He was something of a role model: AB often mentioned derisively how Major had left school at sixteen and didn't go to Oxbridge, yet he was now leader of the BFS; it gave me hope that, despite my unconventional education, I too could achieve great things. Great things, that was, beyond becoming AB's minister for children.

I thought often about Major. When I'd been younger, I'd been frightened to like something AB didn't, but now I almost took a perverse pleasure in it. And as I fantasized about Major in his grey suit and square specs, it seemed inconceivable that every night he tucked a napkin into his collar and devoured a newborn, as AB had always described. Earlier that year, I'd taken courage from my new-found thought freedom and even articulated it: 'They don't eat babies!' I had scoffed, when AB was mid-rant against the SWG.

He pinned me with a glare. 'Don't doubt me,' he'd threatened. I had said nothing more. That always happened: any dissent was crushed so thoroughly that there was no dissent at all.

Except in my mind.

In truth, I wasn't *completely* certain AB didn't have the power to read my thoughts. He often said: 'I allow you to express and *lull* you into thinking you have got away with it, so as to catch you on *bigger* crimes. *Then* I will punish you so that you will become a *self-sacrificing* soldier of AB, and will *never* violate my authority in anything at any time, anywhere in the entire universe . . .' So part of me was worried that he was clocking up each and every thought violation and would one day show his hand.

Yet I also thought: *If Bala does know everything, then he knows I'm thinking about Major . . . and he's not angry, so he is all right with it. Perhaps he secretly* likes *Major after all and his denouncing of him is a test, just like he did with Mao. Perhaps it's even* good *I like Major because I am passing the secret test . . .*

I could tie myself up in knots about it. It was a lonely dilemma, because I couldn't ask anyone for help in unravelling it; Tap and Toilet offered no insight at all. Carefully, I assessed every move of AB's: the way he allowed Aisha to start sleeping in my bed again at the beginning of 1993; the way he increased my good percentage to 70 per cent in September. Ultimately, I decided to trust my instinct. Perhaps things were not quite as controlled as I'd always believed. The thought was a happy one.

Certainly, the Collective seemed rather uncontrolled at the moment, as I accompanied them to the Lambeth housing office. I knew they'd rather have done anything else but bring me here, but the alternative was to leave me in the hotel, which was equally unacceptable.

'Stay here,' they had hissed at me, some distance from the counter. I wasn't to accompany them to speak to the official. Now I watched from afar as the group of comrades moved up the line, getting closer to the mixed-race woman sitting behind the desk.

I viewed her cautiously. She was an out-and-out fascist agent, working for the BFS. With no comrades employed any more, we had been forced to come here to be rehoused by the state – but we all had to be on our guard as we carried out this heroic interaction with our enemy.

Though my head had become a sanctuary for me, Outside was still as scary as ever. I didn't understand my relationship with it: I loved to *be* Outside, and often thought the people I observed there seemed very nice, yet I also had nightmares about the neighbours. I felt as though I swung back and forth about it like a body on a gallows, corpse creaking in the wind but always rooted by the noose: the knowledge that Outside *had* to be dangerous because of all I read each day in *The New World*.

Earlier that year, in January, I'd had a wake-up call about my fascination with Outside. Very naughtily, I'd spent several days pouring water into the airing cupboard, hoping the Collective would think there was a leak and call a plumber. (Anything to break up the monotony of my life.) The 'leak' was soon discovered, but I was identified as the culprit. AB was so incensed that he threw me Out of the house, just as he had when I was four.

I was older and wiser now. Aged four, I'd been overwhelmed; aged ten, it was much, *much* worse, because now I had crystal clarity on all the perils that awaited me if AB didn't let me back in. I banged as hard as I could on the locked door, delirious with danger.

When AB had first opened the door again, my spirits had soared, but he'd merely stripped me of my tracksuit top and thrown me back Out again into the freezing January day. I was beyond distressed. He only let me back in when he considered I was suitably terrified.

I had learned my lesson well. No matter what, no fate could be worse than the idea of leaving the Collective. So, that October day in 1993, I spoke to no one in the housing centre – but I *was* keen to listen. Despite the comrades' instructions, I slid off my plastic chair and began edging closer to the desk, wanting to hear what they were saying about our new house.

Although the Collective was now eight-strong (AB, Chanda, Shobha, Sian, Josie, Aisha, Oh and me), the comrades were discussing a property for just four people: Chanda, Shobha, Sian and Oh. The rest of us were not on the list. I hated being excluded from official paperwork like this.

I could hear the woman behind the desk speaking now. She had a bossy tone and everything about her manner screamed self-importance. I could sense the comrades' dislike of her because I knew them well, but she may not have known. Only if there was an issue – if they thought someone was probing a little too closely into their affairs – would they show the other side of themselves and go on the attack.

'Who is *she*?' I suddenly heard the bossy woman ask. I glanced up to see that she was pointing a finger straight at me.

As one, the comrades' heads swivelled and they all stared angrily down at me. No longer was I standing at a distance from them as they'd directed – I had walked right up to the desk.

'Oh, she's just staying with us for a few days,' the breezy lie came. 'Her parents are coming to take her away soon.'

The woman nodded and bent back to her paperwork: curiosity satisfied; explanation accepted. Though the lie chimed a little bit off with me – AB always insisted on honesty – I believed they had done it to protect me from the BFS. If the SWG found out where I was, I would be kidnapped and killed. What was one little white lie in the face of that?

I tried to bury my instinctive feeling that lying to the woman was wrong. Everyone else thought it was right, so I took my gut feeling to be a Maozi wave; my desire to listen to it evidence of my 30 per cent. Rather than the lie being something the comrades had done wrong, I believed it was my reaction to it that was wicked.

The reference to parents intrigued me, though. AB had told me by now that I hadn't been born on to his hand after all – I was a test-tube baby, born of machine rather than of man. But what was strange was that despite this explanation, which made sense to me, any time the comrades lied about my origins to Outside they *always* gave me parents, as though everyone had to have them in order to be born. In the run-up to the eviction – perhaps anticipating that questions might soon be asked – AB had even drilled me in the explanation I must give if anyone ever interrogated me. He and Comrade Sian had sat me down one day and directed me to write the following:

My father was a Peruvian Communist freedom fighter who died in a people's war. My mother was an Englishwoman who died giving birth to me. They were friends of AB, which is why he is now taking care of me.

I knew it was a story but I *wished* it was real. Lately, I'd decided I would like to have parents, despite all the trouble the comrades had with theirs. To know where I came from would have given me some substance, a child born of *someone* and not just shadows, but I knew it was impossible. I came from a test tube; there was nothing behind my origins but empty glass.

I'd written out the story of my so-called parents happily, excited to be given something imaginary to inscribe. The unsettling thing about the episode had been Comrade Sian's reaction. As she'd been dictating the story to me, the words had kept stopping; mid-sentence, I'd looked up at her to discover the reason for the delay.

Comrade Sian was crying.

Comrade Sian *never* cried, unless AB hit her head too hard, she was the sheepdog, she made *others* cry.

'W-what's wrong?' I'd asked, cautious in case she snapped my head off.

'The story of your parents is making me emotional' was what she'd said.

I knew better than to pursue it.

AB had issued several other mysterious guidelines in the run-up to eviction. 'Don't smell AB Outside' was one; 'Don't tell anybody AB beat you' was another.

As it turned out, however, there was no one for me to tell anything to. No one I encountered asked me any questions at all. With a final flourish, the housing officer signed off our application. Smooth as silk, Comrade Sian ushered me out of the housing centre, walking fast so I struggled to keep up with her, in order to express her displeasure that I'd dared show myself to the woman behind the desk.

So quickly did she escort me out that I only had time to capture one last, fleeting look at that office of authority: the staff behind their counters, the piles of paperwork, the filing cabinets filled with form after form . . . Everything was a blur of bureaucracy: a world of which I had never been and would never be part.

One last look . . . then the door closed softly behind us.

14

We moved into our new home in Wembley, north London, on 5 November 1993. Unlike our previous houses, which were relatively large and self-contained, this was a tiny three-bedroom flat on the ground floor of a low-rise apartment block. With eight people living in it, we were at close quarters. AB commandeered the box room, Chanda and Shobha shared, and the rest of us slept in the third room.

In this house I saw much more of Comrades Chanda and Shobha, who had previously kept their distance. It was fascinating for me to observe the interaction between AB and his wife – because Chanda didn't worship him as slavishly as the others. She would even dare to say, 'Hold on!' when he called her name, rather than scurrying to attention the moment he shouted. It was eye-opening, as extraordinary to me as if a planet suddenly broke from its orbit around the Sun.

Perhaps because of Chanda's increased presence, morning singing stopped in Wembley. My interpretation of it was that AB did not seem keen to let Chanda hear our songs, maybe because Comrade Sian organized them and there seemed such a strange relationship between those women. For the same reason, Sian's constant bullying of me was curbed too – though it did not stop entirely – as though she disliked Comrade Chanda seeing too much of our affairs. I was also no longer forced to write my diary every day.

In Wembley the rules were also relaxed at a mind-boggling rate. The very first day we got there, AB taught me how to use the peephole at the front door. I was to be permitted to open and close it in this house for the first time in my life, but *only* when I was sure it was the comrades coming home. I was also allowed to speak on the telephone to AB or the comrades if they had gone Out or vice versa. The women would hold the receiver for me so I didn't physically touch it.

I believe the ethnicity of our neighbours had a lot to do with the regime change. Rather than being surrounded by ugly dirty whites, as we had been in all our previous homes, Wembley was full of people from ethnic minorities, and the Collective, initially at least, were much less hostile towards them. For my part, I still found the adult neighbours frightening – and there was one man in particular who terrified me. Once when I was gazing Outside, he glanced up at me from his basement flat below: his face was a grey-green colour in the shadows of his dreadlocks and seemed almost to loom up at me. I called him Uenis Cieppo, a name that, for me, captured his shadowy colour.

For all my new liberties, however, by far the best thing about Wembley was that I got to go Outside much more. Previously, AB and I only really went Out when the relatives came, which was a maximum two or three times a year. But in Wembley, because the property was owned by the BFS, housing officials visited *once a month* – and, naturally, my existence had to be concealed each and every time.

Nor was it only my existence, but also the fact that eight people were living covertly in the tiny flat. We routinely removed excess toothbrushes from the common holder in the bathroom, piled pillows up on beds to conceal the truth of their multiple occupants; tucked away Oh's fold-up bed and Aisha's sofa bedding. Once the place looked as if just four people lived there, AB and I would take our leave, only returning when the coast was clear.

The property didn't have a garden, but there were beautiful communal grounds. I longed to be able to stroll around them, but I went in them just twice in all the years we lived there. I used to sit in the back bedroom and gaze forlornly out of the window. I had more time to do this than before because another relaxed rule was that I was allowed to change my clothes alone. I also had an hour to myself to do AB's exercises (which involved lying in bed and stretching out my arms towards my legs until I reached the tips of my toes).

For a while, I followed AB's instructions to the letter, but my little-used body struggled with the stretches; in particular my tummy, which was often poorly (perhaps with anxiety), always hurt when I bent my body in two. Very quickly, I realized that my alone time was far too precious to be spent doing exercises. I started to secret-read instead. For a long time now, I'd yearned to read something other than Chinese children's books or *The New World*. I'd tried to read the books AB did, but he'd told me brusquely not to copy him. However, when I was supposedly doing those exercises in my bedroom, AB wasn't there to stop me . . .

In the room was a cupboard filled with books. Books about China, Hinduism, leading figures of the Western world . . . AB's philosophy was that you had to *know* what you hated: he liked to learn all about the things he detested so that he could repudiate them with authority. So at my disposal was a wealth of knowledge, though I could only read in snatches at a time, and always cautiously, in case a comrade came in and caught me.

I began by reading books on Hinduism and the Indian mystics, Sri Ramakrishna Paramahansa and Swami Vivekananda. I fell in love with Hinduism: the colourful clothes, the food and the festivals, the divine trances the faithful had. I thought how nice it would be to fall into such a trance myself; I'd thought, before now, that my cocoon with Major and Mao was fun, but what a way this would be to escape the drudgery of my existence! I prayed – I wasn't quite sure to whom – that one day I would get to feel as those mystics did. In fact, that polytheistic element added to the appeal: everyone should be free to worship the gods of their choice.

Imagine having a choice, I thought, eyes wide with wonder.

While alone in the room, I also used to open the window, so I could get a rare chance to feel the heat of the sun or the coolness of a fresh breeze fluttering on my face. I'd have a really good time looking Out, for as long as I could get away with it.

With the window open, it wasn't long before the laughter of the neighbourhood children reached me. There were perhaps six or seven other kids living in the apartment block and someone had rigged up a homemade swing for them opposite my window: a hanging bar that was just the right size for an eleven-year-old like me.

It looked so good! And if the breeze through the window was welcome, I could only imagine how nice it would feel to climb aboard that swing and sail through the air, my legs and arms and body all flying . . . The other children played on it all the time, soaring backwards and forwards. I used to watch them and cry.

'Why can't I play on the swing?' I asked AB tearfully one day.

'It's too dangerous,' he replied in a kind, protective tone. 'People might notice you.'

I had to stay in the shadows instead.

I felt so sad about it. The other children used to shout and run about and I'd sit silently in my room, watching them, *wishing* I could be part of the group. Bala ordered me to ignore them, but time and again I was drawn back to the window, unable to resist temptation.

One day, while I was jealously staring Out, one of the little Indian girls saw me looking. She raised her hand eagerly; not to wave, but to beckon. Even to me the meaning was plain: *Come and play with me* . . .

I backed away, terror firing my feet. With the Collective now on warmer terms with the neighbours, I couldn't trust that she wouldn't mention my existence to her mother, who might say something to Sian, who would say it to AB, who would beat me for not keeping myself hidden.

I didn't think *she* was a fascist agent, but I knew, nonetheless, that she could not be my friend.

15

One February day in 1994, I carefully stepped up on to the side of the bath and reached up to the window. At eleven years and one month old, I was a tall child – AB said 'too tall', but that was perhaps because I was now almost the same height as him – so I could just manage to hook my fingers round the bar and push the window open. The bathroom window was opaque, so to see Outside I had to do this.

I was very, very cautious every time I did, fearful that if the Collective caught me they would impose time restrictions on my bathroom visits again. I'd been delighted to find that my old friends, Tap and Toilet, had transferred their loyalty to our new address; I may have been forbidden from forming friendships with other children, but AB had no sway over me and my mates. Consequently, I thought of the bathroom as my home. It was a beautiful place to be – when I was alone. For despite all the rule-relaxing happening in Wembley, one remained sacrosanct: I must be watched by the comrades in the bath.

I hated it. Unlike in our previous house, there was no shower curtain here, so there was nowhere to hide. A string ran over the bath for drying laundry, so I'd try to conceal myself by hanging my towel across it, but it wasn't very effective. It felt particularly oppressive because my body had started to change: beneath my nipples small breasts had begun to bud. I didn't want the Collective to see, yet nor could I mention my distress; Bala used to say, 'If I find out you don't like something, I will do it more until you subordinate.'

I let out a sigh of satisfaction as I peered Outside: I hadn't missed him. One of the highlights of my day now was watching one of our upstairs neighbours leave his house. The bathroom looked out on to the main road, as well as the apartment block's parking spaces, and this particular neighbour had a motorcycle. I loved watching him get ready to go Out on his bike in the morning. On would go his gloves, then another pair of sturdier ones, then a huge helmet . . . and only then would he swing his leg over the bike and make the engine roar. I'd begun timing my visit to the toilet so I could see him. I adored the sheer freedom of it: he was not closed in, as in a car, yet still had the ability to zoom off!

I had no real idea of where he, or the other neighbours I saw coming and going, went every day. Other than the Science Museum, the Commonwealth Institute and London Zoo, where *did* people go? Yet I felt envious all the same. *How lucky they are*, I thought wistfully, *they get to go Out every day*.

Distracted, I wobbled a little on the edge of the bath and clutched at the window to steady myself, heart pounding. I found, these days, that it was sometimes hard for me to keep my balance; I used my body so little that when I was upright and moving, I experienced the physical exertion in a kind of head rush. I'd begun to fear I might fall over; I didn't trust my body.

I regained my balance and craned my neck to see out of the small window again. It was a wonderful view. The road was always busy. As well as the neighbours coming to and fro, I loved to watch the traffic, especially the bright-red double-decker buses thundering past.

I stepped down from the bath with a satisfied sigh. I just had time for one more game . . . Quietly, I dug into the laundry bag, hunting through the dirty clothes . . . *Bingo*. With a triumphant grin, I pulled out one of Chanda's beautiful salwar kameez.

Seeing more of Comrade Chanda in Wembley had made me even more aware of the hierarchy in the house. It had jarred with me even as we'd unpacked: Chanda, Shobha and AB got one cupboard each to put their things in, whereas the five of us had one cupboard between us. More obvious, too, was what I took to be Comrade Chanda's intense dislike of me.

'Will you and Comrade Shobha be joining us for dinner?' I'd asked her one evening at Comrade Oh's direction. Sometimes, she and Shobha ate alone.

But she had not responded. I'd cleared my throat and asked again, a little louder. Yet she'd ignored me completely, as if I was a ghost.

Her response – or lack of it – was particularly hurtful because I already felt so much like an unperson, always skulking in the shadows. Now, even within the Collective, I'd spoken aloud but my words hadn't registered. I couldn't think what I'd done wrong to make her treat me in such a way. *It must be something inside me*, I'd thought. *I am wrong, not just my actions.*

Knowing time was against me, I hurriedly pulled on the salwar kameez, drawing it on over my shirt and trousers, playing dress-up in Comrade Chanda's dirty clothes. Oh, it was so gorgeous, despite the smell! The fabric floated around me in a vibrant pool of purple. I twisted and turned to show it off to better effect, attempting to dance across the bathroom and quietly whispering, 'Woo! Woo!' to myself. It was *such* a nice feeling. I felt glamorous and feminine . . . I wanted to see myself.

There was only one mirror in the bathroom. It was positioned so that Chanda could see herself, but with my new height I'd discovered that if I stood in the bath I could see myself too. Holding the salwar kameez carefully, I stepped into the bath and turned to face the mirror.

Wow. Is that me?

A person stood before me: brown eyes, brown hair, big smile. I could just see down to the swell of my developing breasts, and the sight of *my* body clad in that forbidden dress was fascinating and thrilling. Comrade Sian said in disgust that the lumps on my chest were 'dirty fat', but *I* liked them. To me, they were more evidence I *was* a girl, and that was something to cherish. It was a shame my hair was so short, only a few inches long, but maybe I could do something to improve it . . .

I stepped out of the bath again and crossed to the cabinet. Chanda and Shobha wore delicious-smelling oils in their hair; sure enough, I soon found the luxurious-looking bottle. I poured out the tiniest smidgeon and rubbed it all over my head. It smelt wonderful. *That* was better. I grinned in pleasure at my new game and quickly changed out of Chanda's clothes before I got caught.

AB soon wiped the smile off my face.

'You are a criminal!' he roared. He'd noticed the sweet-smelling oil in my hair and immediately realized I'd 'stolen' it from Chanda. He grasped a fistful of my hair and yanked, pulling it out.

'Stick *this* in your diary,' he ordered, throwing the ripped strands at me, 'to remind you of your crime.'

I did so obediently. Yet these days I wasn't always *quite* so obedi-ent as I'd been before. Inspired by Comrade Chanda's more relaxed interaction with AB, I aspired to copy her, hoping such behaviour might win me more respect as she was the most highly regarded woman in the house. So I began to dally when AB summoned me.

Yet he merely screamed for me in an increasingly imperious man-ner, as though I was a dog and he my master, until I came to hate every nuance of my name.

I tried another tack. When AB gave me his daily creepy cuddles, I began to pull away. He was furious: I was *his*.

'OK,' he huffed. 'You don't want me to touch you? Then you can't touch me either.'

I lasted only a few weeks before I caved. Without AB's touch, I got none at all, and life to that measure of loneliness was impossible to bear. The women were all still banned from touching me; Bala accused me of 'neglecting' him if I paid particular attention to them. Very occasionally, Oh now let me tickle her hand as she lay beside me on her fold-up bed, but if anyone caught us AB denounced us as 'lesbians' – whatever that meant.

Yet in some ways – only some – AB was not quite the same implacable tyrant I'd always known. Having so many Indian neigh-bours seemed to make him reconnect with the Outside world in a way he hadn't for years; it seemed to prompt memories. He and Chanda often joined us for lunch (another new development) and, because there was no kitchen table in the tiny flat, we would sit together and eat from our laps. To my surprise, I observed that when he and Chanda ate, they *talked* to each other. As they did so, I heard, perhaps for the first time, the lilting, back-and-forth lullaby of a *respectful* conversation.

It was extraordinary! They didn't just lecture or obey – they exchanged stories, sparked off different topics of conversation, and wound their way around words with a casual indirection that you simply didn't hear in AB's sermons.

There was another, very strange thing about the way AB and Chanda talked. Unlike in Discussions, when the women would be torn apart for all they'd done before meeting AB, *these* were recol-lections to be revered, taken out like special treasures to be exclaimed over. I could hear it in their voices: the warm way they would recount an anecdote, as though giving a precious jewel a polish. In such delighted tones, they used to talk about their childhoods and the fun they used to have.

Until then, because of what I'd heard in Discussions, I'd thought that no type of childhood but mine had any merit. Yet these childhoods sounded pleasant; something you *would* want. Having so recently seen the children Outside playing on the swing, this idea that there were actually different *good* ways to grow up made a lasting impression.

I also heard stories of how the comrades used to help people in the community, back when the Collective was based in the Mao Memorial Centre on Acre Lane in the 1970s, well before I was born. I learned there had been fifteen comrades back then: they used to flyer on the streets of Brixton as well as selling Marxist and Maoist tracts for pennies and hosting public political meetings at which AB would preach. AB used to talk about the conferences they'd all attended.

I dared to wonder aloud why we, as a group, didn't do any of that any more; I would have liked to help people and sell them books. It was explained to me that when I was born in 1983, they'd had to go underground to protect Project Prem: from that point on, our activities became top secret; all public interaction ceased.

But as I listened to those lunchtime chats, I realized that public interaction had once been a big part of AB's life – of *all* the comrades' lives. Perhaps because of hearing AB and Chanda talk so warmly of their formative experiences, I now listened more closely when the comrades talked of theirs. Comrade Sian had been a postgrad student at the London School of Economics; that was where she'd met AB. Bala encouraged her to talk about her past – he said she needed to 'cleanse' herself by telling him about it – so I had lots of opportunity to hear her recollections. I heard about her childhood growing up in Wales, about holidays in the Mediterranean, about riding a horse in the splash of the surf. Though always recounted in a derogatory way, these stories were nonetheless bursting with colour.

They took root in my imagination: the fierce gallop of a horse's hooves; the crack of a cricket bat in a freshly mown field; the chink of wine glasses on a summer's day . . . They lodged there in my mind, beside memories of a bright-red slide in next door's garden, of children playing on a swing, of a man on a motorbike zooming down the road.

None of it seemed dangerous.

None of it seemed wrong.

So I started to think: *why can't I experience any of that, when everybody else has had the chance?*

By far the worst thing to hear about, however, were all the friends AB and Chanda made when they were young. There was no mention of fascist agents, old-world ideas or the need to keep your distance, such as I was always told. In my world, a sheet of glass always fell between me and others, but AB had once run with his friends and played with them in the street. He wasn't separate from the world, despite his divinity – he'd been part of it.

I wanted to be part of it too.

Because, as I listened, I was starting to realize something – an idea that grew stronger with every anecdote I heard. Outside wasn't *all* about danger. Yes, there was murder and mayhem, but there were also picnics and ponies.

And if Outside had been good enough for AB as a child, why couldn't I at least *try* it?

Before, I'd always felt grateful to the Collective, thankful for my protection from Outside. Now, listening to the comrades speak, for the first time I didn't feel defended, but deprived.

16

Though I was not permitted friends, AB had them, and in Wembley I got to meet one of them.

His name was Comrade Simons. A Jamaican man, he had the most beautiful white-toothed smile. He was part of the Collective – often helping AB and the comrades by driving them about – yet apart from it too. I loved it when he visited, for his natural niceness seemed to encourage everyone else to be much nicer too. He was never nasty to me; instead, he had a quiet, placid way about him I found rather peaceful. He visited twice a week on Wednesdays and Sundays. Immediately, they became my favourite days of the week.

Everything was better when Comrade Simons came. AB presented a different side of himself to Simons; he never offered to beat the Maozi waves out of *him*. In fact, there were no beatings and no nasty tongue-lashings when Simons was around; instead, we ate food together and talked about the world. Comrade Simons shared the same views as the others and adored AB. I suppose that emphasized the truth of what I'd been told about the coming Overt, because Simons believed it too and he came from Outside.

AB always told me to wear a long-sleeved shirt for his visits, so my bruises weren't visible. It was an advisable precaution because I loved nothing more than to be *seen* by Comrade Simons. Whenever he visited, I liked to show off to him at every opportunity, in love with the novelty of his presence.

So I'd stand in the doorway while he sat on the sofa, melodramatically beating eggs with a fork while I grinned inanely at him. *Look at me! Look what I can do!* the clatter of my fork seemed to say. Or I'd beg to be the one to serve him his food, rushing up to him with his plate and then standing back and staring at him, so agog at this new face in my midst that all I could do was gawp. Comrade

Sian used to get so mad at me – 'Stop showing off!' she'd hiss – but I'd do anything to get one of Comrade Simons' smiles.

'I'm going for a shit!' I announced loudly one afternoon when Comrade Simons was visiting. I was following orders – I had to do this whenever I went to the bathroom alone – but to my confusion Simons looked mightily embarrassed at my words.

Later, Bala said I had to be 'polite' when Simons came. Apparently, it wasn't the done thing to announce one's bowel movements to the room, although I'd been taught I always must. Instead, AB said, I should only tell the comrades in the kitchen now; or, if we were all together, simply say, 'Excuse me, please.' I noted the revised instruction, but little understood why it had been given.

During those visits from Simons, in Discussions and over lunch, AB began to describe in detail the reality of his planned new world. When I'd first started helping with our homemade newspaper, I'd realized exactly why the old world *needed* to be replaced, but I hadn't given much consideration to what AB would be replacing it *with*. In Wembley, I found out.

The new world, AB declared, would be a 'Communist Terrorist Dictatorship' with him as GPCR (God, President, Chairman, Ruler). If anybody committed the slightest indiscretion they would be subjected to EAT (Execute, Arrest and Torture), no matter the triviality of their transgression. To AB, violence against one's own people was laudable. Although he'd denounced Mao, his issue was not Mao's track record on so-called human rights. AB thought the torture and oppression of one's opponents was *exactly* the right way to behave (indeed, AB claimed that because he was the natural centre, *he* had overseen the Chinese regime that carried out such activities, and it wasn't Mao's initiative at all).

The massacre at Tiananmen Square in 1989 (what AB called TAMS) was held up as a victory of AB's too: extreme hard-line Communism triumphing over disgusting Western liberalism. Every time he talked of TAMS, his voice would ring with mocking hatred of 'democracy' and 'human rights'. He almost licked his lips at the thought of the bloodbath, seeming to anticipate with glee one day having the Overt power to do the same. He often went into graphic detail about how he'd like to torture all his enemies, including the unborn babies and pregnant women in their midst. And though he'd usually work himself up, spitting and shouting, what I found most chilling was the casual way he would describe the mass murder that would happen in his new world. He celebrated it even in the old world; to him, terrorists were martyrs, champions against the West.

In AB's view, 'Which Side Are You On?' was the question that divided life and death. If you went against him, you were less than human and should be crushed like a cockroach. His was a black-and-white world, coloured only by the blood of his betrayers.

But even at eleven I was starting to see the world in shades of grey, something that only increased as time went on, directly in line with the number of books I secret-read from the cupboard. One of those books was about the Chinese military leader Peng Te-Huai, who'd been tortured to death for daring to challenge Mao. Reading about his fate in the book, rather than learning it from AB's lips, put a different spin on the situation. Previously, I'd only ever heard AB's account that torture was correct, and that fitted with all I'd learned about Maozi waves and my 30 per cent: people *deserved* to be beaten. I'd squashed down all my gut instincts that told me such violence was wrong or unfair. But in the books I read, the authors seemed to take that instinctive opinion of mine and unashamedly spread it all over the page, as though it wasn't something to be battened down, but a viewpoint to be celebrated. In the books, torture *wasn't* endorsed; quite the opposite. And when I read Peng's story, I felt sorry for him. It made me feel rather differently about my friend Mao, too. I was really upset with him for his part in it and couldn't condone his actions. Yet my anger was primarily reserved for AB as he was the one, so he said with pride, who was *really* behind it all.

Ever since birth, AB had told me that when his leadership became Overt I'd have everything I'd ever wanted – *and* more. So, ever since birth, I'd *longed* for that day – the day when I'd have no more need to fear fascist agents, when I could walk in the sun and every-body could know that I *existed*. No more need to hide in the shadows. Oh, how I *longed* for that day. But as I listened to AB outline these details of his new world, and paired them with what I was learning from the books, another sensation overtook me about Overt. Though I *loved* the sound of the liberty I'd have, I was chilled to the bone at the thought of all those deaths.

I don't want happiness if everyone else can't share it too.

95

For I knew better than anyone what it was to be lonely and afraid. I didn't want anyone else to feel as doomed as I so often did.

I thought about what AB had always said: that if we followed him properly, we too could live long lives, perhaps even achieve the eternal life he so enjoyed. But now I dared to think the wayward thought: *Would I want to live forever in a world like that?*

I couldn't express my nascent resistance – everywhere I looked, the comrades seemed in full agreement. As always, they spoke with one voice, eyes shining with awe, voices lifted in fervent passion: 'YES!'

I started, subtly, not to join my voice to theirs. Yet the small rebellion was hopeless in the face of the inevitability of AB's rise to power. As we sat in the living room for Discussions (the standing circle being another relaxed rule), AB showed us articles that he said foreshadowed the Overt. Then, he would ask us, 'WHO is coming to WHOM?'

'THEY are coming to YOU!' we would chorus in reply.

I was only eleven; I couldn't compute all this. I began spending more time in my mental cocoon, trying to lose myself in happy fantasies of John Major (who hadn't, to my knowledge, murdered 75 million people like my old friend Mao). Dissociated from the world around me, I felt in a dream a lot of the time. But, always, AB's beatings and the subsequent isolation would burst my bubble. Then, I'd have no choice but to face up to the pain.

I began retreating to the bathroom – this time, not to play or look Outside, but to face myself in the mirror and look frankly at the tears running down my cheeks. My feelings were so often belittled by AB that I found a certain comfort in allowing myself to *see* them, even if no one else cared to look.

A few years before, there had been a lot of newspaper coverage about confessional interviews that Ronald Reagan's daughter, Patti Davis, had done on TV, talking about how her parents had treated her badly. It gave me an idea. In the bathroom, I started standing before the mirror, imagining I was seeing myself on a TV screen. I decided I was going to tell the world about AB and what was happening; about how badly I was treated, being beaten black and blue.

Since I'd been able to think a bit more for myself, I'd become more confident in my hesitant belief that AB's beatings *were* bad. Though I still believed *I* was a bad person, I no longer believed hitting it out of me was going to help – not least because it kept happening.

I found it really helped to talk to the 'camera'. I would whisper all manner of truths that I could tell no one else, watching as if from a distance as the tears tracked down my cheeks. Knowing that AB said the BFS was always listening, part of me hoped that someone might be able to hear; that maybe they'd come and put a stop to it.

Yet that idea was also tinged with fear (I was still scared of fascist agents and the neighbour from the basement flat) and also with confusion – for if they were listening, why did they allow AB to continue with his plans? After all, for all AB's insistence on 'no talking' and 'KQ', he lectured us *every day* in Discussions; if the fascist state was listening in, it would be pretty obvious they'd found their man. Perhaps they were gathering intel; maybe that's what it was.

That idea made me feel hopeless too. To think that Outside was listening in but didn't want to save me was perhaps the bleakest realization of all.

17

Those bathroom retreats were a lifeline. The 'TV interviews', the dressing up, the motorcycle man and Tap and Toilet: *these* were the things that made life worth living.

That was why I would stop at nothing to protect them.

One windy day when I opened the window, the bathroom door started shaking on its hinges as the gusts blew through the flat.

'You must have opened a window!' one of the comrades accused when I came out.

My heart started banging in my chest. If they realized what I was doing, somebody would tell Bala. I dreaded his reaction: he might revoke the private toilet privileges and ask a comrade to be with me *all* the time. I couldn't go back to a life like that. I swallowed. I had a choice. I could lose every drop of freedom that I had, or I could *lie*.

It was a big step for me. I hated lying, but there was no choice. It was a strategy to survive. So I arranged my features into what I hoped was an honest expression. I couldn't be sure I would get away with it because these people had watched me almost every minute, every hour, every day of my life. But nevertheless I had to try.

'I didn't,' I fibbed, holding my breath afterwards . . .

To my relief, they accepted it, and after that the floodgates opened. If the comrades interrogated me about something I was doing wrong, I was able, if needed, to lie to save myself. In Streatham, I hadn't been able to keep the neighbour's wave from them, but now I was better equipped at keeping secrets. It still felt wrong to do it, especially to someone like Aisha or Oh, but to my mind it became a necessary evil.

It was into this climate, just as I was relishing my ability to think and lie, that the lightning bolt I'd been dreading came. In the spring of 1994, everything changed. JACKIE had arrived.

★

JACKIE stood for Jehovah, Allah, Christ, Krishna and Immortal Easwaran, but was far more powerful than any of them. He was the latest incarnation of AB's mind-control machines – and the most deadly of them all.

I'd grown up with the idea of AB's machines. When I was a young child, they weren't that much of a big deal; we didn't talk about them every day, only now and again. I wasn't frightened of them. I was much more frightened of Bala.

Over the years, they had become more prominent. They developed over time – first called the BFSMM (Beautiful Field Synchronizing Media Machine), then JCH, then JACHI . . . until finally JACKIE arrived. Through all these twists and turns, the machines were upgraded. By the time JACKIE burst on to the scene, he had become invincible.

From the start, JACKIE was different. JACKIE, we were told, had even greater wrath than AB. When Bala beat us now, he was doing it to protect us from JACKIE. If he didn't step in and smash our faces up, JACKIE would do far worse.

'Focus on AB,' he said now, 'otherwise AB's JACKIE will torture you to death . . .'

From the very first moment AB told us JACKIE was here, he was a real force of fear in the house. JACKIE could read our minds and he knew everything we were doing; he even knew what we *wanted* to do before we actually did it.

'JACKIE is testing you,' AB warned. 'But you should be able to resist. Focus on AB, and when JACKIE tests you, remember the guidelines and stay strong.'

If we didn't, we'd feel the force of JACKIE's wrath.

His power stretched everywhere, just like AB's own. JACKIE controlled *everything*; in a way, I suppose he was the enforcer of AB's will: it was JACKIE now who sparked the damp electrics; who started the wildfires; who murdered dignitaries in their beds. As evidence of JACKIE's power, AB pointed to the death of Jackie Kennedy Onassis when it happened a few months later on 19 May 1994. He said she'd died because AB had finally told us the truth about JACKIE. (JACKIE had actually been born on 1 May 1970; it was just that AB had only now told the Collective about him.)

Our lives changed overnight. Though no one else questioned the arrival of this machine, *I* noticed that it didn't tally with what we'd been told before.

'Where is JACKIE?' I asked AB. 'Can I see him?' I think I wanted proof, to see him with my own two eyes.

AB chuckled at my innocence. 'No, you can't *see* him,' he said mockingly. 'JACKIE is here, he's there, he's everywhere. He is in everything: he's in the smallest thing and the biggest thing at the same time.'

From the start, JACKIE was adopted by the Collective as if he had always been around. Though things didn't tally, I was told to 'have faith'. Now, when the women fretted about something, they would say, 'We have to be careful about JACKIE.' Once, to reassure me when I was upset, Comrade Aisha soothed: 'Don't worry, JACKIE is in control.'

That was not a soothing thought. I had come to believe that AB could not read my thoughts, but JACKIE now could. 'AB said he's inside me,' I wrote in my diary. I wanted to scratch that spirit out, but everyone else seemed in awe and I didn't know enough to swim against the tide. I got swept up and I too became terrified of JACKIE – a new faceless demon to haunt my dreams.

Nor was mine the only mind he stalked through. 'Comrade Aisha was screaming in the night,' my diary noted that spring. From the moment of JACKIE's arrival, all the comrades were on best behaviour – which meant reporting more.

The situation was made all the worse when I learned I was the first of my kind. AB now said that in the new world all people on earth would be killed and he'd replace them with 1 billion children of JACKIE, which is what he told me I was. To me, it seemed a bleak thought – though I quickly tried to unthink it.

The one good thing was that my days in Wembley involved a lot of sitting with Bala. That plan I'd had in earlier houses, of trying to be with him more so he'd see I wasn't all bad, could finally be put into practice. In the tight constraints of the Wembley flat, we were thrown together by dint of the limited furniture: we sat together at the single table doing our important work for the new world.

The proximity to Bala had a rather lovely upside. I now had a front-row seat for whatever he was reading! The book or paper was always turned away from me, but I taught myself to read upside-down and scanned everything on the page. I loved to fill my mind with different things. AB read a lot of newspapers and magazines – *Asian Age* and *National Enquirer* – and I'd look at the images in delight too, loving the different clothes people wore in the pictures. *I'd like to dress like that*, I'd think, casting a mournful look down at my unisex tracksuit.

Around this time, I tentatively tried out a new name for AB too. I called him Papa.

Everybody else had someone to call Father, I reasoned, and as AB was the only man around (and he'd been, in a way, both mother and father to me), it seemed a natural thing to do. AB didn't like it at first, but he accepted it after a while. I was absolutely forbidden, however, from using or even *wanting* to use 'Balakrishnan' as my last name.

I wished I had someone to call Mama too. The older I got, the more I longed for a mother. I felt the stab of her absence every time I heard the others talk of their parents, or saw the children Outside being comforted and loved. But the closest thing I had to a mum was Comrade Sian, and she was the *least* motherly figure in my life. In eleven and a half years, I could count on two fingers the times she had been nice to me – once, her voice had been a bit kindly when I was poorly (a total surprise); another time, when Comrade Josie and AB had been berating me, she had intervened and said, 'This is getting too much: it's humiliating.' (AB had said, 'Nonsense, she needs a strict hand,' and Sian had acquiesced.) I yearned for her love and kindness, but she always pushed me away.

As 1994 unfolded, my closer relationship with AB seemed to pay off. On 25 May 1994, he agreed that I could bathe alone as long as he was in the house. I was so delighted, I didn't care at first that the new privacy came with new rules attached. Before my bath, I now had to tell Bala I was going to have it, and he would ask, 'Body wash or hair wash?'

Yet the best treat of all was still to come. For months, ever since we'd moved into Wembley, I'd been begging to be taken to a playground. Seeing the children on the swing every day was torture, and though I knew AB would never permit me to use the one at the apartment – the comrades were becoming hostile to the neighbours again now, and fascist agents lurked in every shadow – I hoped he might allow me to play on equipment further from home. Though I went Out once a month in Wembley, in a way the more regular outings made things worse for me; the more frequent tastes of what I was missing made me hunger for more. I started circling the word 'Out' in my diary when AB promised me a trip, the ink imbued with my longing and anticipation.

On 31 May 1994, I finally got my wish.

I was utterly thrilled when AB, Sian and Aisha accompanied me to Hyde Park. It was a baking hot day and the scene before me almost shimmered in the heat. Like an oasis in a desert, there shone a children's playground – swings and slide and so much more.

Eagerly, I ambled over to the equipment. I would have run, but I never ran, having been beaten too many times for doing so, so even my excited pace was snail-slow. I headed straight for the swings. Below bright-red bars, a plastic platform swung on heavy chains.

Almost holding my breath with the intensity of the moment, I gingerly plonked my bottom down and clutched the chains between two fists. *Oh! I am sitting on a swing!* I thought happily. I never, ever thought it would happen.

For several seconds, I simply savoured the moment, enjoying the unfamiliar seat beneath my bottom and the still air around me.

Now what?

I glanced over at AB, looking for direction, but he gave me none. I racked my brains to remember what I'd seen from the window, and lifted my legs off the floor.

The swing swayed slightly from the motion, but I didn't move back and forth.

Nonetheless, I felt a bit sick: afraid of the gentle movement; scared I might fall off. I gripped the chains tighter – and steeled my nerves. I had *begged* to be allowed to do this; I had to take my chance.

I lifted my legs again. Nothing. *How do people do this?* I wondered. The other children had made it look so easy, sailing through the air, but I couldn't do it. I wanted to learn, but there was no one to teach me.

In the end, I had to give up. I walked glumly back to AB and the others, only to find they were looking behind me, back at the swings. Another little girl was playing on them now. With ease, she kicked out her legs and leaned back, and the swing started to move. Higher and higher she flew, the chains now squeaking happily, an under-score to her flight.

'Look at her!' AB remarked. 'Look how high she's going!' He gave me a glare. 'Why can't you do it like that?'

I crumpled at his words, inadequacy rather than blood running through my veins. *But she's probably been swinging for years*, I thought. *This is my first time.* Yet AB made no allowance for it; nor was it the last time he compared me to others in this way. I felt useless.

My shoulders sank as we left the playground. I felt broken. Though I begged many times to return to the swings, wanting to try again, we never did. I felt it was extra cruel to have given me a glimpse of what I wanted, so that when it was denied in future I felt the absence that much more.

So focused was I on my inadequacy that I didn't give a moment's thought to the implications of that incident on the swings in Hyde Park. For once, AB had let me do what I wanted – only for me to find that I did not have the skills. I *could* not swing, much as I yearned to.

Even when the glass was gone, I was trapped just the same.

18

'Comrade Bala told Comrade Prem not to say she wants to be a "girl",' I wrote in my diary in the summer of 1994. The age-old guideline – but unfortunately for AB, my body didn't get the memo.

When I looked at myself in the mirror now, the swell of my breasts was undeniable. They were big, too – already larger than many of the other comrades' – and so heavy that my back ached. I looked with envy at Comrade Sian's bright-pink brassiere drying on the laundry rack. I wasn't allowed to wear a bra, even though the other women could; it was an old-world concept. I wasn't supposed to need one, anyway, not when I was a child of JACKIE – a child of the new world.

'Who needs a bra?' AB sneered when I hesitantly requested one. 'You don't need a bra! Don't you *ever* talk like that!'

He wanted to deny that my body was changing, even when the evidence was right in front of him.

At AB's insistence, I continued to wear only androgynous clothes, the comrades now ensuring that my tops were high-necked and excessively loose so that the womanly curves I loved so much were never, ever on show. Hidden though they were, I think the Collective guessed how much I adored my breasts and the identity they gave me. I think that was why my boobs became part of my punishments.

It happened that summer. There'd been a huge argument between Comrade Chanda and the other women one day because we'd run out of bread. As the women could only go shopping in pairs, and at regimented times (because AB insisted we all follow a daily schedule from which we could never deviate), if we ran out of something it was a disaster. The comrades couldn't just pop out even though the shop was only a hundred yards away.

'Where is the bread?' Chanda roared at the comrades; her temper could be short.

It was not an uncommon scene. Though I knew JACKIE would have something to say about it, I thought, *Why is Chanda making such a fuss? Why do we have to be talked to like this? If she wants bread, why doesn't she just go and get it herself? Why do we have to jump to her command?*

Unusually, I did even more than think those thoughts: I kept talking over Chanda as she was remonstrating with the others.

'Comrade Prem, NO TALKING! Remember you are subordinate!' came the complaint. It was a familiar one: that I did not know my place.

So, I had to be put in it.

That evening, Sian informed Bala of the altercation, explaining I'd been disrespectful to his wife. Often, Bala exploded at the first mention of a misdemeanour, but this time he was calm, which was in fact worse. In measured tones, he said to Sian, 'If she carries on like this, you should ask the other three women to hold her down and then you take a knife and chop her boobs off, OK?'

Sian nodded: a fitting punishment.

I was horrified. Though I'd been only five when I'd seen Leanne pinned down by the others, the memory was as fresh as if it had happened only yesterday. I really believed Sian was going to hurt me, and that the others would help her. In the face of JACKIE, who could dare refuse?

Sian shared a bed with me when it was her shift. I took to lying there in terror, listening out for her creeping up to the bed. Sometimes I heard a metallic sound as she walked towards me, and my guts would tighten in fear, my arms placed protectively across my chest. *My God, that sounds like a knife coming; my God, my God, she's actually going to chop my boobs off . . .* Only when she placed her mug down and stirred her hot drink with the spoon would I realize what I'd heard.

On 30 July 1994, I started bleeding from my wastehole. I had no idea what was happening to me, but I don't recall being unduly concerned; I was used to the sight of my own blood from Bala's beatings. At first, Sian told me I'd soiled myself, but when the blood appeared in my knickers for two days running, she talked to AB.

Afterwards, in a hushed whisper, she told me something miraculous: 'This is what happens to all the women in the house once a month.'

All women . . . That meant *I* was a woman too! I LOVED it! Here was *proof* – proof of what I'd always hoped for – that I *was* a girl and not just a unisex, genderless *thing*. It meant I was like other people and not a strange freak. I was so proud of myself and my body for that.

But AB was far from proud.

'You've messed up the programme!' he roared at me a few days later. I wasn't supposed to get my period, or grow boobs, but thanks to my hateful 60 per cent – according to the latest rankings – I had fallen prey to negative female energy.

Long ago, I'd been told by Comrade Sian that if I was good I'd have a body like Bala's – now, it seemed, I had fallen.

I was delighted. It was empowering, too, to know that *this wasn't supposed to happen, but it did*. For all JACKIE's power – which I did believe in – *this* was something that neither JACKIE nor AB had been able to control. Though AB ranted that it was *my* negativity that had caused the derailment, either way his little genderless soldier was gone.

I was a woman now.

With my body declaring independence, I dared to continue to do so in my mind. Despite AB's threats about Sian cutting off my boobs, his attempt to dominate me drove me further from him. Rather than becoming more obedient, I became better at hiding my waywardness. I'd plan made-up excuses for my bad behaviour in advance, so if anybody asked, I'd be ready. I was fearful of what JACKIE might do, but I carried on regardless, believing it was worth the risk.

The new year, 1995, ushered in another relaxed rule. To my delight, I was informed that I would now be permitted to write poetry. The idea, of course, was that I would put my pen to good use in praising Bala.

From the word go, I fell in love with poetry. It was like growing your own perfect piece of fruit, a bite-size way to make your reader taste your mood. I loved learning how to layer up lines and stanzas and creating the rhymes and rhythms within. I wrote my first proper poem when I was twelve. It was about God – but *not* about AB, although I still believed our leader was divine, for he clearly had great power.

The inspiration for my poem was my secret-reading about

Hinduism. Carefully, I inscribed my original words in rust-coloured ink – using my left hand for some reason, as though the controversial content rendered my right unusable. It was another declaration of independence: me doing my own thing and praising who *I* wanted to, rather than AB. Helpfully, however, both Sian and Bala believed that my 'God' in the poem *was* AB, so I got away with it. But *I* knew the truth.

I wrote poem after poem after that; some of them secretly about John Major, whom I still admired so much. They stacked up, the pages forming a pillar, as though I was building a new school of thought and these were my basic building blocks. Seeing my felt-tip pen sketch out the words I felt a little less like a shadow-woman and a little more like *me*.

That summer, I couldn't help but notice that there was a lot of stress regarding our housing situation again. The Wembley flat had only been intended as temporary accommodation, so the council was attempting to rehouse us, but the Collective rejected every property proposed. As time passed and still no suitable home had been iden-tified, AB began to suspect that the fascist state might evict us and not offer another house as we'd already refused so many. Out of the blue, he had ordered Sian to reconnect with her mother, Ceri, and declared that, if this dire scenario came to pass, Chanda, Shobha and Oh would move in with Chanda's relatives and the rest of us would remove to Sian's mother's house in Wales.

I was excited by the activity; intrigued by Sian's conversations with her mother on the telephone. AB began building on his master plan and briefed Sian that – if and only if we did have to move to Wales – she must tell her mother that I was her 'daughter', strictly on a 'need-to-know' basis. From the vast piles of paperwork in his box room, AB now produced a piece of pink card stamped by a hospital that I'd never seen before. It bore my name – though, unexpectedly, it listed my surname as 'Davies', the same as Sian's. In a section headed 'relationship with child', Sian had signed her name and writ-ten 'Mother'. This card, AB said, should be shown to Sian's mummy if we had to explain why we were coming to stay.

Even as AB displayed it to me, he explained that the card was misleading. It didn't really mean Sian was my mother, for I had no mother: I was a child of JACKIE. Rather, the form indicated that Sian had 'claimed' me for the Collective, as though I was a waif on the wayside she had picked up for AB.

How that fitted in with the test tube I'd come from, I could not really fathom.

I tried to overhear Sian's conversations with her mum, but I did not get very far. *If Sian had been my mother, that would have been my grandmother on the phone*, I reflected wistfully. I *wished* I had grandparents; just someone who was mine and who would look out for me.

My parentage kept playing on my mind that summer. In *The New World*, AB shared some articles that referred to unmarried parents.

'Unmarried parents?' I mused aloud to Comrade Sian. 'That's like AB and you!'

I merely meant that they were *like* mother and father to me, but Sian was not AB's wife. Yet all the colour drained from Sian's face at my words. She hushed me instantly, pale and shaking.

'Don't *ever* say such a thing again!' she hissed, her voice simultaneously disgusted and afraid, as though I had dared to speak the unspeakable. I was completely baffled by her reaction.

I soon had bigger things to worry about though. Chatting with Josie one day, I foolishly let slip my admiration for John Major. I think it got AB wondering about the true subjects of my poems because he suddenly ordered Sian to raid my writings. Weirdly, I was almost happy about it because part of me *wanted* my love for Major to be public; I wanted the comrades to look at me and think, 'Prem likes John Major.' I guess it was a way of asserting my identity: I was not just an unperson, I was a John Major fan!

All my poems – there were about twenty – were hauled out for examination. In some ways I enjoyed the attention, for I loved my writing to be read: it was a *connection* to people, where normally I had none. So there was a grain of pleasure amid all the pain.

'Get on your knees,' AB growled; he was furious at my insurrection. He told me I was 'unfaithful' and would die of '*mening*itis' because of letting other '*men in*' to my mind.

As he ranted at me and forced me into submission, the comrades looked on silently. 'You will not disrespect me,' he spat. 'You will say . . .' He paused, deliberating which words would cause me the most hurt. 'You will say, "Death to John Major."'

I shook my head; I didn't want to do it. John Major was the man I loved! I didn't want to denounce him!

But AB brooked no argument. I was allowed to love no other man but him. On my knees, head bowed, I had no choice. Tears trickled down my cheeks as, through gritted teeth, I was forced to say the words that broke my heart: 'Death to John Major, death to John Major . . .' I had to say it two hundred times and with every single syllable I felt I was betraying the man I loved.

It was my mind, in the end, that came to my rescue; that saved me from abject humiliation and shame. As my mouth formed the hateful words into a rhythm, my brain interjected at the relevant point: 'Death to—' (*haters of*) '—John Major. Death to—' (*haters of*) '—John Major.' It was the only way I made it through.

Bala was extremely hard on Sian when it was discovered I'd been writing those poems. AB expected her to be on top of my training: she should have noticed I was excited about someone else and put a stop to it long ago. He now beat me in front of her, all the while castigating her, 'It's *your* failure that this sort of thing happens. *You* are the cause of all this.'

Comrade Sian redoubled her efforts to keep me in line. Matter-of-factly, she explained to me the reason why my crime was so out of order: 'You were betrothed to Bala at birth.'

She didn't mean I'd been promised to AB as a second wife – AB was immortal, above all such earthly things. Rather, my betrothal to him was spiritual, just as nuns in the Catholic church commit themselves to God. From what I'd read, however, nuns were elevated by their love, whereas my betrothal was more like an emptying out. I was to have no will, no mind, no feelings of my own; I was to meld myself into Bala's will until I didn't know where I ended and he began.

I hated the idea. Previously, when Comrade Sian got angry with me, I would knuckle under. But I'd been thinking my own thoughts for a good while now, and neither JACKIE nor AB had stopped me. That emboldened me even more. In fact, I felt defiant about it. If JACKIE *could* hear me, I now thought boldly: *Well, let him hear, he should know what I think!*

And with that barrier completely gone, I grew more daring. Until now, while I'd written things in praise of other people, I'd never dared actively to criticize AB: that was evidence I could ill afford to create. A poem about John Major would get me into trouble, but it wouldn't get me killed.

Yet the more AB and Sian tried to crush me in the months that followed, the more emboldened I became. I think it may have been in the winter of 1995 when I first dared to do it. I'd been praying – perhaps to Bala? It was all mixed up in my mind – that things would change. But my prayers went unanswered. I *knew* AB had the power to change things if he wished, so I got angry at him for not listening.

Really angry.

I was supposed to be doing exercises in my bedroom, but I grabbed a piece of paper and a pen instead. I took a deep breath and pressed pen to paper.

'How come,' I wrote heatedly, 'you *idiot*, you *god*, you let these bad things happen?'

My heart was racing – but, oh, it felt so *GOOD*! It was as though the anger boiling in my body seeped out into the ink on the page.

I was incredibly glad it had left me – but now it was on the paper for all to see. Hurriedly, I scribbled all over my angry words, scoring through them so heavily that the paper almost tore. Only when none of the letters could be deciphered did I stop scrawling. Then I tore the sheet into tiny, tiny pieces and threw them all away.

Afterwards, I was frightened at first, but then I felt empowered. Having dared to do it once, I dared to do it twice. On to those scraps of paper I poured out my heart, in the same way I still gave 'TV interviews' in the loo. But this was better. This was tangible. This felt *real*.

I destroyed each and every one, usually just moments after I'd written it. I'd have loved to keep them, but I knew I didn't dare. Nonetheless, each time, they got a little bit longer and a little more frank.

And once I started fighting back, there was no stopping me.

19

'We are surrounded,' AB ranted, 'by enemy agents! Listen to their music!' He paused for a second so we could all appreciate the neighbours' music travelling through the walls. 'This is a deliberate act of war from the fascist state against the Collective! But we will never forgive and we will never forget!'

The comrades' voices rose and fell in a murmur of agreement. Their former friendliness to the neighbours was no more: suspicion tainted every interaction.

When I looked Outside, I shared that fear and paranoia when it came to enemy agents. I think I trusted my instincts on it: my motorcyclist seemed a good Outsider, but the dreadlocked Uenis Cieppo from the basement flat was bad. Uenis made me so anxious. I think he was simply the kind of character who makes a person unsettled; the type of man even non-Collective members crossed the street to avoid.

AB concurred with my opinion and frequently denounced him. Every time he did, I would enthusiastically join in, adding my voice to the chorus of hate that filled the sitting room every night.

It was so easy to hate in the Collective. It was the one emotion that fuelled us all. We hated each other, because of all the reporting, but what united us was hatred of others. Maybe that was why everyone joined in so ardently – because it was the one time we weren't all at each other's throats.

That winter of 1995, AB was on high alert about enemy agents. On his way home from his weekly shopping trip in central London one day, he had spied Uenis Cieppo chatting with the fascist police. For what possible reason could Uenis, a down-and-out, be having this conversation? It was obvious: he was undercover police passing his recordings of AB's conversations to his handler.

The observation got AB's hackles up. Not long after that, Bala spotted a police car parked in the driveway of our block of flats as he was walking home. As he entered through the doors, Uenis jumped a mile – clearly Uenis had been skulking around, waiting for his chance to connect with the police in the driveway, but AB had caught him red-handed!

'Outrageous!' I exclaimed, when AB filled us in during Discussions. AB nodded in agreement, satisfied by my spirit, and launched into a full-scale denunciation of the agent.

Later, though, I started thinking more deeply about this story. If Uenis *was* an undercover spy, why would the police make contact with him in a marked car – and do so openly, right in front of the intended target? Something didn't tally . . .

AB often railed not only against agents, but those who softened their hate into forgiveness. He called them weak. 'Peace is like piss,' he would mock. He thought Gerry Adams, who was currently leading the Irish peace process, an out-and-out traitor.

Now that I was almost thirteen, I'd begun to form a different view. The books I'd been secret-reading talked about forgiveness too – but they said it was a good thing; something that gave you strength. I thought it sounded rather beautiful, whereas the scenes in the sitting room were always ugly.

I mulled over what I knew of Uenis. I was no longer wholly sure he could be an informant – but even if it was true, I decided it was time to forgive; I wanted to try out what I'd read in the books. My decision was compounded by all the rants I was hearing about him; *this is a bit much*, I thought. I was ashamed I had joined in.

So I held a formal Forgiveness Day in my mind; the first of many. It felt incredibly cleansing to decide to start anew with someone; to put aside all the hate and distrust I'd held inside me and wash myself clean of those horrible feelings. If I'm honest, too, I enjoyed it because it was another small act of rebellion against AB.

More and more, as winter turned the corner into spring, I valued the difference between my emerging viewpoints and those of Bala. I became passionate about reconciliation and rehabilitation, as opposed to retribution and punishment, which was what AB adored. From secret-reading, new heroes took the place of AB in my mind: Mahatma Gandhi, Nelson Mandela and Martin Luther King. Knowing more about it, I felt even more outraged and out of place when I heard AB glorify torture and capital punishment and everyone agree.

I remember feeling so isolated. I couldn't articulate my evolving opinions to anyone, which made me uncertain those opinions were right. The only thing that gave me any hope that I was on the right track were the books I read. Those books gave me other voices to listen to, where before there had been only one.

None of my new opinions was easy for me to form. I felt as though I was a butterfly emerging from a chrysalis – into a nest of butterfly-eating ants. If I'd dared to express any of the ideas percolating through me, I'd have been beaten to within an inch of my life.

It was very lonely, being the only butterfly in the world. Nevertheless, I thought to myself, *I hope I never become like them.* Even if I was eaten, it was better than being an ant.

I made myself a fervent promise, too. *If ever in the future there comes a time when someone needs my help and friendship, I will willingly give it. I will never let anyone be in the position that I'm in now, so alone and friendless. From this point forwards, I will not join in with bullying. I will never let anyone feel alone.*

I didn't know it then, but it was a promise that would save my life.

20

On 7 May 1996 we moved house again, the council having finally found a property that was to the Collective's satisfaction. That piece of pink card with my name on was put away, Sian's mother banished without knowing of my existence, and the Outside world retreated once more.

Our new home was a three-storey terraced Victorian property in Brixton. From the moment we moved in, I adored it. There was so much space! In contrast to the tiny flat in Wembley, it felt as if we were living in a palace. Downstairs had two living rooms, where we did Discussions and preparation for the new world, and Sian and Josie slept; the middle floor hosted the kitchen and Bala and Chanda's bedroom; and on the top floor, up a steep little staircase with no rail, were the bathroom, Shobha's room (which she shared with Oh), and the room I shared with Aisha.

Sharing with Comrade Aisha was the best arrangement I could have hoped for. We slept together in a kingsize bed and, unlike in the other houses, it was *always* Aisha who was with me at night: no more taking shifts. Well knowing she was the most liberal comrade in the Collective, I dared to stroke her hair at night almost as soon as we moved in and she *let* me; sometimes, she'd even stroke mine as well. It was such a beautiful treat.

To my disappointment, the view from the window was nowhere near as exciting as in Wembley. Both my bedroom window and the bathroom looked out on to the gardens at the back. No more red buses; no more Mr Motorcycle! I missed the constant action of the road. That had been a lifeline for me in Wembley, but now it was no more.

There was one key difference to my looking Out now. For the very first time, when my eyes alighted on our new neighbours, I did not believe that any of them were enemy agents. No longer was I scared. My experiences in Wembley with Uenis Cieppo had changed me. While I still believed in AB's importance and his role in the new world, I didn't think any more that these ordinary people were out to get us – whatever Bala said.

AB's paranoia was as great as ever, however. Sadly, in Brixton, he rolled the rules out again: no more phone calls, no more front-door opening; he even banned me from being on the ground floor alone. When I asked why, he said it was in case fascist agents snatched me.

I no longer believed that, and my mindset had altered on something else, too. Soon after we moved in, Comrade Sian made some comment about a story in the news – a political prisoner, perhaps, who had spent a long time in jail.

'If that happened to me,' I remember saying, in a matter-of-fact way, 'I wouldn't find it too difficult to cope. I've already spent all my life in prison.'

It was the first time I'd ever thought of it that way. I wasn't angry about it; it was just the way things were. Knowing that AB was the covert leader of the world and that one day it would be Overt, I considered my imprisonment now as excessive preparation for my role in that new world. I was like a debutante, waiting for the ball, and in the meantime AB kept me hidden away. He didn't need to, because those fascist agents weren't going to snatch me, but he'd decided to restrict my access to dancing and people nonetheless, so that the ball would be special and unspoiled.

I was still only allowed Outside if AB was with me. The Brixton house had a big garden at the back, with a small square concrete patio. I was thirteen and a half years old, yet I wasn't allowed to go in it alone – and the ground-floor ban meant I could never get out anyway. AB was particularly cautious about our trips to the garden because two of our neighbours were teenage lads. They used to smile in a friendly fashion at me sometimes when AB and I were in the garden.

Yet he needn't have worried. What need had I of teenage boys when John Major was in my heart? The more Sian and AB berated me for my affection for him, the more I loved him – another form of insurrection. Since my forgiveness days, too, I had so revised my erstwhile opinion of Uenis Cieppo that he too had become a favourite. I wrote poetry for him. I hadn't forgotten my personal promise that no one would be alone if I could help it – and my first act of kindness was to give my love to my former foe. I saw in him a kindred spirit as, like me, he was frequently the focus of AB's ire.

Even though we had moved away from Wembley, that rage against Uenis continued – probably because I was so rebelliously overt about my affection for him. No matter what AB and Sian said, I refused to be browbeaten. I made it clear I was not going to give him up.

'I don't know why you waste your time,' AB jeered at me. 'Uenis was revolted by your appearance. You're so ugly no one will ever look at you.'

I felt the words as a mortal blow to my self-esteem. I already disliked my appearance, but this attack left me reeling. For a long time afterwards, I couldn't forget his words. They became a part of my everyday attitude: the stitching in all my robes of self-hate.

I saw much less of AB in the Brixton house, which as always was both good and bad. No longer did I get to overhear his convivial chats with Chanda over lunch, nor could I attempt to persuade him through my presence I had some merit. I saw him for Discussions, for our creepy hugs and – a new 'privilege' – when I brought him his food on a tray. He ate in his room with Chanda now and every mealtime except breakfast I would knock on his door with his food.

It was always wrong. It was either served the wrong way – in a bowl when it should have been on a plate; on a plate when it should have been in a bowl – or there was too much of it; he often said the comrades were putting too big a helping on his plate and making him fat. 'I'll throw the food in your face!' he would threaten. I tried to get in and out as quickly as I could.

The other drawback to the new place was that Comrade Simons didn't visit any more. Around the time we moved, however, he did too, downsizing to a smaller place, and our larger house became filled with books he'd been storing for AB. Many of them came from the time when the Collective had operated from the Mao Memorial Centre, and AB gave them to me to read because they were all about China and the Cultural Revolution: he wanted to educate me in its brilliance.

Bala encouraged me, when it came to the fascist state, to think critically. Repeatedly he told us all not to believe everything we heard or read in the mass media. For once, I did as I was told. As I read about the Cultural Revolution, *I thought critically.*

I remember reading about a girl who'd been dragged into the street and had her hair forcibly cut by the Red Guards. The soldiers smashed mirrors and held public denunciations of those wearing elegant clothes. The government imposed the most nonsensical restrictions on people; everything artistic and entertaining was banned, from music to parties to films. As my secret-reading had already exposed me to the more liberal, tolerant and enlightened attitudes prevalent in the West, I was aghast by what I read. *I don't like all this*, I thought – a rebellious attitude indeed within the Communist Collective.

What I was reading about had happened in the past. Yet I knew that this was the vision AB aspired to for the future. This was another catalyst that made me question the Collective's ideas. I thought everyone should be allowed to do what they wanted, more or less, as long as they were not harming others. Having been so deprived myself, I was against the idea of banning anything that made people happy. I knew only too well, from the way the Collective denounced Uenis, whom I loved, exactly how it felt when that happened.

'When it is Overt,' AB told me cruelly that year, 'I will build a pyre and put Uenis on it and I will ask *you* to light the flame to kill him . . .'

When it is Overt . . . When *would* it be Overt? That summer of 1996, the Olympics were staged in Atlanta, USA – the same Olympics that AB had once said would never be staged as he'd be ruling the world by then. Yet he seemed to have forgotten. I'd been so young when he'd first said it that I don't think I was fully aware of the discrepancy, but nonetheless it made an impact, implanting a nagging doubt. *Why aren't things as he said they would be?*

Sometimes, he blamed his followers for things like that: 'You people don't work with me properly.' Certainly, no one seemed to question *him*. A butterfly alone, I felt I could not trust my intuition on it.

Yet time and again that year, things happened that made me question more. Still writing my secret denouncements of AB (and then destroying them afterwards), I thought one day as I angrily scribbled, *How come this pen is working while I'm writing these things if everything is controlled by Bala? Surely he or JACKIE would have made it not work so I couldn't write against him?*

Then, on 13 November 1996, AB's mother passed away. This, too, was not in the programme. When I'd been younger, AB had sometimes said that I would one day meet his mother; knowing how much I longed for new people in my life, he'd dangled it almost as a carrot, telling me that it would happen when I was 'good' enough. Amma was, in my mind, a sort of grandmother to me, even though she didn't know I existed. The way AB talked of it, it seemed certain that one day it *would* happen. But now she was dead.

AB said JACKIE did it – to punish Comrade Sian. It was complicated, but on AB's parents' last visit to see him back in 1979, they had got on very well with Sian, and Amma had commented that she and Sian were alike. AB now declared that JACKIE had killed Amma to make Sian pull her socks up: in killing the person *like* Sian, it was a warning that Sian would be next if she didn't watch out.

'My mother died and it's all *your* fault!' AB ranted at Sian.

It was horrible to watch him do it in Discussions. Comrade Sian worshipped AB *and* his parents. She was distraught by his claim. AB was putting more and more pressure on her; not helped, I will admit, by my continuing rebellions, which were *also* her fault. Sian had once been the favourite comrade. Now, it was her turn to fall from grace.

She was so devoted to him I think it was too much for her to bear.

'Comrade Sian, your food is getting cold,' I ventured to her one day, perhaps a month after Amma died; a month of Sian being denigrated every single day.

'I don't deserve to eat,' she replied. 'I'm a bad person; I should die.'

Her voice sounded strange: louder than normal and distressed. Comrade Sian was usually a self-controlled person – it was one of the scariest things about her – but now she started talking too loud, too fast, too much all the time. It was so different from how we knew her that everybody was alarmed.

Everybody – it seemed to me – but Bala. Even when Sian acted out of character by talking back to him, he said she was just playing games. He'd told her, 'Be quiet!' when she was rambling, but she was in such a strange mood that it seemed she *could* not stop talking in her weird robotic voice, even when God himself had ordered her to do so. AB had slapped her, and she'd started crying. For a while, at least, she fell into silence.

She was so messed up, she even eased up on me. It felt as if the tables were turning in a way – she had bullied me for almost fourteen years for the slightest misdemeanour, but now *she* was the one in trouble with AB. Yet she was behaving so peculiarly, it was disconcerting. I was worried about her, though the others seemed to take their lead from AB, dismissing any concerns they may have had.

Perhaps my worry stemmed from the things she said to me. On 19 December, she made me get my diary and ordered me to write in it: 'It is thanks to Comrade Sian that you're alive!'

'Write,' she said in that strange high voice, ' "Comrade Sian, my darling *mother*." '

I did what she said. I was scared – her voice was weaving up and down like a siren, almost as if radio signals were coming in and out, as though someone else was speaking through her. I was confused by what she was saying; not least when, days later, in a different, more self-destructive mood, she told me to grab the diary again.

'Write,' she ordered, ' "Bloody prostitute! She was not my mother. I was MAD to think so. Comrades Bala and Chanda are my parents . . . Only AB has given us all life, not prostitutes like Sian!" ' She told me to cross out what I'd written before.

I couldn't understand what was happening. On 21 December, I woke in the night to hear Sian screaming. I wanted to go down to the kitchen to see what was happening, but Aisha said we should stay put. (Only several days later would I learn what had happened: Sian had tried to stab herself with a knife in the middle of the night, but Josie managed to stop her.)

It was the day afterwards, however, that the most confusing thing of all took place. AB called me to him: it was just the two of us in the room. At last, he seemed concerned for Sian.

'She's going really bad,' he told me. Almost to himself, he added: 'How can she say such things?'

Sian had filed a new report, he said. I didn't see the slip of paper till months afterwards, but AB now planned to tell me what it said, intending me to denounce her for her crimes. *This* was new – I was never normally allowed to say one word against Sian, even when she'd fed me my own vomit – but such was the depth of her disobedience this time that AB had decided enough was enough.

My mind was racing. *What could she have said?* I'd ranted against

AB on my scraps of paper for not listening to my prayers; for beating me unfairly; for being overly hostile to Uenis Cieppo. How would Sian have gone against him?

'If you are a god,' Comrade Sian had said, 'why are you ageing?'

21

Shock doesn't even cover my reaction. Nobody *ever* questioned AB's divinity – not even me, with my forgiveness days and my love for others and my doubt he could read my mind. This was a much bigger thing. Of *course* AB was a god – look at the Synchronizations. Why did all those things happen in the world if AB and JACKIE hadn't caused them?

It was undeniably true, however, that AB *was* ageing. I had noticed that. When he gave me his hair to stick in my diary now, some strands were white. When we'd celebrated his birthday earlier that year, AB had turned fifty-six. His rotting teeth were almost all gone by now. He claimed, however, that the decline in his teeth was due to us; he was falling apart because he had to put up with all these bad people around him.

Yet *that* didn't tally with his claim to be invincible . . .

I tucked Sian's sacrilegious comment away in my head, not knowing what to do with the bombshell notion. That same day, I snuck into the downstairs back room, where Sian slept on a fold-up bed. Unusually, she was still in it, lying there in her turquoise pyjamas.

I edged into the room. It wasn't Sian's private bedroom, but a communal space, almost like a warehouse, stacked high with boxes of newspapers and magazines, books and notepads, as well as supplies for the house. A little window looked out on to the concrete patio beyond, but the curtains were closed that day.

Though Sian had always been an enemy of mine, I couldn't help but feel sorry for her. Perhaps my forgiveness days were paying off . . . She'd always frightened me before, but no one could be frightened of this broken woman in the bed.

I sat down beside her. Hesitantly, because I knew it was forbidden, I reached out a hand and softly stroked her hair. I wanted to say something nice to her.

121

'You look lovely,' I whispered.

Her face creased with anxiety. 'Don't say I look nice! Don't say things like that!'

I couldn't work out if she was scared we'd get in trouble, training me in what was right, or maybe even trying to protect me from AB's beatings, by warning me to stop. Whatever it was, she was clearly agitated. Once again, she began to talk rapidly, scarily, so I quickly left the room. I hadn't intended to distress her.

More strange things happened. Loitering outside the bathroom, I heard her crying while sitting on the loo. *I thought only I did that.* Another time, I came up to my bedroom to find her on her hands and knees, kissing her sandals, which she'd removed and which I knew were similar in style to the shoes AB's mother had worn. Sian was muttering gibberish, but I wondered if perhaps she was trying to say sorry to Amma for having killed her; her manner had that apologetic flavour.

And then, on 23 December, I woke in the middle of the night to hear an awful lot of shouting coming from downstairs.

'What's happening?' I whispered to Aisha. This time, together, we slipped out of bed. From the room she shared with Shobha, Oh had done the same, and the three of us huddled at the top of the second-floor staircase, listening to the row developing downstairs.

'Comrade Chanda, you are not a good team player!' I heard Comrade Sian yell.

I turned my head away from the others, my movements sharp with shock. Comrade Sian *never* challenged AB's wife. Yet I was glad, all the same, that she was finally speaking up because she'd allowed Chanda to dominate her all my life.

'Shut up!' Chanda shouted back at her. AB chimed in too.

But Sian didn't shut up. Her voice rose again with its uncontrolled accusations and I felt a surprising sensation of the situation escalating: AB did not have her under his control.

'Shall we go and see what's going on?' Oh whispered. Unsure if we were meant to, we crept hesitantly down the stairs.

'Stalinist!' I heard Sian shout as we reached the first floor. AB roared back at her in rage. As I followed the comrades down the second staircase, sounds of a struggle coming from the front room reached us.

Then Sian started screaming her head off. Just as suddenly, her voice stopped eerily dead.

Oh was ahead of me. As she pushed her way into the sitting room, I heard AB cry impatiently: 'Hold her!'

By the time I made it through the door, some of the comrades were already in place. As with the attack on Leanne when I was five years old, the puppets needed no preparation. The moment AB gave the command, it was instantly carried out.

Sian lay on the floor, surrounded, a gag in her mouth and her feet and hands being tied to stop her getting away. Muffled cries came through the gag – she was still trying to speak non-stop – and she was struggling against her bonds with almost superhuman strength. As she writhed desperately, I saw her eyes roll back into her head.

AB stood triumphantly over Sian, his feet spread apart while her body bucked between his legs. He had to keep her in her place – because Sian had been trying to escape. The shouting we'd first heard had been her aborted attempt to run out the front door.

Later, he said he tied her up to protect her. She'd tried to run out in her bare feet on a cold December night; she was, he said, in no fit state to leave.

I said nothing, just took in the scene. I'd always known it would happen again – the comrades physically turning on each other – but it was still sobering to see. Sian was so distressed that when AB explained she would be in danger if we let her free, I accepted it without question. I took a seat, next to where she lay.

She was calmer now; her muttering had stopped. Cautiously, they removed the gag – but as soon as they did she started shouting again. I wasn't supposed to hear such ideas so I was whisked out of the room. Aisha and I went upstairs to the kitchen and hung around, listening to the rise and fall of the voices below and wondering what was happening.

When we ventured downstairs again Sian had been untied. She was sitting up in bed, calm again – for now.

'AB, can I have a phone?' I heard her ask. 'Can I speak to Ceri?' She couldn't say 'Mum' because that was banned.

'I've already told you,' AB replied. 'No!'

Sian seemed resigned to it, and did not ask again. She did not seem to notice my presence at all: she was completely focused on Bala.

We slept in till 8.30 a.m. the next day after our disturbed night. It was Christmas Eve, but we did not celebrate that holiday in the Collective – AB's birthday was our Christmas. Once again, I was woken by shouting; Sian had tried to burst in on AB and Chanda, and Josie and Oh were holding her back.

The situation called for desperate measures. AB instructed Josie and Oh to go Out and get her some Kalms medicine. *Medicine* – what an old-world idea. Aside from that gesture, however, AB appeared unperturbed. He placed no value on other people's emotional experiences. He was the natural hub so everything must be centred on him: Sian was just pushing him to see how far she could go before he beat her; she was not genuinely in distress.

Indeed, once the medicine had been given, he announced: 'Everything is all right now. Everything can go back to normal.'

Though Sian's behaviour had been unsettling, I felt rather disappointed when AB said that. *Great, she'll probably be back to bullying me soon.* My life was so mind-numbingly dull that the excitement of the past few evenings had made for a welcome change, despite the horror.

Exactly as AB had directed, things did go back to normal. Later that same day, Oh and Josie went out shopping and returned with a vanilla swiss roll. We never did anything as nice as all eat cake together in the Collective; each person just helped themselves when they wanted some. However, as it was coming up to teatime that day, I happened to walk into the kitchen to find Sian there with the sponge roll, a sharp knife in her hand.

I stopped in my tracks. She'd been so unstable lately . . . *Oh my God*, I thought, eyeing the knife in alarm, *what's she going to do now? Is she going to stab* me*?* The blade glinted and I backed slowly away.

Yet she merely asked: 'Would you like to have some?'

I wasn't put at ease. For all AB's words about 'back to normal', Sian still wasn't *quite* herself. There was something vulnerable about her, as if she needed affirmation or affection. I wondered if it was a trick; I didn't trust her. Was she only being nice so I'd come closer – so she could stab me with the knife? I'd been so rebellious lately; would she think hurting me was a way to get back in Bala's good books? I assessed her coolly from the doorway.

'Do you want some of this?' she asked again.

I couldn't understand the messages in her voice. She sounded needy, as though she wanted my acceptance. Over the years, I had yearned for this woman's love and kindness, and she had always pushed me away. She had *always* reported; *always* betrayed. Despite the promise I'd made myself, I found I didn't have it in my heart to forgive all of that.

Instead, I wanted to give her a taste of her own medicine. I wanted to punish her for all the cruelty she had shown to me over the years. So I said abruptly: 'No, I don't!'

She took a small step backwards, perhaps surprised at my undisguised animosity. 'Why are you being like that with me?' she asked.

Though the question was interrogative, to my confusion she *still* wasn't the sheepdog; in fact, she sounded plaintive.

But almost fourteen years of misery was impossible to shake off. I'd had it up to here. I'd had enough of *her*.

I turned my back and walked away. Revenge and retribution were mine.

It was only about an hour later that it happened. I was downstairs with Josie, at about 6 p.m., when we heard screaming. *Here we go again* . . . It was the fourth such incident of late.

The noise was coming from upstairs, so we took to our heels and began running up the steps. On the first floor, I saw AB and Chanda, having just come out of their room, looking up towards the bathroom. Aisha was there, yelling desperately: 'Downstairs!'

Downstairs? I thought. *It's not downstairs. The screaming was coming from upstairs.*

But we all changed direction and pelted down the steps. I heard someone say, 'Outside,' and all of us burst out the back door. I went so rarely in the garden that as I crossed the threshold I was momentarily lost in that delicious sensation of being Outside.

And Outside in the dark . . . *How magical* . . . For the first few seconds I focused only on the white moon above me, slipping in and out of the passing clouds. I didn't notice that everyone else had stopped dead on the concrete patio.

There was a tree in the corner of the garden; it made the moonlight dappled. It made it hard to see. What *was* that beneath the gently moving patches of light and dark, lying twisted and broken on the floor? I didn't understand when AB said in a sober voice, 'Call an ambulance.'

Without a murmur, Comrade Josie slipped inside to make the call. The rest of us – me included – stared silently at the scene before us.

Comrade Sian was lying on the patio. I blinked as the moonlight passed momentarily across her, lighting up her pale face. A mysterious black stain was spreading slowly beneath her, though the concrete floor was usually a clean light-grey . . .

Everyone else seemed frozen, but I walked over to her, like an enchanted girl brought to life in a sleeping forest of figures. I walked slowly, because when the moon dipped behind the clouds I couldn't see much. Carefully, I bent down next to her. And sneakily, just as I'd done in her bedroom a few days before, I reached out to stroke her hair. My fingers fumbled through it.

Wet. It was wet.

In the dappled moonlight, I glanced down at my hand.

It was slick and black with blood.

And that was the first time I realized what it was. Not a shadow, conjured by the clouds: the patio was black with blood.

I gasped.

'Don't touch her,' AB interjected. 'It may be used as evidence. Somebody may say we pushed her.'

She had tumbled from the bathroom window, three storeys above. As I crouched beside her, she moaned a little, slipping in and out of consciousness as the moon slipped through the clouds.

AB was standing near to her; perhaps she felt his presence. For as she stirred, she began to chant softly: a message just for him.

'Kill me. Kill me. Kill me.'

22

I could not take it in. Nothing *ever* happened in my life, and now there was all of this. It was overwhelming. I stayed on the patio, stunned, staring blindly at Sian in her pool of blood as AB told her not to talk nonsense and asked her urgently if she could wiggle her toes. Comrade Sian had been a giant in my life, but now she was bloodied and broken. Everything was wrong.

I was so adrift that my senses stopped working. I didn't hear the ambulance sirens coming towards us in the December night air, getting louder and louder, but the comrades did. Suddenly, I was whisked inside.

Yet when the paramedics arrived, they were so focused on Sian they paid me no attention. I hung about downstairs, guarded by Aisha, eavesdropping.

'She just fell,' I heard someone say.

Even in the midst of my anguish, I remember thinking, *That doesn't sound right* . . . Given Sian's state of mind over the past few weeks, in *my* mind there was no mistake. *She threw herself out.*

The paramedics spent a long time in the garden with her. Eventually, they lifted her up on to a stretcher and carried her out through the house. It was at that point I burst into tears. I was in shock, I think, but there was also something else.

I was thankful to see her go.

I didn't know what was going to happen to her, but whatever did, I knew I was guaranteed at least a break from her horribleness. It sounds terrible to say it. But every day of my life I'd lived beneath the piercing glare of her critical eye; when she was carried out on that stretcher, I felt a weight lift off me. So, yes, I was shocked and sad and it was a dreadful thing.

But principally I thought: *I'm glad she's gone.*

*

AB didn't go with her to the hospital; he said he wanted her to feel that he had abandoned her. I wasn't surprised: after she'd questioned his divinity, she was the lowest of the low. Josie and Oh went with the ambulance and phoned AB with updates. I remember him writing notes: *She is paralysed on one side . . .*

AB summoned Aisha to report on what had happened, as she'd been the last person to see Sian before she 'fell'. Aisha said she'd heard Sian go into the bathroom and lift up the sash window, which was unusual; we kept the windows shut as much as possible to keep the fascist agents out. She'd called out, 'Are you OK?' but Sian had not responded. After a few moments, Aisha had knocked on the door and gone in – and all she saw was Sian's feet, tumbling out the window. That's when Aisha started screaming. She said nothing could shock her any more after she'd seen that.

Comrade Josie was put down as Sian's next of kin at the hospital; Ceri was not informed. In fact, in the weeks that followed, the comrades told Sian's family she had gone to India to do some charity work and breathed no mention of the 'accident'. Ceri had no idea her daughter was lying in a hospital bed in London, paralysed from the neck down.

After Sian had gone, it was easier to feel softer towards her. I kept running through my last memory of speaking with her in the kitchen. I felt an overwhelming sense of regret. Why hadn't I forgiven her? Why hadn't I kept my promise to myself? I wished with all my heart I'd just hugged her.

Because: what if it was me walking away that made her do it?

Though I wondered if I was at fault, Sian herself blamed someone else. On Christmas Day, AB finally went to visit her in hospital.

'All this happened,' she apparently said, 'because I broke from you.'

Eight little words. But what a difference they made. What had happened to Sian happened *because she did not believe in him*. JACKIE had tested her and she'd failed the test. AB repeated her words almost every day, and would cite them again if ever there were any disagreements in the Collective. Sian's broken body became a beacon: *you better believe or else* . . . Ever since JACKIE had arrived, he'd wrought destruction all over the world, but the hurricane had just touched down closer to home. *Here* was JACKIE's power in all its glory. *Here* were the

128

connections for all of us to see: the proof I'd once requested, viewed with my own two eyes. *All this happened because I broke from you.*

Life was very, very different after Sian fell. Not only were Sian's eyes no longer on me, but with Sian requiring daily visits in hospital, the eyes of the other comrades were also looking elsewhere. Every afternoon, AB would go to the hospital with two of the women – usually leaving me at home. (I accompanied them once a week, a regularity of Outside trips that was beyond my wildest dreams.) I had never felt so free in my life. I felt almost alone in the large house: only three other comrades were left with me, and Chanda and Shobha kept to themselves. I used to sing to myself as I pootled about, little poems I'd written that I turned into tunes.

I also had much more time to look Outside. Shobha's room looked out on to the street, and sometimes I'd go in there while she was distracted having her food and peer Outside – even daring now to lift up the net curtain. In the house opposite was an elderly black man who seemed to spend much of his time sitting by his window. One day, he waved at me – *and I waved back*! Just quickly, a flash of my hand, but it was magnificent to have found a friend at last. I called him Peeper. Every time he waved, I felt a little glow inside that kept me warm for weeks.

Without Sian around, mealtimes were different too. Without her there to silence us we began to talk over our food; it was very nice sometimes. Aisha and Oh even let me discuss Uenis, which previously would have been out of the question. During afternoon nap, which I sometimes shared with Oh, I managed to persuade her to hug me. It was heavenly!

We still had to be careful. Comrade Josie unexpectedly came into the room one day and was so upset when she saw me cuddling Oh. 'I will tell Bala about it if you do that again,' she threatened. It seemed to me that Josie, always so devout to AB, wanted to hold on to the way things had been – but with one comrade down, the running of the house took up much more time and she could not pay close attention even if she wanted to. The women had a strict schedule to keep to – cleaning the bath for AB before he used it; making sure his bathwater was warm; picking up and drying off the damp mat afterwards; not to mention all the shopping and cooking and cleaning – and that took priority above all else.

I began a new tactic: part strategy and part striving to be a better me. I began to chat to Josie more, in the distant hope she would report less if we were on friendlier terms. It worked. Almost as soon as Sian went to hospital, there was much less reporting from everyone, and consequently we all got beaten less. Every now and again, AB would slap or smack us – when he became angry, there was still no stopping him – but there weren't the same huge explosions there once had been. Though it should have been a tragic time with Sian so ill, it was in fact the best life I had ever lived.

By far the finest thing about those giddily free days, however, was that I got the chance to secret-read.

With people going out more, and all those household responsibilities spread so thinly, I daringly decided to become more ambitious. Why confine myself to a single cupboard of books? I had a fair amount of free time now – up to three hours a day – generated both when the comrades went to visit Sian and when Shobha needed caring for, as a couple of comrades would help her twice daily with her ablutions. At those times, it was often only me and Aisha left downstairs. I began to say to her, 'My boobs are itchy, can I go into the front room to apply some cream?' She'd readily agree and I'd take a bottle of baby lotion into the room with me. I'd shut the door behind me, for 'privacy' while I 'applied the cream'. Aisha never seemed to notice that the lotion never went down. In fact, I never even opened the bottle. I had much more important things to do.

The front room was almost like AB's study, but at these times he was never in it. Everywhere I looked there was reading material – as far as the eye could see. AB's books were placed in stacks about a foot high on the desk, and then there were *more* stacks of books on top of the boxes dotted around the room. The room also had a small walk-in storage cupboard – which was filled with yet more books! In addition, there were huge stacks of magazines everywhere. Pure heaven . . .

I almost didn't know where to start. The room had a sofa and three chairs (two of them white plastic garden chairs; the furniture was always mismatched) so I'd choose one to sit on and pick up the nearest book. There were biographies of world leaders, medical encyclopaedias, books on psychology and philosophy . . .

Every time I opened a book, I was transported. For a girl who rarely went Outside, it was the ride of my life. No longer was I sat in prison, on a garden chair in a cluttered front room. Instead, I sat with world leaders at state banquets; walked in tandem with political prisoners freed from jail; delved into the synapses of the human brain with the world's foremost psychologists as my guides. It blew *my* brain. I read about the justice system: how everyone has the right to a fair trial and is innocent until proven guilty. What I read resonated with me deeply. Bala wasn't interested in assessing 'evidence' or hearing both sides of a story.

But as I read more and more, both sides of the story were *exactly* what I got. In fact, I deliberately sought out different books on the same topic, stimulated by the mere notion that one could take a balanced view. Even more than I'd done in Wembley, I took against AB's ideas about totalitarian control and state violence. I thought we should be kind and tolerant and try to understand other people instead. When I read that Gandhi had written, 'An eye for an eye till the whole world is blind' I added my own line: 'A life for a life until the whole world is dead.'

I didn't just read books, I read newspapers too. With Sian in hospital, our daily task of laying out *The New World* went by the wayside; now, AB just passed around the chosen articles. He'd throw the rest of the newspaper away, into a box beside his desk. But once AB was in the bath, I started saying, 'I'll just clear that box up . . .' and while doing so I would read as much as I could of the articles he *hadn't* selected.

A few months after Sian's fall, while she was still being cared for in hospital, I pulled one of the medical books off the stack and settled down to read. Before this, I'd read another book that discussed something called 'embryos' and 'pregnancy' and had been stumped. *How do babies get into wombs in the first place? Is the womb a kind of test tube such as I was born in?* I was perplexed; I needed something else to complete the puzzle.

In that medical encyclopaedia, I found it. Over the years, I had learned the difference between male and female wasteholes. AB had explained that the act of 'poking wasteholes' was what the old world was based on; he was protecting me and the other comrades from *such heinous acts* and therefore from *evil* and *death*. The way he described it, I thought men were violently poking knives up women;

131

he didn't talk about cocks and cunts. I remember thinking, *That sounds so painful. I don't want to go Out in that world!* Any physical intimacy was dirty to AB; if ever we saw two people kissing, he would say, 'Yuck!' and tell me to look away.

But, I now read, in fact sex gave us *life*, not death! *This* was how babies were born! Every child came from an egg and a sperm. And *every* child had a mother and father.

For a shadow-child such as me, it was a revelation. *I* do *come from somewhere. I am not just a child of JACKIE.* Yet in some ways the knowledge made me more rootless still, as I now wondered who my parents might be. I had no one I could ask about it; I couldn't tell anybody I knew about this now, as I wasn't meant to know such things.

I believed I understood why they'd kept it from me – because of AB's prudish attitude (I'd learned about such people and views from secret-reading). Now, a memory came back to me, of AB and me when I was ten and he was trying to teach me Malayalam, the language of Kerala. There was a glossary of words and he'd pointed to one of them and said, 'That's you. You're always going to be a *virgin*.' I hadn't known what it meant then, but I did now. I hated the idea – I wanted to marry Uenis Cieppo and have three lovely children. But as I was told time and again, that was not my destiny: I was betrothed to AB, my life to be dedicated only to his cause.

After I read that book, my new knowledge was like a little secret burning inside me. I became a detective, alert to clues, trying to find out who my mother might be. After the business with the pink card, my number-one suspect was Sian.

I'll confess: I was disappointed by the idea. She was such a beastly person. I'd longed for a mother for years now, but I'd always imagined her as kindly. That wasn't Comrade Sian.

My weekly visits to the hospital became charged with curiosity. When I heard Sian remark to a nurse that she'd brought me up, I thought: *Is that a confession? Or does she just mean she's my foster mother?* AB had interrupted hurriedly.

It was very important that no one at the hospital thought I was Sian's daughter; I'd picked up that much. I believe my relationship to her was billed to the staff as that of a 'family friend'. Largely, though, the Collective seemed unconcerned about the people in the hospital seeing me; I think AB was confident in his ability to explain away my presence if needed. I was a teenager now and no one looked too closely.

Sian was recovering well after her 'fall'. She'd been in ICU initially, and on my first visit had been unable to speak, struck dumb by a tracheostomy, but by now, in April 1997, she had been moved to a ward on a high-dependency unit. She had her own room and could talk and eat, but her body was still immobile. The doctors said they thought she would never walk again.

She didn't pay me much attention during my visits. As she'd always done, she had eyes only for AB. She was repenting, and most of the time I sat quietly by while the two of them talked, just delighting that I was Outside for once. To be in a hospital was such a novel experience that I wished I could drink it all in, but AB kept telling me not to ogle and to follow behind him, my eyes fixed firmly on the back of his anorak. I was banned from talking to the nurses.

Whether it was because of the encyclopaedia or the forgiveness days or just because she wasn't on my back all the time, I was feeling a lot kindlier towards Comrade Sian. Memories fade, and with my secret-reading inspiring me I was determined not to be the sort of person to bear grudges. I remained anxious that one day she might return at full strength and I'd lose all the precious freedoms I'd gained, but while she was at arm's length, she was far from being a foe.

On 16 April 1997, AB, the comrades and I went to the hospital as usual. I sat beside the woman I suspected was my mother and all I could think about was whether or not she was. So when we left that day, I did something I knew AB would disapprove of, but I felt it was too important to desist.

As I looked in Sian's brown eyes on my way out, I said, for the first time in my life, 'Bye bye, Mummy.'

Her expression changed. It was a bit like the time she made me write in my diary that she *was* my mother. Just for a moment, I glimpsed another Sian, a very different woman shining through. An unfamiliar but undeniable tenderness glittered through her expression; there was even – *dare I say it?* – love.

I had never seen her look like that at me before.

She parted her lips. 'Bye bye, baby,' she said softly to me in reply.

I was so thrilled by those three small words. It still didn't solve the case, but it was the first time in fourteen years that Sian had ever acknowledged she had anything to do with me. I felt AB stiffen beside me at our exchange, but we were in public and he did not interject. I kept the memory of Sian's look and words as a talisman: a sign that someone somewhere cared.

I would have loved to speak more to her; would have loved, eventually, to ask the question outright: 'Comrade Sian, are you my mother?'

But only five days later, JACKIE struck: punishment for our moment of connection. Comrade Sian began having epileptic fits, then fell into a catatonic state.

The comrades said they didn't want me to see her like that.

So, I never saw her again.

23

Sian Davies died on 3 August 1997. I can still remember Josie's reaction when she took the call from the hospital: 'What nonsense.' For almost two decades Sian had been AB's most devoted acolyte – and those closest to him would achieve long, possibly eternal life . . .

Sian had died when she was only forty-four.

All this happened because I broke from you.

A sign of JACKIE's power? I didn't know enough to challenge it. A horrible mix of fear, loss and – shame to say – gratitude about Sian's death was my reaction. Never again would she bully me; never again would she look at me with love. I drew a picture for her, a crimson rose, and for a short while wore some of her clothes, including a long, mock-mohair cardigan she'd liked. But AB grew angry I was becoming 'too attached' to her and ordered me to stop. The only item I managed to keep was her bright-pink bra, which I'd squirrelled away to help support my aching back. That was my first bra. In a way, it was her parting gift.

AB expressed no grief that I saw about Sian's death. He despised people who showed emotion; to him it was a sign of weakness. He made an odd announcement in the wake of her passing, though. 'If anybody comes to the door or phones asking for Comrade Prem,' he instructed, 'you must say: "No such person living here."'

I was confused – why would anyone suddenly come looking for *me*? – yet I also viewed the announcement through narrowed eyes. Ever since reading that medical book, I'd been studying AB. Was my 'Papa' actually my biological dad? If Sian *was* my mother – I was still not wholly sure – it seemed unlikely that my father could be anyone else because Sian had always been so devoted.

Recently, I'd stumbled on a book during my secret-reading sessions that, to me, almost certainly proved his paternity. The book was about Janet Jackson; AB enjoyed reading about celebrities as he said when it became Overt all these 'bombshells' would be his spokeswomen: he was keen to know all about them so he'd be able to control them when he ran the world. The book happened to mention that Janet's mother was angry when Janet's father had committed adultery and spawned illegitimate children. And there was something in the description of her mother's reaction that I recognized only too well. I thought, almost in wonder at the revelation, *That sounds like Comrade Chanda . . .* It was only my opinion but, for me, that was the moment it all fell into place: *No wonder Chanda always looks at me as if she wants me dead: I am living proof AB had an affair with Comrade Sian! He* is *my father! I am his bastard child!*

With the seed planted that I was AB's daughter, I began to realize something else, too − something that started ticking away in my brain again as I listened to AB's instruction to the comrades to deny I lived at the house. If I *was* living proof of AB's extra-marital affair, then I really was something to be hidden. I started to wonder: did my imprisonment come about not to protect *me* from the fascist state − but to protect Bala's *reputation* for when he became leader of the world? The Collective had always said they'd had to go underground when I was born − but perhaps AB had kept me inside not to shield me, but for shame. He didn't want people to ask questions. When he ran the world, there couldn't be any gossip about his private life.

I knew from secret-reading that when people died, there was usually a funeral. So I expected the Collective to start making arrangements for Sian but, unexpectedly, it was taken out of their hands. I don't know how it happened, but Sian's family found out she was dead. They insisted they would organize Sian's burial − and refused to allow the comrades to attend.

I have no idea how Ceri reacted to the news her daughter had died, nor what she thought when she discovered she had never been in India as the comrades had said, but had in fact spent the last seven months of her life paralysed in hospital after 'falling' from a third-storey window. What I do know is that two days after Sian died, there was an authoritative knock at the door of our house.

The police had come to call.

'She's just staying with us for a while,' AB told the police officers as they looked curiously in my direction, scribbling down the names of every member of the group. We'd had no warning of their visit and there'd been no time to hide me: I sat with the others as two officers explained they'd come to investigate Sian's death.

Though I was sitting right there during their visit, I cannot tell you more of what they said. As always happened with anything new, I couldn't take it in. People from Outside even *smelt* different so I was concentrating more on the assault to my senses than on the topic of conversation. Whatever it was, it had Bala shaking with rage, though he was careful to conceal it from them.

When they left, saying they would return soon, he did not hold back.

'Bloody fascist state trying to make trouble for us!' he raged. 'These bastards are trying to say we murdered her! They will pay for this!'

It seemed there was some suspicion Sian may have been pushed from the window. As she had now died of her injuries, a murder investigation had been launched. I suspect Ceri may have reasoned: why else had the Collective concealed the truth from her? Why hadn't they let her visit her only daughter – given her a chance to say goodbye – unless they had something to hide?

I knew Sian hadn't been pushed, but I didn't understand why the Collective didn't tell the truth about the fact she had probably jumped. She had been so desperate that December – it was clear to me that when she went out the window she was either trying to commit suicide or escape. But perhaps if suicide was thought of, people might start digging into what had driven her to it . . . AB could bear no such intervention from the BFS.

The police had said they would be back – and they were, time and again that August of 1997. Though the women were stroppy with them, the investigation continued apace, with every group member but me subjected to an interview. I watched in fascination when they visited, the novelty of new people actually coming *into* the house miraculous to me.

I was never allowed to be near the officers on my own, so I never had an opportunity to speak to them. Their very presence was so overwhelming I had no time to think. I know that even if my brain had allowed me to conceive of it, I wouldn't have dared do it. So much kept me silent: a fear of JACKIE, of AB; an age-old distrust of these uniformed 'fascist dogs'. But, even beyond all that, my life

137

had become so comparatively free since Sian had fallen that I didn't dare risk rocking the boat. I was so grateful about being able to hug Oh (secretly) and have a conversation over dinner. I didn't know any different so, for me, that *was* freedom.

I sat mute every time the officers came.

AB, however, seemed concerned that they might be interested in me. He kept throwing out different stories that the comrades should share. 'If worst comes to worst,' he said, 'tell the police that Comrade Prem is the product of a relationship between Sian and Comrade Simons.' Then he said: 'You should say that Chanda and I have adopted her.' And finally: 'You may say that Prem is a result of my relationship with Comrade Sian.'

At which point, I exclaimed loudly: 'YES!' I took this as confirmation of all my suspicions.

Yet . . . this was just one of *several* things he'd said, so I still wasn't 100 per cent sure. I later asked him, one to one, if he *was* my dad. I wanted to hear him say it, so that I could put my shadow-feelings to bed and *know*: *I am the daughter of Sian and AB.*

He refused to give me that certainty.

'Be patient,' he said instead. 'I will tell you all in good time.'

But 'in good time' never came. Whenever I asked him outright, he'd 'um' and 'ah' and dodge the question. He *did* start to say that my 95 per cent (good) was him and seemed to suggest the 5 per cent (bad) was Sian and my 'Welsh heritage', but I wasn't wholly sure what that meant. Was AB just trying to claim credit, as he always did, for everything in my life?

I wanted so badly to believe in my theory – I wanted to *belong* – but until it was confirmed by an adult, I could not be sure. If he was my dad, why didn't he just say so? Or was he actually *not* my dad and *that* was why he refused to commit? Was he claiming to be the source of my 95 per cent so I didn't start looking for my *real* father?

It was reasonable, I concluded, that he might just have *said* he was my dad to keep the fascist state away: if he claimed to be my birth parent, they would leave us alone.

But, in the end, no one even asked about me; I was just a 'guest' and therefore not a focus of the police inquiries.

Yet I think AB was irritated that I'd started asking questions. A few weeks after Sian had passed away, he went on the attack.

'You do know why she's dead?' he asked me. 'It's *your* fault, Comrade Prem. You said "Mummy" to her. JACKIE was VERY angry about that: it's anti–AB. *That's* why she's dead.'

My little talisman . . . My one nice moment with the woman I *thought* was my mother. That look of love . . . The tiny candle I'd been holding inside me – the memory of that scene – flickered and burned out. Ever since she'd died, I'd been thinking: *Maybe we shared that moment because Sian didn't want to die without letting me know she cared*. Now, that one nice thing was destroyed, tainted by the knowledge that I'd killed (my mother?) with my selfishness. Forget 5 per cent: *all* of me was bad.

And JACKIE had one more sting in the tail. Though the murder investigation concluded that summer without any charges being brought, AB would not tolerate such vicious harassment from the fascist state. And so, on the night of 31 August 1997, at around 12.23 a.m., JACKIE sent a black Mercedes spinning in a subterranean tunnel across the Channel in France. It hit the thirteenth pillar at 65mph.

In retribution, JACKIE had killed Diana, Princess of Wales.

24

I observed the two-minute silence for the princess without anyone knowing I was; they probably thought I was following AB's no-talking guideline, but in my head I was thinking of her. The newspapers from Outside were full of conspiracy theories as to what had killed her – the drunk driver or the paparazzi? Not one of them identified that JACKIE had struck, which was what AB told us.

It was a terrible time. AB was on the warpath. As if Sian's fall and her death had not been warning enough, this was an awesome demonstration of what JACKIE could do. AB kept reminding me, over and over, of JACKIE's anger at me, saying my actions had forced him to kill Sian. It was an impossible situation for me to be in. I felt responsible.

Because it wasn't only AB telling me it was my fault: a small voice inside me kept reminding me I'd walked away from Sian, an hour before she 'fell'.

As summer segued into autumn, I became more and more distressed. AB bullied me constantly. I became desperate, my suicidal feelings rising up again; once, I even opened the bathroom window myself, thinking that I'd like to join Sian beyond AB's reach . . . Balanced by the open window, I looked shakily down at the concrete patio; it seemed so far away.

But I didn't have the courage to do it; something else that made me feel useless. I was scared of falling and not dying. If I was paralysed, I knew I'd be even more under AB's control.

Just as Sian's family had directed, none of us went to her funeral. I remember overhearing an angry conversation on the telephone between the Collective and Sian's relatives about it. Both Ceri and Sian's cousin, Eleri, had called: their raised voices snapped from the receiver like the negative Maozi waves I'd been warned about. It turned out that Eleri actually lived in London, not far from the hospital. She'd been devastated to learn she'd not been able to visit Sian while she was still alive; in fact, the only time she got to see her was when she identified her body. Ceri shouted of AB, 'He took her over!' She meant he'd brainwashed Sian; something she'd said before and which had been mentioned in Discussions over the years, when Sian had been forced to denigrate her mum. Sian used to say, mocking her mother, 'If the brain is dirty, you *have* to wash it.'

After this heated conversation, Ceri had put the phone down on Josie. There was much chatter within the Collective of what a rude, hateful mother Sian had had.

I'd listened with so much interest to that phone call. If Sian *was* my mother, these people were my family. Though Ceri knew nothing of my existence, I found that a small part of me hoped she'd find me, somehow, and take me away. I would have *loved* to have a grandmother. Yet after that angry phone call, Ceri cut off all contact with the Collective, and even changed her phone number so they could never ring her.

But maybe one day I would meet her. Maybe one day . . .

There was one final piece of fascist-state bureaucracy the Collective had to complete in the wake of Sian's passing. In mid-October, official letters arrived for all the comrades; as usual, I was the only one without. They'd been summoned to the coroner's inquest into Sian's death on 15 October 1997.

AB issued instructions beforehand: the comrades must lie under oath.

No one was to say that Sian threw herself out.

And if they asked if she had any dependents, they must say, 'No.'

I wonder what dependents are, I remember thinking. I didn't know it meant children; nor that if Outside suspected Sian had a fourteen-year-old daughter they would want to make sure she was safe, now that her mother was dead. To me, it meant nothing, aside from an awareness that Bala was asking them to lie about her 'fall'. That riled me. I wanted them to tell the truth, as I was always told to. It seemed the least that Sian deserved.

But they were lying to keep the BFS away and, in their minds, that end game justified their means.

Nor were these the only lies they told. Comrade Sian had occasionally talked to the neighbours, and they had all started asking, 'Where's that tall woman these days?'

It was incredible, the ease with which the comrades said: 'She's moved away.'

Even though it wasn't murder, the cover-up was complete.

On the day of the inquest, a miraculous thing happened: every comrade in the Collective went Out, as demanded by those letters from the BFS. They were adamant I could not go with them, but of course I couldn't be left alone. So Comrade Simons came to watch me. It was so nice to see him again: it was a rare treat for me to see anyone but those same six faces, so I studied his features with a fascinated gaze. However, I'd been warned by the Collective not to get *too* close to him, so I made sure I kept my distance all day. I spent most of the time secret-reading.

The coroner's court should have been the end of it. But journalists became interested in the story; I guess they thought it strange, the way the comrades had misinformed Ceri and barred her from her daughter's deathbed. 'Why did you keep Sian's mother in the dark?' one reporter demanded; he ambushed the comrades on their way to the launderette. The phone kept ringing non-stop; the media wanted to speak to Comrade Bala.

One day, a man in a blue jacket even came to our front door. I was upstairs doing AB's exercises at the time, in my room at the back of the house. So I didn't look Out, but I couldn't help but overhear the confrontation.

'Could we speak to Comrade Bala please?' the man politely asked.

Comrades Josie, Oh and Aisha – the only non-family comrades left – dealt with him on the doorstep.

'You're part of the fascist state!' Josie asserted. 'And if you don't stop harassing us, we'll call the *open* fascist state on you!'

'We would just like to ask you some very simple questions. Why won't you speak to us?' he pleaded.

'You are just showing,' spat out Josie, 'that you are part of the fascist state!' As proof, she cited the fact that the man had arrived at the same time as the milkman – proving they were *both* enemy agents.

The comrades soon retreated indoors and shut the door in his face.

Why don't you just tell the truth? I wondered. I had tears in my eyes: I knew this was only happening because Ceri wanted to know what *really* happened to her daughter. Yet, at the same time, I *knew* why:

because they didn't want outside agencies to have anything to do with the inner workings of the group.

So the door stayed shut. The phone fell silent. AB, expert at talking his way round, was eventually satisfied that he had seen off all Outside intrusion: the police, the courts, the media. A woman had died, but the fuss was over. Though difficult at times, he had explained it all away. The officials stopped investigating: no more questions asked.

No one looked up to the second-floor window, where I stared out wistfully at the world.

Part Three
Clipped Wings

25

'I'd like that one, please,' I said, pointing a trembling finger at the ready-to-wear salwar kameez hanging in the shop. It was 21 December 2001 and I'd been permitted to choose an outfit for my upcoming nineteenth birthday. It was a gift indeed: the first time in my life I'd been able to choose something for myself in a store. The fact that it was an Indian dress of the type I'd always longed for was an additional miracle. Though Dad – AB – stood over me while I chose, making me feel uncomfortable, and I selected only what I thought he'd approve, it still felt like a big victory.

I didn't know why he had suddenly allowed me to wear Indian dress, but over the past few years things had changed a lot at home. After Comrade Sian died, Dad asked Comrade Chanda to take over my training. For a while, things improved – Chanda bought me clothes in feminine colours, stopped Dad forcing me to my knees in subjugation and, for one year, even insisted he took me Out to the garden *every three days*. I began to call her 'Mum', hoping for the mother/daughter relationship I'd never had; JACKIE issued no punishment. On the contrary, Dad seemed pleased I was rejecting my negative 5 per cent. I went back through my old diaries, adding my name to my childhood diagrams of AB's family tree, scribbling proudly: 'Prem Balakrishnan.' AB permitted me to call him Dad.

I didn't think much about Comrade Sian as I embraced this new family. I still had no real proof she was my mother, and even if she was, after the way she'd treated me I felt no loyalty to her – just as she'd shown none to me. Because, if she was my mother – I sometimes thought on my darker days – why had she not taken me with her, to the better place of death, when she'd thrown herself out of that bathroom window?

To my disappointment, my new mother/daughter relationship with Chanda didn't last. I felt she began to relish the control she now had over me. When it came down to it, she had no space in her heart for the cuckoo in her nest. I wanted to love her, but all she did was give me hateful looks powerful enough to fell an elephant. Though I continued to call her Mum, I did not consider her to be one. In her own way, I felt that she was even more controlling than Dad.

'Right, let's go home,' Dad said as soon as the shopkeeper had wrapped up my brand-new salwar kameez; every time he took me Out, he wanted to return home as soon as possible. I hadn't tried the outfit on, instead Josie had efficiently picked out the size for me; I had no idea what size I was, having never shopped for myself. She'd accompanied us not just for that reason, however, but because Dad wouldn't let me go any distance Outside without a female comrade present. Although I was not watched in the bathroom at home, Outside I was always accompanied to the toilet for fear fascist agents would snatch me. Josie or Aisha or Oh would loiter outside my cubicle, waiting and listening. I always felt so robbed of dignity. In fact, it spoiled the rare occasions I got to go Out because it reminded me of my invisible chains.

Despite today's treat, those chains were tighter now than they'd been before. I'd always been afraid of Dad, but now I was older I had more awareness of what he might do. The year before, there'd been an enormous scene when I'd revealed I was in love with the politician Ken Livingstone (the London mayoral elections had been going on at the time and I was besotted with him, much as I'd once been with Uenis Cieppo and John Major). 'One day I am going to marry Ken,' I wrote. 'I will be Mrs P Livingstone! Is there anything greater than that?'

Dad's face had contorted with anger when he'd realized I was going against him: I was betrothed to *him*. Instantly, he'd raged towards me, his hand already outstretched for a beating. That was all too familiar, but this time as he landed his blows on me, his face barely an inch from mine, he said something new: 'No one knows you are here, Comrade Prem. So don't chance your luck. I'll torture you to death and what can anyone do? If I killed you, I'd just bury you in the garden and nobody would know.'

As I'd cowered on the sofa, trying to shield myself, I'd recognized the chilling ring of truth. Nobody would know. Nobody knew I existed. My name was on no official database. Unlike Sian, whose welfare had been enquired about by the neighbours after she died, I was permitted to speak to no one on the rare occasions I left the house, so no one would ask after *me*. If Dad wanted to, I was certain he could get away with murder.

'Thank you very much!' Dad said now as we exited the shop and walked out on to Upper Tooting Road. I watched him with my usual perplexed feelings. How could he sometimes be so nice, and sometimes such a monster?

I'd spent a lot of time thinking about it over the past few years: shut up inside every day, I had a lot of time to think. I couldn't understand what made him – what made *all* of them – so nasty, when they could all be nice if they wanted. Even Josie, who had once been such a keen reporter, had become a friend of sorts; she had taught me to knit, and now regularly entranced me with tales of her childhood in the countryside – stories I listened to with enthrall-ment and envy in equal measure. Each of the Collective members would almost take turns to pet and cosset me, and for a time it could seem as if everything was normal – but there would always come a time when someone would report again. Then, they'd turn into a pack, heartless and sadistic. I started to think of whatever took them over as being like some kind of evil spirit, infecting everybody.

Yet what could it be? It wasn't as if Dad drank a potion to trans-form. It was when the *group* connected that bad things happened.

Back in 1999, I'd come up with a theory for it. *The one thing they all believe in is Communism.* I decided what was making them horrible must be this – this 'deathly stinking poisonous diabolical Commie evil', as I called it. I used to imagine that one day I'd write an article in a prominent newspaper entitled: 'Communism – The Religion of Hate'.

Identifying the culprit didn't make life any easier, though. If any-thing, it exacerbated my loneliness – because they all believed in it and I (secretly) didn't. I had never felt more like the only butterfly on the planet. Now I was older, I couldn't take comfort in the bath-room utilities any more. My only friends were the dogs I saw from a distance in the neighbours' gardens – Tommy, a black-and-white Collie two doors down, was a real pal – and my writings. Peeper, the elderly man I'd once waved at, was long gone; about a year after I'd started waving to him, a hearse had left his house, the flowers along its side spelling 'Grandad'. I'd cried to see it and Dad had crossly asked me why I was so upset.

'We were friends,' I'd told him.

'*That's* why JACKIE killed him,' he'd snapped back.

To be a good soldier in the new world, I could have no connections in the old.

Dad, Josie and I walked in single file along the high street, me in the middle for protection. As I'd always been taught, I stared only at the back of Dad's anorak and did not allow my eyes to slide left or right. Aged eighteen, this habit was so ingrained in me that the comrades no longer needed to hiss, 'Don't ogle!' as they monitored my movements.

Their surveillance aside, however, I knew I'd find it too overwhelming to look at anything but the collar of Dad's coat. I was used to viewing only the rooms in the house and the outlook from its windows – the experience of walking down the high street, with so many strangers around me in so many interesting clothes, with so many shops you could enter, each with its own bright sign, was overpowering. I now went Out maybe once a week or once every two weeks, but only to the garden or perhaps up the road if Dad was in a good mood. We never went as far as the high road unless it was a special occasion. Now I was eighteen, I was no longer taken Out when the housing officials came; Dad said that if I was seen, the comrades should say I was caring for Shobha. Now I was officially an adult, it did not matter so much to Dad if others saw me.

Indeed, since I was sixteen, Dad had started allowing me Outings on my birthday. We'd go into central London to a bookstore so he could buy books, or do something else that was different. Today's trip to buy the salwar kameez was so that I would have something to wear for my birthday in January. These events were the highlights of my year and *almost* made all the misery in between worth it. I was so grateful to be allowed these treats – huge in scale to me – that I always felt guilty for thinking any bad thoughts about Dad.

'Don't dawdle!' he snapped at me, as though wanting me to resist the instinct to think well of him. I was making painfully slow progress along the street. The truth was, I didn't *want* to walk faster – I wanted to prolong the trip Out – but Dad always castigated me for my pace, saying I was lazy. Now that he was sixty-one, however, his own pace was diminishing, so I was increasingly able to take the unhurried steps I preferred.

Yet the crowds around us were walking fast, their coats buttoned up and their bodies bent into the cutting cold of the December air. The weather was usually poor when I went Out, especially in the summer – as though Dad chose those days specifically, the better to reflect his own dark mood at having to take me Out in the first place. I spent months begging for each excursion, and Dad found excuse after excuse to delay. In the end, we'd only go Out when the weather was awful, so I frequently caught a cold – which then became another excuse to keep me in, because I always got sick from Outside.

Of course, Dad didn't have to grant my requests at all, and he tried his very hardest not to. 'After Overt you will be able to do what you want,' he would say expansively. 'Why are you so impatient?'

The coming Overt was my saving grace. It was the only reason I got to go Out. I'd cottoned on to Dad's Achilles' heel: his reputation. When it became Overt and I was allowed out of the shadows, how would it look if I then began to badmouth him, saying he *never* took me Out in the old world? So it seemed he'd decided to throw me a bone every now and then to keep me happy. 'Now you can't say I don't take you out!' he would say triumphantly on our return.

If it was a ruse to keep me in line, it worked. That evening, back at home, I reverentially picked up each piece of the salwar kameez and eased it on to my body. Brown with rust-coloured embroidery, it was the most beautiful piece of clothing I had ever worn – and it was *mine*. I couldn't believe my luck.

We had no full-length mirrors in the Collective, so I tried instead to catch a glimpse of myself in the darkened window. My reflection came in and out of focus, shimmering in the glass like a ghost.

I squinted at my reflection, then frowned. Although I was in love with the Indian dress, I *hated* the rest of what I saw. I looked ugly and unhealthy: extremely pale skin from never going Out; dark circles around my eyes, which were bloodshot and putty; dry skin and lips. But my greatest shame was my hair.

When I was sixteen it had started to fall out. It was now very thin, with balding patches, and I knew I'd soon have to cut it all off. How I *wished* I could get a tan or wear make-up or dye my hair, like I read about in magazines! But such things were a freedom too far.

Yet this salwar kameez was nice. In this salwar kameez, I could *imagine* I was beautiful.

My imagination was still my very best friend, my cocoon as much of a sanctuary as it had always been. Gifts like this salwar kameez were a further feather for my mental nest, allowing me to forget I was being kept prisoner. I lived in my head most of the time, in blissful and intentional ignorance. In my head, I wasn't Comrade Prem, but Preethi, a free girl. Sometimes, Preethi would even wave her arms in the air when alone to convince herself of that. *Look – no invisible chains! If I wave my arms around, it feels like I am free. I can do what I want because I can move my arms . . .*

From my secret-reading – which I was still doing several hours a day – I had stumbled upon a quotation I thought described my sanctuary. 'Schizophrenic behaviour is a special strategy that a person invents in order to live in an unliveable situation,' wrote R. D. Laing in *The Politics of Experience*. I knew what I was doing was mad, but I took so much comfort from it I could not stop.

In a way, though, recognizing the insanity of my actions confirmed something I'd begun to suspect – that the *real* reason the Collective kept me hidden was *because* I was mentally ill. Perhaps I was kept in the shadows not to protect me, but others. Perhaps I wasn't fit to mix with people outside the group; perhaps no one else would be as forgiving and supportive as those who cared for me in the Collective. I thought differently to everyone else I knew – wasn't that a sign of madness too?

Being so happily enmeshed in my cocoon, I only came back to reality when I had to: when a comrade reported and Dad beat me; when the general election was held and for the first time I'd had to acknowledge that the reason I couldn't vote was not my age but Dad's refusal; when four planes were hijacked in America on 11 September and Dad was jubilant about the colossal loss of life: he said this was JACKIE's revenge for all the crimes America had committed in the world . . . I remember wondering what crime *I* had committed in my past life to have been landed with a man who took such pleasure at the mass murder of innocent people.

9/11 was a very bad day, a day when even my cocoon could not save me. I'd had to hold back my tears for more than two hours while Dad raved about it, to avoid being beaten for my contrary views; I could cry only when I went for my bath. When I came out, Dad challenged me, asking aggressively why my eyes were so red.

'I got shampoo in them,' I'd lied, but I'm not sure he believed me.

It was at times like those that my carefully constructed cocoon got torn into a million pieces – a cobweb caught in a tornado – and then I couldn't help but see the stark reality of my situation: I was trapped here until it became Overt, but when Overt arrived it would bring no relief, as when Dad ruled the world things would be a million times worse.

The thought of everywhere being as dismal and funereal as the Collective was nightmarish. I'd stand at the window, wishing the glass would vanish so I could get Out *now*. I'd stare at the neighbours sitting on their patio, having a nice drink in the evening, and dream I could do the same – but I knew I'd never be able to, because when it was Overt such things would be banned. I felt the future was a cul-de-sac: no way out.

Standing at the window, my hand pressed to the glass that I wished would melt away, I also gazed enviously at the goldfinches and blue tits. I'd fantasize that I too could fly free like them . . . But that was not my destiny. That was not Dad's plan for me.

I felt so isolated that I took to communicating with my younger self: I went back through my diaries, commenting on old entries. When a seven-year-old Prem had parroted Bala, writing of the Queen: 'Why does [Britain] have cult Loony Liz? She is a blood-drenched criminal!' I scored through it and corrected: 'No, she's not! She's a lovely elegant lady who commands great respect from all noble, decent souls.'

I felt more confident about keeping records of my controversial views now. Though the comrades were strict with me, their surveillance was nothing like it had been in the days of Sian. I kept my writings in a folder called 'Not-to-look-at files' and informed the comrades I was preparing a special surprise for Dad's birthday that I didn't want them to see. At that, they respected my privacy, believing that this was an act of worship between my dad and me. I was good at lying to them and keeping secrets now.

Perhaps the biggest secret of all was that, like Sian before me, I was beginning to doubt my dad was *actually* a god. Could he *really* be immortal when he was so clearly getting old? Sian's words had

153

stayed with me through the years: *If you are a god, why are you ageing?* As though the slip of paper she'd written it on was a seed, I felt the branches of a different ideology growing steadily inside me.

My writings – my true thoughts – were like my babies; sometimes, I'd even hug them to me, paper pressed to skin. I cared more for those pieces of paper than I did for anyone in the house.

It was just a shame they didn't ever speak back. I tried to get them to, sometimes. 'Hello! Where are you? How are you?' I wrote in my diary one day. But the page stayed blank after my questions. No one messaged with anything to say.

On that evening of 21 December 2001, I removed my salwar kameez with sadness as I got ready for bed. I wished I could wear it *all* the time. It provided armour against the reality of my life: a friend made out of fabric.

Little did I know that I was about to meet perhaps the greatest friend of my entire life . . .

His name was Harry Potter.

26

If Dad hadn't wanted me to become his minister for children, I don't know that I ever would have met the boy wizard. But in January 2002, Harry Potter was taking the world by storm, with the first book in the series lighting up cinema screens. Dad decided that we should go to see it, so that I could repudiate it and advise the children of the new world to avoid it absolutely.

The trip to the cinema was my Outing for my nineteenth birthday. It was one of the happiest days of my life; we also went to McDonald's for lunch beforehand. I even got to have some birthday cake as a girl on the next table was celebrating *her* birthday and shared her cake with us! My first-ever birthday cake!

Yet the icing on the cake of the Outing was the film itself. The experience blew me away. I was able to follow the story, something I'd struggled with before, perhaps helped by the fact that, in the past year or so, I'd been permitted to watch some television with Shobha, keeping her company in her room. I wasn't allowed to watch it on my own, and was only permitted to view programmes Dad approved, but it was a mind-bending experience nonetheless – for Shobha liked nature and holiday shows.

Oh my goodness. What I saw on those programmes was mind-boggling, so far removed from anything *I* had seen that I could hardly comprehend it. Oceans! Deserts! Rainforests! *Fields*! I'd been to the park on occasion, but this was literally another world. I used to yearn to visit some of those places, and would fall asleep dreaming of flying above them, of diving into the sea and tasting the saltwater. Staring up at the screen in the cinema, Harry's world was equally magical.

Dad thought so too. He changed his tune. After we watched the movie, he declared that the books were actually about *him*. Harry – Arry – Ara – Aravindan Balakrishnan! The narrative of a seemingly ordinary boy who is actually a wizard perfectly described Dad's own role in the world: a seemingly ordinary man who was actually a powerful god and who was – little known to the 'Muggles' – the covert leader of the world.

Eagerly, I asked if I could read the books. The idea of reading a novel was exciting; there weren't many in the house because of Dad's dislike of ISA (Imagining, Speculating, Assuming). Dad had to give it serious consideration – he hated to approve anything that might make me happy, because *non*-serious life would not help to build AB's new world – and I could see the cogs turning.

I played on it. 'But they're about you, Dad! *Please* let me, I want to read all about you!'

So he acquiesced: a man who fondly chorused, 'I LOVE myself! I WORSHIP myself!' was too much in self-love to say no.

From the very first word of the very first chapter, I was spellbound. To begin with, I was comforted by the story, thinking that we in the Collective were a bit like wizards: we couldn't let the Muggles Outside know anything about our secret world, and *that* was why I had to be hidden. But as I read on – one book after the other – I felt as though a different kind of spell was being cast. The books became like a magic mirror and as I saw myself and the Collective reflected, I learned to see life in a different light.

Up until this point, I'd questioned Dad's ideas for how to run the world, but I'd never been sure I was *right* to do so – because everyone I knew agreed with them. Perhaps *I* was the one who had got things wrong; perhaps *I* was the evil one. And even though I shakily suspected his ideology was the wrong way to proceed, I didn't have an alternative: I was a bit unclear on what was *right*. But, in Harry Potter, I finally found a framework to go by; a yardstick by which I could measure Dad's behaviour and assert it came up short. My hero in all of this was Harry's headmaster, Albus Dumbledore. Kind, merciful and patient, he shaped my way of thinking and inspired many of my core values. He was the perfect beacon of 'tolerating all but intolerance' and advocated the absolute opposite of Dad's love for hate. I wanted to emulate him.

I also saw parallels in the story with what was happening in the house. Our two-tier hierarchy, for instance, which had always made me uneasy: why should Mum and Dad be waited on hand and foot while Aisha, Josie and Oh worked themselves into the ground? When I met the enslaved house-elves in book two I recognized the injustice of the situation. In addition, I saw my relationship with Dad's precious legitimate family echoed in Harry's experiences with the Dursleys: the way they belittled everything precious to him; the way I never received a single letter either. In Chanda's hateful glares I now observed what I perceived to be the beastly eyes of the basilisk.

All these insights were incredibly helpful. For years, despite everything, I couldn't keep from craving acceptance from Dad's family because there was no one else in my world. I was torn two ways: wanting to belong, yet also *not* wanting to, because belonging meant joining something that felt ugly. But after seeing these people through the prism of Harry's world I decided that, if I had to pick sides, I wanted to be part of the house-elves and not part of the 'Dursleys', no matter how many privileges they could offer.

I started to live in Harry Potter. The characters were so real to me I celebrated their birthdays. My cocoon grew new rooms to relax in: the Gryffindor common room, the Weasleys' kitchen, the Great Hall at Hogwarts for a spectacular feast! I read the books again and again; I read them aloud to Josie, Aisha and Oh. I began to embrace British culture more – to Dad's disgust – discovering a fondness for the joys of Christmas and watching people 'snogging' Outside with much more interest. I didn't think it looked 'yuck' at all, as Dad always said. Instead, I used to wish with all my might that somebody would kiss *me* like that, though I think it was really the love I saw between those kissing that appealed. No one had ever loved me in such a way. I couldn't imagine someone kissing me; another person coming so close. The only 'kisses' I'd ever had were Dad's 'big smells' on my cheek.

Engrossed in reading, I became much happier staying indoors, and nagged Dad much less about being taken Out. I think that was why, in September 2002, he permitted me to read *The Lord of the Rings*. Well, for that reason – and because, once again, the books starred him: *Ara*gorn, a future leader in exile, was clearly modelled on *Ara*vindan Balakrishnan.

Dad was right, in a way. The more I read of both Harry Potter and Tolkien's masterpiece, the more I saw Dad within the pages of the books. But it was in the portraits of the *villains* – Voldemort and Sauron – that I recognized him.

'I never forgive and I never forget': that was Dad's motto. But it was Voldemort who took that position; Voldemort who fixated on the idea of immortality, just as Dad did. Both Voldemort and Sauron insisted on total subjugation from their followers and terrorized them into obedience. And it was perhaps in reading about those followers – the Death Eaters and Black Riders – that I discovered the most chilling parallel of all. For the Black Riders *were* those soldiers Dad aspired to have: people emptied out of self, with no mind of their own except the will of Sauron. They had no relationships, no hearts: nothing inside but a desire to serve him. Had I not been trained to live a life just like that? Was that not what the comrades appeared to aspire to, with their self-criticisms and their brains and memories that needed to be scrubbed clean? I began thinking of the comrades as Black Riders, and once I started seeing them that way, I couldn't stop.

Perhaps the most fascinating element of *The Lord of the Rings* to me, though, was the idea of the power of the One Ring. This was an evil so commanding it made even the nicest people turn bad; even the hobbits in the book were affected! Did not the same thing happen in the Collective? The comrades, so nice at times as individuals, turned into slavish orcs at a word from Dad: the One Ring of Communism was powerful indeed. In Gollum, perhaps the character most affected by the Ring, I recognized shades of Josie, for Gollum had, in my mind, the same obsequious manner that she always assumed when speaking to her leader.

The books cemented my view that *something* must be affecting the Collective: they were not *all* bad. Because, while I saw my dad in the villains, it was only the bad *side* of him I thought they portrayed. The dad who took me to buy salwar kameez was not the father who beat me: I refused to amalgamate them in my mind. Dad had been brainwashed by his ideology and *that* was why he was nasty. At his heart, he was a good man – he was just misguided. He had been poisoned by Communism: affected by the One Ring. I didn't hate *him*; I hated the evil that had him in its grip.

But – I now thought – what if there was a way to loosen that grip? As I read and reread throughout 2002, I took courage. For the books told the stories of little, seemingly powerless people who nevertheless had the power to change the world. Could *I* be the one to make that change?

I started thinking: what if Dad held these horrible views simply because no one had ever challenged him? What if I showed him a different, more liberal and tolerant way to live? Could I persuade him to be a better person?

Once I had the idea, I couldn't shake it. It kept me up at night, lying awake beside Aisha in our kingsize bed while the thoughts ran round and round my head. But could I dare to do it – to share my deepest, most heartfelt convictions with Dad, to say I believed his treasured dominance and violence were wrong – when I knew it was blasphemy in this household? I was scared not only of him but of JACKIE, for JACKIE still held sway. This was not a move for the faint-hearted.

My view of JACKIE had changed a little after reading the books, however. I now thought of him as a kind of 'black magic' Dad could do; indeed, I started asking the comrades to buy Dad 'Black Magic' chocolates on my behalf for Father's Day, an 'in-joke' that only I appreciated. Somehow, the idea of Dad being able to do black magic sat much more easily with me than the idea of him having an invisible mind-control machine. I just had this nagging feeling *that* was somewhat farfetched.

To speak to Dad or not? My quandary gave me headaches. Yet I kept circling back to the cul-de-sac of the future. My only hope for freedom lay in Overt, but I shuddered to think what a hellhole the world would become if Dad was left unfettered.

But what if I *could* fetter him? What if I could work with him to limit the reach of his harm? Could I exert my influence as his adopted daughter to make a change for good, to make him kinder and more liberal? Then everything would be fine when it became Overt: the world might even be a better place.

I took a deep breath as the knowledge hit me.

I might be the only person who can save the world.

So, despite the threat to my own life and person, on 30 January 2003 I stayed up late into the night. A headache burned my brain, as though JACKIE was attempting to make me stop, but I ignored him.

Instead, I picked up my pen and began to write.

27

It was Dad himself who gave me the opportunity to share my views with him. Recently, a new entry had appeared in our regimented daily schedule: all comrades had to watch the 6 o'clock news in the evening and then listen to Dad's dissection of current events. He used to shout and curse about what was happening in the world; eventually, I nicknamed these vitriolic lectures 'Vampire Puking' – because his views poured forth like vomit.

In January 2003, the news was full of deliberation about whether or not the UK and US would go to war against Iraq. Saddam Hussein was a hero of Dad's. My father was virulently opposed to the fascist dogs attacking a regime he'd long admired. I felt conflicted about it, because I hated war, but despised even more totalitarian dictatorships. Living under one myself, I saw an instant parallel to my own situation – and I knew that I *really* wished a 'Blair' would intervene to stop my suffering. In the end, I decided that I could not instantly denounce the military action, even if I didn't like the bullish way they were going about things, because of the 'greater good' of overthrowing a tyrant.

I dared not fully articulate my opinion, but my face often betrayed my feelings during Vampire Puking.

'Are you the one in eight who supports Blair?' my father asked me on 30 January, suspicious of my silence when I didn't condemn the fascist dogs.

I didn't exactly give a reply; luckily, as he was mid-rant, he didn't exactly expect one. Yet I identified in the direct question an opportunity to tell him how I really felt. So, that night, I stayed up late writing a no-holds-barred account of my true feelings: my genuine response to his question. The following day, heart in mouth, I gave it to Dad, handing over four handwritten A4 pages that revealed my darkest secrets . . .

I have been wanting to say all this for a long time, but dare not, in case you get too angry. But I have to be honest, and tell you the truth.

After reading books like Harry Potter *and* The Lord of the Rings, *my attitudes to things have changed dramatically. I absolutely loathe these totalitarian, repressive regimes, where someone's a self-styled Overlord and everybody is forced to worship him or suffer . . . After reading these books, I just cannot bring myself to speak one nice word about such monstrous people.*

. . . In my opinion, if someone's really doing good, they are not afraid of opposing views . . . Only those who know that they're in the wrong, and are terrified that others will find out, will seek to stifle all dissent. Events, like the cruel massacre in Tiananmen Square, really make me dislike this kind of Overlordism. I just can't bring myself to support it, however much I have tried. That's why my face always falls whenever you talk about such things . . . I can't understand why you support these bad things. I hope you won't be angry with me for being so forthright, but it really beggars belief.

It was direct and unashamed. Yet never was it antagonistic; not intentionally, anyway.

I hope that this will help us to understand each other better. I have never managed to convey all this to you, though I have wanted to, many, many times. It's high time these issues are addressed, I think.

I went right back to basics. For the first time, I confessed that I had long despised the ideas behind China's Cultural Revolution, which AB wanted to emulate in the new world.

I really hate the way the government imposed the most nonsensical restrictions on people . . . These totalitarian elements, they just can't appreciate a happy, artistic lifestyle . . . They just like to spoil everything, to tear everything to pieces. And they want to replace it with . . . only blind, slavish worship to their mad theories, which aim to build a so-called paradise on earth over the shrivelled minds and tortured bodies of their ever-so-willing followers . . . I absolutely hate and detest it!

161

I think it was the bravest I had ever been in my life. I ended on a conciliatory note, reaching out the hand of fellowship to my father, only hoping that his good side would reach a hand in return.

To my amazement, Dad wasn't incandescent with rage when he reviewed it. How *relieved* I was . . . Instead, like the teacher he considered himself to be, he went through it diligently, writing his notes in the margin.

In place of rage was a mocking condescension. 'You are wrong, dodo,' he wrote, using the nickname that conveyed the archaic nature of my views. 'What do you know about it?'

In some ways, I think rage would have been better – rage would have afforded my perspective some respect, signalled that he felt threatened by my opposing opinion. Instead, his reaction communicated his disregard for my beliefs. Dad – and all the Collective – saw me as an eternal child, even though I was twenty. What I'd written was to be taken no more seriously than the scribblings of a toddler. Dad scoffed at my thoughts and feelings in this regard just as he did when I asked to be taken Out more. After all, I lived within the inner circle of the future leader of the world: wasn't that enough? Why did I always have to be hassling him for privileges such as a breath of fresh air?

I felt deflated – and concerned – when I realized my attempt to influence him had failed. Yet this was a long game: right up until it became Overt, I had opportunities to try again. But as I continued to assert my views overtly, Dad gave a stronger response.

'If you carry on like this,' he threatened, 'when I rule the world you won't be part of my government!'

As if that was a bad thing!

I wished I could get a proper job instead, or use the few skills I had mastered in the house to earn some independence. I found it hard to have confidence in anything I did because I was never praised – and I was still disciplined if I dared take pride in my own achievements – but I wasn't bad at knitting, if I had Josie's help. I started dreaming that perhaps I could sell my wares in a little shop; I had a book of knitting patterns written by a woman who did just that and thought it sounded idyllic. Yet I knew Dad would never allow it – not even when it became Overt.

My hesitant fantasies of alternative lives were making me

increasingly aware that I couldn't make things happen myself, however. I relied on Dad and the comrades for so much. If I wanted to move to the Scottish Highlands and open a knitting shop, how would I go about that? When I considered it, it was as though someone had cast a Confundus charm on me: my mind was a blank fog of nothing. No familiar landmarks even lurked within that smog for me to snag on to: I had never even once bought a ticket for a train. Where was the train station that would take me to the Highlands? How could I get there? What would I say or do when confronted by the sales clerk? How would I pay? I had no idea where to begin with such an adventure, let alone any concept of the necessary steps to take along the way.

I felt very disabled by the things I didn't know, though I tried not to think about it, preferring instead to pretend to be Preethi. With my real views now espoused to Dad, however, I began pushing the boundaries a little more. I was twenty years old. Why did I have to stay in all the time? Why couldn't I get a job?

'You have no qualifications. That means you're unable to work,' Dad explained to me once.

I could have gone to college to gain those qualifications I'd been prevented from getting as a child, but when I kept on pushing those boundaries – once even daring to suggest that perhaps I could put the rubbish out on my own – Dad finally broke some news to me that he'd been protecting me from for all these years.

'You're not capable of looking after yourself,' he told me. 'You don't have the *capacities* necessary. *That* is why we are protecting you.'

I wasn't just mad, it seemed. It was worse than I'd feared. From what they said, I now understood: it was plain I was also retarded.

28

In a sign of my stupidity, in that spring of 2003 I began to wish that an immortal man would die.

If you are a god, why are you ageing?

If you're not a god, I hope you can die.

When Dad and Mum went out in Comrade Simons' car these days, I used to wish they'd have a terrible crash and that Dad would meet his end. That sounds awful, doesn't it? It *felt* awful, especially because it was only Communism making him act the way he did. But with my appeals to him falling on deaf ears I couldn't think of any other way to get free.

The seed that Sian had planted had flowered now; my dark hope grew with it. Every day I saw signs that Dad was getting older: his shaky handwriting, his slow steps. Perhaps it wouldn't be a car crash, perhaps he'd just keel over one day from a heart attack. At last, I gained the confidence to dismiss outright in my mind the idea that Dad was a god or would live for ever. Frankly, and as heartless as it sounds, the notion that he *could* be killed was the only thing that gave me any hope a better day would come.

On those car journeys, Mum and Dad were looking for a new place to live. The council wanted to convert our house into flats – and we were soon to be evicted.

I was devastated. This house had been my home for seven years. I'd gained so many new freedoms during my time there and I was fearful of losing them in a new house. What would happen to my secret-reading? What would the view from the window be like?

As an eternal child, I was not consulted in the choice of property or invited to join Mum and Dad on their trips to view the homes the council offered. They would make the decision on my behalf – as they did with every other aspect of my life – and expected me to accept it. Without any say, all I could do was pray that the place they chose didn't make my life too hellish.

So much for prayers.

We moved to a tiny ground-floor flat on 3 June 2003; it was even smaller than the one we'd shared in Wembley. With only four people officially living there, there weren't enough bedrooms for the seven of us. Only the family were permitted them: Josie, Aisha and I slept in the large sitting room, Josie and I in a shared set of bunkbeds placed behind a pale-green curtain. (Oh slept in Shobha's room, as she was required to be on call 24/7.) How I missed my nights sleeping next to Aisha; in this flat, I used to bang my head on Josie's bunk every time I sat up.

The new flat was incredibly damp: black mould grew all over the walls. Having little opportunity to breathe any fresh air, I soon developed a hacking cough, which provided Dad with another excuse to keep me in. Once again the electrics seemed dangerous: I didn't trust Dad not to use his black magic to harm me through them, so I avoided using the appliances, just as I'd done since I was small. The dampness brought bugs too – silverfish that got *everywhere*. Dad said their presence was the fascist state attacking him and point-blank refused to do anything about them.

Worse than all this, however, was the fact that my secret-reading was no more. I tried to keep it up, sneaking into Dad's room when he went Out and reading as much as I could. But the opportunities were fewer because we all lived on top of each other.

There was no garden, just communal grounds. From time to time, I dared to throw bread from the window for the birds. The grounds were home to a green woodpecker, great and blue tits, wrens, robins and dunnocks. On occasion, even mallards, a heron and an eagle passed by! I loved watching them, vicariously enjoying the birds' freewheeling freedom as they soared across the sky. I wished I could do the same, but on the rare occasions I went Out now, I could no longer enjoy it so much, for I developed a frustrating habit of getting headaches. The noise and the colours and the *newness* of everything was too overwhelming; my temples would start to throb and I'd have to fight through the pain, determined to try to get some pleasure from the Outing, as I didn't know when the next one might be.

I told no one of my headaches, worried they'd say I shouldn't go Out at all. Apart from those few Outings, I spent all my time at home. My favourite place to sit was beside the front door; there, I could hear what was going on Outside, but also the TV in Dad and Chanda's room. When I wasn't sitting there, trying to piece together stories from the sounds, I watched the neighbours through the living-room window.

That was the single benefit this flat brought. In our previous house, my bedroom had looked out on to sparsely populated back gardens. But my view in our new flat took in the path leading to the front door of the low-rise apartment block, so I could easily observe the comings and goings of all our neighbours.

They became like characters to me, as real and with lives as excit-ing as Harry Potter and his friends. There was the lovely black family headed by a matriarch whom everyone liked; she had two children who loved loud music and flashy cars. There was the snooty lady who thought she was a cut above the rest; the friendly Muslims whose womenfolk wore the niqab; and the white family, a mum, dad and two young children who lived above us.

Perhaps because I could hear their every movement, I became par-ticularly interested in the family upstairs. I used to like listening to the rock music the man played and hearing him hammer when he did DIY. Dad was swiftly enraged by this 'attack' of noise by these 'fascist agents', but I found it entertaining – and not just because I enjoyed the different sounds, which made for a change in my never-changing life, but also because the noise irritated Dad. It almost felt as if the man, whom I called Peregrine McConaughey, was my champion and he was punishing Dad on my behalf. Whenever Dad hated someone, I took them to be my ally. And Peregrine was *everything* Dad hated – he even displayed flags of the Union Jack in his window.

The more I watched him, the more I liked him. His life became my own personal soap opera: I'd hear the dramatic sound of some-one falling over upstairs, and then the next day Peregrine's ankle appeared purple and swollen. An injury like that gave me weeks of interest: I would record in my diary each day how bad his limp was and whether the swelling had gone down. I felt an intimacy with him, worried for him when he went to the toilet more often than usual or brought up phlegm as he brushed his teeth. Monitoring Peregrine through sight and sound gave my meaningless life some meaning. It was just a shame that I could only see the neighbours through the window and never interact with them. They were all as remote from me as if I *had* been watching them on TV.

By far the hardest thing to see through the window was when Josie or the other comrades talked to them, these neighbours whom I had taken to my heart but with whom I was forbidden to communicate. To see the comrades enjoying privileges I was denied was extremely difficult. But Dad insisted I had to stay in the shadows.

With the flat so small, and we comrades so many, life quickly became very nasty indeed. In the Brixton house, there had been enough rooms that we could spend our time largely separated, which made for a much more harmonious atmosphere, as it was only when the group came together that the nastiness ensued.

As the months passed in this new 'home', I grew more and more depressed. I longed for the freedoms of our old house and felt the sting of the comrades' betrayal whenever they curbed my liberties at Dad or Mum's request. Josie had told me that whenever she was nice to me it was only because she was 'working at the level I was at', rather than because she liked or respected me; I couldn't bear to look in her eyes after that. I avoided eye contact with everyone, because every time I looked in their eyes I seemed to see only hate. The pain of each betrayal – when I was reported for talking nicely of the neighbours, for example – was palpable, like a beast clawing at the inside of my stomach, fighting to get out.

Nonetheless, despite the pain and isolation, I refused to stop speaking my own truth. On a daily basis, I saw evidence of my father's prejudice: for example, just because people played loud music, he declared them to be the devil incarnate and threatened that all manner of torture would befall them when it became Overt. He soon began vendettas against my new friends – and I nobly refused to take any part in it. Instead, for the first time, I actually dared to defend them. I saw doing so as my duty: part of my campaign to try to influence Dad to become a better man. Forget minister for children – I was going to be the champion of the disadvantaged!

I was accused of being an apologist, belittled and mocked, but I reso-
lutely didn't care. If being just and fair meant being an apologist, I
was *proud* to be one.

Yet it was hard, being the only bastion of good in a world of evil,
and I was not a courageous person. Weak-kneed and faint-hearted,
I was still too easily influenced by a kind word from my father or a
fellow comrade. I felt as if I was a yo-yo. I was trying to break away
from them, but the moment they were pleasant I was reeled back,
desperate for any affection. I only wished I had someone who was
like me, open-minded and open-hearted, to whom I could speak
about these things, but the only real friend I had was the paper on to
which I poured out my heart . . .

> *I should be proud of what I am and not let my happiness hinge on*
> *whether a stupid Commie agrees with me or not. It's hard, but the cor-*
> *rect things are often hard, and that's what I must do . . . I should in fact*
> *court their disapproval! Because I am way ahead of them . . . Though*
> *I have been drowned in the Morgulduin of Communism since birth, I*
> *have had the courage and the ability to throw it away and totally purge*
> *myself of it . . . I should be happy that I'm far ahead, even though I*
> *have known little else – you can say I was born with the Ring of Sauron*
> *on my finger! Yet I've thrown it away! And if that's not something to*
> *be proud of, I don't know what is.*
>
> *They may scoff at me. So what! Did Gandalf . . . and Dumbledore*
> *back down when [people] scoffed at them? No, they did not! So I am*
> *going to be proud of what I am, and I'm going to follow in the footsteps*
> *of my trailblazers!*

Christmas 2003 approached. Sat at my window, I watched as the
neighbours went about their preparations, bringing back bags laden
with shopping and fir trees ready for decorating. Our upstairs neighbour Peregrine was a social sort and, to my delight, he often went out
at night. Even better, though, was when he stayed in, as he sometimes played music until 2 a.m. I called his exploits 'Oin', my own
made-up word for 'entertainment'. Peregrine gave me so much Oin
during the winter of 2003 that I fell head over heels in love.

That was why, on 23 December, after months of Dad denigrating
'that man upstairs', I finally reached the end of my tether.

Peregrine was drilling that evening. It was two days before Christmas and it was clear that he was just getting ready for his family celebration, but Dad saw it differently.

'Listen!' he ranted to me and the comrades, his finger pointing above his head and shaking with his rage. 'That man upstairs is deliberately harassing me on the orders of the fascist state!'

'Dad—' I began, wanting to defend my friend.

He turned on me. 'This is your fault, Comrade Prem! Your softness is letting the enemy attack the Collective!'

As Peregrine's younger son laughed loudly upstairs, Dad's eyes narrowed further. 'I should kidnap that child and kill him,' he said.

The boy was five. But no agent of the fascist state would escape my father's wrath.

'Dad—' I tried again, but he interrupted me. He cast his eyes around the group, making sure every woman was hanging on his every word. For months now I'd been defending the neighbours, yet also happily chattering away about my 'soap opera' to the comrades (when they were in a good mood). It was the only Oin I could generate for myself, to discuss these people whose lives were now a part of my cocoon. But Dad would not countenance any such fun.

'When Comrade Prem talks of the antics upstairs,' my father now said brusquely, 'you are not to entertain her insubordination. If you ever hear her say one word more about this family, you must report straight to me.'

His words acted as a prison door, clanging shut to keep me even deeper in his dungeon. It felt as if all the little freedoms I had managed to secure since Sian had died were being taken away. The way it worked in the Collective was that if Dad *specifically* outlawed something, the Black Riders would never cross him. But if he hadn't precisely laid down the law, I had a bit of wiggle room to, for example, have a conversation with Aisha about how Peregrine's leg was healing. Such details were my only source of amusement or social contact. To have that taken away was more than I could bear.

I said nothing more in Discussions, biting down on my tongue, but that evening I nursed the hurt, picking over my feelings as if I was picking at a bloody scab. I felt violated. I knew the comrades would implement Dad's decree with gusto: there was to be no relief and no escape for me.

I couldn't live like this, not any more, where I was at the mercy of others and had no autonomy at all. I sat on my bunkbed, a note-pad on my lap, shaking with rage and crying at the injustice of it all.

Then I started to write. I was a proud, independent lady and I decided I *had* to stand up for myself.

At that time, Dad was in the habit of asking me what I wanted for my birthday. He wouldn't often grant the wish *exactly* as I described it – when I'd asked, for my twentieth, to have a cake served in a res-taurant, like the girl we'd seen in McDonald's, he'd said I could only have it at home or not at all – but at least there was an opportunity to state my wishes. In the New Year, my twenty-first birthday was coming up . . .

So I decided, that December night, to ask for what had been in my heart for many years now.

For my twenty-first birthday, I would like to leave the Collective.

29

I don't know if I would *actually* have had the courage to give the note to him, but in the end the decision was taken out of my hands. Josie, in the form of Gollum, as I liked to think of her, crept behind the pale-green curtain while I was lost in scribbling down my thoughts. Always watchful, she snooped over my shoulder and spied what I'd written. The next morning, a whisper entered into the ear of our great leader, and I was summoned to his room to explain myself.

I was scared as I walked in, but he was not as angry as I'd expected. In fact, he seemed chastened, as if he had an inkling that he had overstepped the mark and lost me. I had asked many times to be allowed more trips Outside and more freedom – to use the telephone, to answer the door – but he had never seemed worried before that his refusals might lead to a request to leave altogether. He still saw my resistance as part of my infantile disorder, and he believed when he dismissed those requests that I had learned from him. He was so sure of the power of his own voice: he thought all he had to do was tell me not to be so silly as to want more freedom and my desire for it would go away – much as, in *The Lord of the Rings*, the persuasive voice of Saruman made men fall into line. But while his voice seemed to have that power over the others, it did not work with me.

He was actually reasonable as we discussed what I'd written, however. Immediately, I felt pangs of guilt. Would Dad be hurt I wanted to leave? My tender heart could not bear the thought of having caused pain. The promise I'd made to myself as a child never to let anyone else feel alone was more important to me than ever. Was I breaking it in telling Dad I wanted to go?

But now that the thought of freedom had been planted, and Dad even seemed willing to discuss it, it was too good a prospect to let go.

As I faced my father in his room, having a one-to-one conversation for once, it felt as if, if I played it right, freedom was within grasp.

'I feel your treatment of me is callous,' I ventured.

'Why?' he asked. 'What is it you don't like?'

'I feel overshadowed all the time,' I explained. I took a deep breath. 'I want to go because I can't continue to live like this, when my life, health and happiness are all subject to someone else's whims and fancies.'

'But you must be patient, Comrade Prem,' he said – no anger in his tone, just logic. 'Wait until it becomes Overt. Then you will have all the freedom you want.'

But I want freedom now . . .

I continued to write more letters to him, and to talk to him, throughout that day, telling him honestly and frankly how unhappy I was. At one point he said he still loved and respected me in spite of all this, and at that point I felt seriously guilty, for he had never spoken to me like that before. He even agreed that he would tell the others to let me talk about the goings-on upstairs: a measure both of how shocked he was by my rebellion and of the scale of it.

Then a miracle happened.

'OK,' he agreed. 'I'll arrange for you to have your own place. Maybe we could go to the cinema on your birthday and I can just leave you there.'

There was a threat behind his words – just as there had been when he'd told me, as a child, that if I wanted to play on that bright-red slide next door I *could*, I'd just never be able to come back home. It was still a scary idea as I had no clue what to do Outside without him but, despite what Dad thought, I was no longer a child. I thought to myself: *You may not know now, but you will learn!*

I was so thrilled we had reached an understanding. I started imagining all the wonderful things I would be able to do once I got free. I could go to the cinema whenever I liked; I could go *Out* whenever I liked. I could sleep in my own room and go to the toilet without an escort. I could go shopping for my own clothes! (The salwar kameez was a one-off; I was still not permitted to join the comrades when they shopped.)

'GOING AWAY is on!' I wrote exultantly in my diary that

Christmas Eve. 'I've gone away in my heart a long, long time ago, and now the real, practical part is coming!'

I could almost taste the freedom, the damp air of the flat seeming to lose a little of its mouldiness as though a fresh wind was blowing through. And how wonderful, too, that it was my *negotiation* that had brought us to this point! I had hoped that Dad was finally learning from me, that he was appreciating compromise and tolerance could have a place in his new world. Even though I was leaving, I *had* made my mark for when it became Overt. I felt very proud of that.

When I woke on Christmas Day, I felt as if I was waking into my own new world. I washed and dressed with a new purpose, imagining the time when I would do all this every day in my own place. It was almost inconceivable, the idea of having such freedom.

'Comrade Prem, a word,' Dad said that morning.

My heart began to beat faster. *What is this?*

The One Ring had taken him. The good man of yesterday was gone.

'If you leave, I will immediately move house so that you cannot contact me or the Collective ever again. You must agree to wait until it is Overt, right this moment, or the old world will begin to blow up.' He fixed me with his dark eyes, glowing behind his glasses. 'The choice is yours.'

Choice? What choice? There *was* no choice. At his words, I became terrified. JACKIE had the power to bring even *America* to her knees – what chance did I stand against him? I pictured earthquakes tearing up the land; buildings blowing up with people still inside them. Dad would stop at nothing to hurt whoever went against him. He had said it proudly many times and I believed him utterly. My request to leave the group was the first time I had ever dared challenge Dad on such a massive scale; I had no doubt he would wreak his revenge in an equally big way.

What can I do? I had no support or guidance from anyone. Even beyond my fear of JACKIE, there was lots of harm Dad could do. He'd threatened, two days before, to kidnap and kill the boy upstairs; having been beaten by him since I was a baby, I well believed him capable. There was no one Outside I could turn to – beyond my not knowing anyone, Dad always jeered, 'The police cannot get me, I *am* the police!'

I believed that too. Hadn't he run circles around the authorities when Sian had died? Hadn't he fooled the housing officials into never knowing he lived in their properties? I knew he could talk his way out of anything.

What else might he do? Take his revenge on those closest to me? Report Aisha to the immigration authorities, as he often threatens, to get back at me? What about his threat to kill me and bury me in the garden? He could do it, I know he could. No one knows I exist . . .

In the end, I concluded not one of these possibilities was worth the risk. I couldn't condemn others to death simply to pursue my own selfish desires.

He was still waiting for an answer.

'OK,' I said eventually, not meeting his eyes, each word bitter to the taste. 'I agree to wait for the Overt.'

I didn't give up on my dream of freedom. Every day I prayed to be free of the cultist maniac I felt my father had become. Repeatedly, I openly voiced my rejection of him and his ideas, but his conceit was so great he couldn't get it into his thick head that I was sick and tired of him. He flattered himself that I was interested in him and kept talking in the most maddening way about our future together, when I had told him in no uncertain terms I wanted nothing to do with it. I had no problem with him and the comrades believing what *they* wanted to believe, but I detested the fact Dad forced me to stay when I didn't share their views. In his mind, though, he was keeping me caged for better things.

Increasingly, I did feel caged. I kept thinking about the animals I'd seen at London Zoo. On a second trip there in 2002, I'd finally got to see the aviary, with its owls and weaver birds, imperial pigeons and lorikeets. I'd felt an affinity for them then, but with Dad having now slammed shut the door that had been edging open, I felt the connection even more.

'I feel like *I'm* a caged bird,' I said to Josie one day.

She turned her ever-staring blue eyes on me and I quickly looked away. She often looked at me as if she thought I was mad. Josie simply couldn't fathom how anyone could *not* worship Dad and his cult (as I now thought of the Black Riders) – especially someone who, like me, had 'benefited' from his leadership since birth.

Despite Dad lifting his ban on me talking about Peregrine, Josie kept harassing me about it, as though wanting to prove her loyalty.

She told Dad what I'd said.

'Caged birds live longer,' Dad told me when we discussed it, as though that made everything all right.

But what surely matters is not the quantity of life, but the quality, I thought. *What's the use of living a thousand years in a pit of hell?*

I tried to find my happiness where I could. With the Black Riders on full alert to report me, my only salvation came in the form of Peregrine McConaughey. To my delight, he seemed to signal that he reciprocated my affection. When I coughed at night, he would wake and go to the loo; if I bounced a ball disconsolately indoors, he would bang on the floor to show he'd heard me; once, we were both in the toilet at the same time and flushed together! Our mating dance was carried out by means of this aural call-and-respond: I listened eagerly for his Footstepping above me, for his Cooing as he sang along with his music, for the *tick tick tick* of his spoon against his plate. I concentrated so much on the sounds upstairs that it almost became as if I was no longer living with the Collective after all – my body was there, but my heart and mind were up above.

I called him Master – partly inspired by Sam in *The Lord of the Rings*, as that was what he called his friend Frodo, but also perhaps because the only love I'd ever witnessed was the subjugated devotion shown to my father by his followers. Like them, I refused to hear a word said against my beloved Peregrine. I began making lists of all the beautiful events in my life where I'd witnessed Peregrine doing something, just as I had once copied out AB's Synchronizations. I wrote songs about his blue hood and his red jacket; recorded the registration plates of his visitors' cars; noted down if he was walking or cycling when he went Out, and how he wore his hair.

He had wonderful hair. With thick, dark curls covering his whole scalp and falling beautifully over his forehead, he reminded me of Frodo.

'O! You can't believe how All-Sexed-Up I felt when I watched young Peregrine putting his hand through his thick hair – it looked so sexy, so gentle, so natural, sooo appealing! I love him! I worship him!' I wrote enthusiastically in my diary. 'I saw him moving the fingers of his left hand, touching his side a bit,' I recorded another day.

I was fascinated by his hands. Apart from Dad's creepy cuddles, I was still rarely touched by anyone else, so the way Peregrine touched himself filled me with envious curiosity. How might it feel for him to touch *my* side or *my* hair like that? My whole being yearned for that human connection: for a touch that would make me more than shadow. Peregrine was my sunshine, the perennial fragrant blossom in my heart. I worshipped the ground he walked on.

I had an inkling, I think, that my love for him was a form of protection. 'He fills the void in me,' I wrote. 'There is clearly something vital for me in him.' In Peregrine, I found somewhere to hide from the villainy of my father. It was because Peregrine was not imposed on me, but *chosen* by me – me, who never had any choice in life. In loving him, I didn't feel crushed and stifled, manipulated and coerced, as I always did with Dad. I felt myself for once – I felt like Preethi, or Bryony as I'd begun to call myself – and not a pawn in someone else's hands. To love him was a declaration of independence; he became a symbol of my refusal to be put down.

I felt his protection in other ways too. My deep love became a talisman I carried around. It strengthened my resolve not to be sucked into my father's cult, even though to shun the comrades and their beliefs forced me to be alone. Loving Peregrine made me *immune* to the evil propagated by my father, because the spectres of darkness surrounding me could not endure such emotions of the light as love and kindness. Those emotions humanized me and stopped me from becoming a Black Rider. As in *Harry Potter*, I discovered that love truly was the best antidote to black magic.

I think some small part of me did recognize that my intense connection to him was a kind of madness. Ironically, however, it was also the only thing that helped to keep me sane.

I watched and listened for him every day – and night. After Josie had climbed on to her bunk to go to sleep, I used to slide out of bed to stare out of the window into the wee small hours, hoping I'd catch of glimpse of Peregrine coming home. I tried to keep myself hidden but sometimes, as though he felt my eyes on him, he would glance in my direction. Then I'd beam shyly at him, inwardly cursing my appearance, but hoping he could see through my ugliness to my true, good heart. Once or twice, he even said hello to me! I hankered after any affection, so deprived of it that the smallest drop made all the difference; it was all the medicine I needed to make me well.

If only Dad allowed medicine in the Collective . . . For a while now, I'd been worried about Comrade Oh. Though only small, she did a lot of heavy-lifting, helping Shobha from her wheelchair to her bath and back again, as well as carrying the shopping home. She'd been complaining of pain in her neck for years, and now started saying that if she ever looked down she felt very strange. She vomited; developed a cold. She said she just didn't feel right.

'Don't talk nonsense! You don't need to see a doctor, just talk to Comrade Bala,' some of the other comrades enthused.

She did.

'Focus on me,' he advised.

On 11 May 2004, Oh and Josie were working in the kitchen. Their relationship was still as acrimonious as it had always been; I had tried for a while to step in as a peacemaker, but their rows could be intense: a complete personality clash. On this day, I was sitting, writing, on my bunkbed in the living room when I heard Oh shouting angrily: 'It just shows what you are!'

I ignored it; she and Josie were always sparring. I heard nothing more for about twenty minutes, when I heard Oh shout again, in a very weird voice: 'Call the doctor!'

I could hear muffled, raised voices coming from the hallway. It sounded as if everyone was getting involved, the vultures on the attack, so I stayed where I was.

'Nobody bangs their head and then refuses to speak!' I heard Mum say. I thought she and Dad were just having a 'good struggle' with Oh; that wasn't unusual.

What *was* unusual was that I couldn't hear Oh: she was the one who sometimes spoke back. But there was nothing but silence from her as Dad and Mum ranted and raved.

I would have stayed out of it entirely if Aisha hadn't come to get me. 'Look what's happening,' she said.

I assumed she meant Oh was being disobedient: having been summoned, I would be forced to bear witness. Reluctantly, I got to my feet and edged into the hallway.

I was completely unprepared for the sight that greeted me.

Comrade Oh lay on the floor like a dead thing.

30

No one called an ambulance. Mum and Dad just stood over her, shouting.

'Come on, let's move her!' Dad said when he saw me.

Like puppets on strings, myself among them this time, at his command we all picked Oh up and moved her from where she lay in the open-doored bathroom to the hallway. Her body was rigid, her eyes closed. My arms strained as I grasped her shoulders; though Oh was small, she proved heavy. I couldn't understand what had happened. I felt numb.

As I gently lowered her to the floor, my face came close to hers and I realized she was barely breathing.

'She's not—' I began.

'Shut up!'

I couldn't even raise the notion of her being unwell – because everything could be cured, so long as we followed Dad.

For about an hour, Oh lay unattended to on the hallway floor. Dad and Mum were muttering above her prone body in a disgruntled fashion about her 'tantrum'. They seemed to think her inability to speak was a refusal: it was Oh being Oh. I surreptitiously stroked her hair, but she did not respond even to that kindness.

In bits and pieces, the story of what had happened emerged. Josie had unwittingly left a cupboard door open in the kitchen while she cleared cups from the draining board; Oh had been crouched down beneath that same cupboard, unaware of what Josie had done. When Oh stood up, she cracked her head, hard, on the open door. Twenty minutes later, Oh had started vomiting and suddenly shouted, 'Call the doctor!'

But AB would not let us. Only after about an hour, an hour of Oh lying silent and still, did Dad say we could phone for an ambulance.

I was ordered to wait in the living room when the paramedics came. Dad went with her to the hospital. She was alive – but only just. They hooked her up to life-support machines; still, she didn't regain consciousness.

It was that same evening, after Dad had returned from the hospital, that there came a knock upon the door: the police. They ran blue-and-white crime-scene tape around the kitchen and summoned us together.

'We want to interview everybody,' they announced. 'We're going to take names. What's yours, miss?'

I started at the unfamiliar sensation of a stranger speaking to *me*.

'Prem Maopinduzi,' I said. I felt my heart, itself a caged bird, fluttering within my chest. I wanted so badly to tell the police what was going on; about how Dad hadn't called the ambulance for ages. *I hope they interview me on my own: I can't speak out in front of him.*

But Dad cleared his throat as the policeman scribbled down my name in his notebook. 'Prem was not in the house when Oh banged her head. She was out with me,' he said.

The puppets all nodded their heads. 'Yes, she was out. Bala and Prem know nothing about what happened.' The Collective never used the 'Comrade' prefix when talking to Outsiders.

Anger filled me at being silenced – but I could do nothing, not in the face of the group. If I spoke up (which I didn't really know *how* to do; I'd *never* had a conversation with anyone Outside), then I knew Dad would be able to outtalk me. How easy it would be for him to say I was autistic or mad and for the police to dismiss me . . . If I even tried, I knew JACKIE and Dad's revenge would be terrible. I stayed silent and listened to their lies.

The police took more details of the accident. Josie had to go to the station to make a statement. Afterwards, the police came back and removed the crime-scene tape, their inquiries over.

Unlike with Sian, I wasn't permitted to visit Oh in hospital. Perhaps Dad thought, after all my recent requests for freedom, it was a risk he couldn't take. The other comrades went to see her but I stayed home.

Midway through the evening after Oh's accident, on 12 May, the phone rang while I was having a shower. I heard Josie answer it but couldn't hear what was said. Nonetheless, a feeling of trepidation gripped me. I took my time scrubbing myself clean and rubbing myself dry, as if this could cancel out any bad news beyond the bathroom door.

When I came out, into the living room, everyone was sat round on the mismatched chairs. There was a peculiar atmosphere.

'Comrade Prem,' Dad announced. 'The fascist state has murdered Comrade Oh.'

The hospital had turned off the life-support machine, saying there was nothing more they could do. Oh's autopsy would show she died of a cerebral artery atheroma – essentially, a stroke.

Poor Oh, I thought, strangely numb. Having never been allowed to have feelings for the comrades, I didn't know quite how to respond. I wasn't encouraged to grieve. This time the comrades organized the funeral, deliberately preventing Oh's family from receiving her ashes, even though they requested them. I was not permitted to attend. Yet I knew I would miss her – miss the intermittent treat of her warm hugs and especially the way she dared defy Dad on occasion.

As though reading my mind, Dad soon started cursing Oh for 'killing herself' by 'refusing to focus on him properly'. As Sian had been before her, Oh now became an example to us all of what might happen if we didn't submit fully to his authority. Dad had it both ways: it was the fascist state *and* Oh herself who was to blame. He even berated Josie, because she left the cupboard door open; taunted her cruelly, falsely saying that she had murdered Oh, which soon became another stick with which to beat her in Discussions.

But of his own role in her demise, he said nothing.

There was a terrible bittersweetness about Oh's death. We had been too many in our tiny flat: when she passed away we all had more space. Aisha moved into Shobha's room, though it was Josie who took over Oh's duties. I'd have much preferred Aisha to stay with me and for Josie to go, but as usual I had no say. The other, huge change was that I was finally permitted, at the age of twenty-one, to join the comrades when they went to the shops.

This change in routine was not a request, nor an invitation, but an order: I was required to pull my weight to help with the running of the Collective. Dad needed me to step up to take Oh's place. Frankly, I didn't care why he'd removed the rule, I was just delighted to be allowed to go.

Though I was now permitted to shop, the rule remained in place that I could not leave the house without Dad. On a weekly basis, I would now accompany him and another comrade to the local shops; once a month, we went to the big Tesco nearby.

As it happened, the May Tesco trip was scheduled just days after Oh's accident, so on 13 May 2004 I found myself in Comrade Simons' car en route to the supermarket.

What an extraordinary experience. As we entered the cavernous store – far larger than the tiny corner shops I'd previously been in – I found myself feeling glad for once, instead of resentful, for the way the comrades surrounded me. It was so BIG! I was fearful I'd get lost; I stayed close to Josie. Aisle after aisle stretched before me. My gaze darted this way and that, reading the huge signs hung over the aisles, the brand names that banshee-wailed from every box. Brightly coloured price tags shouted about 'discounts' that I could not comprehend, while end-of-aisle 'special offers' grabbed violently for my attention.

But most of all my eyes were out on stalks at the shelves and shelves and *shelves* of goods – never had I seen anything like it. There were *so* many products! Dad didn't like to try new things, so the shopping I saw at home always comprised the same foodstuffs. Here, there was a multiplicity of choice. Strangely shaped vegetables, exotic coloured fruits, surprising ready-made sandwiches and whole aisles dedicated to the beauty lotions I would have loved to try for myself. I blinked fast, unable to take it all in, one of my Outside headaches coming swiftly on.

Though I was ostensibly there to help, I don't know how much assistance I provided. I trailed around after Josie, as she consulted her shopping list and efficiently deposited the items in the trolley. When she was finished, we walked to the checkout and I methodically helped deposit items on the conveyor belt, following her lead. It was Josie or Dad who took care of the bill, handing over notes and coins that were foreign to me. I was as clueless about money as I had been when we'd lived in Streatham fourteen years before. What did all the different coins *mean*? To me, they were just scraps of metal. And what were the paper notes?

Dad could be a different man when we went Out – another pleasant thing about shopping. It almost seemed that in leaving the flat, which could be a vortex of evil, the good side of him came out, like a mole emerging from his tunnel, nose sniffing cautiously at the air. Sometimes, he would even say agreeable things about the people we met, as if he forgot to be nasty.

I would have liked to join him and Josie in exchanging a few words with the shopkeepers, but I was encouraged not to speak. If I attempted it, the words were like loose pebbles in my mouth, so that I stumbled over them. I didn't know *how* to strike up *any* kind of connection with someone who was not a comrade. Always, Josie or Dad would step in and take over so I didn't get a chance to talk.

It left me feeling more convinced I must be retarded, as Dad now often said; since my request to leave on 23 December, he'd repeatedly reminded me of my low IQ, to warn me that, even if he granted my request, I would undoubtedly sink Outside, not swim. And in a way these shopping trips served to convince me I *was* ill-suited to a life Outside. Though my existence *felt* like a cage, *was* my seclusion for my own good?

After Oh died, though, he got nastier and nastier. The biggest flashpoint was my flagrant affection for Peregrine: Dad simply couldn't bear it.

'*Why* do you have to have crushes?' he would roar. 'Look at Comrade Josie, look at Comrade Aisha – they are *devoted* to me. They don't want to marry another man!'

But they are not your daughter! I used to think, too scared of his violence to speak out. I'd grown up with him as a father – it wasn't fair to expect me to be like the other women, nor to feel the way they did. On the contrary, Peregrine was everything to me – all I had to live for – and I refused to give him up.

In the face of my continued defiance, Dad took revenge in his own special, wounding way.

That summer, my Oin from Peregrine abruptly ended. He stopped playing music late at night; nobody came to visit him in their car; he didn't go out in the evening either. In early August, his Cooing ceased and his temper calmed (previously, I could hear him scolding his kids, but now the sweet sound of his angry voice had vanished). It was rare, now, for him even to walk past my window; days would go by without my seeing him. It felt as if the Golden Old Days were over – and I knew exactly who was to blame.

'It's my dad's evil Black Magic against him!' I wrote angrily.

'Father can't take the fact that I have dared to fight the iron manacles he has tried to chain me up with! And he takes it out on my master, to whom I have proudly and constantly defied him.'

With Oin devastatingly beyond my reach, I started to embark on my own small acts of rebellion. I managed to persuade Josie to buy me some fishnet tights, which I'd seen Peregrine's partner wear and thought looked nice. Just having them made me feel less caged; another feather for my mental nest. I only wore them under long skirts and trousers, so Dad did not know. It felt like a big victory.

As did the day, in autumn 2004, when I managed to buy an alcoholic drink; though Dad had told stories over the years of how he used to get drunk in his youth in Singapore, as with everything else he'd ever enjoyed, this experience was to be denied to me. Dad had waited outside the shop one day while Aisha and I went in, so I secretly picked out a cold shandy from the drinks cabinet rather than a Coke; I don't think Aisha even looked at it so I managed to get her to buy it, sneaking it out of the shopping bag as soon as we got home.

That afternoon, once Dad was busy entertaining Comrade Simons in the living room, I sat in my favourite spot in the hallway and drank it all down. It gave me such a thrill! It was not the best drink I'd ever tasted, nor was its alcohol content high, but it was nice, and the very best bit was that I was doing something Dad would not approve! It made me very happy indeed: later that afternoon, when I went back into my cocoon, Bryony felt just a little bit more normal, more like other young people, because I'd finally had a drink.

In December, I grew bolder and sneaked a Christmas cake into the trolley. It wasn't quite as controversial as it sounds; the year before, I'd managed to put up a few decorations in December without Dad taking me to task, so I hoped the idea of having cake at Christmas was not something that would be outright banned.

Dad didn't say anything as the Tesco checkout lady scanned the item, so the next day, when he asked when we would have it, I cheerily suggested, 'Christmas Day!'

His face darkened. It was one of those awful moments that often happened in the cult: Dad had changed the rules.

'Why do you want to celebrate Christmas? Celebrating Christmas is celebrating the fact you're *British*!' He spat the last word as if it was profane. 'Those imperialists are always trying to put down Indians, and you want to celebrate their customs?' He continued, spit flying from his toothless mouth, 'One day you will get down on your knees and apologize to me.'

I looked at him, this man who always denigrated me yet expected worship in return.

'No, I won't,' I replied. To my surprise, though I was shaking, my voice was resolute.

'Yes, you will!' he roared, outraged.

'No. I. Won't.'

His hand powered across my cheek. Yet even through the stinging pain, I also felt *pride*. It felt good to say no to him.

'You'll pay for your disobedience,' he hissed.

I didn't have long to wait. Exactly one year and three days after I'd asked to leave the Collective, on 26 December 2004, JACKIE caused a major earthquake off the west coast of Sumatra, 'in revenge for my disloyalty'. The third largest earthquake in recorded history, it generated a huge tsunami that swept unstoppably across the Indian Ocean, arriving at the shoreline with waves 100 feet high.

By the time the waters receded, more than 250,000 people had been killed.

My first feeling was horror – horror that my suspicion Dad was evil was undeniably true. He seemed now, to me, a lunatic – a psychopath. He was using his power to murder hundreds of thousands of innocent people. Dad always talked of JACKIE as a force for good, but here was evidence he only ever used his power for evil.

I felt a strange rumbling in my mind too, as though the aftershocks of the earthquake were reverberating through me. I glimpsed something – a nascent idea – which bobbed up and down like it was drowning, but I was unable to grasp it and pull it clear from the weeds of my upbringing. It was just a hint – but I apprehended, somehow, that Dad was using this as a form of control.

Is that all it is? Does he really have that power?

Is he really who he says he is?

The questions had been building for a while, in the same way the pressure had been building beneath the earth. *The Overt that never came; the things that didn't tally . . .* I felt the first whispers of doubt and disbelief, but they were so quiet I could barely hear the words.

Nor did I listen; I didn't want to. For if I doubted Dad and JACKIE, I doubted *everything* – including the fact his leadership would one day be Overt.

But I *had* to believe in Overt because I wanted to get free. It had to be real – otherwise, what was I waiting for? Where was my hope for freedom?

Though the deadline was indistinct, to know that one day Overt would come, that I would finally get to step out of the shadows, was as important to me as my cocoon, as essential to my survival and my sanity.

So I didn't listen to that nagging doubt. I had to have hope. I had to have trust. I had to have faith in my father.

31

On 1 January 2005, I turned to the first page of my brand-new diary and wrote:

The day I escape from the prison my father created will be the day my life really begins.

On 7 January, I turned twenty-two. We went to a café and I boldly ordered a shandy. *I am a grown-up; I should be allowed to do this.*

But as soon as Dad saw it he said: 'You can't have that.'

'Just a little bit . . .' I wheedled, disgusted I had to beg.

'No!'

Aisha signalled the staff and they took it away. I felt mortified, my cheeks burning. *I am twenty-two, not ten.*

The humiliation acted as a catalyst, making me long to break away from his restrictions even more – even if I couldn't yet fathom how.

Come mid-January, the view from my window was populated by workmen: scaffolding went up against the building to allow them to repair the roof. I spent hours watching them, the activity a welcome change from the tedium of my days.

One of them noticed me. While I was standing at the window one day, he came up to me and asked politely if I could refill his water bottle for him. My delight at him speaking to *me* was swiftly curtailed as I realized with a sinking heart that the cult members were all in the flat. I knew there was no way I could have carried out his request without being noticed, and they certainly would not have approved of such an act of kindness: I'd have been denigrated instead for my 'softness' towards these 'fascist agents'.

So I shook my head, unable to speak, having no words to explain my predicament, and dropped the net curtain to conceal myself from view.

The incident made me *extremely* upset. I was tormented by what I'd done for weeks afterwards. I hated to be rude to people; in my mind that made me as bad as the Collective.

A peculiar thing happened in the wake of these experiences, though. My despair was turning into an unbelievable rage. I couldn't talk about it, of course, but I would shake with wrath at the way the Collective behaved and the way they were treating me. I started to snap at them, to push past them roughly. My behaviour reminded me of the way Cindy had behaved before she'd left the Collective; I felt a sudden swell of sympathy for her, feeling guilty now for ever thinking her unpleasant, for I saw it wasn't her fault. When you're stuck in a place where people are nasty to you *all* the time, it's very hard not to become nasty yourself. Actually, *that* was what I was *most* angry about: the only thing I hated was hate, yet the Collective made me hate them when I only wanted to love.

After Mum and Dad, Josie was the primary target of my ire. She seemed to see my falling in love with Peregrine, a white man, as a personal affront. It was as if she feared Dad would somehow blame *her* for it – much as he'd once blamed Sian for my misdemeanours – so she went out of her way to report and to attack both me and Peregrine verbally. Despite me begging her not to, Josie continually harassed me, brooking no arguments and trampling over my feelings. She'd even bully Aisha to be stricter with me, and compiled a log of Peregrine's previous 'anti-social noise', perhaps to give one day to the police or housing association to get him evicted.

For months now, I'd been perplexed by an enigmatic change to Peregrine's daily routine; finally, I realized he must have got a job and was going to work when he left each morning. Though the loud music and late nights had stopped, at times I could still hear Master burping or coughing above me: these were treats as precious as gems.

He remained the only light of my life. Which is why what happened that spring was so very, very dark for me. One evening, Peregrine went out at 10.15 p.m. Naturally, I waited up to see my master return, standing for more than an hour by the window in my pyjamas, staring out fanatically, not wanting to miss the chance to see my beloved.

Would tonight be the night he might recognize my love and sweep me off my feet – and away from my father?

I stood like a spectre by the window. Peregrine staggered a little as he walked up the path; I think he was tipsy. He glanced in my direction and saw me there – saw me where I always was when he arrived home or left for the day, watching his every move. I tried to hide, but it was too late.

'What are you fucking looking at?' he shouted angrily, then stormed into the house.

Those six words smashed me to pieces. A fraction of them were humbly grateful he had *noticed* me; most wanted to die.

I called the incident Black Midnight. And though I castigated myself for my actions, I saw clearly, too, that this disaster had come about only because my father kept me in my cage and never allowed me to interact with other people.

As though my father had cast another spell, shortly after Black Midnight Peregrine cut off the luscious locks I loved so much. His hair was not as thick as when he'd worn it long; without his curls, too, his receding hairline became more apparent. *He's getting older,* I realized. *If I stay in my cage much longer, Peregrine will go bald and I will never get to be with the young and handsome Master. You are fading, Master, and I'm fading with you* . . .

It was another catalyst, a cog in a wheel that was driving me relentlessly forwards.

WHY am I trapped in this HELLHOLE? All my problems are directly due to my dad's folly. All of them. I'm SICK, SICK, SICK of him. WHEN will I be free? . . . Father knows how I feel, yet he conveniently, accidentally-on-purpose forgets and torments me endlessly. He never gives me even a shoulder to cry on – my pen and paper are my only friends, the only ones I can pour out to . . . I must realize, once and for all, something I hate to admit – the fact is that as long as my horrid father is alive, I will NEVER be really happy. He'll never set me free, never. Talk of 'giving space' is only a ploy to pacify me. I'll die a prisoner, as I have lived.

I have no courage to take a step to freedom – at least this is the 'devil I know'. If I try to escape, I'm sure my dad will use his Black Magic to ensure my life is total hell . . . What am I to do? I'm dying, I'm wilting here, to death, death, a miserable death! . . . I have no one to turn to as I languish and flounder every day in my utter distress . . . And

it's all your fault, father, you CRIMINAL! . . . I need help, I need
change . . . I'm dying, and no one ever will help me!

Even in my sleep, there was no salvation. I dreamed one evening
that I met Peregrine – but he looked *scared* at the sight of me, instead of
angry. Feeling perplexed, I turned away, hoping to catch a glimpse
of my reflection in the glass panes of the door behind me. When I
saw myself, I screamed. For it was not my usual reflection: it was
Witch-king, the Black Rider, from *The Lord of the Rings*. I had
turned into him because I had spent too long under the influence of
the Dark Lord. My subconscious had realized the truth before I did:
consumed by hate for my captors, I was becoming someone I did
not want to be.

And if I did not escape my cage soon, I feared the independent,
kind-hearted me that I'd struggled so much to create would be lost
to me, for ever.

In April 2005, my father's bitter attacks against the neighbours
changed focus. On 3 April, friends of the sons of the lovely black
family buzzed our flat a couple of times to ask to be let into the
building. Twice, Josie acceded to their request, but when she told
Dad about it he launched into a fit of rage against the family.

'They are fascist agents! All of them! Don't open the door next
time, don't let them in!' He was full of hatred for the entire family –
and that included the toddler in their midst. 'I wish that child would
just DIE,' he growled.

How can you say that? I thought, too depressed by his callousness
to defend them. *How can you call them fascist agents when they're clearly
not? How can you say that they all should die?*

I thought they were a really nice family, especially the matriarch,
Debbie, who seemed to manage to get on with everyone in the
block, rising above the petty arguments between the various neighbours. I saw her as something of a role model, as I aspired to be a
peacekeeper too. For Dad to start attacking her, someone who did
no wrong but only good, was a red line for me.

Sometimes, looking out the window, I'd see Debbie walking
with her grandchild. The toddler would laugh and reach out to her
with fat little arms and Debbie would hold the child tight in return.
Seeing the affection she showered on her grandchild always made

something tighten in my stomach. *I never had that. Dad always denied that to me.*

The day after this rant, on 4 April, Josie and Aisha visited the shop on the high road. Debbie had recently worked there; when they went in, she was already there with her grandchild, chatting animatedly with her former colleagues. But when the comrades reported this to Dad, he hit the roof.

'Proof!' he cried. 'This *shows* she is a fascist agent – because she was in the shop at the same time as you! That family is going to get what's coming to them, I tell you. That child is going to be executed and tortured to punish them . . .'

I remember standing there listening to this bile, turning my head away so I didn't have to see his wicked face any more. But I could still hear him. I stared blindly out of the window, seething with rage at the injustice and sheer fucking madness.

I can't stay here any more, I thought abruptly. *No matter the consequences, I have to go.*

When Dad had finished shouting, I stood up, walked to the bathroom and stared at myself in the small mirror. My usual unhealthy appearance was reflected back at me – pale, dry skin and bloodshot eyes – but I didn't care about my ugliness in that moment. Instead, I looked beneath my skin to my spirit. For despite my exhaustion and depression, what I saw in that mirror was neither.

Instead, I saw defiance.

'In one month's time,' I whispered fiercely to my reflection, 'I will *not* be in this house.'

32

From that point on, my every waking thought was concentrated on my Flight to Freedom, as I nicknamed it; it seemed apt for a caged bird. I knew it was going to be tough because I had no knowledge of the Outside world and no support. Though it was a huge mountain I did not have the first idea how to climb, I remained determined to do it. I simply could not survive in this madhouse any more. I set a leaving date of 18 April and began my preparations.

My first priority was packing – primarily, all my writings and poems. Luckily, I had so many that it had become a habit to have a regular tidy-up of all my papers. The comrades thought nothing of it as I methodically chose those dear friends who would be joining me on my flight. I began scavenging coins from our shopping trips; occasionally I'd been invited to be the comrade to hand over the note, and I now sneakily kept back a few of the coins the shopkeeper returned to me in change. Though I didn't understand money, the one thing I'd grasped was that I couldn't survive Outside without it.

For once, the mind-numbing predictability of Dad's rota became a blessing. I knew I'd have to pick a time to run away when no one else was around and, by studying our schedule, I found one. Every two weeks, on a Monday morning, Josie and Aisha went to the high road to shop, a little further away than our local stores, which meant they'd be out for longer. At the exact same time, Dad religiously took his bath, so he'd be occupied too.

Now that 'Mum' seemed to want nothing to do with me, except to give me what I felt were evil looks, both she and Shobha were not a concern.

I had no idea where to run to. Fleetingly, as if my brain seized on a distant memory, the idea that I could stay with Sian's mum, Ceri, crossed my mind. But as I didn't know if I really *was* Sian's daughter, it seemed a foolish idea and I quickly dismissed it. Even if Ceri didn't reject me – this half-Indian bastard child from a cult she despised, who might in fact be nothing to do with her – would I merely be jumping out of the frying pan and into the fire? Dad always said that Sian's family were horrible.

As I packed and repacked my things in a multi-coloured raffia laundry bag and a pink shoulder tote, I felt excited and terrified at the same time. 'Things feel strange, different now,' I wrote in my diary.

> *Like I'm my own woman, like I've somehow been liberated. Just the thought of 18 April does that to me . . . I'm going to change things. Make them different, hopefully better – of course they will be better, because I will be free! I'm not interested really in material wealth . . . what I really want is freedom, liberty from my parents' mad restrictions . . . Sometimes I think of dad/mum like ogres . . . And they wonder why I'm sick and tired of it? Well, I'm going away – I am prepared to sacrifice all for my freedom. On April 18, as it stands, I'll be gone from this cage. Clipped wings or not – I'll walk all the way, even if I can't fly.*

The more I planned, the more conscious I became that my wings really were clipped, the better to stop me flying away. I didn't have any money of my own, I didn't have a job, a home, any qualifications; I didn't have any friends. What would I do in the Outside world? How would I survive? I think my worst fear was that I'd somehow be sent back, or have to come crawling back, because I couldn't manage without the Collective – and then Dad would kill me for trying to escape.

Perhaps the most important part of all my preparations was to write my leaving letter to my dad. Believing in Overt as I did, the responsibility to try to change him for the better still sat heavily on my twenty-two-year-old shoulders. With my yo-yoing affection, too, I felt I owed him at least an explanation. Still I saw my father as being as schizophrenic as I was. The nice dad he *could* be was the one I wanted to appeal to. For I knew he wasn't *all* bad; I couldn't leave without letting him know.

> *Dear Papa,*
> *This is a letter I wished I never would have to write. It is hard to write. Because it conveys the sad message that, due to circumstances out of my control, you will not see me again, at least not for a very long time. I*

have higher duties than mere filial piety – duties to my own conscience, to my principles . . .

You seem to me, unfortunately, to be growing into a very cruel, evil Dark Lord, like Voldemort and Sauron. And the others are acting like very proper Death Eaters and Black Riders. I, thank Heaven, shall not be one such character. If I continue to stay with you, and listen to all your mad diatribes . . . I shall go mad myself. I will not be culpable, I will not stand by and turn a blind eye to such things. Voldemort and Sauron grew because good people didn't do their duty. And I shall not be like that. I will do my duty, come what may.

I am not brave, not by nature. But I have to learn to be . . . I am going away, as I said I'd do on 23 December – only I didn't have the courage then. But your madness has pushed me too far. I can't bear watching my beloved father, like Dr Jekyll, turning into an evil, Satanic Dark Lord. You can do all the black magic you want upon me – but I'd rather be the victim than the conniving perpetrator. I want absolutely nothing to do with you and your lot's rubbish . . . I have more sense of right and wrong, good and evil, than that.

You will hate me, I know, for being so frank with you. But it is my duty. And I don't care, frankly, what you think of me. On my part, I will only love you. But let me say this, as your only daughter: you are self-willed and self-deceived, and surrounded by silly people (like Aisha and Josie) who worship you and are totally blind to your faults. As the old saying goes, it takes a child to see that the king is naked. And I am pointing it out. This world has no place for Dark Lords and their followers. No world I want to live in, anyway.

. . . There are also other things, other reasons why I'm just totally unable to bear being a caged bird. You talk absolutely endlessly about yourself in the most arrogant, conceited way: it disgusts me no end. Often I have to stop myself from vomiting . . . The type of world you want to build – where everyone is your slave, and no one has a mind of their own! I do not want to live in such a hellhole . . .

. . . Papa, have you a conscience? Do you know what shame means? I would hope you do. At least you ought to . . . I have told you repeatedly what I think about all this, yet you persist in subjecting me to all your verbal shit. Just because I'm your daughter doesn't mean you don't have to respect my wishes. I am utterly sick of all this – so I'm going to take steps.

By the time you read this, I'll be gone. I so wish it hadn't come to this . . . It pains me endlessly to do this. Because I love you so much. But I hate, I absolutely revile and detest all this Commie puke.

. . . I hope in the future we'll be able to meet again, as father and daughter . . . I am not a Commie, I'm not your cadre, I want no part in your Dark exploits. No part. I'm your daughter, full stop. If we can't be just father and daughter, then I'm afraid there's going to be no relationship at all. Never, never will I ever succumb to your madness and become an evil monster, delighting over dead bodies. Never, Papa! Not on your life! I have that much dignity at least!

. . . I'm ashamed of you, father . . . But I still love you. I love you, not your Commie shit . . . I'm a very tender person by nature, and I'm forced to be so hard, which is not at all easy!

. . . I still hope, though, that in the future we will be able to make it up . . . Whatever happens, we are still father and daughter, and I'll always think well of you, unless, of course, you give me reason to do otherwise.

So, farewell for the present, father. I don't think I could ever convey to you how sad I feel that it's come to this. And I'll miss all the others too . . . O, I really can't bear this! Farewell, my father! I go to find Heaven on Earth!

At the bottom, I signed my name in Malayalam characters: a peace offering of sorts.

And then I counted down the days with a growing sense of anticipation. A week to go, five days, four, three, two . . .

'Comrade Prem, you must see Comrade Bala in his room at once.'

What is this? It was unusual to be summoned. Our household ran like clockwork: I saw Dad morning and night in the living room ('Body wash or hair wash?' he would still ask, with his creepy hugs), but not at other times. My mouth dried as I stood outside his door. Nervously, I knocked to gain admittance.

Dad had received a report, he said. I'd been too confident about the comrades not noticing my packing: Josie, ever suspicious, had sneaked a look in one of my bags. It wasn't just my writings I had put in there by now: clothes and underwear nestled alongside my notepads. It struck her as odd. She had scurried straight to Dad.

'Are you thinking of leaving?' he now asked me straight.

I could hear my heartbeat pounding in my ears. Silently, I thanked God for all my years of subterfuge and keeping secrets, for they had prepared me for this moment. Despite my anxiety, I pasted a wide smile on my face. Long before now, I'd learned to have an answer for everything if ever I was caught out, so the lie rolled smoothly off my tongue, as sweet and black as liquorice.

'Why would I leave you?' I asked in feigned surprise. 'I love you. I love this place – this *beautiful* place. Why would I ever want to leave?'

There could have been a real risk, given my emphatic rejections of his views in the past year, that he would see through me. But I laid it on as thick as marmalade and his ego was such that he couldn't resist; couldn't help but feel flattered. Perhaps he even thought my infantile disorder was cured at last! He swallowed it: hook, line and sinker.

He didn't let me leave without throwing out a threat, though – just in case. He issued so many, hour on hour, that to do so was by now second nature.

'If you do go,' he said lightly, 'lightning will strike you dead or you might spontaneously combust . . .'

I nodded: I knew all about JACKIE's powers.

But while I chose to move my leaving date back by two weeks, thinking it unwise to make a run for it when Josie was on alert, in a way his threats made me more determined than ever.

'I'm going,' I wrote in my diary, 'even if I do die in the process because of evil black magic. I won't let *anything* get in the way of my quest for freedom!'

33

The front door closed behind Aisha and Josie on Monday 2 May 2005 with a click that sounded different to normal. It was the sound that signalled the start of my escape.

Dad was already in the bath. So, the moment I heard the front door close, I shrugged on my coat, inside out, which was part of my master plan: it was a multi-coloured coat I had knitted myself and the comrades knew it well. With only the black lining showing, I'd be less recognizable. I also draped a black dupatta headscarf across my thinning hair.

The very last thing I did before leaving was to take out the note I'd written Dad. I *was* sorry it had come to this . . . Yet I brushed aside my emotional ties to him, strong as they were, knowing that the Dark Lord inside him was growing more powerful and that if I didn't leave now, I may never have another chance. I left the envelope propped up beside the back door.

The key was already in it: a benefit of Dad's paranoia. He used to say that the fascist state could easily get a key made to fit the lock as part of the conspiracy against him, so he kept the key in the door at all times to make sure nobody could get in from Outside. I didn't need to pick locks or scale walls to escape: all I had to do was turn the key.

All I had to do . . . Yet I was balanced on a precipice and the moment my fingers touched that key, I could begin to fall. Visions of all JACKIE's vengeful attacks over the years haunted me, each one of his millions of victims screaming a warning I was (foolishly?) choosing to ignore. I remembered, too, Dad's many threats to move away if I ever left him, so that I'd never, ever see the Collective again: these people who were my only lifeline, who had taught me everything I knew. The idea of being without them in the world was as terrifying as it was liberating, just as an astronaut might feel as he steps out into the vacuum of space. The wonder of it would be captivating – until my lungs began to burn without air. I started sweating as I stared numbly at that key, wondering if I truly had the courage to do this.

But, taking a deep breath, I took the weight of my bags. I had packed everything I thought I might need Outside, everything that was precious to me after twenty-two years of captivity, and the bags were heavy. I felt weighed down by them as much as the magnitude of what I was doing. With a trembling hand, I reached for the key. The metal was cool and unfamiliar. I was so worried it would rattle or squeak and give the game away. But I said to myself: *Just do it. If you think about it, you're going to chicken out, so just do it.*

Somehow, I did. I turned that key and I pulled on the door handle and the back door swung wide . . . I felt fresh air on my face. *Freedom.*

But first I had to cross the threshold. Peering Outside cautiously, I took in the fact that the May day was sunny, the sky a crisp bright blue. It didn't look possible that a lightning bolt of JACKIE's would come out of that beautiful sky to strike me dead. Steeling my nerves, I decided that even if it did, I would rather die standing up for my beliefs than to live a life that was a lie.

So, with a deep breath, I stepped out of that back door. I went fast, too scared to do it slowly: I lumbered out of that door and into my future. I burst out on to the residential street; I didn't burst into flames. It felt like a miracle: I was all in one piece, even though I'd broken through my bonds. I blinked rapidly, stunned as much by the sunshine as my survival.

But there was no time to take in the fact I was still living: I had to get as far away as possible. Frantically, I looked left, I looked right . . . but without a shoulder to follow, I didn't know which way to go. I had never, ever been Out in the world on my own before. I felt overwhelmed, not knowing what to do, only knowing I didn't want to go back.

In the end, I walked where my feet took me. I thought back to the books I'd read in the Collective. I'd read a few things about kind people who took in strangers who were homeless. Maybe I would meet one of them? I could do their washing for them, or something, as a way of paying them back.

Without knowing in which direction I was walking, I took more stumbling steps along the suburban street. It was the most peculiar feeling in the world not to be surrounded. If I looked in front of me, I did not see Dad's anorak, as I had every time I'd gone Out for the past two decades. Instead, a whole vista of Outside was spread before me, looking much as it did through the window – but the view was different, ever-changing, and *there was no glass*. It was frightening; I wasn't sure I liked it. There was too much of everything: too much light, too much space, too much to take in. I kept my head down and heaved on my heavy bags.

Then – a person. A person before me. I kept my eyes fixed on their feet.

'I've run away from home,' I said.

There was a pause. 'What do you want me to do?' the woman replied, then kept on walking.

I stopped one or two people – but nobody was interested. I was starting to despair. *What am I going to do?*

By following the complex warren of paths in twists and turns, I managed to get to a main shopping street; not the one Josie and Aisha had gone to. Maybe here I would find a kind stranger who could help? By now, my bags were such an encumbrance I could barely walk. Somewhat to my surprise, after all the people who'd ignored me, a short elderly man came to my aid.

'Do you want any help?' he asked kindly.

'I've run away from home,' I said to his feet, feeling uncomfortable about looking in his – or anyone else's – eyes. For what would I see there? I wondered. The fear and revulsion I'd dreamed Peregrine possessed? The hate and disparagement I always saw in the comrades' gaze? It was best to look down, I decided, so I did not learn what Outside truly thought of me. 'What can I do?' I asked his feet.

To my amazement, the gentleman answered my question. 'Why don't you go to the police station?' he suggested.

'Where is it?' I asked. I spoke with hesitancy, almost expecting Dad or Josie to cut into the conversation, as they always had when I'd tried to speak before. But I was on my own now, cut adrift from both their surveillance and security. *I like this*, I thought, as the man and I exchanged our separate sentences in a verbal dance that delighted me.

I thrilled a little that I was actually communicating with someone from Outside.

'It's beyond the traffic lights,' he replied and swiftly walked on.

I knew *what* traffic lights were physically, though I could not comprehend what the different colours meant. But how to find them on this busy street was beyond me. It was all I could do to fix my eyes on the narrow strip of high street right in front of me – to look left or right or see anything beyond my immediate location was impossible. All my life, I had been actively discouraged from looking beyond Dad's shoulder – 'Don't ogle!' had been the constant refrain – and I could not start now. My eyes had not been built for such things.

I stumbled on. Everything was strange. Even with the man's clear directions, I was unable to navigate my way from A to B. My heart started pounding again. I hadn't known escaping would be *this* hard. Now that I was allowed Out shopping, I'd thought I'd gained a good grasp of the world Outside, but being Out without the comforting if constricting presence of the comrades, I was realizing, with an increasing sense of sickness, that I didn't have the first clue.

I stopped a few more people. 'Where is the police station?' I asked, again and again. I kept asking and I kept walking, until eventually someone said: 'It's right there.'

I surveyed the building with awe. *I found it.* I felt awash with relief and achievement. Yet this was only base camp. I still had a long way to go to reach the summit.

Still heaving my bags, I walked up to the front door of the station. I hesitated before I went in. *Is this the right thing to do?* I'd had years of Dad warning me about the 'fascist dogs' who policed the BFS, and while I no longer feared or even disliked the police myself, it went against every instinct to go to them for help. Yet I had no other ideas. Taking a deep breath, I pulled on the door handle and entered in.

I was so overwhelmed to be Outside on my own, and to have made it this far, that I can barely remember anything about that police station. The entrance lobby was small and, I recall, red; maybe the floor was red. It had been bright and sunny outside, but inside the police station it was dark and cool. There was a desk immediately in front of me when I stumbled in.

What I do remember is the woman sat at the desk. She wore plainclothes and she had her black hair twisted into cornrows. She wasn't motherly, but she seemed kind.

'I've run away from home,' I told her plaintively. 'What do I *do*?'

She looked up from her papers and asked me why I'd run away.

Where do I even begin? Twenty-two years of captivity were too many to boil down to a single sentence. Faced with the officer, too, I suddenly felt a keen responsibility towards Dad and the others. For my open heart tolerated everything except intolerance: I didn't want the police to break up the Collective, as the comrades were entitled to believe what they wished. I just wanted to be free of it myself.

So I chose my words carefully, knowing I couldn't break Dad's trust about the Overt, nor wanting to get him into trouble.

'It's too restrictive,' I said in the end. 'I'm not allowed to go Out.'

I made no mention of his violence, nor the way the comrades marched in step with me every time we went Outside. Most importantly, I didn't tell her about Dad's black magic, which was the scariest aspect of all. I wanted no conflict to come of this: I simply wanted to start a new life for myself.

Though I tried to communicate my desperation without words, the officer – I'll call her Sarah – didn't seem to take me too seriously. I had no other words to be able to make her listen. The mere fact of speaking with an Outsider was so alien to me that it was as much as I could manage to have said those first nine words.

She told me I could phone some refuges if I wanted. 'It's a bank holiday, though,' she warned.

A bank holiday . . . I'd heard of them, but I didn't know what it meant. I didn't know that offices shut down and that many places would not be manned to take my call. If I'd known, perhaps I'd have delayed my Flight to Freedom.

I managed to get through to one refuge. In halting sentences, I tried to explain that I needed a place to stay, but I was really thrown by the act of using a telephone: it had been many years since I'd spoken on one and everything about the exchange was odd. The refuge did say they could take me, but then they started explaining how to get there . . .

As with the man on the high street, their directions made no sense at all. My mind felt scrambled just by listening. I gathered that

I would have to take a bus *and* a train . . . I felt a grim sense of help-lessness sinking through me. There was no way I could do it. I had never travelled on a bus alone: never bought a ticket, chosen a destination, known where to get off, known where to get *on* . . . I had battled even to get here, ten minutes down the road on foot – the idea of taking public transport was akin to embarking on a round-the-world trip without an atlas. It was impossible. I had never been taught how to do it; I couldn't even consider undertaking such a complex journey on my own.

I hung up the phone with a very heavy heart. A man in the police station, who'd been listening to the exchange, came over to me.

'You know what I think would be best?' he said.

I shook my head.

'I think we should phone your family. It's best to tell them what's happened. Perhaps they could come and get you.'

I mulled it over. I knew how much Dad hated the police. *Perhaps*, I thought hopefully, my spirits rising a little, *if the police are involved Dad will give me a bit more freedom – in order to stop the officers delving deeper into his affairs.*

Another thought occurred to me. I was almost certain, given everything he had always said about people leaving, that Dad wouldn't actually want me back now. The moment I'd stepped over the threshold, I had crossed from black to white. Surely I'd be as dead to him as Cindy and Leanne? In my heart, I was desperately *hoping* he wouldn't want me back. *Perhaps*, I thought now, *if we call and he rejects me, the police will help me more.* All I really wanted was to get out of the Collective and find somewhere else to live. Everything that had happened so far today had shown me I was hopelessly out of my depth. I couldn't do this on my own – I had to accept help from *someone.*

And this man was offering help. I don't know, now, if he was an officer or just a man who happened to be passing through. I liked that he wasn't aggressive or domineering; rather, his attitude seemed to be: 'Don't you see this is the best way?'

As I couldn't see *any* other way forward, I could do little but agree.

'OK,' I acquiesced in the end. 'You can phone my dad.'

34

I paced up and down while Sarah made the call.

'I want to start a new life,' I kept saying to her, 'I don't want to go back.'

I still felt confident as I said those words, buoyed by a surge of hope even as Sarah spoke to Josie on the phone and explained I'd run away. Because I knew things would *have* to change now that the police were involved.

I've done it, I thought triumphantly. *I will actually start to live a new life.*

Sarah hung up the telephone. 'They're on their way,' she said. She suggested I got myself some food while I waited for them.

I nodded without words, not knowing how to explain I'd never done such a thing before. Nevertheless, inspired by the knowledge that this would be the first meal of my new life, I cautiously made my way down the steps outside the station and saw there was a KFC nearby. I went in with my mismatched collection of coins gripped tightly in my hand, a mess of bronze and silver and gold I had no idea how to decipher.

Above the counter was a lit-up display board with a confusing array of items listed. I felt the overwhelming panic of *not knowing how* rising inside me again. Hesitantly, I walked further into the restaurant, looking around me for clues.

There was a woman in the line in front of me, waiting to be served. She was slim and white, with honey-blonde hair. When it was her turn at the counter, I closely watched everything she did and memorized each word she said.

Then, when it was my turn, as though I was a parrot from a story-book, I imitated everything that had just happened in exactly the same order. *I hope they don't think I'm funny*, I remember thinking.

Even if they did, the magic words she had muttered worked for me, too; the coins I cluelessly slid across the counter seemingly providing sufficient payment. I managed to get a cup of Pepsi and some chips. I took them over to a table, cradling them in my hands like treasure. I sucked on the straw and felt the cool drink slide down my throat as I swallowed. I plucked a chip from its paper bag and tasted its salty tang on my tongue.

It was the nicest drink and the nicest food I had ever consumed. Because they didn't just taste of Pepsi and potato.

They tasted of freedom.

After I had finished my food, I went to use the loo. For the first time in my life Outside, I went to the toilet on my own. I remember thinking, *What a wonderful feeling this is, to be able to do this on my own!* There was no one standing outside the door, waiting and listening. It was just me and my body, free to do as we pleased.

I really like this, I thought. *I like going Out on my own. If only there was somebody around to give me some help to learn things, it would be the best thing in the world to be free!*

With that thought in mind, I returned to the police station to wait for Dad. I felt hopeful. With the police on my side, there was now a new dimension. Dad would have to consider what I was saying and even agree to it.

They soon arrived. To my shock, both Josie and Dad enveloped me in a hug; Josie seemed to have missed me and it felt like a genuine embrace. Dad, on the other hand, seemed to be putting on an act. I wondered if the police would fall for it . . .

I watched nervously as Sarah spoke to them on my behalf. I believe she thought they were well-meaning but strict parents; that she only had to talk to them and they would come round. She suggested that they let me take a trip to the shops alone or go on the bus independently every now and again. My heart stuttered a little as I heard her speak, for she clearly didn't realize how bad it was – that I wasn't just not allowed to do those things, but had never been taught how to do them. I think she thought it was a culturally restricted life I was living; that an Asian father was protecting his daughter from the Western world.

Still, I said nothing. I watched Dad's reaction closely. He seemed to give the appearance of someone who didn't know he'd done wrong, as though he was just a parent who was trying his best. He admitted he was restrictive: 'Yes, I have been keeping her in,' he acknowledged. He was very persuasive and believable – but then, he'd always been good with the authorities.

After Sarah had pleaded my case, Dad gave a tight-lipped acquiescence of sorts. 'I'll think about it,' he said, in response to her appeal for a little more leniency.

OK, I thought. *Maybe this isn't so bad . . .*

Unexpectedly, Sarah then looked at me. 'Is there anything you want to talk about without them here?'

I could feel Dad bristling at the suggestion from where I was sat across the room from him, but bravely I ignored him. 'Yes,' I said.

Sarah asked them to step outside and they went.

I stood up and started pacing again. 'I don't know what I'm supposed to do,' I said desperately. 'I don't really want to go back. I don't know if I can; I don't know if I can bear it . . .'

'Well,' she said reasonably. 'It's a bank holiday. Why don't you go back and think about what it is you really want to do? Otherwise you'll have to sleep on the streets tonight. Maybe you can go back home and discuss it with them, and then make a decision.'

At her words, I panicked. *Sleep on the streets . . .?* But what about my friends, my writings: if it rained, they would be destroyed. They had sustained me throughout my prison sentence: I could not abandon them now. I was not really too worried for myself – I had been prepared for JACKIE to kill me if I left – but I did not feel I could subject my friends to that.

My brain was desperately trying to think through all the possible consequences of this major decision I now had to make. What if I said no to Sarah? What if I refused to go home? What would happen then?

I imagined Dad's reaction: 'There is NOTHING I won't do to punish those who go against me!' Standing there in that police station – which prompted memories of what had happened to Sian and Oh – wild thoughts ran through my head: what if Dad lied to the police that I had killed Sian and Oh? He had suggested as much during a quarrel in the house. Josie had also once said something about me being reported as an illegal immigrant; though I'd been born in Britain, I knew so little of Outside I didn't know that meant that I could stay.

These thoughts were terrifying. And here was Sarah, who clearly had so much more experience than me, suggesting I went back and talked things over. I was still a big believer in talking things through. After all, I'd *nearly* persuaded Dad in Christmas 2003 to let me leave – perhaps now, now that I'd dared to take this step, he'd be even more shaken up and *have* to acquiesce? My spirits lifted again. Hadn't he just promised as much in front of Sarah?

Though I could feel the truth of what was really going on in the house on the tip of my tongue, I didn't want to get anyone into trouble. I doubted Sarah would believe me even if I did tell the truth, not with Dad around to tell her otherwise. I was without guidance and friends, and I didn't know anything about the Outside world . . . In the end, despite racking my brains, I simply couldn't think of a better way to proceed than what she was suggesting, even though every cell in my body militated against doing so.

If everyone is telling me to go back, I concluded, *maybe I should. Maybe that* is *the right thing to do.*

Nevertheless, I think my desperation showed in my eyes. I don't know, now, whether she or I initiated it, or perhaps it was both of us at the same time, but Sarah and I started hugging each other.

It was such a beautiful feeling. I *loved* it. Since Oh had died, I'd barely had any hugs at all. I craved that human touch like candy; it tasted just as sweet. Sarah was warm and soft and I held on to her tightly. It was so lovely to have somebody hugging me, *especially* a woman who wouldn't turn into a monster in a few minutes' time. Unusually for me, I felt I could *trust* her. I wasn't used to trusting people. So I held her tight, with everything I had, not wanting to let go; not wanting to go back.

But I couldn't hold on to her for ever. Eventually, we broke apart and she gave me a half-smile.

'I'll call you in a few days to see how it's going,' she promised.

I nodded silently.

Sarah called a cab to take us home, my bags really were heavy. Josie, Dad and I got into the car and it pulled smoothly away. In just a few short minutes, all the distance I'd put between myself and the house where I'd been held prisoner was eliminated.

Yet I returned with a sense of hope. Now Sarah was involved, things would be different.

When I walked through the door, Mum – for the first time ever – embraced me.

'Welcome home,' Chanda said warmly.

I felt a sense of shock as she wrapped me in her arms. *Maybe they really do care about me*, I thought in confusion. *Maybe I've been imagining that Dad is a nasty person. Perhaps this is all in my head and I'm as retarded as they've always said. I know so little about people – have I misread all the signs?*

Dad sat me down on the mismatched chairs in our living room while the others thronged about us, watching. Dad seemed in a state of shock too.

'How could you do this to me?' he asked in bewilderment: the hurt patriarch deceived by his kin. 'I've done everything for you. I've tried my hardest to care for you. How could you think of leaving me? Of betraying me?'

I felt *so* guilty when he said that. He *had* done everything for me. But I couldn't let this opportunity go without begging him to change things; I knew I couldn't carry on as before.

So I tried to talk to him. At that moment it seemed like he *could* be talked to.

'I want to change things,' I declared passionately.

Dad fixed me with a wise gaze. Somehow, beneath it, I became a child again; a child who knew nothing of the ways of the world. 'We can't take the risk,' he told me, patting my hand sadly.

But that wasn't an outright no . . . I thought, if I was clever about it, that everything could still change.

Because nothing was as Dad had said it would be if I left. I was alive, for one, but secondly, to my surprise, everyone was so very kind to me that evening.

'What a big long day!' I wrote in my diary as I crawled tiredly into my bunkbed. 'They were surprisingly sympathetic – it seems they were all crying when they found out I'd left . . . But I made clear I'm only coming home on the condition that they'll let me free.'

When I got up the next day, it was in the knowledge that my prison was surely now at an end. Things were going to be very different indeed in the future.

I was so confident, so happy, that my father, even after all these years, was able to take me by surprise.

'Traitor!' he hissed at me that morning. 'Fascist agent!'

Without warning, he gave me a backhander across my face. The slap sent me reeling. I brought my hand to my cheek, feeling the heat there, the redness already beginning to rise.

It was silly to be shocked, after all the many beatings that had come before – but I was, all the same. I felt tears pricking at my eyes. Yet I wasn't crying for the pain, I was crying because I knew, in that moment, that there was no way I was *ever* going to get Out. He wouldn't take this risk again. He wouldn't let me free. And after yesterday, I knew I couldn't do it on my own. Those iron vices around me might have been invisible, but they were no less real. I cried because I felt them digging in, digging into my brain and body, tighter and harder than they'd ever been before.

I was trapped: a caged bird who couldn't even sing her way to solace. A caged bird with wings so clipped that, even when I'd had the chance to fly, I'd failed.

Part Four
Enlightenment

35

I was right: I was trapped. Sarah kept her promise to call, but the comrades surrounded me when I spoke with her on the telephone, breathing down my neck, so I couldn't say the words I wanted to – I could only repeat the phrases Dad had drummed into me, a script to keep me caged: 'I don't want to leave here any more. I'm going to stay.'

I doubt Sarah was suspicious of my change of heart; I believe she thought I was just a young girl who'd had a tantrum. I remember her saying, 'You have to do what *you* want in life.' That was such an empowering statement; no one had ever said such a thing to me before, it was always, 'You have to do what you're *told* to do.' But I had no idea how to go about it.

So time passed, with no further involvement from the police. It was a week since my escape attempt, a month, a year . . . We moved again, into a newly built ground-floor flat in Brixton. I yearned every day to be free, but had neither the courage nor the capability to try to escape again. For I remembered all too well that disorientating journey from the house to the high road: I knew I was not equipped to survive Outside alone; not least because the move meant all the streets were new once more. So I stayed with the Collective by force of necessity, against my will, because my father had made it so that I *couldn't* go. I had to put up with it, if I was not to find myself homeless, friendless and penniless.

Nor was the lack of opportunity solely driven by my stupid self. On a supernatural level, I still feared JACKIE; on a practical one, the rota swiftly changed so that I'd never have another chance to flee. My Outings in general were drastically curtailed; Dad said I didn't deserve to go Out any more because of my 'crime' of running away. Cruelly, there were even birthdays of mine where he went Out but left me behind. He also refused to let me watch the movie adaptations of *The Lord of the Rings* – even though *he* did. 'I see myself chained for life,' I wrote dully in my diary. 'And there's no one, no one in the whole wide world to turn to.'

Even Peregrine McConaughey offered no salvation, now that we had moved. I kept him fed and watered in my mental nest, however, refusing to let my love for him die, even if fate had conspired to keep us apart. Though the years passed – 2005, 2006, 2007 – I kept him alive in my heart throughout, trying to nurture the relationship that, to me, represented my independence and my moral decency. But his light was fading, the talisman he proffered becoming overwhelmed by the darkness I seemed destined to endure.

Though I was still caged, I was not quiet. I appealed to Dad for clemency time and again and begged him to keep his promises.

Oh, my father's promises . . . So many times he swore on his honour as a father that he would relax his rules, but he did not: one flimsy excuse after another kept me chained. He was full of glib, honeyed words, but they were always empty. It was painfully cruel, for I banked *everything* on his promises of change, even though some small part of me suspected they were sedatives, administered to keep me quiet. When I complained about his broken vows, he said I must have faith.

Perhaps strangely, I tried to. 'I believe you will set me free,' I wrote to him, 'and save me from this hellish existence.' I was so habituated to believing him that I struggled to do anything else. Though it was hopeless, I kept on hoping. It was torment of the worst kind.

Yet Dad said it was *I* who was torturing *him* by complaining. How could I hurt him so, when he had only ever had my best interests at heart? He shut me down when I tried to speak up. I was ungrateful and selfish, he said. Because he had brought me up, he expected me to follow him without question.

In many ways, I still did. I believed in JACKIE, I believed in his covert premiership of the world, and I pathologically believed in the coming Overt as, now, it truly was my only path to freedom.

'I know we should be patient,' I wrote to him of the Overt, in yet another plea for mercy, 'but I can't die of misery while waiting for the Heaven of freedom either . . .'

Most of my appeals were met with slander, derision and abuse, both physical and verbal. Occasionally, however, the odd bone was thrown; I would salivate over it with all the dignity of a starving dog. For instance, I was allowed to join Dad and the comrades on their trips to the launderette to help with the weekly wash. It was the highlight of my week. Dad would say, with the beneficence of a kindly king, 'I'm *slowly* teaching you how to do things!' But at the rate he was going, I'd be eighty by the time I'd learned everything I needed to be able to live a life Outside.

I was also permitted to watch *Doctor Who* and other drama programmes on television, though only in his company ('who' in Malayalam apparently meant 'Ara', so the show was allowed because it was about him). This entertainment was desperately needed, yet with bleak recognition I saw my upbringing in the metallic march of the Cybermen: an army of genderless, heartless machines with one sole purpose – to serve their master. They truly were children of JACKIE; nothing like the disappointment I had proved to be.

Occasionally, Dad would indicate the Overt was coming. Whenever an Argos van went past the window of the flat, he would jump up and down, because in AR Adiction 'Argos' meant 'Ara goes!' And 'Ara going' was apparently the first stage of Overt, because Dad would go back to India before he took over the world.

I used to watch him every time he did it, thinking, *You keep saying you're going, but you never do, you're still standing on top of me!*

If it hadn't been for the other comrades, I don't know how I would have survived after my escape attempt failed. Josie and Aisha changed quite a bit after 2 May. I think they were shocked that I'd felt distraught enough to run away, so they were a lot nicer to me after that. They reported less, and even Josie let me talk about Peregrine. The two of them formed a sort of 'outer cocoon' for me, so that I at least had someone to talk to. I think they actually began to consider how I felt: a direct contrast to my parents, who afforded me no respect.

The closeness of my new bond with the comrades came about in part because of my parents. Recently, I'd come up with another theory to explain how my good father could possibly be such a demon. The answer – gifted to me by centuries of folklore – was my creation of an evil stepmother. I'd watched Bala and Chanda together and come up with what seemed to me a reasonable theory that she sometimes put him up to his attacks, egging him on and using him as her mouthpiece. Perhaps it was just easier for me to think that, but

213

it seemed a reasonable theory. Could it be possible, I fancifully suggested to Josie and Aisha, that when Dad was mean to us and beat us *unfairly*, it was because Chanda had cast a spell on him?

I'd never have got away with this if Dad hadn't often acted on 'reports' from Chanda that were patently false – for if Josie or Aisha thought he was beating them *fairly*, they still embraced the benefits of his 'good struggle' with them. But when he attacked them on false reports, *that* wasn't educational in the least . . . it made sense to the comrades that it *couldn't* be our noble leader himself who had gone astray: someone must have led him there. My stepmother was the obvious choice for prime suspect.

With Dad perceived to be at least partly under her spell, reporting then decreased yet further: the comrades felt less inclined to report as none of us wanted our misdemeanours to get back to Chanda. So as the years after my escape attempt passed, we three little house-elves grew closer. We even secretly started giving each other gifts on our birthdays as a sign of our affection; previously, gifts had been a privilege only afforded in the Collective to members of Dad's legitimate family.

Had Dad known about our increasing intimacy, I suspect he would have stepped in and put a stop to our 'anti-party clique'. But he relied on Josie and Aisha to tell him what was going on and, at that time, they didn't. Nevertheless, I engaged with them on a knife edge because I never knew when the Black Rider inside them both might rear its head and betray me. I could never *really* trust them. In my heart, I knew the truth: leopards do not change their spots, and neither do servants of the Dark Lord.

So although I now shared a fragile friendship with the pair of them, my *real* friends remained my writings. I'd read that Ernest Hemingway once said, 'There is no friend as loyal as a book,' and how right he was! My diary was the only true friend I had; my imagination a magic carpet that still transported me away. I wrote poems and stories that truly expressed my pain, though I feared my creations were rubbish: the mad scribblings of a non-brain. 'I know nothing about writing,' I lamented in my diary. 'It's my dad's folly for not sending me to school . . . I love writing more than anything else in the world, but I can't do it.'

I would rail against the Collective for never giving me a chance to further my dreams or fulfil my hopes; for keeping me locked up so I would never even gain the life experience I needed to become a *real* writer. But I had experience enough. Often, the only way I could make sense of my strange world was to write about it:

> *Living with loved ones who are apt to fall into madness — or, in many cases, pure, downright evil — is not an easy thing to do. But it was a sort of natural-born art for the unlucky Claretta Frobisher . . . All she had to do was to withdraw into her room, take up a pen and paper . . . and write . . . She would feel a measure of hope, of happiness — a rare and welcome sensation in her unbelievable situation.*
>
> *And then the truth would hit her, hit her like a thousand-ton boulder, driving her to the ground and pinning her under its murky colossus. She was stuck out here, alone and friendless, in the company of insane people.*
>
> *Insane people with a propensity for evil.*

36

On 1 January 2008, six days before my twenty-fifth birthday, the sky outside exploded in a rainbow of colour.

It wasn't JACKIE, making the sky fall down; somebody was letting off fireworks. I edged into Shobha's room so I could see them better; the coast was clear as she and Chanda had gone to the other room to call their family to wish them a happy new year.

Such phone calls always made me jealous and morose. If only *I* had some family Outside I could call . . . The devastating thing was: I now knew I did.

The truth had come out, in whispered conversations, in the wake of my escape attempt. It was Aisha I had asked, because she had always been the most understanding comrade. Though my parentage had been something I'd wanted confirmed for years, the question had always been dodged before and, previously, I couldn't push it for fear of the consequences. But with Aisha and me on friendly terms and my bid for freedom in ashes, I felt I had nothing left to lose.

'Was Comrade Sian my mother? Was she pregnant with me?' I'd asked her directly one day.

Aisha had tried to evade the question – but for once I wouldn't let her. After I'd wheedled and begged, she spoke haltingly, as though some long-ago command was tampering with her tone. 'Yes,' she conceded at last. 'Sian was pregnant with you.'

It made such a difference, to hear someone confirm it. I had almost felt the roots shooting out of me at her words, anchoring me to the world. Not just shadow: someone's daughter, after all. Though I'd had pretty concrete suspicions for years, I had never heard anyone *say* it before. There had been nothing more painful to me than being an unperson, but now I *finally* had a place in the world. It was something to hold on to, something that was mine, when everything else was denied to me.

216

In dribs and drabs, Aisha had told me the whole story. When Sian's body had begun to balloon in 1982, Dad had told her that she had gas. She believed him, of course. It was only when they went to the hospital on a snowy January night that she and the comrades had found out there was a baby inside her. When she came home with me, Dad instructed the comrades to clean the bathroom very carefully – he said it was possibly because the bathroom was not clean that Sian had fallen pregnant; as though I was some dirty thing that had infected her. *Is that all he thought of me?* I thought when I heard that – wounded by it, even after everything.

I didn't ask if Dad was my father; I was pretty certain of that, too, even though he still wouldn't openly admit it. My thoughts were full of Sian instead: full of my *mother*. The further away from Dad's influence I'd come over the past few years, the more I'd felt drawn towards her, as though I was turning my back on the Indian part of me and embracing my inner Welsh dragon.

I thought nonstop about my mother after Aisha had confirmed it; I used to dream about her constantly and I'd always wake up crying, just wishing there was a way I could have known her as a proper mother – could have known her when she was nice. I felt so sad that she had died without our ever being mother and daughter, despite the fact we'd lived side by side for almost fourteen years.

For a long while, I was angry with her: for choosing 'Beloved Comrade Bala' over me. But I understood in time that she didn't really have a choice. She had become a Black Rider: her soul had been emptied out by her desire to follow AB. Ultimately I decided she had been a victim too. The more I reviewed our time together, the more I remembered of those few occasions when she had been nice. Perhaps, I thought wistfully, she became Dad's worst disciple *because* she loved me so much: in order to prove to Dad she didn't, she *had* to go out of her way to punish me. Maybe her love for me was something she constantly had to struggle against, and *that's* why she behaved as she did.

Over and over, I replayed my memory of our one nice moment together in the hospital: 'Bye bye, baby,' she had said. Did she sense she was going to die, and didn't want to leave without letting me know she cared? I felt like crying when I remembered that moment. Because I knew, in that fleeting glance I'd seen in her eyes, that I had seen the *real* Sian then, and not the Black Rider I had usually known. I felt proud she was my mum; I felt proud she'd let me know. We had been deprived of so much together, but nevertheless we had managed to give each other a glimpse of what could have been.

While Sian was long dead and buried by the time Aisha confirmed her motherhood of me, the news did change things, for I now *knew* I had a grandmother out there somewhere: Ceri. How I *longed* to make contact with her! I spent hours fantasizing about her discovering my existence, somehow, and coming to my rescue. We would live together in her house in Wales. We would take trips to my mother's grave, arranging yellow flowers as we both cried and mourned for Sian.

But despite my increasingly desperate fantasies, Ceri had so far not come to my door. So well hidden had my father made me that even my own grandmother could not find me. That New Year's Day, as I listened to the rise and fall of Chanda's voice speaking with her relatives, I felt a familiar twist in my gut. Why was she permitted to have that which was denied to me? I knew why, really: it was because I had no family that *knew* of my existence that Dad could abuse me as he wished, because he didn't have to answer for it; he was hardly going to give that up.

I'd become increasingly bitter over the years about the way Dad had forced me into the shadows. Now I knew Sian *was* my mother, my illegitimacy was obvious, so I knew to my very soul that the *real* reason for my caged existence was Dad's shame about his bastard child and desire to cover it up. I was his guilty secret, kept forever in the shadows: proof he cared more about his own good name than his daughter's happiness. And he said *I* was selfish!

I sighed deeply as I stared out the window, my face lit by the fireworks but feeling only dark inside. Never in my life had I felt so miserable. My existence was so drab and monotonous: nothing interesting *ever* happened and I had nothing to look forward to. Just the same four walls: reading, eating, sleeping, watching dull TV. I couldn't even bring myself to write, for I had no inspiration. And what was the point anyway? It would never be published or even read because Dad was so controlling. Even looking out of the window – for so many years a source of entertainment – had become too painful. *Why can't I have a bit of that?* I would think jealously as I saw people walking to and fro: couples, families, friends. Everybody had somebody but me.

I was always kept from people I wanted to befriend. At the launderette, there would sometimes be Caribbean people there with earphones in and they seemed so cool – I wanted them to be my friends! But although I was now allowed to say a few things to people Outside, such as, 'Don't put your money in that machine, it's dodgy,' if the conversation ever moved on to anything personal or contentious, Dad would step in. I could never chat freely because he was always there, listening to every word I said. His favourite excuse to curtail a possible friendship for me – for example, if someone suggested that we meet for a coffee one day – would be to say, 'We are looking after a disabled person, we can't do such things.' He made it sound noble and self-sacrificing; often people praised him. I would seethe with rage, thinking, *You bastard, you're lying to these nice people and making them think you're good when you're just evil, keeping me prisoner! Just because we look after Shobha, that shouldn't mean I can't have a friend!*

I longed to be able to tell people what was *really* going on, but I was scared they wouldn't believe me – or that they'd confront Dad. If he knew I'd dared to say something, I would lose the few privileges I'd scavenged. It wasn't worth the risk.

By that January day, I'd given up hope of things ever changing. A few years ago, I had found my first grey hair. *I am old before I've lived*, I'd thought morosely. Though my hair was slowly turning grey, Dad and Chanda still insisted on handling me like a child. He did not believe I needed respect, only 'guidance', and treated me like a dog on a leash who should only go where its master wants. They tried to break my spirit, rather than encouraging it to flourish. I denounced him as a 'fuddy-duddy' and 'killjoy' in my diary, but the truth was he was a lot more cruel than that. I called him the Dark Lord Monster too.

I heard Chanda exclaim on the telephone and threw a look back over my shoulder at the noise. I wasn't entirely devoid of sympathy for her. how hard must it be to live with your husband's bastard child when you had no children of your own? Sometimes, I thought Dad had ruined her life as much as mine. But I could not forgive her for the way she deliberately excluded me, to the pettiest degree: arranging family meals where I was banished from the table; buying pastries just for herself, Shobha and Dad; labelling their special food with

'SCAB' (Shobha, Chanda, AB) to dissuade us house-elves from eating it (the one benefit of *that* was that the unpleasant-sounding acronym gave me a good giggle). Though I didn't entirely begrudge Chanda her animosity towards me – I felt it was understandable – as Dad wouldn't let me leave the Collective, this was the only home I had. I was treated as an interloper by my only family, yet prevented from finding any other friends. Stuck with them as I was, her unkindness cut deeply and left me feeling even more that I did not belong.

Sometimes, I wished Dad *had* killed me for running away. Initially, I'd put his lack of action on that front down to the police involvement in my failed attempt. Since then, however, I thought he'd come up with another plan: one that wouldn't leave him with actual blood on his hands.

'He's hoping to drive me mad, and he is succeeding,' I wrote in my diary. 'I think he's hoping I'll go round the bend and commit suicide like my mother did, then the final blot on his reputation will be removed – kill the bastard child so there never can be any evidence of her existence!'

And as the rest of the world celebrated the coming of the New Year, I felt as if I couldn't face one more second of this life. For me, 1 January did not denote a new start, but another tally on the wall of my jail: another year behind bars. As I listened to the bangs of the neighbours' fireworks, each one sounded like a gunshot that I wished would blast my brains to bits.

I gazed at those fireworks: dark-gold, green and turquoise sparks exploding against the black night sky. *If I am going to kill myself,* I thought numbly, the decision made, *I might as well watch them one last time. Because I will never see New Year's fireworks ever again.* I smiled wryly. *Let's go out with a bang . . .*

Shobha's room was at the back of the apartment, so it looked out on to the communal bins. As I stared sadly out that evening, I heard our neighbour's front door suddenly open as he took his rubbish out. I'd seen him around and thought him rather groovy, but of course we had never had a chance to connect.

The light was on in Shobha's room, so I think it caught his eye. As he made his way back from the bins, he glanced over at me, standing there lifting the net curtain so I could better see the fireworks. And as our eyes met, as he *saw* me, he gave me the hugest smile I had *ever* received. *I am so happy to see you!* that big, white-toothed smile seemed to say. In that instant, I felt liked and valued as I *never* had in the Collective. It changed everything, as I later wrote:

> On the First Day, on New Year's Day,
> He came to me, in deep twilight
> And bore aloft, to light my way
> His flame, a candle in the night;
> He graced me with his gentle glance
> And gave my soul a second chance.

37

I fell in love. Truly – no longer imaginary, as it had been with Peregrine McConaughey. My sweet cherub had smiled at me with such joy that there was no doubting his feelings for me. I had never known anyone quite as downright perfect. From that moment on, I revered him. I started following his football club to be like him and when he broke a green glass bottle outside the flat, I scavenged one of the shards as a memento.

My delight at my new friendship was matched only by my intense sadness at my inability to deepen that friendship because of my captivity. It was exquisitely painful always to be loving, but never loved in return. For although Roddy (that was the name of my beloved) beamed at me from afar, what more could he do to express his affection? Mr Monster – my father – had ensured I was beyond his reach.

Immediately, I began recording Roddy's movements in my diary, as I had with Peregrine before him. This did not go unnoticed by the Dark Lord, and Roddy immediately became the focus of Dad's daily Vampire Puking, as well as subject to his old black magic intended to keep the two of us apart.

'He will rob you! Rape you! Kill you!' ranted Dad, putting his foot down. 'He is not interested in *you*, he is a fascist agent working to infiltrate the Collective.'

'It's not fair to say such things—'

'Fuck off!' my father swore at me.

The problem for Dad was that the moment I took a step out of his reach, he became even *more* irrelevant to me. The Dark Lord simply couldn't bear to see me happy, for then he seemed to feel his strangling power over me loosen. He feared that lack of control intensely. Even after all these years his plan for me had not changed: he wanted to subjugate me to his will. He was used to every woman around him worshipping him; to him, I was just another woman and should have no other man in my life but him.

'Why is he so frightened, so fucking cowardly, that he cannot dare to give me a chance to choose?' I ranted to my dear friend Diary. 'Surely, being the great man he claims to be, nothing can stop him? Surely he has nothing to lose by GIVING ME A CHANCE?'

I begged him from the bottom of my heart to let me have an opportunity at least to speak to Roddy. Just to be permitted to say hello to him when we went to the shops or the launderette would have been a gift indeed.

But he wouldn't listen, not even when I told him that Roddy had saved me in January, when I'd felt so close to taking my own life. Whenever I told Dad I felt suicidal he merely laughed. I had no doubt this nugget of information fuelled his hatred for Roddy, for my beloved had spoiled all Dad's carefully laid plans for me to top myself.

As the months passed and still nothing changed, I grew desperate. From my secret-reading, I'd heard of blood sacrifices. So in April 2008, I took a razorblade from the bathroom and smuggled it into my room. Baring my large boobs – which I considered my prize asset and therefore worthy of this task – I deliberately pressed the hard metal blade to their flesh. Breathing deeply through the almost delicate pain, I slashed a series of thin red lines. *Please let me be free*, I begged as the blood bloomed beneath that blade. *Or, at the very least, please let me have some opportunity to connect with Roddy . . .*

It felt like a release: pain and prayer bound into one. And I don't know, now, if the universe answered or if I took courage from a different source, but in May I decided I would write Roddy a letter to thank him for saving my life. I'd never been brave enough to do this with anyone before: to reach out beyond the window.

But I didn't have the first clue how to start. *How do people write letters Outside? Is it like the letters I write in the cult or is it different? Will he think me freaky if I get something wrong?* Too unsure of myself to act alone, I took Josie into my confidence and she helped. Though she was not comfortable about doing it, I said I'd tell Dad in the future about it, but I didn't want Chanda to know. That, she could understand.

I wrote Roddy a poem. 'You are an angel who tarries in Brixton/ . . .Your courage and valour inspire one/ To forget Misery and challenge Despair.' I did not sign it: I did not dare, in case Roddy later made some reference to it and the Dark Lord discovered my crime.

On 29 June 2008 (it took me a long time to build up my courage), I was finally ready to send it. I planned its dispatch as a military operation. On those occasions when Dad and I went food shopping together, it was our habit to take the rubbish out at the same time. I saw an opportunity in that: while Dad took the bag over to the bins, I could loiter by the flats, next to Roddy's door, and post the letter to him covertly, fingers fumbling behind my back.

My heart was pounding as I did it. I was breaking through the window! I was speaking to a friend! I had *never* done such a thing before in my life. Those stilted conversations in the launderette didn't count: they were a bone Dad threw me and he monitored every one. Yet he knew nothing about *this*. The paper envelope felt as illicit as a drug, my act as criminal as smuggling. As it left my fingers and disappeared into the box, it marked a milestone for me.

I was stepping out of the shadows at last.

After I'd sent it, I kept looking out the window at Roddy (when I knew I wouldn't get caught). Of course he didn't acknowledge my poem because he didn't know it was from me, but as he went about his way he kept catching my eye through the window. Often, I merely gazed dreamily at him; other times, when I dared, I would cheerily wave.

Unlike with Peregrine on Black Midnight, my darling was the friendliest angel you could imagine. Roddy would eagerly smile and wave back to me. And then, just a few weeks after I'd sent the poem, on 11 July 2008, a miracle occurred.

He was standing by our gate as I was gazing out from the kitchen, looking as divine as ever, when he raised his hand and *beckoned* me to come Outside to join him!

Gosh!

Of course, I immediately and frantically shook my head. He made as though to enter through the gate to come and talk to me; urgently, I windmilled my arms. *Come through the gate? Was he mad? Dad already thought he was a fascist agent!*

As it happened, both Dad and Chanda were out shopping that day – but I was still scared Shobha might see him and report. Using hand gestures, I signalled that he should come round the other way, over the wall; with some bemusement, he followed my directions.

I felt so excited as he made his way round! A puppy on Christmas morning; if only I'd had a tail I could wag! Aisha was in the kitchen with me, but I knew she wouldn't say anything now. Josie was another matter – she was in the corridor – but I decided I would deal with her later.

I could barely believe my eyes as Roddy walked right up to the kitchen window and smiled at me. Having watched him from afar for so long, I couldn't believe he was this close. I could see the large ovals of his beautiful dark eyes and the pores on his nose. With shaking hands, I opened the window, letting both fresh air and his fragrant smell inside. I inhaled surreptitiously. He smelt of cigarettes.

'Come out,' he encouraged, a smile in his voice.

If only he knew . . . To step outside the door was impossible without permission.

'I can't,' was all I said.

I'd daydreamed about this moment so many times it was hard to believe it was actually happening. In *Harry Potter*, the boys and girls had sometimes been tongue-tied when they spoke to those they loved, and I'd imagined that I would go red and shake and be unable to meet his eye. But Roddy was the sort of person who made me feel at ease, so I was already busy talking to him before some part of me stood back and shouted internally: 'Look! *You are having a conversation!!*'

Aside from my attempts to ask for directions on 2 May, it was my first-ever one outside the cult without the Dark Lord's surveillance. I realized that, for all my fears my crush would leave me tongue-tied, it was actually far *more* awkward having a conversation when Dad was eavesdropping. Then, I always had to watch my words. Now, I could just watch Roddy. Glorious, beautiful Roddy.

The most special thing was that he had come here *just* to speak to *me*. I had never, ever had that. No child had ever called to play with me; no personal invitation had ever arrived; I had no friends who were *mine*. Though Dad was happy for the comrades to speak to the neighbours, I always had to be pushed to one side, blending in with the furniture, never the focus of attention. But Roddy, now, was looking only at me. It was exhilarating. It was hands-down the very best experience of my life.

I didn't have trouble making eye contact with him. I drank him in: his youthful skin, his full set of bright white teeth. Everyone in the Collective was old and toothless – but here was a Bright Young Thing! To be talking to somebody my own age for a change *and* to a boy and most of all to someone who was *not part of this freaky cult* was the most refreshing thing I had *ever* experienced.

'What's your name?' he asked.

'Rose,' I half-whispered, giving him the name I currently called myself in my cocoon. I refused to use Prem: whenever I heard Dad or Chanda call me that, I felt robbed of dignity. Prem was their property: Rose was free.

'Rosie, eh?' he said.

Rosie! A nickname! How I *loved* that.

'Did you get that poem?' I ventured, still speaking in a hushed tone in case Josie was snooping. I was very aware that she kept ducking her head into the kitchen from the corridor and then retreating again. I could feel disapproval emanating from her, though she did not stop us speaking.

'Yes!' he exclaimed merrily. 'I thought it might be from you because you're always smiling and waving at me.'

But *he* was the one smiling now. He grinned nonstop. *I think he's got a little bit of a crush on me!* I realized in delight. I thought of him as my boyfriend straight away because of that chemistry. So I wasn't alarmed when he suddenly said: 'Where's your bedroom?'

'It's round the other side,' I answered innocently, swooning inside. I'd read about passionate love affairs and this was straight out of a storybook! He couldn't resist me!

As I knew from my observations that Roddy already had a partner, I now cast myself in the role of the *real* love of his life. *I will be his mistress*, I decided dramatically, warming to my theme. There were plenty of literary heroines for me to model myself upon, not to mention my own mother in her illicit affair with AB.

But this afternoon was not the time to commence our ardent passion. Even as we whispered to one another by the window, I was fearful the Dark Lord Monsters might return. When I didn't make a move towards my bedroom, Roddy instead said, 'Shall we have a hug?'

He ducked under the open window – a bit awkwardly – and opened out his arms. I threw myself into them, driven by the urgency and longing that twenty-five years without love will instil in any woman's heart. As I felt the pressure of his warm, masculine arms around me, it was like no feeling I had ever had on earth. Though day in, day out, Dad still gave me his creepy cuddles, this was about as different as could be. I held on tight, as amazed by the feeling of holding him as I was at being held. I breathed in deeply and the scent of his cigarettes surrounded me: an aromatic armour to protect me from my father.

I have no idea how long that hug lasted. If it was up to me, I would still be there now, the two of us squeezed beside the window frame, bodies pressed close enough to kiss. It was a truly miraculous event: something I had long given up hope would *ever* happen to me. Wrapped in his arms, I almost lost the sense of fear I'd had that Dad might come back and discover us. I felt, with Roddy beside me, that I could take on the world. No matter what happened next, I knew I could now stand up to Dad and fight against it.

Because, for the very first time in my life, I had finally found a friend.

38

Two days later, I wrote to Roddy again to enthuse about my happiness and to fret in case I'd behaved in any way oddly, given I'd never had a solo conversation with an Outsider before.

'I hope I behaved properly with you, and was not rude or standoffish – I've been worrying about it ever since!' I confided. 'I would rather die than lose you!' I signed the letter 'Your No. 1 fan' and gave him twenty-five kisses.

Then came an agonizing wait before I could see him again. I was so scared of the Dark Lord Monsters (DLMs) finding out about our Great Love Affair that I was barely brave enough to glance out the window when Roddy wandered by. I didn't want to attract any unwanted attention. But having had a taste of what could be, there was also no way I could not connect with him again.

By the summer of 2008, I had a bedroom of my own. Although Josie and I had started out sharing when we'd first moved to this flat, she'd never been the easiest of bedfellows – I think she was as scared of intruding fascist agents as AB and in my opinion it made her neurotic. One night, she'd reared up in her sleep and grabbed me fiercely round the throat. After *that* incident, she'd said she'd sleep in the living room, so I had the bedroom to myself. I absolutely *loved* it: it was so free! And although the DLMs would frequently barge in without knocking, in the small hours of the night I was undisturbed.

It was like it was meant to be . . .

'HELLO, IT'S ROSIE!' I wrote to Roddy, in only my third letter, on 27 July 2008.

Can you come to my window after midnight on Thursday 31 July? Please turn off your mobile and don't come through the gate . . . We have to be extremely quiet!! These guys here are very ALERT!! And if we're caught – WE'RE DEAD!!!!

. . . I will be waiting for you! . . . Come to me, darling, at the time we arranged. I've got something for you!

After that, all I could do was wait.

I'd chosen that day and time especially: it was the exact same time that Hagrid in *Harry Potter* had arrived to take Harry away from the Dursleys, whisking him off to his new life as a wizard. Given Roddy was going to do the same for me – for our love was so great I knew nothing would keep us apart – it seemed more than appropriate.

I got myself ready with a tingling excitement. After washing my short, dark hair I pulled on a black velvet skirt, yanking it up above my breasts so it looked like a dress. I also donned my fishnet tights and black underwear. Daringly, I thought, I left my arms naked.

Although, in all honesty, I was mainly looking for a friend, I'd guessed from Roddy's behaviour at the window two weeks before that sex *might* be something he would want from me. I was really flattered. Dad had always said no man would ever love me because I was so ugly. Though I only knew about sex from books, if Roddy asked me to do it with him, I already knew I would be more than willing to show my friendship in that way. For he was my darling cherub and I adored him with all my heart: to gift my body to him, when he already had my soul, did not seem such a big step to take.

Carefully, I applied my make-up. I wasn't allowed proper things, so I had my own DIY version. I used a felt-tip pen to fill in my eyebrows; my foundation was made from a mix of henna and orange food colouring. I loved my make-up – with it on, I could imagine I was just like anyone else – so I was always fearful Dad would ban it. But in using the food colouring on my face, which was an ingredient in his favourite curry, I knew it would always be available to me. I needed it desperately, for my honey-coloured skin looked grey – perhaps because I went Out so infrequently and because I often felt unwell.

After I'd finished, I stood nervously at the window, staring out and waiting for my beloved. I *really* hoped I looked OK. As I didn't shop for my own clothes and had so little understanding of the norms Outside, I was terrified of making a fashion faux pas. Even in daily life, I relied heavily on Josie to help me dress. But I could hardly ask for her assistance with this.

I pondered Josie for a moment while I waited on that sticky summer night. After she'd seen me speak with Roddy at the window, I'd sensed a painful internal struggle. I used to call her Jekyll and Hyde because the two halves were always battling. I truly think she wanted me to be happy – but at the same time she did not want to disobey.

I squinted into the shadows, hoping Roddy would be careful. My greatest fear was that the DLMs would find him and kill him. Dad already threatened Roddy with murder in his nightly rants, so I knew he'd have no hesitation in striking should he find him in my room. I had told Roddy none of this, of course – I yearned for him to think me normal, for ours to be a simple love affair between boy and girl with none of the cult's nonsense to spoil it – but I had stressed that my home-life was extremely strict. I could only hope he would heed my warnings.

I waited for minute after minute – but he did not come that night. I was disappointed, but my twenty-five years in captivity had taught me nothing if not patience. 'If you can't make it before 1.30 a.m.,' I'd written in my letter, 'we can meet the next night.'

So the following evening I once again prepared myself. Once again I stood at the window at the witching hour, my eyes seeking a shadow that might morph into a man.

There he is! Athletic as a jaguar, he climbed over the gate as I'd instructed and loped towards me. Mine was a large window, almost like a door, so I opened it right out so that he could climb into my room. My heart was pounding so hard. *He is here! He is coming Inside!*

He looked and smelt gorgeous, wearing a casual T-shirt and jeans. Too keen to feel that delicious embrace again, I put my arms around him as soon as he was inside – and *he kissed me!*

Oh! What a surprising sensation!

It didn't feel anything like it looked Outside, when I'd watched people kissing from the window. My lips moved weirdly against his. It was very wet and his tongue surged forcefully into my mouth. *He must be an Alpha male*, I thought wisely, *he just goes straight for the kill.* I didn't know what to make of it all: it was a bit yucky, I thought, and all I really wanted to do was hug him, but I was willing to put up with it if this was what was required to have him as my friend.

I tried to savour all the different, new sensations. *This is so strange . . .* I could feel his heart racing beneath his T-shirt and his breath, in between his kisses, was going *huh-huh*, hot and urgent on my neck. His desire for me was overwhelming. *Dad was wrong*, I thought with a kind of wonder, *Roddy* does *like me. He* really *likes me . . .*

'I'll show you,' he suddenly said. I didn't know what he meant, but he moved further into the room and pulled the mattress off the bed, placing it on the floor. We pushed the blankets to the bottom of the mattress and I lay down beside him. I felt so excited, but terrified at the same time that one of the DLMs would hear. My heart was pounding so hard I thought the whole neighbourhood must be able to hear it.

As soon as Roddy pulled me towards him, though, the fear was held at bay. Once again I experienced that heady rush: that certainty that as long as he was with me, I could take on the world. To have a boy lying beside me in the dark was the best feeling I had ever known – and by far the best bit was imagining the looks on the faces of the DLMs if they knew what was happening!

'Feel,' he said. He took my hand and placed it on his groin.

Now, I was a very well-read young woman. I had read several Catherine Cookson novels, as well as medical encyclopaedias from cover to cover. I had seen diagrams of the human body and illustrations that taught me sexual intercourse. But in every one, there had been nothing that taught me scale. So I'd always imagined the penis to be a small, slim thing.

'Wow!' I whispered in some shock as I touched him through his trousers, thinking all the while, *That can't go inside me! It's too big!*

'Do you want me?' Roddy asked.

If I hadn't already been lying down, I think I would have fallen. It was the first time someone had *ever* asked for my consent. All my life, every decision had been made for me *without* my consent and often *against* my wishes.

'Yes, more than anything in the world,' I whispered passionately.

I was still reeling from his question. Roddy was the first person in my world who had ever treated me with genuine respect. I was humbled by it; grateful for it. For here was love and honour – not derision and abuse.

'Do you want to suck on me?' he asked.

I willingly agreed, but being faced with it was not quite so straightforward.

231

'OK, let's try something else,' he said in the end.

I kept my velvet dress on; perhaps a good thing as my scars from my blood sacrifice still showed on my breasts and I felt self-conscious. He kept his T-shirt on too, but I could still feel the touch of his beautiful arms and legs, his head and face as he leaned his body over mine, quickly slipping on a condom.

I couldn't believe this was happening. This was the first time I'd ever had a friend in my room and suddenly there was all of this! *This is what I've seen in the drawings*, I thought, almost remotely, as though I wasn't part of what came next. *This is what other people do.*

Other people . . . and now me too. It was such an incredible feeling to think that, for once, I was doing as others did. I wasn't apart, I wasn't alone and different: I was about to connect with the Outside world in the most physical, intense way anyone could. The glass was gone. In its place was me and a man and this moment.

Despite my overpowering emotions, or perhaps because of them, I still felt tense, especially when I thought of that big thing in my small place. Roddy did not know it was my first time, of course. So passionate was he that he simply ploughed straight into me without a further second's hesitation.

It was *much* more painful than I'd expected, but at the same time it was something so *new* that I was very glad to have it. That raw humanity was heady, shocking me out of my shadows, demanding a response in a way I'd never had to give before. After the controlled, sterile environment of the Collective, the heat and blood and pure lust were full of colour and life. Though in some ways it wasn't pleasant, in others it was the best thing I'd ever, *ever* experienced because it was a *normal* relationship – and it was what *I* wanted. I felt as though, for the first time, I glimpsed the fullness of experience that life could offer.

In the midst of it, I spared a gleeful thought for AB. 'You're always going to be a virgin,' he'd arrogantly told me when I was ten. I remember thinking in elation: *You are not controlling me any more, Dad, my body is MINE!*

I put my arms around my Roddy as he ploughed on. *That* was nice. Armfuls of soft, warm, fragrant boy! There was so much to take in, so many things happening all at once after a lifetime of nothing. My dreams *never* came true, my prayers were *never* answered, but here was my beloved, after more than half a year of unrequited love, in my arms at last. It was more than I had ever dared hope for.

Afterwards came the best bit. When he'd finished, he sat next to me on the mattress and I got to chuck his cheek and stroke his face. He was the cutest thing I'd ever seen. I couldn't believe my luck: all those horrible nasty old people in the Collective, and here I was with this gorgeous young thing! Every now and then, I wrapped my arms around him and hugged him. To be able to hug someone I loved at will, when I wanted, was mind-blowing. The BEST experience in my whole life, without doubt.

As we sat together, lit by the light of the moon, we held hands as we whispered to one another. I wanted to know everything about him – where he was from and his job and his family. He stayed for about half an hour and we talked like mad about all sorts of things. I felt as though the words were tumbling out of me, undammed after twenty-five years of censorship – I could have talked for days without cease. He was the first person who actually listened to me, and to whom I could tell everything!

Hesitantly, for the first time I told someone outside the cult what had happened to Sian. 'My mum committed suicide,' I said nervously, knowing the DLMs would kill me if they knew I'd told.

He was so kind and sympathetic. He patted my arm, then hugged me.

His compassion inspired me. 'You saved my life in January,' I told him. 'I was thinking about killing myself.'

He looked concerned. 'Don't think like that,' he begged me with a loving tone. 'Please don't think about killing yourself.' He gently reached out and touched my hair: 'Do not let those bad thoughts in.'

As I relaxed, I confessed to him that this had been my first time. He seemed surprised; I was twenty-five. He didn't make any comment as I recall, though, and that suited me just fine. I wanted things to be as normal as could be.

'I've got to go to work now,' he said after a while. 'I'll see you again?'

Yes please!

Ever the gentleman, he helped me to put the mattress back on the bed. We shared a final hug and kiss. It wasn't a wet kiss this time: his passion had been sated so it was a nice kiss on the lips, much more like I'd always imagined.

'I'll come back when I can,' he told me.

'Whenever you are free,' I replied devotedly. 'I'll be waiting.'

He climbed out of the window and back over the gate, and disappeared into the shadows like a secret.

39

When I woke the next morning, I was still bubbling with joy. I had never known such joy in my whole life. Nor was the experience of the night before the only source: the fact that nobody in the Collective knew what had happened made my own new knowledge just that little more delicious. I floated around on cloud nine, clever enough to conceal it from the comrades. My memories were my most precious possession – for no matter what happened next, I knew I would always have them and nobody, not even my powerful father, could take them away. Though I did not have a penny to my name, I was now rich beyond measure.

Each night, I prepared myself for Roddy's arrival and waited by the window. Though night after night went by without him visiting, I never lost faith. I knew he would come to me again, one day.

I took such strength from my new identity: *I am Roddy's mistress.* As with my learning that I was Sian's daughter, the role gave me roots that tethered me firmly to this world. *I am somebody's something. I am* not *an unperson.*

The difficulties of our being together – the fact Roddy could not come again so soon – only fuelled my love for him, for was this not what Romeo and Juliet or Beren and Lúthien had endured? What Great Love Affair was without its trials? I felt the power of Roddy's love in every cell of my body. I'd had a hint of it with Peregrine, but the immunity I now received from the Dark Lord's evil was off the scale. 'Loving [Roddy] ensures that this evil Dark Lord dungeon cannot suck the humanity out of me like it has done to the others,' I enthused in my diary. 'Thanks to my Ringdove [my nickname for Roddy] I have not lost my grip on sanity . . . Love is the greatest magic! It is the purest emotion and a talisman against evil dark sorcery!'

On 8 August, to my delight, I had a midnight visitor again. How cute my darling looked! Once more we made love and then talked and embraced. I would have been happy just to spend hours hugging him. That's all I wanted, really: a cuddle buddy.

Nevertheless, I couldn't ignore the fact that Roddy and I were soulmates. After his second visit, I was keen for our life together to begin. Why wait, now that we had found each other? I had been waiting twenty-five years already and I was impatient for Roddy to put the next stage of his passion into practice. I began to write him notes to inform him I was ready. Once again, I snuck the letters into his flat when Dad and I went Out shopping.

My lord, my life, my saviour! . . . You have proven that you love me and care about me – all that remains now is for us to live together . . . I want to get away from here . . . I want to stay with you! . . . If you ask that bitch [Roddy's partner] to go, then can I live with you? . . . I worship you, Angel!

Greatly to my surprise, he didn't immediately respond. On the contrary, when I occasionally managed to snatch a daytime conversation with him through the window, he seemed distant. No longer did he meet my eye. I waited for him every night, spending hours standing at the window and searching the shadows, but days and then weeks passed and still he did not come. *What has happened to my Ringdove?* I couldn't understand it. *Is this more of my father's black magic?*

I tried to apply what I'd read in books to our relationship. I couldn't possibly be moving too fast, for Romeo and Juliet had sworn undying love to one another just after meeting. I'd read that Marie Curie had bluntly told her lover to leave his wife, so I demanded Roddy did the same. I sent letters every Sunday. But rather than my impassioned appeals prompting a response, I sensed only a withdrawal. Roddy did not even acknowledge my notes.

August became September and I continued to be disappointed. For a whole month I had maintained my nightly vigil, but my lover had not yet re-materialized. *I know the path of true love is supposed to be rough*, I thought, *but is this just a little too much?*

Rather than putting me off, however, I became even more desperate and impassioned. I confessed to him in a letter that I was kept inside all the time, that I couldn't even step Outside without my 'armed guards' . . . but still he did not act.

I had one last hope. In early September, drawing on all my know-ledge of love and romance, I asked him to get me pregnant. I thought I might get some help from someone Outside if I had a child: some-one who could home me in a sort of halfway house and help me learn what I lacked. Plus, babies were always the crowning glory of love affairs in books. It seemed the obvious next step.

And. It. Worked. On 12 September, my heart leapt as I stood at the window. *Here he comes!*

But as he climbed inside my room he seemed different; uncom-fortable. He still wouldn't meet my eyes, nor did he make any mention of our imminent Flight to Freedom. Perturbed, I flipped the light on, wanting to see him properly, perhaps even hoping that the extra illumination would help me to understand what on earth was happening to our Great Love Affair.

'Put it off,' he said at once. I quickly obeyed.

Though he did not have the same ardour as before, he still pulled me down with him on to the mattress. We had protected sex at first and then he took the condom off. I was so glad. I was hoping a baby might be a way out, as well as a precious something to call my own. I had no clue at all about the actual responsibility of caring for a child. They never really talked about *that* in the books.

In the days after Roddy had departed, I hoped so much that it had worked. To my frustration, the medical encyclopaedias that had once proved so educational had long ago gone to our Access Self-Storage lock-up, but Dad had a book that mentioned embryos so I secret-read that, as well as the dictionary, to gen up on my potential impending motherhood.

Perhaps it was the hugeness of this possible new role that prompted what I did next, or perhaps that bubble of joy that had been simmer-ing inside me since July simply exploded, but towards the end of September I made the decision to take Josie and Aisha into my con-fidence. I think, in my excitement, I'd already let out little hints of my blossoming romance, unable to keep it to myself. I'd say enig-matically, 'I've changed down there . . .' But on 27 September I whispered: '*I got laid!*' (I'd picked up the phrase from a book.)

I didn't witness Josie's reaction; I wasn't making eye contact. Yet they both seemed all right with it, that first day, and I think Aisha especially was glad to see me happy. Despite the risks involved, I was over the moon that they finally knew I was Roddy's girlfriend. I felt centred, for once, anchored in identity.

Just a few days later, though, Josie seemed uptight. She'd had too much time to think. What would Comrade Bala say if he knew someone was coming into the house? The number-one rule was that no one must breach the defences of the Collective – and here I was *inviting* him in! Nightly, Dad ranted that Roddy was a fascist agent. In staying quiet about my midnight visitor, was Josie aiding and abetting an intruder? I could see that she was torn, Hyde shifting uncomfortably inside her. Nevertheless, it was still Josie I turned to when I started to feel sick in the morning, giddy and with sensitive breasts.

She suggested I take a pregnancy test. As Dad stood unwittingly outside the chemist, guarding our trolleys that were loaded with clean washing, she and I slipped inside and covertly picked one up in the early weeks of October.

Josie was clearly *very* uncomfortable with all these developments. I'm ashamed to say I manipulated her. 'If you tell them,' I'd threatened, 'I *will* commit suicide!'

As I'd already confided that I'd cut my breasts, she took me seriously.

She took the idea of the baby seriously too.

'If you were pregnant,' she told me, '*I* would look after the baby.'

It could have been a chilling thought. *Another Project Prem . . .?* But *I* wasn't like Sian, *I* was fiercely independent. I would make sure my baby was brought up the way I wanted . . .

Once we were home, I told Josie that I wanted to take the test alone. On 9 October, I smuggled the test into the bathroom – for so many years a sanctuary of mine – and prepared to find out my future.

Those were the longest few minutes of my life. I didn't know what was going on with Roddy and me but a baby, I knew, would give me something to live for, even if he didn't want me any more. If I had a baby, I would be able to get out into the world.

Blue line.

I frantically checked the packet.

A blue line means a baby.

Though I was barely a month gone, it was suddenly as if I could feel my child within me, such was the surge of hope I felt so deep inside. I looked down at my body – my *womanly* body – with a kind of wonder at its power, and curved my hand around the swell of my belly. For twenty-five years, I'd had no connection to the world, but never had I felt more rooted. I'd been a soldier, a daughter, a mistress, a friend . . .

Now, I was a mother.

Now everything would change.

40

I didn't tell a soul about my secret; not even my diary. I lied to Josie that the test was negative and wrote fake diary entries about how gutted I was that I wasn't pregnant; trust was still a scarce commodity in the cult and I couldn't risk someone doing some secret-reading of their own. I was so fearful Dad would insist I had an abortion if he found out too soon: I wanted my baby to have a chance to grow until it was too late for anyone to stop him or her coming. I felt a mother-bear protectiveness towards my unborn child from the very beginning.

My midnight visitor came to see me twice in October, but I did not share our happy news, although I was sorely tempted. As he'd seemed so distant of late, I did not want him to think I had somehow trapped him. Yet it was such a lovely feeling, to know we had made a child together. I badly wanted to share the secret; had he not had to rush off so soon after he'd finished, I think I might have let it slip. As it was, I planned to tell him around Christmastime, and thought we could then tell the DLMs together.

'You had visitors, didn't you, last night?' Josie hissed at me on 16 October, the night after Roddy came. To my concern, she looked stressed. 'I'm being tortured in my mind!' she said.

I could almost see Hyde battling with Jekyll, the two locked in hand-to-hand combat. She hated betraying Bala, as she saw it, by not telling him about my friend.

'Let it go,' I urged her. Day after day, I kept talking to her, trying to butter her up and calm her down. 'I'm happy at last,' I whispered to her, keeping my voice low for fear the DLMs might be listening. 'This will be all right. I *promise* I will tell Bala soon. I just don't want Chanda to know . . .'

She wrung her hands together anxiously, but nodded. 'Yes, I

shouldn't fret too much,' she said in a tight voice. 'You know what you're doing.'

I only hoped I had done enough.

In the early hours of 4 November 2008, I turned away from my window with my customary sigh of regret. No Ringdove had fluttered his way to me tonight. I closed the window and drew the curtain across before crawling back into my lonely bed.

Rat-a-tat-tat!

My Ringdove was knocking on the window . . . *The DLMs might hear!* Made nervous by his knocking, I frantically kicked off my blankets and rushed to greet my beloved. In warning, I pressed a finger to my lips as I opened the window wide.

I shivered a little in the autumn air: I was wearing only a black bra and knickers and the hot nights of summer were a distant memory. Roddy had not yet started climbing in when his mobile phone burst into life. The sound cut through the night like a knife.

'Oh no!' I exclaimed.

Roddy silenced his mobile swiftly and continued to make his way inside – but it was too late. The instant I'd cried out, as though she'd been lurking outside my room waiting for a chance to interrupt us, Josie burst into my bedroom. She said, later, that she thought I was crying out for help, but I think some time in the past two weeks, she'd felt the need to expose us.

Because, although I hissed at her, 'It's all right! Go away!' she coolly opened her mouth and screamed: 'AB! AB!'

First a light flicked on in the hallway, and then Roddy and I were bathed in brightness as my bedroom light burst on. Into the glare of that terrible blaze of light, the Dark Lord and Lady came running, Chanda in her nightdress and Dad in his white robe with royal-blue stripes. Aisha trailed in after them, the whole household startled awake by Josie's treacherous cry.

'Go!' I urged Roddy. I was terrified about what they might do to him.

He didn't need telling twice. All Dad saw was the beautiful curve of his back as Roddy vaulted out of the window and ran.

I desperately tried to go after him. I flung myself at the window and tried to heave myself Out. Roddy had always made it look easy, but as I was not allowed to be physically active – had *never* been physically active – it was impossible for me. Nor was I given a clear run at it: the moment she saw I was trying to escape, Josie was quickly at my side, grabbing my arm and pulling me back. I tried to shake her off but she clung like a limpet, with all the strength of Gollum when he's driven by the Ring. Though I tried to muster my strength to make another attempt to climb out, by the time I did Bala was there too, pulling me with violent force.

The two of them hauled me back into the bedroom and the window was slammed shut.

No way out.

The room was full of consternation and shock. I was shocked too – by the expression on Dad's face. He was pale and *scared*. Given the intensity of the moment, it was only a fleeting thought, but I briefly wondered: *if he has the powers he says he's got, why does he need to be white and scared?*

Both he and Chanda were behaving as if Roddy was a burglar and were threatening to call the police. (They had no problem calling the police on other people; they just never wanted the fascist dogs to turn their investigatory powers on *them*.) I *had* to stand up for my lover. So I shouted passionately: 'That's not a burglar! He's my boyfriend! I love him!'

They rolled their eyes and laughed derisively. 'Your boyfriend? *You* can't be having a boyfriend. Stop making up stories.'

But I kept on saying it. Bala slapped me hard in the face.

'If you carry on like this,' Chanda roared at me, 'you'll get taken to the mental hospital!'

'Retard!' Dad shouted. 'You're a fantasist! You're mad!'

They were soon fixated on the idea of Roddy being a fascist agent. Chanda was glaring at me with her basilisk eyes, her hatred and disgust seemingly unmasked. *Now I see the true you, the you I always knew was there*, those eyes seemed to say. *You: finally caught in cahoots with the fascist state.*

'You ran away on the second of May and talked to the police,' she hissed at me, 'and now they have sent their police agent for you.' She accused me of being a mole, passing information about the Collective to this agent who had infiltrated us; of hiring a hitman to kill AB.

It was ridiculous!

'No, I'm not doing that!' I protested. *'We don't talk about you at all!'*

That was perhaps the most galling thing: that they made it all about them, when my love affair with Roddy was precious precisely because it was *nothing* to do with them.

'You're just fantasizing,' Dad scoffed again. 'You're just imagining that because you like him, he likes you and you have created this fictional relationship.'

I lifted my head defiantly. Had the circumstances not been so grave, I might have relished what I was about to say, but instead I just remember feeling desperate, trying to make him believe me so he would not call the police on my beloved.

'It is *not* a fantasy,' I declared. 'We have had a physical relationship.'

Dad looked as though I had struck him. For the first time, he seemed to take in my appearance: my curves wrapped in black underwear as if I was a gift. But I was telling him I had given myself to someone *other than him*. He looked betrayed. His reaction was not like a father with his daughter: more like a husband with his wife.

'*What?*' he said. 'But you're *mine!*'

He didn't want to believe it. So I told him how our affair had begun, describing how I'd sent Roddy those secret letters on our trips to the shops. I *had* to tell him, because he would not believe me otherwise – and the more I told him, the more I could see that the truth was slowly sinking in.

He started muttering, words like 'adultery' and 'unfaithful' slipping out in a shower of spit. He was enraged. I had *always* been his complete property – *he* decided what was done with me. I could do nothing without his permission, especially not have a relationship, even with the comrades – but now his property had been defiled by another man.

'You're spoiled goods!' he roared at last. 'Prostitute! Whore! Get yourself covered up. How *ugly* you look.'

It was humiliating, standing there in my bra and knickers, but it was more humiliating to have been caged the way I had for twenty-five years, so I did not move to cover myself. In fact, I tore off my bra to show him the scars on my breasts.

'Look!' I shouted angrily. 'I've been slashing my boobs because I feel so desperate at being stuck here in this place!'

He refused to look at me or to acknowledge my confession. 'You're just playing with it,' he retorted heartlessly. 'Like Amy Winehouse. You're just like one of those silly Western women who make an indulgence about feeling depressed and suicidal when actually there is nothing there and you're just doing it for attention.'

He started muttering again about my relationship with Roddy as I pulled my bra back on and got dressed. 'Imagine if you had a child with him!' he spluttered, as though that would be the worst thing in the world.

I felt my secret inside me, snug and safe. *You are wrong*, I thought. *It is the* best *thing in the world. Because now I've got somebody of my own and I don't have to put up with* you.

'I'm going to call the police!' the Dark Lord threatened again. 'I'm going to get them to arrest this agent for burglary *and* rape!' In his mind, the crimes were equal, for in sleeping with me had not Roddy stolen something from him?

'I'm over the age of consent!' I reminded him tartly. 'They're not going to ask the parents, they will ask me! And I *wanted* him!'

The Dark Lord opened and closed his mouth like a fish, before beginning on another rant. He realized he couldn't claim rape, after all, but still he threatened to report Roddy for theft. I was so frightened of that, because even though it wasn't true I knew that Dad excelled at lying. What would happen then to my Roddy, wrongfully arrested, who was so noble in spirit he would probably fight back? I had visions of JACKIE ensuring that Roddy would die in custody so I would never see him again . . .

The Dark Lord glowered at me. Never had he looked more menacing. 'I want to burn you where you stand!' he told me.

I only wanted to protect Roddy. If I could take the flak from him, then even if I died it would be for a noble cause. I faced up to my father. 'Well, burn me then!' I shouted back.

His face went black with rage and he thrust it into mine, howling wildly in fury . . .

. . . but, despite his intense anger, no lightning bolt came from the sky to turn my skin to black.

Abruptly, I felt a tiny flicker of something, as though a distant radio signal had connected with my brain. My synapses snapped to attention: a light switched on. It was a little like when my mother had gone mad, and her signals too had come in and out of range. Because as Dad stood there impotently, threatening to burn me *but not doing it*, I thought: *You* can't *do it. That's why you don't do it, it's because you can't . . .*

The light snapped off; the radio signal went out of range.

'Don't try me!' Dad said. I was supposed to be grateful for his mercy, but instead I wanted to spit on him.

All my life, up to now, I had been torn between love and hate for my father, but the way he was raging against Roddy and desecrating our love was too much. *I will be a coward no more*, I thought. I drew myself up to my full height, which meant I was a touch taller than the Dark Lord. I pictured my Ringdove, urging me on, riding with me into battle. He gave me courage. So I shouted at the top of my lungs: '*I HATE YOU!*'

It was the first time I'd dared to say to his face that I didn't like *him*; the first time, that is, since I was two years old.

In response, he started flailing at me. I don't think he did it deliberately – I think he was so enraged he was hitting out at any target and did not direct his fists – but in a punch that left me reeling, he belted me violently in my tummy. I doubled over in pain.

As he hit me, Chanda went on the verbal attack too: 'You're so bloody pampered,' she hissed to me: for daring to speak my true feelings; for daring to want a partner as she herself had.

I was done with holding back. 'You are jealous of me because you hated my mum!' I spat at her, my voice a bit shaky but resolute nonetheless.

I think I'd struck a nerve because she went quiet and seemed to go red in the face. Never before had I dared acknowledge it: *I think you hate me because I'm the evidence your husband fucked someone else behind your back.* She could put me down all she liked, but I was done with being a beetle she wanted to crush beneath her feet. I hadn't asked to be born. It wasn't *my* fault.

I think Dad was still too shocked to retaliate immediately for what I'd said to Chanda. Instead, he continued to insult me and threaten Roddy.

'I will torture you both to death!' the Dark Lord shouted with sadistic glee. 'I am going to curse him till he's dead!'

I begged Dad on my knees to spare him, howling: 'I'll die if you harm him! If you want revenge, kill *me*, but leave him alone! *Please!*'

It was the longest night of my life. The Dark Lord kept shouting and cursing until around 5 a.m. I remember my mouth being so dry I couldn't even beg for mercy in the end. It was my worst nightmare come to life: Roddy discovered, the Dark Lord on the warpath, and all that stood between my Ringdove and destruction was whatever words I could muster. As AB threatened torture and execution, I became hysterical. After his beatings and his blow to my belly, I felt horribly sick. Fearing I might vomit, I rushed to the toilet and shut myself inside. I needed to calm down. I needed just a few minutes' peace on my own.

When I returned to my bedroom, I saw them fiddling at the window. They had a shifty demeanour, and my stomach flipped with fear, but I had more important things to concentrate upon right then.

Because I wanted to strike a deal with the devil: my obedience for my lover's life.

To my immense relief, the Dark Lord agreed to my terms. He would not go to the police or kill Roddy as long as I agreed to stay away from him for months. I had to meet three guidelines: 1) Don't meet up with him. 2) Don't communicate with him. 3) Don't talk about him.

'If you care about Roddy,' Dad threatened, 'don't go anywhere near him. Don't try to escape, and don't try to report, or I will tell the police about Roddy.'

He had me. Never before had I felt so stuck. If he'd said he'd harm *me*, I would have given my life gladly in my lover's defence, but I could not allow my darling to be hurt. I would do anything to protect Roddy.

Perhaps the most painful thing was knowing that I wouldn't be able to explain all this to my lover. What would he think of me? Would he believe I had willingly given him up? I would be unable to send a single sign of my continuing affection, for that would put him in mortal peril.

'How long must I do this for?' I asked bleakly. I knew what it was like to endure a prison sentence without an end date, and I knew I *had* to have one for this punishment. Dad tried to wriggle out of setting one at first but I kept at him and at last he agreed to make the deadline Valentine's Day. Then, he said, I could contact Roddy again – assuming I had held up my side of the bargain.

It was the best I was going to get. I felt proud of myself for saving my lover.

After all our negotiations, my mouth was dry as dust. While the others waited in my bedroom, I went to the kitchen to get a drink of water. Something was niggling in the back of my brain – something about their shifty behaviour when I'd seen them at my window. With a creeping sense of horror, I approached the back door. The lock, which had always previously held the key, was empty.

The key had gone.

I went to the cutlery drawer, where we kept all the keys: windows, back door, front door. *The entire set was missing.* Though I searched the flat high and low, that night and in the days that followed, no door or window key could I find.

I felt my stomach fall as I stood in the kitchen on that night of horror. I felt stupid: *Why didn't I run before, when I had the chance . . .?* I had never thought they would sink to such depths. Because it was one thing to be tied by invisible chains, but now I truly was a prisoner: locked in my cage with no recourse to freedom.

How am I ever going to get out of here now?

41

Something snapped in me that dark night in November. For the Collective to banish Roddy, the only sunshine in my life, and lock me up was more than I could endure. There is only so much misery a person can take and I felt full to the top. Both my cocoons, inner and outer, abruptly shattered.

Oddly, the moment I realized they had physically imprisoned me, locking all the doors and windows, something strange happened. My heart and soul felt *freer* than before, as though I'd been tethered to these people, but in slamming shut my escape routes they themselves had cut the ties that bound me to them.

In banishing Roddy my father had crossed a red line, from which he could never retreat. That was when I gave up on him. No longer was I going to try to work with him, to negotiate or make the best of a bad situation. Though I would abide by the terms of our agreement to save Roddy, on all other counts it was all-out war.

'He thought destroying my relationship will bring me closer to him – not on your life!' I wrote heatedly in my diary. 'I will never ever think well of you again [Father], and from today I DISOWN YOU!'

Predictably, in the days after Roddy's banishment the Dark Lord soon set about rewriting history. He claimed JACKIE had been testing me and would have executed me that November night had he not intervened. Yet even the threat of JACKIE lost its sting in my cold new world. 'He can kill me if he likes,' I wrote defiantly, 'but he'll never break my spirit.'

The Dark Lord soon warmed to his theme, positing himself as my protector, and my lover as a villain, describing my physical captivity as being in my 'best interests' and ordering me to be 'grateful'. Instead of being cowed or accepting, I silently jeered at him.

'I could excuse all this as being the early onset of senile dementia,'

I wrote, 'if I didn't know it was something a lot more sinister. Threatening to murder your daughter's boyfriend is not the sign of a sane man . . . He threatens and intimidates me nonstop, trying to frighten me with death about a hundred times a day – the dying gasps of a bankrupt old loser who can't accept he is finished.'

But while I was not taken in by him, to my great distress the comrades were. Those fragile friendships had vanished the moment Josie opened her mouth and screamed for AB, and I suddenly found myself living in a nest of vipers. Aisha took Bala's side, seemingly seduced by his portrait of himself as my saviour, while Josie seemed to revert 100 per cent to what I called her Hyde, her blue eyes illuminated by what felt like a bullying light I hadn't seen in a long time.

When Bala realized the women had known of my assignations with Roddy, his temper knew no bounds. He kept threatening that when it became Overt he would go back to India and leave them behind. Nothing terrified them more than the thought of being without him, so they threw themselves into punishing me with gusto.

While I despised them for it, in other ways I rationalized their response. I used to think of it as similar to that torture method where persecutors place an upturned receptacle over a victim's stomach with a rat underneath. They then apply heat to the receptacle and the rat, desperate to save itself, burrows into the victim's stomach and tears them apart. That's what it felt like the women did to me.

It made me very ill. Several times a day, I suffered vomiting and diarrhoea, my stomach churned by fear and betrayal. I used to hear Josie and Bala whispering about me, deciding how best to bully and control me, and when I heard them hissing like demented snakes, my stomach would dissolve and I often soiled myself. Sometimes I was so scared that I even passed out. In the months after Roddy's banishment, I lost two stone, unable to keep down my food. I was also plagued by crippling headaches and mouth ulcers.

Cast adrift from my cocoon, on a daily basis I veered wildly between abject misery, hysterical laughter, gut wrenching fear and an overwhelming, murderous rage.

There's no expressing the intolerable anger I feel. I just wish I could dash his brains out – disembowel him with a red-hot poker – tear his heart out – bathe in his putrid liquid shit that poses for blood – tear out his entrails and feed his stinking remains to the worms . . . When he has the nerve to add insult to injury by so shamelessly praising his own crimes, I just wish I could grab that smug bit of filth by the throat and squeeze until he is dead dead DEAD.

But, to my eternal dismay, it wasn't Bala for whom Death came calling that autumn. About two weeks after the Dark Lord punched me in my stomach I started bleeding down below.

I knew the baby had died: I had miscarried. The sight of that blood gave me the worst feeling – because it wasn't just my baby I was losing. *Everything* had now been lost.

I began to review things – all the way back to my childhood. The baby and Roddy were just the latest in a long line of things I'd loved that had been taken away from me: what about my yellow blanket and Maria Franklin, the Lego doll? The Dark Lord had always banished anything that made me happy.

The realization made me all the more determined to cling to my feelings for Roddy. Bereft of allies – I had essentially been put in solitary confinement, for my crime was such that no one would speak to me – I quickly recognized that Roddy was now my only living friend. As I put it in a poem: 'The only person I have got/ Who doesn't wish I'm what I'm not.'

The Dark Lord's ultimate weapon of injury was to keep telling me that Roddy did not love me, but by now I had stopped listening. He could talk all he wanted, but he could not erase my memories. And when I remembered Roddy's beautiful face and his words to me on the first night we lay together as lovers, I felt my strength returning to me. As long as I loved him, I could retain my dignity, no matter what they did to me.

I soon began writing my Ringdove letters in my notebook, many times a day: letters I would never send, but without which I could not have survived my ordeal.

'They hope to kill me with misery, but they're not going to get their way,' I told him.

Thoughts of Roddy made life much more bearable, but they could not save me completely. The thing I found most difficult in the wake of that November night was living alongside my former friends. When those you have confided in and trusted turn round and betray you, it is a betrayal like no other. Yet I knew I shouldn't have been surprised by their behaviour. All my life, this had always been the way. The shock, really, was that it hadn't happened sooner. In an instant, the years had been rolled away, and it was back to the bad old days of my youth: the pack of vultures picking greedily at my flesh.

But while their actions were familiar to me, especially after seeing what had happened to Leanne, and Sian, and Oh, I was no longer a scared five-year-old girl who wet herself to see the puppets pulled into action.

'These [people] are so simplistic,' I wrote to Roddy. 'They think that just by chaining us up and keeping us apart, they can subdue us to their will. But no one can chain the mind, not unless the individuals themselves allow it to happen!'

And therein lay the crux of the cult. Amidst my anger, hatred and hurt, around this time I also felt another emotion for the comrades – perhaps for the first time. I felt *pity*, pity that they could not free their minds from the Dark Lord's control. They were doomed for ever to be worm-eating, slavering, squelching beasts – and who would ever wish to be like that? While Aisha and Josie appeared to have so many freedoms I did not – permission to go Out without AB, and possession of the house keys that jangled in their pockets – I knew that I was actually much, much freer because my mind was not chained to him.

Ever since 2 May, Bala had been fond of castigating me for my lack of education – the lack of education that he himself had brought about. He used to tell me how much more worthy and clever everyone else in the cult was than me, with their university educations, and say, 'If *they* choose to follow me, how can an insignificant idiot like you dare to challenge me?' But now I had broken from him once and for all, I found those university educations infuriating, because it wasn't as though the comrades couldn't read and write: they had had brains, once, before he'd scrubbed them clean. Unlike me, who had been born into this, they had *chosen* this mindless existence. I felt contemptuous of that, that they would swallow his nonsense. If I, who didn't even go to school, could see he was a lunatic peddling falsehoods, why couldn't they?

Over the years, my secret-reading and my natural rebellion had made me despise obeying authority without question. If you were an adult, you should think for yourself: that was what I thought. And never had it rung more true. Before, I'd wanted Bala to give me freedom. Now, I was determined to find out how to get free on my own – or die trying.

42

As though I was myself a spy who had infiltrated the Collective, for the next few months I tried to do everything right. Always, the guillotine hung over my neck: if I broke the rules, if I ran for help, Roddy would suffer – whether at JACKIE or AB's hands, or in a cell at the police station, was irrelevant. So although living in Mordor, imprisoned in the Dark Tower with the Dark Lord, was no mean feat, I considered it a price worth paying to save my beloved. If I was to win my freedom, and his, I had to play the long game.

Valentine's Day, AB had said. It was a line in the sand I strove towards, battling for survival. Though I knew AB to be cunning and treacherous, I hoped he would keep his word.

I was clutching at straws. When February 2009 arrived, he told me my request was denied, but I could see Roddy at the end of March if I 'behaved'.

'What is required of me?' I demanded.

'I don't know,' he said mysteriously, dismissing me from his presence.

I tried my best – washing up, helping the comrades cook, doing the housework. With no guidelines to follow beyond the three already laid down, I had to interpret his further directives as best I could. Yet when he saw that I had tried my hardest to carry out his enigmatic instructions, the Dark Lord became fond of changing the rules at the last minute. It was a malicious mind game. Every month my heart would soar at the thought my torture may soon be over, the threat to Roddy's life lifted at last by my dedicated penance, but every month my jailer would deny me. It was a painful pattern, made crueller with every repetition. Yet I found that I could not help but repeat it, over and over again.

The mental torture was interspersed with violent physical attacks. Christmas Day 2008 had been the worst. Josie had reported me for looking out the window at Roddy, which I hadn't done – I'd simply pulled back the net curtain for more light while I'd stuffed a chicken for roasting, and Roddy had innocently walked past about a half-hour later – but AB listened only to Josie.

'Don't you violate my authority!' he had shouted, before smashing both sides of my head in, so hard that I had ringing in my ears for days afterwards; my right ear was never the same again. I was hysterical about it: panicked in case Roddy was about to be killed; terrified because I was trying to do everything right and it *still* wasn't enough. I could never enjoy Christmas again after that incident because it always reminded me of his attack. Another time, in July 2009, when I stood up to him and told him Roddy was worth a hundred of him, he hit my head so violently that I felt something snap.

'I'm just waiting to attend your funeral,' he would say, 'and maybe I won't even go!'

The only changes I experienced were for the worse. Though I was still permitted to go to the launderette – the only time I was not kept under lock and key – my bodyguard detail was tighter than ever, my chance to post letters cut off.

With all the windows locked, even small graces I'd previously enjoyed, such as throwing bread to the birds while I stood indoors, were prohibited. And this was when it was confirmed to me that AB had only ever done what was necessary to keep me *just* happy enough. I was permitted no birthday treats at all, not even cake; trips to central London had long since ceased. Now I was 'spoiled goods', I was to receive no rewards at all.

'I'm swimming against the current and it's pulling me under,' I wrote dismally in the spring of 2009. Remembering my successful blood sacrifice the year before, I once again sliced at my breasts with a razor in the hope that *something* might change but, this time, nothing did. 'I fear that . . . nothing but death can release me from this evil hellhole,' I wrote to Roddy in my notebook.

I was so low, I think I would have killed myself, but for three things. The first was my memory of Roddy reaching out his hand to touch my hair gently when I'd told him of my suicidal feelings. 'Do not let those bad thoughts in,' he had said. I held on to those words like a life raft.

The second was that I couldn't die because I couldn't let Roddy think that I had willingly abandoned him. I had to live, painful as it was, until I got a chance to tell him that my love was as strong as it had always been.

The third was my saving grace: the only way I survived. The pen was mightier than the razorblade, it seemed, and through increasingly impassioned poems and short stories I wrote my way out of the depths of my despair. My writings had been important to me before, but now they were my only loyal companions through the very darkest days of my life. If I hadn't been able to express myself on paper, I think I would have blown up. It is not an exaggeration to say it kept me alive; I called it my 'miracle medicine'. I wrote allegorical stories about my captivity, recasting my situation within a fantasy world where the demons could be defeated. I wrote Harry Potter fan fiction where Voldemort was made good through kindness. It was so empowering to write these things because, for once, *I* was in control. I could fight back in a way I couldn't in real life. I could be victorious, even if I always really lost.

Sometimes, I simply wrote in my diary, as I did one day when the Dark Lord had said in Vampire Puking: 'Think what life would've been like without me and the Collective!'

I had not to think a second before my answer came in my head – I'd have been free. I'd have a family and a career. I'd have gone to school and had friends my own age. I wouldn't have to spend my life in a stifling prison with horrible people who bully me. I wouldn't have endless nightmares. I wouldn't have been separated from my lover. I'd be a mother, I may even be a bestselling writer. I wouldn't look old and worn out as I do. I wouldn't have to spend burning hot days locked up in the house with no interesting people to talk to. I wouldn't be so dead bored. I could come and go as I please, make lots of friends, enjoy life to the full, not always be frightened of being bullied and deprived of any little freedom, not be crushed and picked on so much that I feel so mortified and self-conscious. I wouldn't be so angry and so tense. I'd be able to laugh a lot more. I wouldn't have to put up with a silly old madman puking down my throat every day, threatening me with death. Life would be so much more pleasant and so much more agreeable – I could go Out in the evenings, enjoy the fresh air . . .

I could have written that response for ever and ever . . .

By the summer of 2009, I was desperately lonely. Spending so many hours inside, I'd become aware of all the sounds of the flat and one in particular intrigued me: the scrabbling of the mice and rats beneath the floorboards. *I have no one else to talk to*, I thought, *why not them?*

I began tempting them out with scraps of food. I used to go to the kitchen late at night and get a bit of biscuit and put it out for the rodents. Then I'd retreat to a safe place and wait.

After a while, they would come. It started out as mice, but the rats soon took over. They would only come if it was pin-drop silent, but silence, as a shadow-woman, was my speciality. Up they would come, black eyes shining, noses twitching and brown fur gleaming under the kitchen lights. I used to yearn to pet them, to touch another living creature after so long alone.

The rats became my friends. I went to see them as often as I could. One night, Bala came in and ordered me out; I think he'd assumed I was in there because I wanted to look out the kitchen window at Roddy.

He didn't realize that, by now, I had set my sights much lower. I knew I wasn't allowed a human friend.

All that was left to me were the rats.

That same summer, there happened to be an irruption of Painted Lady butterflies. Hundreds of them fluttered past, as brightly coloured as the Outside world itself. I tried to take their appearance as a good omen: that one day I too would get free and fly away as easily as they.

And, when I did, I was by now determined to take down the Dark Lord. Months – years – *decades* of his abuse had seen to that. AB had, in the end, transformed me into a soldier, but I was joining the opposing side to him. Though I detested war, I was now prepared to fight.

'I'm not going to just fade away like my mother and let him get away with what he's been doing,' I wrote. 'There is nobody else who can stop him – something has got to be done!'

That same summer was also the twentieth anniversary of Tiananmen Square. The Dark Lord was in his element, saying he wished a *million* people had been massacred instead. It was outrageous – and all the darker to me because of the coming Overt.

'I'm going to report him,' I wrote. '. . . It shows that these crooks are dangerous criminals . . . I must tell someone before he does some mad cultist thing like some of those idiots you hear about on the news do – but . . . I have to make sure that my lover is safe [in case] this psychopath and his slaves . . . attack him to take revenge on me for being a traitor.'

I took pride in being a traitor: it was perhaps my finest role.

'I'm going to be the one to stop them,' I wrote. 'I'm *not* going to allow this Dark Lord to rise!'

43

In the late summer of 2009, I lay on my bed for our afternoon nap, beads of sweat breaking out on my forehead. The summer months had proved absolutely sweltering. We'd had weeks of glorious weather, but even when it had been 34 degrees Outside, AB had insisted that the double-glazed windows stayed closed and locked. It made for a death trap of heat.

How I longed for grey clouds and rainy days. All this nice weather merely tormented me, for I could not enjoy it, chained up in my dungeon as I was. It was so hot, so oppressive, so bloody claustrophobic.

I closed my eyes.

What do I imagine?

I see myself out there. The evening is cool and pleasant. The pink-tinged clouds, the soft blue sky. The trees with their budding leaves, whispering in the breeze.

I hoped desperately that if I just imagined it hard enough, all the walls would disappear and I'd suddenly be there in the park.

But even with my well-practised imagination, I could not manage it. The sheer sweltering heat kept me firmly anchored to the nasty, dystopian reality I was living. Even the most comforting cocoon could not possibly protect me from that horrible heat. Try as I might, I couldn't help but be constantly reminded of my plight.

For decades, I had tried really hard not to think about how things were. I'd done everything in my power to avoid it: inventing friends from toilets and dictators; losing myself in my imagination. But I could no longer retreat into the comfort of my own head. Even the sedative effect of poetry was useless against this scorching wall of heat.

Unable to escape it, I found myself unable to do anything but *think*.

By now, we were months and months beyond that original Valentine's Day deadline I had once been promised. In the heat of that boiling room, reality came down to one clear insight: *Bala has been stringing me along. He has no intention of ever letting me see Roddy again, of ever letting me be free. It was just a way of shutting me up.*

Another bead of sweat bloomed on my forehead. It was as though each one contained a new idea. *How could I have fallen for that?* I thought. *I've been so gullible! Why did I never see that before?*

Lying on my bed, sweating in the heat, I cast my mind even further back. I started reviewing one thing after another. I started questioning.

The old Dark Lord Monster keeps saying he is 'going' – he's been saying it for years now, but I'm still stuck here.

He said it would be Overt for the 1996 Olympics; for the 1997 handover of Hong Kong; he promised me that just three months after 2 May my Endurance Test would be over . . . but I'm still stuck here.

The Overt is coming. The Overt never comes.

Valentine's Day was coming. But Valentine's Day never comes . . .

He is stringing me along.

I felt those unsettling rumblings again, the rumblings in the very bedrock of my brain that I'd dismissed after the tsunami in 2004. This time, I didn't do that. I opened up my mind and let the tremors take me. I lay in that scorching room and let myself be burned by the truth. In a way, it was as much of a lightning bolt as AB had always threatened – but *I* was the one with the power.

This is all a big fraud.

He's not going to rule the world. He's got no authority, covert or otherwise. He's just a nasty psychopath trying to control people with all these curses and lies.

I have absolutely no faith in him and his mad ideas any more.

All this had been building for a while; in real life, you don't just get hit on the head with a hammer so that all your old ideas fall out. Each new discovery of mine had, over the years, added a thin layer of understanding, as in sedimentary rock. Now, it all seemed as obvious as evolution.

He tells me I'm a fantasist – when it was him all along: he is the wild fantasist! Every day he indulges in ridiculous unrealities: megalomaniac fantasies about how he rules the world! How stupid! He can't even rule himself properly – can't even control his own madness!

If the Dark Lord was truly the perfect character he makes himself out to be, what is the need for his endless bragging and insulting and threatening?

Good people have no need of that. They know what they are. They don't need to force others to worship them by intimidation. That alone shows the total quackery and fraudulence of the Dark Lord's boasts and assertions. He is impotent and desperate – a clear failure in everything – so he uses empty threats to frighten the weak, the silly, the feeble-minded.

But I have risen above that now.

I cast my mind over everything I knew of AB's life: his 'heroic struggles' against the 'fascist state'; his pride in his prison sentence. Bala was basically a third-rate thug, I realized. It was all very well to go to prison to stand up for your beliefs, but violent assault was an entirely different matter.

He spent *all* his time idling – he did nothing but read papers and watch TV all day and imagine, imagine . . . His 'preparation' for the new world was preposterous. He didn't even do any practical work – the cooking, cleaning, and so on. The house-elves took care of all that. It left him with so much excess energy that he wasted his time demonizing other people and pontificating about how he would do this and do that when he became lord of the universe.

He's lost his marbles! I thought. Long ago I'd thought him mad – but psychopath, he'll-kill-you-soon-as-look-at-you mad, not certifiable, he-is-completely-off-his-rocker mad.

The only authority he had was within the Collective. *That* was why he was such a tyrant to us – because it was the sole sphere of his domain. He loved to throw tantrums about his food just because he could; every day I still took in his trays of food to him and nine times out of ten he would throw a wobbly. I saw now he did so simply to assert his bankrupt 'authority'.

The same went for the rule about the comrades only ever going out in pairs. It wasn't for safety, to preclude an attack from the fascist state, as he'd always said; the fascist state didn't give two hoots about him and the Collective. I realized it was just another form of control – so that each comrade could spy on the other and make sure neither spoke to Outsiders. It was no accident, I realized now, that the only people I'd ever seen successfully leave the Collective – Cindy and Leanne – were also the only people who had ever been permitted to leave the house alone.

If I'd felt gullible for believing him about Valentine's Day, it was as nothing to my rage at myself as I now appreciated how thoroughly

I'd been duped *for my entire fucking life*. Why hadn't I trusted my gut instinct? I was furious with myself for not trusting my intuition and getting out before I was trapped. 'It takes a child to see the king is naked' I had written to him years ago – and yet I'd still been blind. I felt embarrassed and ashamed.

I had already disowned him and declared my hatred to his face, but I now began to despise him with a new passion. To this day he was defending his actions by saying he was 'protecting' me, but there was literally *nothing* to protect me from. The danger had *never* been Outside – the danger had only ever been him! It was a slow inversion of everything I'd been told, yet I didn't feel on shifting sands: the world felt *more* stable, for it was the Collective that was the madhouse. If I ever got Out, I now knew I could join a sane society – and a society that would *never* be ruled by my captor, as I had once feared.

But *would* I ever get Out? With a sinking feeling, I grasped the dark flipside of seeing the light. For as liberating as it was to see through AB at last, I now realized I was more of a prisoner than ever – for if Overt was never coming, then *neither would I* ever *be set free*. For nearly twenty-seven years, AB had kept me captive by dangling the 'carrot' of the coming Overt before me. But, now, I knew that I would never get that chance to step out of the shadows.

I am almost certainly the eternal prisoner of a madman. He is a total liar and psychopath, and he will never rule the world – except in his own head and in the heads of those brainwashed by him.

If I do not get free, I will die here.

I was stunned by the bleakness of my future. And it wasn't just him keeping me captive. Though they were just as much his victims, the comrades were tied up in this too. I felt disgusted with those around him for having believed and propagated his lies to me. They should have known better. Yet I could also see just how much they were under his thumb.

In his deluded fantasies, he was the covert leader – and that was how he justified his abuse. He had to resort to terrors and intimidation to keep people in line, just like Sauron and Voldemort. Though I could see, now, that it was bluff – a bankrupt, lunatic tyrant trying to terrorize and blackmail others into letting him have his way – I knew from my own experience how convincing he could be.

I think it was at this point that another bead of sweat shone brightly in the sunshine that was blazing through the window. *JACKIE, JACKIE . . . Who the fuck is this JACKIE?*

Just a mythical bogeyman created by the Dark Lord to scare the ignorant: 'Do as I say or this supernatural fuck will get you.'

Though I'd had an inkling of it before, I now comprehended that every world event AB had ever used to intimidate us – the tsunami, Diana's death, right the way back to the Challenger space shuttle – was just another aspect of his twisted control. Synchronizations were merely claimed coincidences: nothing more . . .

. . . *Or were they?* I'll be honest: JACKIE was the very hardest chain to break. For although my rational mind did not believe AB could *really* do black magic, I could not absolutely *disprove* it. In the back of my head, even though most of me knew it was rubbish, there was still a tiny nagging voice which said, 'What if you are wrong?' Ninety-nine times out of a hundred, I was sure there was no such thing – but nevertheless there was, sometimes, a shred of doubt.

I wasn't the first in the world to feel that way; to be trapped in the mythology of my childhood even after I had grown. Perhaps lapsed Catholics who still suffer their guilt do so for that exact same reason. Though you don't *really* believe, *something* still taps you on your shoulder, sending a shiver down your spine . . .

Trapped in that sweltering bedroom, it felt as if everything in my life had reached a dead end. There was no way out: the cult was a trap slowly closing around me. I was in a cage with ever-shrinking walls. But once I saw the light, I couldn't unsee it. Once I saw that it was all rubbish, there was no way I could go back to believing it any more. No longer could I kid myself with a cocoon. Nothing filled my mind but my bleak new reality.

I am stuck in a living horror story here. What on earth do I DO?

I didn't know the answer to that question – yet – but I wanted to mark my graduation into flagrant disbelief. So, that year, I wrote out the ugly disgusting swear word that the Dark Lord used to insult me every day: my birth name, Comrade Prem Maopinduzi. Then on my knees, and with God as my witness, I spat upon those evil words, tore them up, scrunched them into a ball, threw them into the toilet, urinated on them and then flushed them away into the sewer.

'Thus God knows,' I wrote in my diary, 'I make a total, total complete break with the evil Dark Lord Monster . . . That Commie cadre, Comrade Prem Maopinduzi, is dead and buried as surely as is Voldemort's Horcrux . . . And this is an Unbreakable Vow – I will *never ever* be a stinking Commie cadre again. I will *never ever ever* be Comrade Prem Maopinduzi again!'

My new name, I decided, would be Roseanne Kathryn Davies.

Rosie didn't yet know how she was going to get Out, but after her birth from the ashes of Prem, neither was she the same enslaved captive Prem Maopinduzi had been. Instead, she was a beautiful phoenix: a bird caged only in body, *not* in mind.

I can remember, from these earliest days of my brand-new dawn, glaring at Bala's back while he went about his 'work', shimmering inside with my new knowledge and potential.

You think you have locked me up, I thought. *But what you have done, Dark Lord, is sown the seeds for your own downfall . . .*

For years now – ever since I was a baby – the Dark Lord had told me I would be his greatest enemy.

By his own hand, as with all Dark Lords, he had made his prophecy come true.

44

After I became Enlightened, I was more desperate than ever to break the borders of my physical cage and escape the madhouse. But it was much easier said than done.

I fantasized all the time about escaping. What if I overpowered the comrades, snatched the keys from their pockets and made a run for it? But there were always too many people around: there was no time when it was quiet and I could be sure nobody would hear. Even night-time was a no-no because AB was now so neurotic that he would come rushing out of his room at the slightest sound. I wondered if I could escape via the bathroom, which had a different type of lock on its window. I was permitted time alone in there to bathe, which might be time enough to engineer an exit, but Shobha's room was next door and she used to call out if anything struck her as unusual. I wouldn't have time to get Out before she started shouting.

Even if I'd managed to overcome those obstacles, I also knew I couldn't run very fast. I'd still be walking down the road when they came after me: I didn't have the physical capability to get away. I dared not even try it, in case I was caught and subjected to worse torment. And my biggest fear of all remained what they might do to Roddy in that instance.

It was so clever of them. If they'd only threatened to harm me, I would not have given a damn, but now Roddy was part of the equation I was trapped like a fly in a spider's web.

I did make some attempts to communicate with Outside. From my wistful looks through my bedroom window, I'd noticed that there was a CCTV camera placed opposite our flat. Perhaps if I held up a note to the window the camera would capture it and who-ever monitored the footage would come and rescue me? I tried it a couple of times, scribbling a message in a marker pen to hold against the glass.

I am being held prisoner here, all windows and doors are locked and I can't get out. Please help me . . .

But no one ever responded. If the neighbours passed by, they never appeared to read the note. I would press it firmly to the clear glass, more conscious of my cage than ever at the touch of the physical barrier. I used to wish there was a Harry Potter in my life who could make that glass melt away like water.

My tragedy was that even when the glass wasn't there – on my dull 'excursions' to the launderette – I still couldn't escape. I did sometimes think of simply running into the street and shouting for help, but I had no confidence I'd be believed and feared I'd only end up having to go back (as on 2 May) and things would then be worse for me and Roddy. As I chattered on an inconsequential level with the people in the launderette, I yearned to tell them what was going on, but overseen by Bala as I was, I couldn't. The best I could hope for was to try to build a friendship of sorts with them: that way, if I did manage to run away one day, I thought I could possibly stay with one of them. But I knew such a strategy could take years.

Nevertheless, I did what I could to be ready for when my moment came. After Enlightenment, I started saving some of the pennies I handled at the launderette, just one or two at a time. I kept the slowly growing bag of bronze coins deep in my wardrobe where no one ever looked. It was only a pittance, I appreciated that much, but it was better than nothing. It gave me a small sense that at least I was doing *something* towards my escape.

If only I could have asked someone for advice, but of course I had no one. I couldn't speak to the comrades or the people I met in the launderette, and that was the extent of my 'social circle'. I would fantasize endlessly about reporting AB to some nameless 'authorities'. 'There are refuge centres for battered wives,' I pondered, 'but what about emotionally abused daughters? I want something to be done . . . I want to get a restraining order preventing these criminals from ever seeing me again . . . He should be locked up in a mental hospital, he is a dangerous psychopath! . . . I must find a way to get him sectioned before he does something . . . I must tell the police!'

This was another frequent fantasy: to tell the police and have Bala imprisoned for his crimes against me. I spent time writing up pages and pages of those crimes, hoping to report him at the first chance I got. I went back over my whole life: the time he stepped on my face and threw me Out for being sick when I was four; the time I was punished for saying Josie's hair looked nice; the time, the time, the time . . . There were almost too many to remember. Somehow, it wasn't difficult to recall them, as it might have been before Enlightenment. Previously, when I'd been busy sedating myself in my cocoon, it would have been far too painful to examine my past. But now there was almost something healthy about doing so, as though my brain and its memories were pus-filled wounds and I had to excise the infection to become clean. In so doing, I realized *none* of these beatings had been my fault, though I'd often thought so at the time. *I* was not the bad girl – *he* was the bad man. He was the criminal who deserved to be punished by the police.

But but but . . . There was always a 'but'.

If I reported Bala, would he not libel Roddy? Even on my good days, when I did not fear JACKIE, I knew from my newspaper reading that miscarriages of justice did exist. It seemed entirely feasible to me that Roddy could be locked up at a false word from my father. How could I fight for my freedom if it meant him sacrificing his? I would not be so selfish. I could not go to the police for fear of what Bala would say about my love, lies though it would be. I knew far too much about my father's skills of manipulation ever to believe the truth would out.

On the first page of my 2010 diary, I filled in 'None' to all the personal details listed at the front: the diary-keeper's passport number, national insurance number and so on. 'I have none of these things,' I wrote, 'because I am a prisoner. I am not registered to be living here . . . I am not allowed to have a doctor . . . I do not exist.'

It had always been immensely painful to be a shadow-woman, but after Enlightenment I truly grasped the callousness – and cleverness – of the way my father had hidden me. Because, unlike in *Harry Potter*, no Hagrid was coming for me. My name was not on a list of wizard-born children: *my name was on no list at all*.

'On the news,' I wrote in the spring of 2010, 'they were saying about how if the authorities had kept a closer watch on people home-schooling their children, poor Khyra Ishaq wouldn't have died [Khyra was starved to death by her mother and stepfather in Birmingham in

May 2008; a Serious Case Review had recently found there was a catalogue of missed opportunities by professional agencies to save her]. I am disgusted the government didn't implement such measures 30 years ago – then the Dark Lord couldn't have taken me off the radar and kept me prisoner! I would have been closely monitored and the DLM would have had to register me – then the police would keep a lookout if I disappear as I have done – it's because I have no official protection that I am a prisoner in this dungeon . . . I am a total prisoner and if something happens to me, nobody will know . . . How did my mentally ill father get allowed to hold people hostage like this? Why can nobody do anything to free me?'

But I knew why – I saw it in action every day. *It was not just my father who had shut me off from the world.* If it was only him, perhaps someone would have questioned it at some point in the past twenty-seven years. But my own mother had been complicit. It was a group effort: a troupe of puppets speaking with one voice and acting to one end.

It left me completely under his control.

'If God forsook his own son,' I wrote despondently, as prayer after prayer for freedom went unanswered, 'how can I expect him not to forsake a complete nonentity like me?'

Ironically, even though I was now Enlightened, in many ways my life was at its very darkest point. 'I have no hope of ever getting free,' I wrote that year. Yet, having come so far, I remained determined not to give up. 'I will hope, even if there is no hope. No darkness can last for ever.'

No darkness can last for ever . . . but for ever is still a very long time. By 2011, I felt worn down. Two years on from Enlightenment, it was hard to keep hoping things would change. Life in my dungeon was one of dodging daily indignities and striving to do so with my head held high. Though I was being held prisoner by lunatics, I learned how to cope, so that there would be something left of *me* when freedom eventually came.

Roddy was my salvation. 'Luckily I have [him] to focus on and hold onto,' I wrote in my diary, 'otherwise the misery of my existence in the DL's dungeon would have either killed me or driven me insane and made me a quivering wreck who *has* to love my oppressors simply to make life bearable. It is my Roddy, child of my heart and soul, who has saved me from all this. Even if I never see him again, he has done enough for me to last a hundred lifetimes.'

Imagine having to laugh when you wanted to cry, having to smile when you wanted to scream, having every aspect of your life nosed into, yet being expected to lick the arse of the Dark Lord doing it – and being insulted and abused if you refused. That was my life. I think enduring it day in and day out made me a very strong person. With Roddy on my side, I learned how to take it in my stride – to laugh off my father's excesses and see them for what they were: the demented rantings of a senile old codger. I began to take pleasure in ridiculing him in my poetry, discovering the power of laughter against a bully. It even had a physical effect on me: my almost-constant headache would disappear, my appetite would return and I would have a good night's sleep after a writing session.

I couldn't laugh it all off. Though the Dark Lord was now seventy-one years old, he could still deliver terrifying beatings; in one, he badly hurt my right eye. When he gloated about it, saying next time he'd pulp my whole head, and shouted: 'I dare you to go to the police about it! The whole old world will blow up if you do!' I took strength from my recognition of his madness. Nothing he *said* could hurt me now. When he attempted to humiliate me publicly, making me stand in front of the others while he mocked and 'disgraced' me, I felt not a drop of embarrassment. He was mad: he was beneath contempt.

His daily Vampire Puking became the bane of my life. As he had done for so many decades, he still passed around newspaper articles with his comments on, and there was still a daily focus within the Collective on working towards 'AB's new world'. I took no part, and would curse under my breath if ever Bala tried to involve me in it. While he lectured us, I would sit with my head in my hands, my middle finger deliberately raised in isolation against my cheek in a defiant, fuck-off sign of what I truly thought of his 'Discussions'.

I think it was the Collective's hypocrisy I found most galling. AB would denounce the 'British fascist state' for its crimes, while he was doing far worse than *any* of the politicians he called out. He would boast how he was always there for the 'common man', sympathizing with the plight of those who suffered misery, all the while inflicting misery on me. What a horrible, self-righteous turdworm! This despicable charlatan railed against injustice, while shamelessly perpetuating injustice himself! I found his double standards very difficult to bear and struggled to control my blinding fury when he banged on and on about how fantastic he and his 'new world' were.

Sometimes, my rage would flash out on my face. Then, the Dark Lord would patronizingly accuse me of 'pulling faces'. I still had the nervous laugh I'd developed as a child and he would bully me for laughing if ever that giggle erupted out of anxiety. Again and again, he would tell me I was 'fortunate' to be here in his house. 'Fortunate' – to be forced to vegetate all the time in the most deathly boring state, never allowed to have any fun or entertainment, doomed to recurring nightmares, not even allowed to see a doctor to check up on my health.

For my prolonged captivity was having a deleterious effect on me physically, too; something that seemed to accelerate in the years after Enlightenment. I now felt ill most of the time, with dreadful headaches, IBS, problems with my womb, and a growing and strange sensitivity to light. I got very red, painful eyes on my trips to the launderette now; it hurt so much that I complained out loud for once and Josie bought me some sunglasses and an eyepatch. But although they helped, they didn't solve or explain the problem. The affliction made me feel as though the shadows had finally claimed me for their own.

Yet 'focus on me' was still AB's constant refrain if he thought I was unwell or unhappy. Focus on what? That lump of nasty horrid shit that had oppressed me and locked me up and deprived me and destroyed my relationships and made my life an utterly boring, depressing living hell filled with nightmares and ill health?

'I'd rather focus on a pig's turd or a worm or a rat dropping,' I wrote in my diary.

As the years crawled by, however, I started to fear what was happening to me. In keeping my defences firm against the Dark Lord's drivel, I myself was becoming hard. I craved human contact, but in order to get it I would have to befriend my enemies. I was resolute that I would not become Comrade Prem again, but the strength of will needed to withstand did not leave me unmarked.

Sometimes, I could almost feel calluses forming on my soul.

Despite my love of humanity and kindness, and my eternal desire to do Dumbledore proud, on many occasions I became so enraged by my captivity that I wanted to kill. When the Dark Lord abused me, I longed to blast open his rotten head and flush his slimy brains down the toilet – *after* shitting on them!

My murderous fantasies were only that – ill-conceived ideas that joined those of reporting him to the authorities or fleeing through locked doors – but the fact I even had them at all was ghastly to one as peace-loving as me.

While my hatred of him kept me strong, I despised what I was turning into. In the summer of 2011, one of my rat friends died beneath the floorboards and gradually rotted away: the stench in our closed-windowed flat was *awful*. To me, the stink reflected the rotten nature of the cult itself – and, I feared, my contaminated, slowly poisoned soul.

'This is something I have to write,' I noted in September of that year.

I cannot speak of it to anyone, not ever – for it is too shameful, too terrible, to be thus communicated . . . The fact is . . . in spite of all I have done to prevent such an evil and destructive occurrence, circumstances have cruelly conspired to make me into the very opposite of which I wish to be. My heart has been steadily growing bitter. It is filled with gall, with a horrible poison that has crept up unawares, with a vicious ill-feeling that is eating away at my sense like a canker . . .

The pain and misery of my existence, courtesy of the criminal Dark Lord Monsters, seems to have finally pushed me into seeking refuge in hatred and bitterness . . . This morning, as is so often nowadays, I found myself shamelessly indulging in these forbidden waters: oceans that may look like welcome refuges at a time of need, but are in fact the foulest and the most dangerous of all. In times of anguish and despair, hatred and anger often become the sanctuary of the wounded soul. But they are like quicksand, a deadly whirlpool; upon entry it is well-nigh impossible to extricate oneself . . .

This is a slippery slope from which there can be no return, if not checked immediately upon detection. This is why I'm writing this, so as to hopefully expunge these evil, cancerous thoughts forever.

Disgusted by my own brain, which had once been a sanctuary but now felt defiled, I tried my hardest to crawl away from that quick-sand of hate. In a way, the Dark Lord himself helped me. 'He's always putting everybody down and bragging about how he knows this and he knows that, the insufferable know-it-all,' I wrote. 'But I think it's more important to be a kind person.'

So I focused on that priority above all others to help me defeat my demons. I didn't manage it *all* the time, but sometimes I did – to the extent that I found I could even pity my deluded father. 'I shouldn't really get angry with him,' I wrote sadly. 'He should be in a mental hospital.'

Over time, I really began to feel sorry for him. He seemed as much a prisoner of his own lies as I was; more so, in fact, because he seemed to believe his falsehoods. He was so afraid of the fascist state coming in that it wasn't only my window that stayed closed and locked: his own did, too. As in my room, it was absolutely roasting and I could smell him, like the rat, rotting away in there. The most horrible stench of sweat emanated from him; his pillows and quilt were stained a dark yellow. His room smelt like a cesspit and any-where he came, the stink followed; it was disgusting, especially as I still had to hug him every morning and night. *What a miserable recluse*, I thought, even as I wrinkled my nose against his stench, *try-ing to cage me up but in the process caging himself too.*

Having disowned my father, I fully embraced my dead mother as my only parent instead. 'I am 100% Welsh,' I wrote, in tongue-in-cheek homage to my father's ridiculous 'percentages'. Through my reading, I pursued my Celtic heritage, taking inspiration from my forefathers' long battles against subjugation; Boudicca and Llywelyn the Last now became my new heroes.

And it may well have been via my fellow Welsh dragons that I first had the idea that I hoped might save my life; at the least, they gave it traction. I read *The Brothers of Gwynedd* by Edith Pargeter and in this learned the story of Eleanor de Montfort, Mrs Llywelyn. In captivity herself in 1276, she resolved to make friends with her cap-tors, partly to make her prison more endurable and partly to win them over to her side. Crucially, although she reached across the divide of her disgust to offer the hand of friendship, she *never* lost sight of her ultimate goal: her release and her reunion with Llywelyn. *That* was the true motivation for her strategy.

As a proud Welshwoman, I felt inspired to follow in her footsteps. I wondered: could I, like Eleanor, work with the cult to further my own ends, even as I loathed them? Could I bring out the best in them while staying true to myself? As ever, Harry Potter had a lesson for me in this: a character in that, too, had successfully and secretly worked with the Death Eaters without compromising their true allegiance to the other side. I would emulate them, I decided.

By 2011, I felt a lot softer towards Josie and Aisha than I had done in the immediate aftermath of Roddy's banishment. I knew, in my heart, they were not evil people, just under an evil spell. It was funny: just as my father did, they both treated me as if I was an eternal child, even though I was twenty-eight, but in many ways I felt they were more like children than I was because *I* was able to make up my own mind about things, whereas they followed everything the Dark Lord said.

I appreciated that it wasn't their fault, however. Both were kept in check by fear of JACKIE; Aisha was also frequently reminded that the Dark Lord had it in his power to arrange her deportation. As for Josie, I had come to believe that she was suffering from Stockholm Syndrome, which I had read about in various newspaper reports about kidnapping.

We discussed the Syndrome in the Collective; AB told me *I* had it – because I loved a fascist agent like Roddy, who was really out to kill me! But I'd thought to myself, *Hang on, I don't think Roddy is keeping me hostage: YOU are keeping me hostage! If I liked you,* then *I'd have Stockholm Syndrome* . . . Immediately afterwards had followed the thought that the *comrades* must be suffering from it, as Bala beat and abused them yet they still worshipped him.

Believing that Josie and Aisha were victims who had resorted to Stockholm Syndrome to keep their sanity made it *much* easier for me to reach out to them again, though I remained ever vigilant. I hoped I could awaken some human feelings in them. To stand any chance of surviving this situation, I knew I had to find a way to neutralize the 'Hyde' part of them that always turned on me, and strive to bring out the 'Jekyll'.

So a new campaign began. I made friends again with Aisha first, for she had always been kinder to me. We bonded over literature: she too liked to read and we nicknamed ourselves 'The Literati'. As we lay together during afternoon nap, we mended our connection to such a degree that I eventually shared some of my poems with her – those I'd written about Roddy and my pain at being separated from him, *not* my rude ridiculing of the Dark Lord!

I think my words helped her to understand my feelings. She seemed very moved, in fact, and often had tears in her eyes as I described how it felt *never* to have been allowed to make and keep a friend. I also discussed with her the idea that ideology should never be put above humanity: if one's beliefs made another suffer, that was wrong. I think this opened her eyes to an extent and made her treat me with more compassion.

But though she was sympathetic, she didn't offer to help me escape, nor did she suggest we try to change things even a little. I think, now, that she was too scared to do so, but at the time I took her attitude to mean that she cared more about her own skin than me; I nicknamed her Wormtail. I couldn't understand how anyone could say they cared about me, as she did, and yet let me stay in that place.

As Aisha and I whispered together, we had a witness: Josie, eavesdropping outside the door. She reported us to Bala, of course. I needed to keep her close and try to help her to understand me too, so that she wouldn't *want* to report. So I started *asking* Josie to lie with me in the afternoons instead: a friendly gesture. Though we were thrown together all the time, as she was often the one charged with watching me, previously I had always and clearly resented her presence. We began making lunches together too, healthy vegetable soups. Josie was an amazing cook and I made sure to praise her skills.

As a child, I would have been harshly condemned for this, but I'd identified in Josie the same craving for appreciation that I myself had. So although she was *very* uncomfortable with it at first, over time she relented and seemed to enjoy having me say nice things to her. It was a rare occurrence in the cult: despite Josie being the one who did most of the cooking, Chanda only ever seemed to criticize her work (often after Josie had spent the whole day slaving away in the kitchen), which meant that a kind word from me was as welcome as water to a dehydrated plant. As the months passed, Josie seemed to flourish. I redoubled my efforts, even when she continued to report, because she was reporting *less*.

I nicknamed the good part of her Alice, and her evil side Patrinnon. 'I do care about Alice,' I wrote in my diary, 'because despite the evil dark spells she has been cursed with by the Dark Lord, she has tried to be as decent to me as her difficult position allows – it is not her fault if she is too weak to properly defeat the evil spells.'

I didn't dare to share with either of them the truth I'd discovered when I became Enlightened. I knew they were mesmerized by AB and would never be able to see that he did any wrong, let alone believe that everything he preached was codswallop. Even when AB beat and bullied them, they still refused to see any wrongdoing in his actions. How I longed for a kindred spirit who would see as I did, but the only sense I got was from books. I felt sad about that for me and for the women. How they could allow themselves to be so badly treated – and not just allow it, but *choose* it – was beyond my comprehension. I'd had no choice, but they'd *had* a choice as to how they lived their lives . . . and they'd chosen this.

I really struggled with that – and with the fact that, even as I set to work on my strategy, Josie and Aisha were actively involved in keeping me captive. *For they were the ones who kept the keys in their pockets.* When I heard the metal jangling, I always lost heart. *Just imagine it's money*, I tried to tell myself, *it's not keys*.

As the months passed and my befriending strategy continued, I could actually see their constant internal struggle, especially within Josie. She was clearly torn between remaining devoted to AB and enjoying the kindness I offered. Seeing that struggle made me feel uneasy. I needed, for my own sanity, to believe she could one day help me. I didn't want to see anything that made me doubt it. Always, I looked away from her and spoke to her indirectly. If I'd looked in her eyes, I think I would have lost my nerve.

For I was under no illusions. Befriending Josie and Aisha was my *only* option – first, to stand any chance of surviving this hellish, friendless existence, but secondly to escape. I knew I'd never make it Out of the cult alone. Though I was bleakly aware such a strategy would take a very long time indeed – and that it might *never* succeed – as the only option available to me, I had to give it a go.

Yet it was painfully slow. Every now and then, Josie would fall back into the simmering cauldron of Bala's poison and start hissing and whispering with him. But despite these setbacks, I remained focused. It was two steps forward and one step back, but I told myself firmly I *was* making progress. I truly believed that Josie was a good person; it was only Bala who seemed able to convince her to act otherwise. All I could do was keep on with my shaky strategy. *This is going to take another hundred years*, I thought, as Josie ebbed and flowed in her friendship like a turning tide.

But while I was deprived of most things, the one thing I did have was time . . .

45

In the winter of 2011, an unexpected – if unwitting – ally joined my ongoing war. As in all great historic conflicts, it would prove a decisive turning point, shifting the balance of the battle in my favour. 'No clique based on doing evil to others can ever hold,' I had written in my diary back in May 2010. 'It will surely wrench itself apart.' Now, I was to learn that my prophecies also could come true.

For a while now, Shobha's health had not been great. Awful as it sounds to say, this had been something of a blessing for me because AB's ire was directed away from me and towards Shobha for 'not focusing on him properly'. But although I think it distracted the Dark Lord's attention from the enemy in his midst – *me* – his fury at Shobha wasn't what helped. Instead, it was Chanda – completely unbeknown to her – who tipped the scales.

After Oh had died in 2004, Josie had taken over being Shobha's main carer. With Shobha now having increased needs, Josie was being berated more and more often for not meeting them. It struck me as wrong, given Josie cared for her very well, unpaid and out of the goodness of her heart. As Shobha needed more help, Josie found herself in the firing line more and more.

It was beastly; I felt for Josie so much. In truth, it was a situation that had been escalating for a while, but it got a lot worse from winter 2011 onwards. Chanda became increasingly tough on Josie for not working hard enough, even though Josie dedicated *all* her time to caring for Shobha, Chanda and AB. Her daily workload was obscene: besides caring for Shobha, who needed round-the-clock attention, Josie cooked, cleaned and shopped for us all. With Aisha being so small, Josie took on the bulk of the hard labour, and with Comrade Simons having passed away and his car no longer available to us, it was Josie now who carried *all* the heavy shopping back to the flat, which was uphill all the way.

I could see Josie was working flat out, at times even making herself physically ill, but it was never enough for Chanda. And what wasn't good enough for Chanda wasn't good enough for AB. I think the thing that cut Josie the most was that Bala *always* took Chanda's side, despite Josie's decades of devotion.

They were driving Josie away from them – but of course, in their arrogance, they believed she would never desert them because she was so 'fortunate' to have a role in their home. As I had done before, I suggested to Josie that I thought Bala must be under Chanda's spell to act so unfairly towards her. I was very careful never to criticize AB, even though I thought him equally culpable.

Bala himself unwittingly helped in this. Though he always took Chanda's side against us, she was not spared his wrath. Sometimes he would say to his wife, 'You're so evil!' Josie and I would seize on this: AB had criticized Chanda, so – between ourselves – we could too, for we were only agreeing with him. When Chanda spoke back to him, as she had always done (and I had once admired), I now framed this assertiveness as an attack on Bala's authority.

'Look how badly Chanda treats my dad!' I would exclaim to Josie. 'What a monster she is, how *dare* she talk to him like that!'

And Josie would enthusiastically chime in, happy to defend Bala against his monstrous spouse. Because she didn't want to believe anything bad about AB, she took the view I suggested: that Bala wouldn't have agreed to beat her but for the fact he was too much under Chanda's spell to be able to see that it was wrong. 'No clique based on doing evil to others can ever hold' I had written – and the splinters were starting to show.

It was at this time that the promise I had made myself as a child – that if someone needed my help and friendship, I would willingly give it – came into its own. Usually what happened in the cult was that we would each in turn be isolated and condemned. If you were in Bala's bad books, you were dead to everyone else too. It was one of the things I hated most about the cult. But when I saw Josie having such a horrible time, I now stepped up to support her – even though she'd never done the same for me. But it was a point of honour with me that I would never now leave anyone, no matter who they were, alone. Because I knew intimately how it felt to be isolated from the world.

So when Bala beat Josie, or Chanda shouted nasty words that cut like knives, I would simply say, 'I'm here for you.' I even hugged her at times. She resisted that physical affection at first but her reservations quickly disappeared as she was so desperately in need of comfort. When she cried, I wrapped my arms around her and gave her the love that had always been denied to me. It did my own soul good to be able to help her: I banished that hate that had been poisoning my heart and embraced affection instead.

For the first time, Josie was able to be empathetic to my situation because she was now enduring something similar. I believe she started to feel ashamed of herself for having done those things to me in the past; eventually, she apologized. It was as if her eyes were being opened and she was seeing the cult in a new light – not the blinding rays of Enlightenment, but the shadows lifted sufficiently so that she realized things didn't *have* to be as nasty and back-biting as they always had been. I went out of my way to show her kindness and she responded to it, as she was starved of affection just like me. It made me feel strong to show her love and not coldness – because I could have abandoned her to her fate, but to forgive was infinitely more rewarding. AB might have taken strength in 'divide and conquer', but I believed unity was more powerful by far.

AB did not seem perturbed by our bond. In a way he was quite happy because he used to say we *should* work together in harmony, the better to prepare for his new world. He much preferred everyone to appear happy, for it suited his narcissistic ego to believe everyone was thrilled to be part of the Collective. By this time, I had long ago given up appealing for more freedom, which to him meant I had given up wanting it. Like the best insider agents in the books I'd read, I kept a low profile. Lulled into a false sense of security, AB became *over*confident he had made everything secure.

There was evidence of that in 2012. Unbelievably, AB passed around a leaflet called 'Stop Adult Abuse in Lambeth'. He said he was trying to show us how bad the old world was and why the Collective was such an exemplary sanctuary, but each bullet point on the leaflet, detailing the signs of abuse, was *exactly* what he was doing to me and the comrades: the physical abuse, psychological abuse, neglect . . . It was all there in black and white: we made a perfect case study. It demonstrated his arrogance and self-deceit that he didn't think circulating such a leaflet might cause at least one of us to identify him as a perpetrator. But that was AB all over.

In the spring of 2012, something extraordinary happened: Outsiders began regularly to come inside the flat. Shobha required such care at that time that Josie's administrations weren't enough: two care workers came to help her; at first four times a day, then twice daily as her condition improved. Before then, only relatives of AB or Chanda had been allowed over the threshold, but these women were *nothing* to do with the cult. I eyed them with a mix of curiosity and hope.

I thought them beautiful: the newness of their faces was as refreshing as a waterfall in a sunlit glen. They worked on a rota but the two who came most often were Constance and Phyllis. Constance was in her fifties and Phyllis in her twenties. Phyllis used to change her hair *all* the time, which I *loved*: straight, curly, black, blonde – once, she even dyed it purple! They were like a breath of fresh air, so welcome in our closed-windowed flat, and each time they came I would edge out of my bedroom and walk past them as they waited outside the bathroom for Shobha, so that eventually they struck up a conversation with me.

I could feel Chanda bristling as they did. She'd be in Shobha's room, putting things away, but when I started speaking the banging noise of drawers would fall eerily silent and I knew she was eavesdropping, perhaps fearing I would spill the secret of what was really going on. Her silence on the other side of the door made me tongue-tied and awkward.

The care workers couldn't help but notice that certain things were odd about our set-up. As the weeks passed and the weather grew warmer, all of us sweated in the sauna of the flat and they exclaimed in surprise: 'Why are the windows always closed?'

'Because Shobha feels the cold,' Chanda said brusquely; they didn't question it after that.

They were curious about me, though. 'Why are you always indoors?' they asked. 'Why do you never go out?'

I had my answer rehearsed: 'I'm doing writing,' I said. It was plausible, I guess – many writers worked from home – but I hated having to lie.

I'm not sure I did it very well, for they still seemed concerned about me. They took to hugging me; I was so overwhelmed by that, that a month into our friendship I wrote to Constance, who was a particularly warm woman, to declare she was like a mother to me. If I didn't come to see them, they would knock on my door and ask, 'What happened to you?'

One day, Constance said to me, 'Do you have a mobile phone?'

I shook my head. I had seen them on TV adverts and in the hands of people Outside, and *longed* to own one, but of course that was impossible. 'It's not my thing . . .' I began.

'I want you to go out this afternoon and buy a phone for yourself, so that when we leave we can keep in contact,' she told me.

I squirmed, feeling so awkward. How could I explain to her why I couldn't do that – without making her ask *more* awkward questions? How could I say no without appearing rude? I would have *loved* to stay in contact but I knew I couldn't. 'I'm not technological,' I said weakly.

It was while the care workers were coming that things came to a head between Josie and Chanda. One evening in mid-April 2012, after Constance and Phyllis had left for the day, Chanda started ordering Josie to do more chores. 'You're not pulling your weight!' she declared – outrageously, given all the work Josie did.

'I'm sorry, Comrade Chanda,' Josie replied politely. 'I've got a terrible pain in my arm.' It was a repetitive strain injury, I think, from carrying all that heavy shopping. 'Is it OK if I ease off just for a bit, and when I am better I will start again?'

'How can your arm be hurting?' Chanda scoffed. 'You don't do any work!'

Josie and I were in the living room later that same night when Bala came charging in angrily.

'Why are you being nasty to Chanda?' he demanded of Josie. 'Why are you refusing to work with her?'

Usually, Josie would meekly kowtow to AB, but Chanda's account of their exchange was so clearly one-sided, making no reference to Josie's injury, that this time she didn't stay silent. 'Sorry, AB,' she began. 'I just said—'

BOOM. Bala smashed her face in – once, twice, three times. Her head whooshed backwards with the force of his blows and her whole face went red.

'Nobody comes between me and Chanda! Cherish AB's family!' he roared.

I was horrified. I wanted to scream, to stop him. I couldn't do anything in the moment, but it was at that point that I thought: *I am going to tell Constance and Phyllis about what is going on!*

As if AB's violence against Josie wasn't bad enough, at that moment Aisha popped her head around the door to see what was happening. Just because she was there, AB smashed her up too; she nearly fell over. She hadn't even said a word. He hit her just for coming in.

'You bastards!' he roared. 'Always violating my authority and not being subordinate to Chanda!'

Boom! Boom! Boom! He hit them over and over.

Even if AB hadn't brought home the leaflet about adult abuse, his attacks on Josie and Aisha that night would have made it clear to me that this was domestic violence. There was a case in the news around that time, centred on a woman called Tina Nash, whose eyes had been gouged out by her boyfriend, and Tina had said that people should not tolerate domestic violence.

I decided to be inspired by her bravery. *No way am I keeping quiet about this*, I thought. So, after AB left, I went straight to my room and began writing a letter to Constance and Phyllis.

46

I have got something to tell you. What I am doing is extremely dangerous; if anyone in this house finds out about what I am going to do, my life will be in mortal peril. I am going to tell you about the dreadful things that go on in this place, and I want you to report to the authorities anonymously and hopefully something can be done.

There is a very evil, mad man who lives here, who is not meant to be living here [AB was not on the housing list either]. He keeps two women as slaves. I am his illegitimate daughter and he keeps me a prisoner here. He has unhealthy attachments to me – he never has allowed me even to go out on my own, or without his permission. He won't let me have friends, he won't let me work, he never even let me go to school . . . This man suffers from delusions of grandeur, and the women in this house are brainwashed and ensnared by him.

Last night this evil madman beat up his two slaves – both my dear friends . . . I too am scared for my life. He has locked all the doors and windows in this place and threatens to harm my friends if I try to escape . . . Because I have no other family, I am completely under his control – there is no one to protect me. I am not on any official document at all . . .

I am a very frightened person and I have never dared to act before, but seeing him braining my friends is more than I can bear. He is wild and demented and dangerous, and I want him locked up in prison or mental hospital . . .

I have no say in my own life, my own future. I am completely at the mercy of this mentally ill person and the others who are spellbound by him . . .

They are so much older than me and when they die, what is to become of me? They don't let me do anything – not even answer the door or the phone – because they don't want their secret to be revealed . . . But I have had enough. I cannot let my friends be killed, and neither do I want to die. I want the police informed. Please can somebody help me? . . . I want to go free and be a normal person, and I hope my two friends also will want this, but they are mesmerised by him and can never see that he does any wrong.

But I at least want to go. I want to work, raise a family, live a decent life. I know nothing about the Outside world (how to fend for myself) because I have been a prisoner since birth, but I want to learn. I need help, and so do my friends . . . All I want is to live a normal life – PLEASE HELP ME!!!

When you have read this, please hand it in to the police station, anonymously if possible. I thank you beforehand, you are saving my life. This is very, very serious and I need police protection if I am to remain safe. This man will kill me without batting an eyelid if he even so much as suspects me of reporting him. But victims of evil madmen must come forward, and I hope we can somehow solve this problem. I am really desperate, else I wouldn't do this! PLEASE ENSURE NONE OF THESE PEOPLE GET TO KNOW – I WILL BE <u>DEAD</u>!!!

I signed the letter 'Rosie', which was the name Josie and Aisha now called me; the name my Roddy had used.

When I woke the next morning, I was determined to hand the letter to Constance when she came. But while I waited for her to arrive, I noticed that everything had calmed down, as though everybody had forgotten the terror of the night before, even though I hadn't. In light of the calm normality around me, I started to think again about my plan, especially as I plotted through the possible consequences.

How well did I *really* know Constance and Phyllis? Could I trust them with this – trust them to handle it with the discretion and delicacy required? I knew them both to be strong women who, if they thought something was wrong, would challenge it. Might they be tempted to talk directly to Chanda or Bala about the contents of my letter? Oh my goodness, what a *disaster* that would be! Yet I could see it happening. The women wouldn't know that such a feisty response would put me and the others in grave danger.

Even if they went to the police first, would *they* be believed and taken seriously? They were not smooth-talking English professionals:

they were low-paid ordinary women. Perhaps they'd be dismissed and I'd be back at square one – but even more at risk.

Any which way I looked at it, in the bright light of day it no longer seemed such a good idea. I wrote two letters in the end, but each time I chickened out of handing them over. I was just so frightened. I couldn't trust them or people Outside to help in the way that was needed for this peculiar, unique situation. Though I could feel my opportunity to speak out slipping through my fingers, I remained too scared to act, too fearful of the consequences if things went wrong. After all, look at how my life had changed since 2 May; all the privileges that had been revoked since I'd made my bid for freedom. I wasn't sure I would be able to bear any further deprivation. And if Josie and Aisha found out what I'd done, they too would take AB's side and shun me once again.

No, I concluded. *I am better off staying as I am. I will continue with my strategy. That remains my best hope.*

The care workers came for the last time in May 2012. I gave them a poem each that I had written as a farewell gift. I cried as I hugged them goodbye; they seemed surprised by the intensity of my emotion.

'If you have a phone,' Constance said once more, 'then I can contact you . . .'

But I knew I would never see them again.

Alone again. And yet not – because I now had Josie and Aisha. As 2012 continued, the three of us grew ever closer, bonding over our shared dislike of Chanda but also finding happiness in our mutual affection. We used to hug each other without Bala knowing and that was *so* nice. Those hugs were genuinely caring, not like the creepy cuddles he still inflicted on me.

Towards the end of 2012, the cruelty of the Dark Lord Monsters was demonstrably on show. My health, patchy at best, began to decline rapidly. Though I was eating like a horse, the weight started to fall off me at an alarming rate. Josie was concerned. Each time I stepped on the scales, I'd lost pounds and pounds, then one stone, then another, despite the fact I was eating piles of food. It wasn't normal. Josie became so disturbed by my weight loss that she dared to raise it with AB and Chanda – but they didn't give a damn.

'Oh, she's just anorexic,' Chanda sneered uncaringly. 'She's obsessed about losing weight because she wants to wear nice clothes.'

They were so indifferent we didn't tell them about another ailment: I was itching 'down there'. I had been for quite a few years now. In a funny way, I'd been pleased when it had first started; I'd wondered if it might be a Sexually Transmitted Infection (STI) from my love-making with Roddy: something to remember him by. But when I confided in Josie about it, she did not share my positive feelings. She was worried.

In 2012, when I remarked that I was itching *again*, she informed me that she had once spoken to Bala about it in the past: 'Do you think it is an STI?' she'd said.

But he had laughed. 'She never had sex with Roddy,' he'd said derisively, 'so how could it be?'

Not wanting to believe the truth, he had resorted to fantasy, rewriting history in his mad old brain. His reaction then meant we didn't try to appeal for help again, even though I continued to itch.

With my so-called parents acting so negligently, Josie did her best to care for me herself. She started making me sage tea, which somehow did make me feel a bit better. In fact, I found I needed to drink copious amounts – of sage tea, water, coffee, milkshake, fruit juice, *anything* I could drink drink drink! There were a couple of pint glasses in the house and I would regularly down about seven or eight at a time. Yet no matter how much tea Josie made me, it could do nothing to counteract the dark haze that occasionally blighted my eyesight. I was so exhausted these days that I found I actually needed our afternoon naps.

Josie attended to me with increasing concern; she didn't even tell me to focus on Bala. I started calling her Mum, because I was so grateful to her for her love and care, and because she was listening to me and not betraying me. She even dared to open the windows in the flat to try to get me some fresh air, although she was careful never to leave me alone in the room when she did. Most promisingly of all, even when Bala and Chanda berated her for 'wasting time' by looking after me, she did not let me down.

It was perhaps around Christmastime that Josie made an extraordinary suggestion: that she should take me to a hospital to get checked out. The idea hadn't even occurred to me – I knew there was no way I could have managed anything like that without help – but Josie seemed willing to take me. Inside, I was jumping up and down with glee: that she could even raise such an idea was a fantastic step in the right direction for my long-term strategy. It had been beyond my wildest hopes she would *ever* get to a point where she might defy Bala's guidelines in such a blatant way!

But I also thought, *I don't want to go to hospital and get well and come back to stay in this horrible place.* I was concerned that if we went to hospital and I turned out to have some chronic illness, Bala would use it to control me even more. So I said no to her suggestion, but I was truly heartened by how far she'd come. Could I persuade her to go further – to suggest not just that we went to hospital, but that we left for good?

I knew I couldn't openly raise such a radical prospect. The idea of escaping *had* to be said by her. Otherwise, if she abandoned any plan halfway through, she might say I had coerced her into it. But if *she* had the idea, I'd feel safe.

So I started saying things like: 'I feel like I'm dying here. We need to get my health seen to, but we can't go to the hospital. Chanda won't want me to have that kind of attention, so Bala won't be able to allow it because of the spell. I will probably just die here . . .'

I wasn't working in a vacuum. My mother, Oh and Comrade Simons had all died in circumstances that, had they seen a doctor sooner, could perhaps have been averted. (Comrade Simons had died of cancer in 2006; despite months spent 'focusing' on Bala before he'd decided to go to hospital, of course it had not saved him.) I suspect all that preyed on Josie's mind too. Was it possible, if she didn't help me, that I would follow in their footsteps? Where would that leave her, without my friendship in this bullying cult? Could she live without me, if I didn't live?

Would she have blood on her hands if she didn't act to save me?

'I'm going to be out of this Dark Tower by the end of 2014,' I predicted to her. 'I will either be out as a free person or I'll be out in a coffin . . .'

On 7 January 2013, I turned thirty. We didn't go Out. The day before, Roddy had beckoned me through the window: the incident made me feel so wrought up because I wanted to respond more than *anything* but was too frightened. Yet it became something of a catalyst: *I have to leave the cult so that I can be with Roddy.* Though we hadn't spoken since 4 November 2008 – over four years ago – I was sure he must still feel the same pure love I did. (It was all I had to live for, so it *had* to be true.) All that was standing in our way was AB.

I redoubled my efforts with Josie. I kept saying how sad and desperate I felt. Through chatting with Josie, I'd come to realize that our leaving *might* not harm Roddy – what would Bala say to the police, after all? The night of 4 November was so long ago; surely it would be odd to report an attempted burglary after all this time? Roddy was not a child. I had to hope that if Bala did try anything Roddy would be able to find a way around it. When I realized this, though I remained a little fearful, it was another barrier to freedom that fell by the wayside.

Bit by bit, I kept working on Josie. A sigh here, a cry there, as my body grew still thinner . . . Until finally, sometime in early 2013, she said the words I never thought I'd hear.

'Why don't we find a way out?'

47

Yes! I could barely believe my ears. All my hard work on my long-term strategy had paid off. By this time, Josie believed that AB was under such a spell that everything he did that was unfair – including caging me up – was done at Chanda's behest. She told me how sorry she was for her part in it; she was disgusted that she'd thought she'd been following AB all this time, but instead had been following Chanda!

So to suggest we left wasn't against Bala, it was against *Chanda*; and that was something Josie could support. Josie believed that AB would actually endorse her helping me, because he didn't *truly* want to chain me up – it was only the part of him under Chanda's influence that subjected me to such cruelty. Though Josie longed to, I told her we couldn't tell him anything about our plans as the part of him under the spell still had the upper hand.

We did not tell Aisha of our plans to escape either. Aisha used to get nightmares and scream in her sleep and I was worried she might unwittingly blurt out something that would ruin everything. As she had done ever since I was a child, too, Aisha had this ability to get on with everyone in the house, so because she still had a bridge to Chanda, I was worried the Wormtail inside her might scuttle across it and betray us: scared into sharing the secret, even though she was on our side.

But although Josie had now raised the idea, coming up with a firm plan was not so straightforward. Though Josie knew much more about the Outside world than I did, she too had been part of the closed Collective for over three decades. She had no more made Outside friends in that time than I had; she had denounced her family. Where could we run to?

A possible solution came from an unexpected source: AB. One day, he presented me with a leaflet about Centrepoint, the charity for homeless people, which had come with the *Observer* newspaper. I believe he may have wanted me to study it as part of my duties as his future minister for children; as I'd kept my head down for a few years now, I believe he thought I was willing to become part of his 'government' again.

I pored over the leaflet with my usual enthusiasm for any information about the Outside world – and read how Centrepoint had set up a halfway home for young people who had run away: a place they could stay until they found their feet and were ready to start living independently.

I showed it to Josie. 'I *wish* there was a place like this that I could go to,' I said wistfully. I knew I'd need a bit of help on the Outside and this halfway house sounded perfect.

'Well, maybe there is something we could do,' Josie said, taking the leaflet from me. 'Maybe when I go out shopping with Aisha I could go to the phone booth and give these people a ring.'

She did exactly as she'd promised – but returned with bad news. The homes were only for young people. Aged thirty, I did not meet the criteria. Centrepoint gave her some other contacts, for women's refuges, and Josie tried a couple of them, but one didn't answer and the other relied on an appointment system; an appointment we'd never be able to make, trapped as we were by Bala's schedule and rules. Such a system was unfit for our purpose.

But although it was a setback, and I did feel sad, I did not lose hope. Because I knew from all she'd done that Josie really was on my side now. It felt a little like when Roddy had been visiting me: I felt as if I could take on the world. That's the power of a friend. And it made me feel that I could bear to be in the cult a little longer, until the *right* opportunity came along, because I now had Josie by my side. Together, I believed we could achieve the impossible.

Summer 2013 rolled around. I watched jealously from the window as people Outside donned brightly coloured summer clothing and showcased sun-kissed skin. My own was grey and pale in comparison; I masked it as best I could with my orange make-up, but it was no substitute for a healthy glow, nor could it put meat on my cheeks where there was none. I weighed around seven and a half stone by then, down from nine and a half, and felt very weary and unwell.

The one positive was that Bala allowed me to go shopping with him again. Earlier that year, Chanda had gone to hospital and I'd asked him if I could help out while she was sick. Believing I was offering because I wanted to pull my weight for the Collective, he had agreed and I now accompanied him regularly to the shops. Really, I was just desperate for more freedom – and I quickly put it to good use. Though I could no longer post letters to Roddy via my old route, having stupidly confessed it to AB on the night of horror, I devised a new way of doing it: on our way *back* from the shops, while Bala was busy ahead of me opening the gate, I would take a letter out of my handbag and quickly slip it into Roddy's letterbox.

Oh, how good it felt to be able to communicate with my darling again! In my first letter, I explained everything – how I had been locked up for the past four years and had endured torment to keep him safe. I told him I loved him more than ever but urged him to be cautious: not to confront my captors, nor do anything to try to free me. He followed my instructions to the letter. 'My health is poor,' I wrote, 'but my deep love for you has kept me sane and even happy (!) through all the horrors . . . Everything I do is for you and for you alone, and for the day of our reunion, which I know will certainly come.'

As summer stretched her long golden fingers over us, Josie and I continued plotting for that very day of reunion. I think at first Josie was thinking that I would leave the Collective on my own, but the more we discussed it, the more uncertain it seemed that I'd be able to manage Outside, so she eventually said she would come with me. She was very reluctant, because Bala was so important to her, but in a sign of her true good heart she decided to prioritize the escape for my benefit. We started brainstorming people we could possibly stay with – Josie threw out some names from her past, while I suggested my friends from the launderette. When I proposed that a mobile phone might be a useful tool to assist us, Josie bought one. We filled it with the contact details of those few people we knew, but never dialled a single number. It was too risky: what if one of the people came to the house and gave us away? We vowed not to use the phone until we were Outside and kept it on silent all the time.

But just to hold it in my hand made me feel more free. It was a wonderful sensation. Chanda had a mobile phone, but Bala had always denied the rest of us the privilege. I spent ages just tinkering about with it – it was a black-and-silver Nokia handset – trying to learn how to use it. It was strange at first, but I did manage. I longed to press the button that would connect me to others, but I resisted. There would be time enough for phone calls after our escape.

Yet Josie was struggling: 'I can't get my head round this,' she said to me at one point.

'We will do it at your pace,' I said patiently. I had waited thirty years for freedom; I could wait a little more time yet. 'When do you feel ready to go?'

She took a deep breath. 'June 2014,' she replied.

I was bitterly disappointed – not another *year* in this place! – but at the same time I knew it was wiser by far to have Josie on board and working at her own pace than for me to rush her and ruin our long-held plans. June 2014 it was.

With an end date now in mind, I started fantasizing nonstop about our escape: my first step, my first free journey, my first night sleeping alone Outside; in thirty years, I had never once spent a night apart from the Collective. I dreamed, too, of meeting my grandmother for the first time. I fantasized that Ceri would embrace me when she found out the truth and exclaim, 'My long-lost granddaughter! How long I have waited for you!' And I would say, 'Yes, Gran, me too!' And we would both cry and hug and cry some more . . .

Those fantasies became like much-loved toys. Each day and night I would unwrap them in my mind and play them over and over again, rewinding to my favourite bits and pressing play again. It kept me entertained for hours. I started my own preparations for going, asking Josie to photocopy my writings. Many of my poems were written in an ink which would run if it got wet, and as I anticipated we might have to spend a few nights on the streets, I didn't want my writings to be ruined. They were as much a part of the escape plan as Josie and me: if I got free without them, it wouldn't be any kind of freedom at all because I'd feel as though I'd left the most import-ant part of me behind. I was sure, once he discovered we were gone, that Bala would burn them all as revenge, or pack them away so they could never be found, and I could not bear that idea. That was why our escape had to be planned in such detail: because my writings had to come too. We couldn't just make a run for it.

I also revealed to Josie that I'd been saving money, and pulled the hidden bag of coins from the bottom of my wardrobe. In the four years since Enlightenment, I'd managed to save over £200. Josie changed the collection of coins into notes so that the money would be lighter to carry.

Though I didn't breathe a word to Josie about my true intentions, I began these preparations in part because I hoped to find a way to persuade her to leave earlier than June 2014, but I had to be very careful not to push too hard and put her off. We whispered together all the time about our plans for leaving, always alert in case of eaves-droppers. A new idea evolved.

Perhaps, before we left, I ought to try going Outside alone. Train-ing, if you will, to prepare me for my own new world.

'Bala and Chanda were meant to help you become independent,' Josie said. 'But now I realize that since they are not going to do it, I have to do it instead.'

Even as she spoke, I could see that constant internal struggle going on: she didn't want to disobey Bala, but could also see how ridiculous and sad the situation was, that a thirty-year-old woman was not permitted to go to the shops alone. I guess she felt that she just couldn't keep quiet about it any more.

'It's awful that you can't do these things,' she said sympathetically.

So we picked a day when we knew that AB, Chanda and Shobha would all be Out for several hours. It was 29 August 2013. Josie gave me such a fright that morning. Out of the blue, she passionately declared: 'AB is my saviour and I have no life without him!'

My heart started pounding – I had to handle this so carefully. So I promised her that once she'd got me Out, during the final escape, she could always go back if she wanted ... I really hoped she wouldn't make that decision – first because I was worried about her health and I didn't want her to become another Oh; secondly because I thought she deserved a better life than being treated as a slave; and thirdly because I knew she had so much potential to be a positive influence in the world, and deserved a chance to spread her wings. But life without AB was not, for Josie, the mecca I anticipated. I could see she was seriously reconsidering, but my words seemed to calm her. Together, we went to the door that led to the front garden and, on my own, I stepped Out of the house. Aside from my escape attempt on 2 May, it was the first time in my life I'd ever done such a thing – and this felt *so* different because this time I had Josie's permission.

I turned back to where she was waiting in the doorway. 'This is the first time I have ever stepped Out into the garden on my own!' I exclaimed. It felt so . . . *wow!*

Josie hugged me; I think she appreciated how momentous the occasion was for me. When we let go, I turned away from her and slowly walked down the garden path to the gate. When I reached it, I felt both exhilarated and daunted. *How do I . . .?* It felt so alien to reach out a hand to work the mechanism to release it. But the low, metal-barred gate swung open at my touch and I stepped through. I remember wishing that Roddy was around so I might be able to say hello, but I hadn't seen him all that much lately.

I put my head down and started the short walk to the Tesco Express around the corner. It was a route I'd taken many times before with Bala, so it was relatively easy to retrace our footsteps and figure out the route. I hesitated a little when I reached the traffic lights, though, scared about crossing the two-way street. Bala had always been the one who told me when to cross; really, not even that. I just walked when he walked, and stopped when he stopped. Stood behind him, I'd never taken in the clues he looked for that instructed him in safe passage; I'd always been told off for ogling. Now faced with the crucial decision myself, it seemed so difficult: how *did* people know when it was safe to step out?

Luckily, the road was very quiet and there wasn't much traffic. I waited until there was a clear gap and scurried across, heart pounding fast, first with fear – then with elation that I'd made it!

In the Tesco, I wandered around aimlessly, the £10 note Josie had given me burning a hole in my handbag. *I can buy anything I like*, I thought with wonder. The idea was completely mind-boggling. *Decisions, decisions* . . . Eventually, I selected a pair of tights and something chocolatey. The act of buying *whatever took my fancy* was so liberating! I went to the checkout and joined the queue, carefully assessing what I saw other people doing and copying. When my time came, I thrust the note at the cashier and took the change. Luckily, I had not spent over the budget. I still did not really understand the mechanism of money, but I'd identified the ebb and flow of the exchange.

The trip was a triumph. Walking back to the house in the bright August sunshine, my goods swinging in a bag from my arm, I *almost* felt like a free woman.

Just hang in there, I told myself, *soon, you'll be able to do this every day. Soon . . .*

48

The summer segued into autumn, and as though I too was a fading leaf on a wintering tree, I lost *all* my former vitality, such as it had been. I felt weak, faint and giddy. When I went Out to the shops or launderette, I struggled with the short walks there and back. I felt tired and thirsty all the time, and every now and then a dark shade would drop across my eyes. Though I would have struggled to remember the last time I'd felt truly well, this was way out, even for me.

So poor was my health that I struggled even to enjoy those new experiences of 'training' that Josie continued to treat me with. I did another solo trip Outside, this time tracing the familiar route to the chemist and Low-Price Food and Wine; on another occasion, towards the end of September, Josie and I went shopping together in Brixton – *without* AB! I tried to buy beer in the Sainsbury's, but the cashier thought I was underage; as I had no ID I couldn't prove I was thirty. Josie bought it instead, and we snuck home and drank it with Aisha: three house-elves secretly sipping on some Stella Artois. I was personally disappointed by the taste – on the telly, people seemed to like beer so much, and I thought it should have tasted better for all the fuss made of it. We didn't drink much, as none of us was used to it – Aisha's head went funny and Josie said her legs started going wobbly! – yet it gave us all a good laugh.

I wasn't laughing now, in the middle of October. I was doing my best to concentrate on the 6 o'clock news, already dreading the Vampire Puking that would inevitably follow. As I watched, I found my interest perking up. There was an item about forced marriage; a woman was being interviewed about some ladies she had rescued from it. Her name was Aneeta Prem. *Prem* . . . Though I hated my former name, I couldn't help but wonder: is this some kind of sign?

After the feature, a helpline number flashed up on the screen.

'If anything in this piece has affected you, or if you know anyone in a similar situation, call this number,' intoned an authoritative voice.

I chanced a quick glance at Josie and could see she was thinking the same as me: *this might be an option* . . . The charity rescued women from situations in which they didn't want to be, saving them from overbearing family members who thought they knew best how to run their lives and offered no autonomy. Was not that my situation? We both memorized the number, then after the news we scurried to Josie's room, closed the door and scribbled it down before we could forget.

Over the next day or so, we made notes about what we might say to the helpline. We didn't want to waste what could be our one chance to reach out to someone Outside who might help us. We decided not to give our real names in case something went wrong. If Bala got wind of this, there would be hell to pay.

Once we were ready, Josie shut herself in my room and made the call on our secret mobile: it had to be Josie who made the call because I didn't know how to speak on the phone. She came out after only a few moments and beckoned me in. The helpline number, she said, had connected to a recorded message giving the numbers of several different charities. Which was the best one to call?

The name of one jumped out at me: Freedom Charity.

'Freedom sounds good . . .' I said wistfully.

I went out of the room again while Josie made the call, keeping lookout. When she'd finished, she called me back in.

'Do you know what the woman said?' she whispered. I shook my head. What would someone Outside think of my life? I couldn't imagine. 'She said she had never heard such an awful story.'

I felt like crying when I heard that. I felt believed and *validated*. All my life, I'd been told I was stupid and selfish for wanting freedom. But this woman seemed to dispute that. What had happened to me *was* wrong. Hearing that someone else thought so too gave me a lot more confidence in my feelings than I'd ever had before.

Josie organized a code word with the charity for when we called and told them we could speak only at a certain time: when Bala and Chanda were busy watching their soaps, which we were not permitted to view. We knew they loved those programmes so they were not likely to be nosing about then: it was an ideal time to make the calls. Over the next few days, arrangements began to be made for our escape. It felt miraculous that everything was moving so fast.

Oddly, when I think back to this time now, my memory clouds over the dates and details in a way it has never done at any other time. I can tell you exact dates of events even from very early in my childhood. Because nothing *ever* happened to me, when it did, whether a trip Outside or a particular argument, it became instantly immortalized in my memory. I'd also had years in which to review all my diaries, rereading them over and over, communicating with my younger self every now and then. I knew with pinpoint accuracy the day I went to London Zoo or the day Roddy took his dog for a walk.

But now, with events unfolding so rapidly, I couldn't keep track. I couldn't keep pace with it all, mentally. But perhaps that was what happened Outside, I reasoned. Perhaps Outside worked at a faster speed than inside the Collective – in the same way that, on other planets in sci-fi stories, a hundred years can pass in the blink of an Earthling's eye.

It was rather disconcerting, if exhilarating. I found it hard to believe that it was ever going to work, that we were actually going to get Out, but at the same time I really hoped that it would. Leaving was a leap of faith for me because I could not imagine where I was going to go or what I was going to do. That's why Josie agreeing to come along was such a great comfort – because she knew how to survive in the world far better than I did.

I anticipated that we would have to spend a few days sleeping on the streets. Because of that, I stipulated with Josie that we couldn't possibly leave until *Doctor Who* had been broadcast in November (now we had made contact with the charity, she seemed prepared to bring forward her own proposed leaving date). After all, a TV programme was only on once and if we happened to miss it because we had no TV, I would *never* find out what happened! *Doctor Who* was one of the few pleasures in my life, so it was too important to me to miss it. Josie seemed only too happy to agree, for she was in no rush to leave Bala.

On Saturday 19 October (I think!), Bala and I went to the shops. As had become my habit, I had taken a love letter to Roddy with me so I could post it through his letterbox while we were Out.

297

Shopping done, Bala and I made our slow way home, my anticipation rising with every measured step.

Bala went through the gate and I pulled the letter from my bag. In my confused memory, I can't quite recall what happened next – either I dropped it or the letter was too bulky to fit – but I made some slight sound of unexpected movement. It prompted Bala to turn around.

As quickly as I could, I concealed the envelope and tried to look nonchalant. I injected liquid innocence into my expression and stared vacantly ahead. He seemed not to notice – but could I trust that? Perhaps he was just playing safe. Perhaps he knew everything already! Would he really spare me a third time, after I had tried to flee on 2 May and then betrayed him with Roddy? Was he already plotting my death? I could not put it past him.

My heart was in my mouth. Though Bala betrayed no sign of having seen, I panicked. I obediently followed him inside and went through the motions of putting away the shopping, but as soon as I could I cornered Josie.

'I'm feeling very ill,' I declared emphatically. 'We have to go *soon*.'

After that, our plans snowballed. Josie told the charity I was poorly and they were swift to act. We said we were keen to stay in London after our rescue; I wanted to be able to see Roddy whenever I liked. But they said it was not a good idea to stay so close by and in the end we agreed, for we didn't want to be running into Bala and Chanda all the time at the shops after we escaped. They suggested Leeds instead: they said they could get us to a safe house there, run by a charity called the Palm Cove Society.

Leeds? Even I knew it was *very* far away from London! Though I couldn't say with any certainty what my hometown of London looked like – having never had much chance to see beyond AB's back, and certainly not in recent years – Leeds seemed somehow exotic and foreign in comparison. We quickly said no, we wanted somewhere closer to home . . . but it turned out there wasn't anywhere else available.

'Maybe it'll be good to make a clean break and start anew,' I said to Josie in the end, desperate to get Out now in case Bala was playing dumb. 'We can always come back and pick up with our friends later. Let's just make a fresh start for now.'

By 'friends', I meant Roddy, Aisha and the friends from the launderette. Aisha could not escape with us, partly because we were still fearful of her unwittingly betraying any plan, but also because someone would need to stay with Shobha when we fled, as she was usually left at home when AB and Chanda went Out, and their going Out would provide our only option for escape. I hoped after Josie and I had gone that we would be able to rescue Aisha too, but we couldn't take her with us on this first Flight to Freedom.

Ultimately, we said yes to the safe house in Leeds. A leaving date was set: Friday 25 October 2013. It was a beautiful feeling to be able to count down to it – but I had been in this position before. I was terrified that something would come up that would change it: that AB and Chanda would decide not to go shopping when they always did, or that they'd go to the corner shop and not Brixton and thus come home early to find us half in and half out the door. When Bala fell and hurt his nose the weekend before the set date, a tremor of terror ran through me – were we cursed? Would this mean he would not go Out as we needed him to? But I just had to trust that everything would be OK.

We started packing. Josie had requested that a car came to collect us and our things, but we'd been told to bring only one suitcase each. How can you fit a life of thirty years into one suitcase? It wasn't possible: my writings alone needed twice that space.

I was petrified about leaving something precious behind – a scrawled sentence or a pithy poem – so I combed through every box and bag I'd ever possessed to ensure that even the smallest bit of paper which had my writing on it was put in my files. *No one gets left behind.* My photocopied writings went in document wallets, which I then wrapped in one black bag, then two black bags, then *three* black bags to make sure they didn't get wet. By the end I had filled two huge raffia laundry bags just with my writings.

There was only one element of my penmanship that I decided would stay in the cult: my childhood diaries, which I'd been forced to write by AB and Sian. I was *so* embarrassed by them – and not the usual embarrassment that any adult might feel about their childish thoughts. I felt it as a mortifying shame. For in those diaries, I had believed 100 per cent in Bala: I'd had complete faith in the new world, and in Overt, and in his godlike powers. I wanted no memory of the humiliating way I'd been brought up by the cult to believe in their nonsense; no reminder that I had once thought they were *protecting* me, when it had *always* been abuse. *Comrade Prem is long dead: long live Rosie.* I wanted a clean slate from *all* of that. I took only my adult writings and diaries with me: the writings that *were* me.

Pretty much everything else I owned, however, went into the bags. I packed any trinket anyone had ever given me – even if it came from Bala. If someone had given me a gift, it was precious to me because it was so rare. I treasured such things, even if I didn't like the person giving it. One bag after another was filled: in the end, I had four laundry bags, a handbag *and* a pink duffel bag to take with me; Josie also packed a bag and a rucksack. We decided there was so much stuff to transport we would have to employ the trolleys we used to take the washing to the launderette. The two of us did a practice midweek, strapping the bags to the trolleys to check they didn't fall over. It was a success.

I felt a tingle run down my spine. The next time we did it, it would be the real deal . . .

It was on the Wednesday, I think, that the charity mentioned that the police would be involved. Suddenly, all the excitement dwindled and died, as though our plans were a tape in an old cassette player and the ribbon had got chewed. My former fears for Roddy flared up – but it was explained that the police would be there for our protection. Though we were hoping to get Out while Bala went shopping with Chanda, nobody quite knew how he would react if this plan went wrong, so we were informed that plainclothes police would be dotted about the estate to protect us, just in case.

When they explained it, I felt really touched by that. *The police care enough about silly brainless me to ensure I am safe?* How I loved the idea of their protection: I, who had never been protected all my life.

But Josie thought differently.

'Shall we just call it off, then, if they're going to involve the police?' she said anxiously.

'No!' I exclaimed. 'I understand where you're coming from – we don't want any trouble for anyone – but we need to go ahead with this. I am dying here.' I took a deep breath and spoke frankly. 'For the first time now, *I* make the decision. All my life, the decisions have always been in Chanda's hands, and she made bad decisions about me *all the time*. Now *I* make the decision to leave, and *I* make the decision whether or not to involve the police – that is *my* choice to make.'

I think she understood where I was coming from too; at any rate, to my relief, she agreed we would continue.

And so, the day before we were due to depart for good, I put pen to paper in the cult for what I hoped would be the very last time. I wanted to write to AB. I didn't want him to think we had just vanished: I wanted to explain and to tell him, truly, how I felt.

I would leave the letter on his desk, I decided, ready for him to read when he came home to find us gone. I picked up a red pen – the colour the Collective used for all their most important statements – and I wrote:

For: My Abusers and Tormentors,

    I know I have been acting as if everything's fine for the past few years – but still, I don't think you should be surprised to find that I have gone away – and will <u>never, ever, ever</u> be returning!

    There are <u>no words</u> to describe the <u>extreme hurt and anger</u> that I feel about the <u>totally inhuman</u> way you lot have treated me – chaining me up here like a prisoner, treating me as your private property and personal plaything – controlling every aspect of my life and deciding everything for me with <u>absolutely no regard</u> for my feelings. I am mortally offended about the utter disrespect, the endless indignities to which I have been subjected ever since I was a little girl . . . Caged up like a wild animal, deprived of what <u>really</u> matters to me (and no, I do not mean material things) . . .

    I have, over the years, <u>repeatedly pleaded</u> with you lot not to abuse me like this, but all you have done is brush it aside, and have continued to subject me to even more abuse, expecting me to believe all your ludicrous stories and excuses as if I'm a dim witted, silly little girl. I'm <u>sick to death</u> of being held hostage by you lot. You think you can just fob me off with a few stupid words and tall stories – you just think I feel perfectly happy being treated any old how, used and abused as you fancy. You think I just simply have to take <u>anything</u> you do to me – any cruelty or indignity to which you subject me – and I'm supposed to love

*it and praise it and be grateful for it! You lot have just ordered me to
sacrifice, without my consent – for nothing except your over-bloated
egos!* . . .

*And it's not as if I haven't told you repeatedly how I feel . . . How
many times I have woken up crying, after nightmares about bullying!
How many times I have wished I was dead, just to escape your torment! What a cruel, selfish lot you are! There's no words to describe
the <u>harm</u> you have done to me . . . All you lot really care about is
preserving your comfortable lifestyle . . . while your own daughter suffers and wastes away right in front of you! And on top of all this, you
expect me to worship you and promote you and go along with all your
<u>sick</u> fantasies – well, <u>not any more</u>!*

*You really ought to be ashamed of yourselves – and if you're not, it
means that there is something <u>severely</u> wrong with you.*

<u>Not</u> hoping to see you soon,
Rosie Davies

*P.S. You would have noticed that I have changed my name. I want
<u>nothing</u> to do with my old life – the life of <u>abuse</u>. That name has <u>nothing</u>
but bad memories – of all the times everybody was <u>bad</u> to me. When I
hear that name, I feel robbed of my dignity – it's like your stamp on me,
claiming me as your property. I loathe that ugly name! . . . You must
have heard of abused people who change everything about themselves in
an attempt to distance themselves from the agony they have endured – so
that they can <u>heal</u>. That's what I am doing – remaking myself to rebuild
my life!*

*P.P.S. I would not mind meeting up with you lot in future, but I will
<u>never, ever</u> return to your evil dungeon – you have to treat me with
respect . . . . I may have no wealth, no property, no position, no prestige –
but <u>I do have my dignity</u> and I will <u>defend it with my life</u>! I will let NO
ONE abuse me!!!*

I took a deep breath and exhaled. I put the pen down. *I am done.*
One more sleep until freedom.

49

The day was bright and sunny when I woke the following morning: that's what I remember. I took it to be a good sign. Yet I yawned widely as I threw back the blankets, exhaustion more than excitement motivating my movements. Beyond my now-usual faint feeling, I hadn't been able to sleep properly. I'd tossed and turned all night, terrified something would go wrong at the last moment. *I hope Josie doesn't decide to chicken out now and yap*, I'd fretted. *I hope these people coming to collect us keep their promise.*

All through that morning, Josie and I were careful to keep to our usual rota, cautious in case Bala or Chanda somehow caught wind of our plans. Josie had discussed our schedule at length with the woman from the Palm Cove Society, Yvonne, who was coming to collect us. We'd told her she had to come at 11.15 a.m. *sharp.* Any sooner, and we or they might run into Bala as he left the house, just before 11 a.m.; he and Chanda were fond of taking a turn around the communal grounds before they went to the shops. Any later, and we ran the risk of bumping into him on his way back, if he'd only gone round the corner and not to Brixton as we hoped.

If anything went wrong, we put in place a Plan B: the pick-up would be cancelled, but Josie and I would try to get to Elephant and Castle later that day instead. Finally, we instructed them *not* to come to the house – we didn't even tell them our address – but to wait outside another property around the corner. That was partly motivated by my desire to protect Roddy, too – I didn't want the police snooping on his doorstep just in case.

I was so scared of all that could go wrong, but one thing reassured me: Josie had told me that Yvonne and her husband, Gerard, had made a special point of coming down to London the night before to ensure they would not be late. I thought that was such a nice thing to do. I guess they must have been as worried as I was that they might get caught in traffic on the long drive south. Now, they were only round the corner. We just had to make sure we could meet them.

It had become my habit to have a bath in the morning. I did exactly as I'd always done, which meant, after it, I dressed quickly, pulling some navy-blue jeans over my now-jutting hipbones, and obediently went to meet Bala in the living room.

He greeted me with his usual expectant manner: expecting me to be subservient and submit myself to his will. He looked me up and down with the cool, assessing eyes of a horse-trainer. 'Body wash or hair wash today?' he asked unctuously.

I resisted the urge to recoil from him, to bite his head off and scream: 'I am THIRTY years old, you have NO RIGHT to ask me such a personal question! I AM NOT YOUR PROPERTY!' Instead, I answered meekly: 'Hair wash.' But I thought to myself, *That's the last time you will* ever *ask me that question, you creep.*

It was the last time, too, that I had to edge close to him and submit to his creepy cuddle. Every day, twice a day, for my entire life, he had embraced me like this. I held my breath against the stink of his sweat and let him trail his fingers up and down my back. I can't honestly say that the final embrace meant anything to me: I didn't hug him back because I knew it was goodbye – my final chance to hold my father. I was just desperately trying to act as normally as possible so that he didn't notice anything was different. I couldn't make a moment of our final moment together – because to do so would ensure it *wasn't* the last.

Nonetheless, as I took my leave of him, knowing I would not see him again before he left for the shops, I did feel sad. I felt sad that it had come to this. Because none of this – the secret escape and the police and the need to involve Outsiders – would have happened if he had just given me a bit more freedom. Yet I did not feel regret. On the contrary: I felt glad that I was going to get a break from all his nonsense.

I did a final check of my belongings, and then Josie and I strapped the bags to the trolleys so we'd be ready. At the last minute, I pulled a long black skirt with rose-pink flowers on it over my jeans, wanting to take it with me but having no more room in my bags. Then all we could do was wait: wait for the click of the front door that meant our abusers had gone.

As soon as we heard it, Josie and I went into the kitchen to find Aisha. We spoke in hushed voices for fear Shobha might hear us, but her door was shut and she had her radio on so there was little risk.

'We're going,' I said to her gently, knowing the news would come as a shock. 'Somebody is coming for us at quarter past and we are going. I'm sorry we didn't tell you, but we were so afraid you might scream about it in your sleep.'

Aisha burst into tears. I do think she was glad for us, but at the same time she was so sad at the thought of being left behind with those horrible people.

'We will come for you,' we promised her. By this time, Josie had bought us house-elves a mobile phone each, so Aisha secretly had her own mobile. 'We will arrange it on the mobile phone and we *will* get you Out too.'

We were all crying by then, the emotion too great to be contained within. But even as we cried, the time was ticking by. We had to be quick.

Carefully, I wrapped my burgundy scarf around my neck and then pulled on the red anorak Oh had given me for my sixteenth birthday. I'd gone Out so rarely in the intervening years that it was still in mint condition.

Josie and I wheeled the trolleys out from where we had hidden them in my bedroom; Josie seemed anxious, I thought, but perhaps she was just worried, as I was, that something might still go wrong. We placed our leaving letters, clipped together, on AB's desk. Then there was just time for a final hug with Aisha. *Oh, Aisha . . .* Aisha, who had perhaps been the first comrade to break the rules and *touch* me; Aisha, who had always been kind when she could. We wrapped our arms around each other, both crying our hearts out, and squeezed as tightly as we dared, trying to say without words what in fact could never be said.

'Keep strong,' I told her. 'Everything will be all right.'

'Yes, yes,' Aisha whispered, speaking through her tears. We locked eyes for a moment. Hers had perhaps been the first to see the real little girl inside me: the soul inside the soldier. I stared back at her with love and thankfulness. 'Be careful,' she told me. One last lingering hug . . . Though I really hated to let her go, I had to.

It was Aisha who opened the front door, taking the key from her pocket with that cruel clink that had tormented me for so long. But, now, she used that key to open up the door to freedom.

I hovered on the threshold just for an instant. It was similar, in a way, to my hesitation on 2 May. But this time I didn't pause because I feared a lightning bolt might strike me dead, it was more that I was struggling to believe the moment had finally come. Since the night of horror, Bala had played such mind games with me that it was almost impossible for me to make sense of the fact that something I had longed for had *actually* arrived. This wasn't a fantasy, although I had played it out in my mind a million times. This was real. But only the weight of the trolley in my hand seemed to tell me so. I was gripped by a sense of unreality, even as I lifted my foot and crossed the threshold for the very last time.

I prayed that Bala hadn't forgotten something and was already on his way back; in fright, my brain was painting pictures of what might happen if he suddenly came round the corner. I knew I wouldn't feel safe until I was sat in Yvonne and Gerard's car. But first we had to cross the estate to reach them.

Josie stepped out behind me, wheeling her own heavy trolley. Together, we walked down the path. Aisha kept the door open, watching us go. But as I turned back to look at the building, it was not her that my hopeful gaze sought. Instead, I raised my eyes sky-wards, towards Roddy's flat on the upper levels.

He was not there; not that I could see. Nevertheless, I mouthed to him: 'Goodbye. I'll see you again. Thank you, thank you, *thank you.*' Because even though he was not there to see me leaving, without him I would never have left. Without him, I'd never have had the strength to withstand my torture, nor reached the insight that made me Enlightened. He had truly been my Angel: an angel I'd first glimpsed on a New Year's Day, who had shown me the way to my brand new life. I knew I could never have done this without him.

I turned back to face the way to freedom. Awkwardly, my body stiff and slow from illness and imbalance, I walked away from my love. Step by slow step, Josie and I picked our way across the estate. It felt so different to leaving on 2 May. For that had been heading out into the complete unknown: a shot in the dark that had ended in failure. But, this time, I had a plan. I had a friend. There was a light; and a Yorkshire woman, named Yvonne, who was waiting for me – I hoped – just around the next corner.

I paused before we turned it. I glanced back one last time to my prison, to the place where I had spent so many hours staring out of the window at the world going by without me.

I was on the Outside now.

I raised a hand: to Aisha, still standing in the doorway; to Roddy above, just in case he was there. A wave goodbye to my old life: a caged bird's final flutter of those wings that felt so clipped. As I turned again, it was almost as if they unfurled behind me for the very first time: the feathers scraggy and unkempt, but spreading out in the bright sunshine all the same. I took a step, and then another, and with each one the wings behind me seemed to shimmer at my shoulder blades, making a train behind me to grace the grandest red carpet I had ever seen in the magazines. And as I rounded the corner my wings rose, unpractised, as though I was on the edge of a high cliff, about to hurl myself into thin air.

In so many ways, I was.

It was time to figure out if this caged bird could learn to fly.

Part Five
Learning to Fly

50

I didn't really expect anyone to be round the corner yet, but the moment I cleared it with my lumbering steps, I saw a tall woman in a burgundy jacket waiting for us, just as she had promised. She turned as she heard us coming.

Oh my, she was *gorgeous*! Smooth black skin, long black braided hair . . . She looked nothing like the dour Yorkshire woman I'd expected – and all the better for it.

'Are you Yvonne?' Josie asked as we approached her. We thought she must be, but we weren't sure.

'I am,' she said in her thick Northern accent. It sounded like crumpets and hot tea.

The moment I reached her, I flung my arms around her. I liked her immediately – she was so warm and motherly, and it was such a joy to see her there! She hugged me back and I squeezed harder. I didn't cry – there were too many things going on for me to focus my emotions in that way – but I felt relief and happiness washing through me. Almost simultaneously, I heard a car door opening: a rather jolly, tall white man got out of the black Jaguar parked a stone's throw away and invited Josie to start loading her bags into the boot.

'This is my husband, Gerard,' Yvonne said. 'And this is Leigh.'

I stared as a blonde woman slid out of the back seat of the car and came over to say hello. Though she seemed nice enough, she had a bit of an official manner about her and I didn't warm to her instantly; Yvonne explained she was one of the police officers who had come to help us.

The first thought that came into my mind was: *I don't want Roddy to get involved in this. I don't want you to talk to Bala in case he dishes dirt on Roddy.*

So when she started asking me questions, I said abruptly: 'I don't want my parents to be in any trouble; I just want to be free. I don't want any harm to come to them: my parents are good people.'

I said that even though I did not believe it was true.

By now, Josie and Gerard had finished loading all our bags into the boot. I was so relieved there was room for everything.

'Now I have to go back,' Josie announced.

Immediately, Yvonne and Leigh started protesting, saying she didn't, but Josie cried, 'Yes I do!' and set off running across the estate.

I think Yvonne believed that Josie had abandoned me. 'Where has she gone?' she asked, clearly agitated. 'Is she going back to danger?'

'No,' I answered calmly. 'She'll be fine; she'll be back soon.'

It was part of our plan. Shobha always had a toilet break at 11.30, so Josie had decided she would go back to help her one last time – partly out of kindness, and partly so that Shobha didn't raise the alarm. Though we'd left Aisha there to look after Shobha in case of an emergency, Josie was always the one who helped her on and off the toilet – Aisha was too slight to lift her. Yvonne didn't know our schedule, so she was panicking, but I trusted that Josie would return.

'OK, you get in the car then,' Yvonne said, and I happily bent my body into the vehicle. That feeling was so nice. *At last I'm safe, I'm here in this car, and these nice people are going to look after me. There's no way I'm going to be taken back into that horrible place ever again.*

Yvonne got in next to me while we waited for Josie. She was a little on edge, and no wonder – for her, this was a major police operation, and one of the victims they were rescuing had just run back into the jaws of who-knew-what – but nevertheless she had this amazing warmth that oozed from her like melted chocolate. I felt so safe in her presence that I ventured a few words about what had happened.

'I've been an unperson all my life,' I confided. 'It is *so* nice to be here and safe at last. I've never had anybody to talk to. Nobody would listen to what I had to say.'

But Yvonne was listening now. I can't tell you what that meant to me. I felt elated to be free.

'Are you OK?' she asked me. No one had ever really asked me such a question before.

I said I was, even though I felt faint and slightly sick, because the feeling of freedom superseded all my physical ailments. Before we had escaped, knowing I was poorly, Yvonne had asked if we needed a doctor to be present, but we'd said no. We had no idea what was wrong with me, after all. Perhaps all I needed was freedom to make me well.

There was no time to discuss it further because at that moment we all spotted Josie, on her way back to us after helping Shobha. There was a flurry of activity: Yvonne moved seats to sit in the front, Gerard got into the driver's seat and put the key in the ignition, and Leigh stood outside the car with the back door open, ready to usher Josie into the middle of the seats so we could make a quick getaway.

From the safety of the car, I watched my friend walking. Her face looked different. She was frowning with her whole brow knotted, eyes squinting against the squashed lines of her forehead, and she looked very, very upset. As she slid across the car seat towards me, she gave a huge sigh. Though she half smiled at me, and touched my arm in a sort of 'well done' gesture, she did not seem at all chirpy, as I felt inside. The moment Gerard started the engine and the car backed away from the flats, I felt this soaring sense of freedom, but there was no hint of jubilation from Josie, as I'd always imagined in my fantasies. I think we did hold hands once or twice as the car drove off, but the feeling I got from her was not what I'd expected. It was as if she felt we had lost more than we'd gained, but the same equation in my mind gave me more than I could grasp.

Gerard steered us smoothly down the London streets. Purely by chance, as we drove away I spotted a familiar couple walking on the pavement towards the car.

'They're there!' I exclaimed in horror. I couldn't help but shrivel in my seat, feeling scared at the sight of AB and Chanda. I pulled my scarf over my head and ducked down, so that if they happened to look inside the car they would not recognize me.

'It's all right,' Yvonne said soothingly. 'They haven't seen us.'

And they hadn't. Proof, if any more were needed, that AB did *not* know everything. Literally from under his nose, we were stealing away. I glanced back at them as the car drove on. They were happily shopping. Part of me felt a bit guilty then, that they were going to come home and find us not there. But only part of me.

Gerard put his foot down, and first feet and then miles divided me from my dad. That was a wonderful feeling. It was as if, with every spin of the Jaguar's wheels, a message went round and round in my brain: *He can't hurt me any more.* I wound the window down, rejoicing at my liberty to do so, and felt the fresh air on my face. It was lovely, fabulous, remarkable, extraordinary . . . Despite having read the whole dictionary, I still didn't have the words to be able to describe it.

It was simply the best feeling in the world.

We didn't go to Leeds immediately. Instead, we went to a secret meeting point in south London. Leigh wanted to interview Josie and me, informally, and Yvonne and Gerard joined us.

I could tell Josie wasn't happy about it, talking to the 'fascist state', but I helped them as much as I was able to, though I made sure not to mention Roddy. I could feel Josie trying to 'shush' me several times as I spoke, but I kept talking nonetheless – just in general terms about my captivity, not pointing the finger at my father. I thought if I betrayed AB, he would betray me by hurting Roddy, and this fear held me back, even though I really wanted to tell all. I was also scared that if I started talking about the Overt and JACKIE they would not believe me, as I could appreciate how outlandish it all sounded. If they thought I was a fantasist, might they send me back? I found it very difficult to speak confidently about how I felt so when I wasn't giving my answers to Leigh I directed my eyes towards the ground.

In the periphery of my downward-facing gaze I noticed something peculiar happening to Josie's arm, the moment she realized I would not stay silent. A red blotch that looked as if it was bleeding surfaced on her skin. It appeared, then disappeared. When I glanced up at her, the same thing was happening on her face. She was breaking out in blotches; I think it was a sign of stress. I was a little shocked: I knew she was upset about the police being involved, but I'd anticipated that her affection for me would overcome this concern. She didn't have to take part in it, after all: *I* was the one who was talking. Throughout my long strategy, I'd always hoped that once we escaped and Josie reconnected with the Outside world, she would realize that the Collective was crazy. As I watched those blood-red blotches flood her face and then fade, however, I grasped that she had a long way to go.

'I think Josie has Stockholm Syndrome,' I declared to Yvonne, Gerard and Leigh.

A ripple of surprise almost visibly weaved through the room. I suppose all they knew about me was that I'd been kept captive since birth: they didn't know about my secret-reading and were therefore shocked that I had both the knowledge and insight to discuss such a condition. I think they were astonished, too, that I was less brainwashed than Josie, even though I'd been born in the cult. I felt chuffed at that, and proud I had been so sensible. All those years I had stood alone, refusing to be browbeaten into belief despite verbal, emotional and physical abuse: now I knew it had all been worth it.

Leigh explained that, from the very little I had said, what had happened to me could be classed as a crime. I felt vindication at that; in my diary, I had long called my father a 'criminal', but until I'd got Out I didn't know for sure that I had properly understood the situation. To hear it spelled out, and to know that I was believed, was a great comfort. I didn't think about what might come next, if AB *had* committed a crime; I was just so overwhelmed to be Out and talking to Outsiders. It was such a huge relief to no longer be isolated; to be surrounded by people who thought what had happened was as wrong as I did. All my life, I had been apart, different, and shunned for my opinions. Now, they were being endorsed. It felt as if the world had turned upside-down.

We were offered a 'comfort break' and Yvonne escorted me round the corner to the loos. As I closed the cubicle door, to my surprise I heard the main door of the bathroom close behind Yvonne as she went back to the others.

She had left me on my own.

I stilled in my movements, listening to the strange sound of no one else breathing but me. For only the second time in my life I was going to go to the toilet Outside on my own. A beat later, I started jumping up and down in excitement, even though it hurt my aching body to do it.

I am free! I thought ecstatically as I bounced. *And, this time, I am free for good! YIPPEE!!!!*

I felt as if I was riding on the crest of a wave. I kept expecting it to break, for the icy waters to splash over my head and wake me from this dream, but I kept on surfing. I surfed all the way back to

Yvonne and exclaimed with a broad smile: 'I've never been allowed to go to the toilet on my own!' She smiled back, perhaps with some sadness behind her brown eyes, but seeming to share in my joy at being free.

By now it was lunchtime so we all ate minestrone soup – which tasted *delicious*! Then, after another comfort break, I came back from the loos to find Aisha there in her pink anorak! I was so delighted to see her that I threw my arms around her and squeezed.

Aisha seemed very shocked to be free. Unlike Josie and me, who had been planning this for months and had known the exact date of the escape, Aisha had suddenly been whisked away from all she knew. She seemed stunned, stressed, happy, in awe . . . I think, like Josie, she was also anxious to be away from AB. She had followed him since 1969. It must have been incredibly strange for her to be apart from him after all those years.

We asked her what had happened after we'd left. Shaking, on the verge of tears, she told us AB had been enraged to find us gone; he'd said we were 'too much' – if we'd had issues we should have raised them with him, rather than going to the fascist state (conveniently, he had seemingly forgotten that every time I *had* raised my issues with him, he had cruelly swept them aside). He'd berated Aisha too for 'not noticing' our going (this was what we had told her to say). He was still denouncing us as the Collective prepared to sit down to lunch – and it was at that time that there came a knock upon the door.

It was the police.

'Don't open the door!' Bala had exclaimed.

'We're from Scotland Yard. We've come because of the two ladies who left the property earlier!' they'd shouted through it.

When Aisha told me that, I felt a tingle of delight run through me. To think I meant so much to someone that they would actually investigate what had happened to me!

Eventually, the door had been opened; Aisha had immediately broken down in tears. She said one of the officers had ushered her outside, where they talked to her privately and urged her not to return.

'But I'm too old to start anew,' Aisha had said; she was sixty-nine. 'I've spent too long here to go anywhere else.'

'But you won't be alone,' the officer had reminded her. 'Rosie and Josie are out now and you can join them.'

Ultimately, Aisha had said that if she could be with us, she would leave. She asked the police to tell AB they were arresting her because of her immigration status, then slipped back inside for a final time to pick up a few of her things. I believe she hugged Bala and Chanda goodbye, then she was whisked away by the police to join us at the secret meeting point.

I was *so* pleased Aisha was Out now too, and so soon; I'd felt terrible leaving her behind, but now we three house-elves were reunited!

Very shortly after that, the three of us climbed into the back of Gerard's big Jaguar and began the long drive north to the safe house we'd been promised in Leeds. I stared Out of the window in wonder, seeming to see my home city with new eyes just as I was leaving it. Though I was sad to be parting from Roddy, the sprawling metropolis had no hold on my heart. I'd been Out so little I felt like a stranger in that city, even though I'd lived there all my life.

It was still light as we left London. As we joined the motorway, I stared in amazement at the rushing rivers of zooming cars, and then in astonishment at the huge wind turbines turning in the fields we passed. I tried to avoid looking around too much, however; I was experiencing this weird sense of vertigo at being Out and I was afraid of being sick, especially with the motion of the car.

I found it hard to believe that the motorway just kept going: a ribbon of concrete that seemed never to end. When I'd been in Comrade Simons' car, we'd completed only short journeys. It seemed miraculous that the road kept on unspooling in front of us, no matter how many miles we drove. I *loved* it. My world had always been blocked before – by a sheet of glass or a locked front door. But, in this Outside world, it seemed there were no barriers.

I sat back and tried to enjoy the journey. It was such a comforting feeling to be there in the car, with all my writings safe in the boot and Aisha and Josie both well and whole and beside me as they'd always been. As we put more and more miles between me and the monster who had caged me, I felt free at last – at long, long last. I savoured the sweet cool wind from the window blowing in my face. It almost felt too good to be true. Everything I'd *ever* wanted!

At some point on the journey, we stopped at a service station. I stepped out of the car excitedly at this new experience and walked straight towards the shop. I had no concept of any possible danger; I didn't even notice the cars I walked in front of, nor the way Yvonne and Gerard darted around me, trying to keep me safe. I had eyes only for the twinkling toys and brightly coloured books they sold in the store. 'Oh wow,' I said as I stood before them. I still wasn't used to the range of things that were stocked in shops. It stopped me in my stride: all I could do was stare. I blinked, several times, as I stood before those things. It was strange, but the dark haze I'd sometimes experienced in the house had dropped before my eyes again. No matter how many times I closed my eyes, when I opened them again a slight veil obscured my sight – as though I was wearing dark glasses, but I wasn't.

Eventually, we got back into the car and drove off again. By now, night had fallen. I watched in amazement as lights flickered along the seams of the road. When I looked behind me, however, the ground was dark.

'What are those lights?' I asked in confusion, pointing.

'They're called cat's eyes,' Gerard explained. 'They reflect the headlights.'

Aisha, who had been very quiet, then asked, 'Why are some of the car lights red and some lights white?'

I listened eagerly to the answer; I'd noticed this too, even from looking out of the window in the cult, but I didn't know why it was.

'The white lights are the headlights at the front,' Gerard replied patiently, 'while the red lights, at the back, are the tail-lights; they also show when a car is braking. Red lights are used at the back so drivers can see the cars in front without being blinded by white light.'

We talked so much and I was so happy to have such conversations. It was a total joy for me to speak to people who were not freaky in any way; who didn't want to champion Pol Pot or denigrate good people. We talked about politics and football, which I had followed devotedly because Roddy was a fan of the sport.

'Do you like football?' I asked Gerard.

'Yes,' he replied.

'Who do you like?'

'Oh, the team I like you have probably never heard of,' he said, a smile in his voice.

'Who is it?' I asked curiously.

'Leeds United; we're not really very good at football.'

'Oh!' I exclaimed, nodding my head. 'Leeds United. Don Revie. It used to be a Premiership side.'

I could see Gerard doing a double take as I proceeded to recount everything I'd ever read about Leeds United. There was a fair amount as I'd read the sports section avidly for years now: just in case I ever got a chance to speak to Roddy again, I'd wanted to have something to say. I proceeded to embark on a knowledgeable discussion of Alex Ferguson's recent departure from Man United and questioned whether David Moyes was the right man to replace him. Gerard only just managed to keep the shock from his voice as he chatted with me; I think he was stunned I knew so much about the world when I'd been kept out of it for so long. But all the while I'd been kept in captivity, I had never lost my curiosity about the things that happened Outside.

As the hours passed, the five of us shared sweets and chocolate bars with popping candy. We all relaxed. Yvonne and Gerard weren't the police and I think that really helped the comrades. Bit by bit, Josie, Aisha and I began to talk about what had happened to us.

For the three of us, it was going over familiar ground: complaints and injustices that we'd discussed to death in the house. As such, we fluidly told our story without taking breath. Though I might start a sentence, Josie would finish it, only for Aisha to begin a new statement that I could conclude. We had discussed it all so much in the cult that we each knew what the others were going to say. I saw Yvonne and Gerard exchange a look as we spoke in this way, but at the time I didn't think what we were doing was strange. We had just lived so much in each other's pockets, without any Outside influence, that we had created this way of communicating so that one collective thought was expressed organically by three individual voices.

Aisha and Josie even mentioned JACKIE. Amid their awe at being Out, there was also definite fear. They were guarded in what they were saying because they feared JACKIE would be listening. Though we had escaped Bala, JACKIE had a longer reach and could be reporting back to AB even at this moment. Some terrible harm might be seconds away – because surely Bala would never let us get away with leaving the Collective?

JACKIE was, as I've said, the hardest chain to break. I didn't believe in him, *but . . .* At the back of my mind, in that instinctive part we all have that is not very sane, I still suspected that bad things might happen. I couldn't 100 per cent discount the idea of JACKIE, so I had to keep an open mind. I was respectful of the others' anxiety. The comrades listened apprehensively to the news in case JACKIE had caused death and destruction in retribution. But there was nothing – not on that day, at least.

At about 11 p.m., the black Jaguar slowed its pace on a suburban street and came to a halt. Feeling exhausted now, I slowly stepped out of the car and followed the others into the nearby three-storey red-brick building. Yvonne ushered us into a clean and tidy four-bedroom flat, which also had a bathroom, kitchen and lounge. By now, that dark shade across my eyes was such that I could barely take it in; all I wanted to do was sleep. Yvonne gave me a quick health check, but I reassured her I was OK: though I felt extremely unwell, I'd been poorly for so many years now that it was normal for me.

Before Yvonne and Gerard left, they took out the keys to the flat to give to us. There was a key for Josie, a key for Aisha *and* a key for me. *That* was a surprise.

I stared down at it in wonder: a big gold key clutched tightly in my hand.

'Is this for *me*?' I asked in disbelief. Yvonne said that it was.

Wow. All my dreams, one by one, are coming true. I could hardly believe it. In thirty years, I had never, ever had my own key, nor the freedom it represented to come and go at will.

I blinked hard, feeling the sudden urge to cry. I had been shown more respect, love and kindness by Yvonne and Gerard in this one day than I had by Bala in three decades. It was overwhelming to experience; I simply was not used to being treated as a human, rather than as a possession or a dog.

I got ready for bed quickly after that, pulling the duvet over my body with a sigh of relief. Though everything around me was new and strange, there was also a peculiar feeling of familiarity as I tucked myself in and reflected on the day's events. I had imagined my first night of freedom so often, replaying it over and over in my fantasies, that it was as if I had already experienced it. As such, I found I could take no joy or real emotion from it. The fantasy had become so dog-eared and worn that I couldn't take pleasure in the actual experience. I turned on to my side and stared blindly at the wall.

I'm free, I told myself. *I did it. I got Out.*

Despite my lack of feeling, a bubble of excitement rose up from my belly to my brain.

Tomorrow is the first day of the rest of my life.

51

When I woke the next day, the morning felt full of potential. *This is the beginning of my new life*, I thought, thrilled. Moving slowly, plagued by a tummy pain, I got up and dressed as quickly as I could physically manage. Despite drinking lots of water, my throat remained desperately dry, and the night of sleep had done nothing to assuage my exhaustion.

I tried not to let my sickness dampen my spirits, though. For there was happiness to be found even in those simple morning ablutions. For the first time in twenty years, there was no one to ask me, 'Body wash or hair wash?' when I came out of the shower, and no sweaty fingers crept creepily up my back. In addition, even as I dressed, my golden key shone brightly in my memory, burning a hole in my pocket. I wanted to use it. I wanted to go Out.

For the first time in my life, I could actually *act* on that desire.

My heart pounding with pride and excitement, as soon as I was ready I slipped out of the front door alone, squinting a bit, despite the dark veil, at the brightness of that Outside light. With joy in my heart, I stepped on to the pavement . . .

But then it all went wrong.

I stood rooted to the spot, looking up and down the unfamiliar street. I blinked again in the bright light. During my 'training' trips, I had gone to Tesco and Low-Price Food and Wine alone: both places I'd been many times with Bala. I thought I'd been independent, but all I really had to do was retrace my footsteps, following a route I already knew.

I didn't know this place.

As I stood there, looking up and down the street for clues that might help me take another step – clues that never came – I realized that I had no idea how to navigate my way from A to B. Other than those training trips and 2 May, I had *never* been Outside alone. Though

I squinted at the road signs, they meant nothing to me. The codes I knew were 'KQ' or 'Argos' for 'Ara goes'; I had no idea what the big P meant nor the symbols on the brown signs. I'd wanted to go to the shops, perhaps to buy a drink to slake my raging thirst, but I had no idea which way to go and was too frightened to go it alone. I knew nothing about how to get anywhere, let alone how to get back. The concept of landmarks or techniques for recognizing where I was and where I'd been were unknown to me. I'd never had to learn: all I'd done when I'd gone Out was to follow AB. Without him, and without knowing the route, I was adrift. My fear kept me glued to that spot: supposedly free and yet ensnared by my inabilities.

Bala's words in the cult came back to me: the reason he kept me in was because I did not have the capabilities or the IQ to survive Outside. Though I appreciated I was only like that because he had *made* it so, it made him no less wrong. A horrible sick feeling surfaced in my stomach. All along, I'd thought the only thing standing between me and my dreams was being locked up – but I now realized my situation was a lot more serious.

Because AB wanted to control me, I thought, *he has rendered me disabled. He'd hoped it would prevent me from ever being free. And now that I am free, I am still stuck.*

I felt so angry, frustrated and sad. Unable to do anything else, I walked back into the flat, knowing I would need Josie or Aisha to escort me anywhere we went.

As the door slammed shut behind me, I acknowledged the grim truth.

He couldn't have made me any more disabled if he'd broken both my legs.

After my realization, my first weekend of freedom was spoiled. Nor did things improve when Josie and Aisha took me out. It was not the way I'd expected it at all. In London, I'd believed I'd always walked so slowly because I was forever traipsing behind seventy-three-year-old Bala. I'd anticipated that once I was free I'd be able to walk just like all the other young people I'd seen Outside my window. But that wasn't the case. I could *only* go slowly, lumbering like an old man, struggling to place my feet on the pavement.

Unlike London, which was flat, Leeds was a little hilly. There was a slight incline from the refuge up to the main road and I found I could not manage it without becoming out of breath. My legs ached: pain all over. I felt unsteady on my feet, unable to balance properly, afraid in case I tripped and fell. My fear was not helped by the comrades, who had their own demons to battle. Their fear that JACKIE might strike was palpable. So our outings that weekend were not the happy occasions I'd imagined – me and my friends going to the shops as free people. I was crestfallen to realize that Outside wasn't the happy-ever-after I'd been dreaming of all this time.

I also felt sick all weekend: thirsty, tummy problems, exhausted and dizzy. Still my vagina itched itched itched. When Josie, Aisha and I walked to the offices of the Palm Cove Society on Monday afternoon, which were just down the road from the flat, I was pleased to learn that Yvonne had arranged for us all to see a doctor. She took us to the GP's surgery in her car that same day.

I was excited about seeing the doctor, though a little apprehensive about what might be wrong. I was even more apprehensive that they might say my horrible birth name, which had so many bad connotations for me, but luckily Yvonne had asked them to call me Rosie. That was a great relief. When they called my name, I stood and went alone to the consulting room for my first-ever doctor's appointment.

I felt a sense of unreality again as I knocked on the doctor's door and entered. Could this really be me, seeing a *doctor*, getting a chance to *talk* without somebody else standing on top of me, telling me what I could and couldn't say? The sheer privacy of the doctor/patient dynamic was extraordinary to me.

I had insisted on seeing the doctor alone because I knew I had to mention my itching, which to my mind could be a possible STI, and I didn't want anyone else to know about Roddy and our physical relationship. Luckily, it was a female doctor with a nice friendly face, and she was kind and not at all nosy. I was taken aback by that kindness; it was remarkable to me because I'd spent my whole life being afraid of people, having to tiptoe round them and butter them up so they didn't abuse me, and here she was being lovely when I had done nothing to elicit that approach! That was *really* strange. The itching was the first thing I told her about, before I mentioned my tummy troubles and my thirst and my dramatic weight loss . . .

She gave me something to drink and said she wanted to do a blood test right away to check my blood sugar levels. I felt rather scared at the idea; I thought it would be painful. But the sharp scratch of the needle was not as bad as I'd anticipated and she was soon studying the results.

'I think you're diabetic,' she informed me. My blood sugar level was 23; a normal level should be 4–7. This meant I was hyperglycaemic. The itching was a symptom of this: an infection called thrush, which could be quickly cleared up with the right medication. All that needless itching! I was so angry when I thought about that.

When I mentioned to the doctor that I'd had all these symptoms for many months now, she looked very concerned and said she wanted to do an immediate test for ketones in my urine.

The ketones proved present – and at that point the doctor became urgent in her manner: 'You need to go to hospital at once.'

I didn't really understand what was happening. Yvonne and I went home first, so I could pack a bag for an overnight stay at the hospital; I was to be kept in for several days at least. I remember overhearing her speaking to Josie and Aisha: 'This girl is very, *very* ill.'

Oh! I thought. *I didn't know I was so sick* . . . For although I felt ill, I wasn't collapsing. I was used to battling on. For decades, any ailment of mine had been so downplayed by AB that it was hard for me to appreciate that the things I was feeling were in fact serious.

The doctor had told Yvonne I was on the verge of a diabetic coma; it could have been just hours away. The ketones in my system could lead to DKA (diabetic ketoacidosis), the most serious effects of which include swelling in the brain, life-threatening damage to the kidneys and lungs, loss of consciousness and coma, and eventually – especially if left untreated – death.

I had escaped from my prison not a moment too soon.

What would have happened if Josie and I had waited until June 2014 to escape, as she'd once said? The chances were I would have slipped into a coma this very week; I wouldn't have made it. And would Bala have called an ambulance? He hadn't for Oh . . . I had no doubt that he would have shouted at me, fruitlessly, just as he did her. Perhaps he'd have dialled 999 in the end, but only when it was too late. And when I died, at the age of thirty, he'd have added my name to the list of those people who had met their demise because they hadn't focused on him. I could see exactly how it would have played out.

I think Josie knew it too. She was very upset. She kept hugging me. 'It's so good that we found out, just in time,' she said, 'otherwise you'd have died!'

I was taken swiftly to the hospital, now the centre of attention after decades of neglect. All the staff were so kind and caring, and Yvonne and Gerard were paying special attention to me too. I *loved* it! Though Josie had made me sage tea throughout the past year, this was care on a different scale. And everyone was so concerned to make me comfortable, to consult my opinion, to be sure I was ready for this needle or that drip to be inserted into my body. I'd never been treated as an equal or permitted a right to think before, and now, suddenly, I had all this agency and all these Outsiders being so solicitous! It was overwhelming.

In the midst of my happiness, I was aware of a sense of embarrassment too, especially when it came to Josie and Aisha, who had come with us to the hospital. I believe I was ashamed about being poorly in front of them. I think, in hindsight, it was a hangover from the cult because, in the Collective, to be poorly meant you weren't focusing on Bala. You were a bad person if you were ill. Some vestiges of that clearly remained in me, even though I didn't believe in it any more.

The more time that passed since we'd left the cult, the less bothered I became about Josie and Aisha's opinions. In my immediate world, now, Yvonne and Gerard were the authority figures and I felt drawn to them. I aspired to be like them; I could sense, from observing the way people interacted Outside, that Josie and Aisha still had the funny ways of the cult about them. I wanted to be free of all that. I wanted to be *normal*. The only way I could learn was with Yvonne and Gerard's help, so I paid them lots of attention.

Yvonne was amazing. My biggest fear about staying in the hospital was that I'd have to sleep on a shared or mixed ward. But she arranged a private room for me, so that I could be comfortable. I loved the way she made everything possible with one efficient phone call or a quick word with a consultant.

Yvonne, Gerard and the comrades stayed with me till about 10 p.m. that Monday night as I lay in bed and let the insulin and other medicines do their work to fix me. Eventually, however, visiting hours were over and I was to be left alone.

They all said goodbye and left. I looked around me, still astonished at my situation. Liquids dripped into me from equipment by my bed. Machines beeped and flickered. I felt as if I was in a science-fiction film – so many strange things. But perhaps the oddest of all was that I was in a building with *no one from the Collective* around me. In almost thirty-one years, that had *never* happened before. I had never, ever slept away from home. So despite the fact I was very poorly, despite the fact I'd been poked and prodded in ways I'd never before experienced, I felt pleased. I felt protected.

I felt safe.

I remained delighted when I woke the next morning. The insulin made me feel *so* much better; the dark haze cleared from my eyes. I was so happy to be diagnosed with *something* too. Here was an educated doctor – who, let's face it, knew *far* more than Bala – who had stuck a label on my symptoms and definitively said there was something wrong.

As the doctors continued to test me, however, it turned out that diabetes was not my only medical problem. As Bala had allowed me Out so infrequently throughout my life, I was suffering from a dramatic vitamin D deficiency; I think my levels were 50 or 60, when they should be more like 200. Without that vitamin, I was at an increased risk from osteoporosis – and it was possible it had already affected my bones. Though I was not formally diagnosed with it, a lack of vitamin D can result in osteomalacia, which causes dull, aching pains in the pelvis, hips and legs and weakens the muscles, both of which make walking slower and more difficult. As I'd discovered, I *did* find walking slow and difficult. I didn't walk as others did, even after my diabetes diagnosis improved my general health.

For as well as suffering aches and pains in my legs and finding it hard to keep my balance, I discovered I had no fast or medium speed – it was impossible for me to run for a bus, for example. All I could do was waddle along as best I could, moving in a rather wooden, jerky way and at a snail's pace. The doctors recognized my problems, but committed themselves to saying no more than that I had a 'lack of mobility'.

Yvonne's theory was that because I had spent so much time sitting as a child, she thought it possible that my bones and joints had fused in such a way as to immobilize me. I'd never run about or climbed furniture or trees, nor skipped or leaped about, as other children do from birth. Perhaps it had left a legacy inside my very skeleton.

There was nothing the doctors could do for me now, they said. All I could do was accept it.

I had to accept, too, that my untreated diabetes and my long captivity had left me with lasting damage to my eyes. Though the dark haze lifted, my eyes remained extremely sensitive to the light. I found I had to close them if I stepped Outside; it hurt too much to keep them open. Sunglasses were essential every day I went Out, even if it was cloudy, because the brightness was unbearable. It was devastating in many ways: I was finally free, but I couldn't even enjoy looking around me at my new environment because my eyes hurt so much. It took them a long, long while to adjust to going Out more often.

I was kept in hospital for several days while they monitored my ketone levels and tried to get them back to normal to avert the risk of coma. While I was there, the police came to see me. They were still continuing their investigation, they said. I was nervous about seeing them, petrified that if they arrested AB (which they had not yet done), he would say all manner of bad things about Roddy. I didn't understand the process, nor the need for evidence to uphold a claim. In the cult, AB would dish out 'justice' without trial and, despite my secret-reading, in my panic a small part of me thought it might be like that Outside too.

The police came to ask me if, amid my countless medical tests, I would agree to submit to another: a DNA test. Bala was saying point-blank that I was not his child. Apparently, he was the one who had demanded the test, slandering my mother by saying she used to sleep around and he believed I must be another man's daughter.

I wasn't surprised to hear it. He had no honour. Having kept his guilty secret all these years, I could imagine him doing anything to stop it coming out. In his madness, he seemed to have forgotten that the DNA test was likely to do the opposite.

But then I started wondering: did he know something I didn't? Given he had never acknowledged paternity, was it possible I *was* another man's child?

God, I hope so!

So as the police took a DNA swab from inside my mouth, I found a tiny bit of me was hoping the test would show up another father. AB had been so terrible to me: if he *was* my dad, surely that meant I had bad genes in me – and maybe I was also a bad person?

I'd been discharged from hospital by the time the results came back. The police came to the Palm Cove offices to share them with me. My hand trembled a little as I took the letter. Though I believed I'd solved the mystery of my parentage while in the Collective, there was a chance I'd been wrong. Now I would know for certain.

'I have compared the reference DNA profiles of Rosie Davies and Aravindan Balakrishnan,' the letter read. '[There is] extremely strong scientific support for the proposition that Aravindan Balakrishnan is the biological father of Rosie Davies.'

I let out my breath in a rush. So he *was* my dad, after all, even though he had never felt able to bring himself to admit it. I was glad at last to know who my parents *definitely* were, but sad that such a nasty man was my father.

I don't know Bala's reaction to the results; nor Chanda's, though she later told *The Times* she was 'shocked' her husband had fathered a child with Sian. Yet she brushed it off as a 'mistake'.

'For 99.99 per cent of the time, he is loving me and not these other people,' she remarked defiantly.

I guess I felt a small sense of satisfaction that his paternity was now revealed. If my suspicions were correct, Bala had kept me captive because he didn't want anyone to know he had a bastard child. His desire to protect his reputation had outstripped his humanity. But it had all come to nought.

The truth – and I – were finally out.

52

After my release from hospital at the end of October, I tried my hardest to get my head around my new life. It was nothing like I had imagined in my cage. Trapped behind the window, I had fantasized over and over about all the things I would do – such as going to the cinema or the park or for a night out with friends – but I found I was unable to do much of anything at all as I found the experience of being free overwhelming.

After all the medical poking and prodding, when Yvonne and Gerard suggested I next see a dentist, I had to say no. It was too much, too soon. If they suggested doing two things in one day it was impossible for me; even one task a day was a challenge. I couldn't cope with the novelty; everything was unnervingly new and I felt as if my brain might explode.

Yvonne and Gerard began, in my first few weeks of freedom, suggesting I complete a little activity, however small, every single day, but I had to tell them in the end I couldn't even cope with that. To do something new once a week or maybe once a fortnight was more manageable, so that I could rest and recover in between. If I didn't, my body forced me to stop anyway, paralysing me with headaches that demanded early retirement from activities.

Nor could I be spontaneous. If it was a sunny day and Yvonne suggested we went to the park, I would become anxious and unable to go. This was partly due to my medical problems – I had dreadful IBS, which I believed was a legacy from the daily stress of living in the cult, so I didn't want to go Out unprepared. I needed to know at least the day before if Yvonne wanted to go for a walk, so that I could eat mindfully.

Perhaps, too, it was a hangover from the way Bala had always made me *wait* for days Out. I was used to begging for an outing, and being granted my wish only when AB ran out of excuses. The idea of someone giving me what I wished for in a single instant was alien and I could not cope with the spontaneity.

Even going to the new shops was a struggle. I'd become used to where I'd lived in London: I knew the route, the shopkeepers, the goods on the shelves. The constant repetition, though dull, was comforting and manageable. But now we had a whole new high street to learn, and it was no longer just the grocery store and the chemist I could enter. Each time we went Out, we could go into *whatever* shops we wanted and buy *whatever* we pleased.

It was something I'd always longed to do. But when I accompanied Josie or Aisha, it wasn't the fun girlie shopping extravaganza I'd fondly imagined for decades. Instead, I felt unnerved and anxious, curious yet sick, in the grip of a sensory overload if I went into too many different shops or tried to do too many things. Everything was so unfamiliar that I couldn't enjoy any of it. This happened almost every time we went shopping. It was information overload: having so many things to choose from gave me headaches. No longer were we tied to what Bala liked: we were free to make our own choices. *But I never had*. Because of that, I found I simply couldn't.

I felt like a rabbit in the headlights, the world moving around me yet I was frozen still. I didn't know what to do. Everything was too fast, too loud, too quick. Even relatively simple things, such as knowing when to go up to the counter to be served, or when to open or hold the door for another person coming towards me, wrong-footed me. In the Collective, Bala always went first through the door and I followed. I was afraid to make a faux pas: was it rude to go through first, or did it hold everyone up if I waited? No one had ever told me the right way to do it: I wasn't even allowed to *open* doors in my old life. It was immensely upsetting that I found it so difficult, especially as everyone else, even children, would breezily walk through doorways as if it wasn't the slightest bit tough.

So overwhelming did I find the world that I was forced to adopt the same blinkered outlook when walking Outside that I'd always had. Though no one was telling me 'Don't ogle!' any more, I still couldn't look around. Yvonne and Gerard have told me that they once left work one evening and saw Josie, Aisha and I walking along the high street in single file. Though they slowed down their car to say hello to us, I did not look left or right to see them, even when they were right beside me. I wasn't aware of their presence at all. All I could manage was to stare straight ahead, concentrating on the small patch of Outside that I could see in my tunnel vision.

To do anything else was to be confronted by a giant kaleidoscopic whirlpool that sucked me under. After spending most of my life staring only at four walls, or at the collar of AB's coat, everything seemed so huge and complicated. Every time I went Out, I felt like I was climbing upwards, vertically, without any handholds or footholds. It was terrifying. I had so much to learn that I couldn't even begin to find a place to start.

At times, when it all got on top of me, I wondered if it might have been better if I had died in the cult. It was mainly when I felt especially poorly, or was in a low mood, and generally it was a fleeting feeling, but it was still there. I felt so stupid, especially to be unable to make my way around on my own. *I am useless*, I'd think, *I am not worthy to carry on. Why didn't I just die in Dark Tower?*

Never, in a million years, could I have anticipated how hard it would be. I struggled with *everything*. It was excruciatingly embarrassing, not to mention confusing, stressful and exhausting. Even things that should have been pleasurable, such as the freedom to watch whatever I wanted on TV, came with a price attached, because I had so many headaches when I first left that watching television was agony. It felt as if I had got what I wanted but only at the point when I was past being able to enjoy it. At times like that I felt very sad.

I especially hated the thought of people pitying me because of all the things I couldn't do. I was thirty years old, yet I was as helpless as a child – *more* helpless, in fact. When I realized the extent of my incapacity, I felt so angry at AB for not showing me the world as he should have done; and at the others, too. Why hadn't they stood up to him and insisted that I needed to learn how to cross the road or make a shopping list? In the end, I learned how to do the latter from Aisha, which eventually made things a little easier for me in the shops, but it was a long hard road to walk.

Knowing how much I didn't know, I overthought everything, forever worried about what might go wrong. Even getting dressed in the morning was an ordeal. I fretted so much about whether I was wearing the right clothes for the right occasion. Every day I asked Josie if what I was wearing was acceptable; I had no clue.

All these disappointments made me all the more grateful for my mask of make-up, which I still applied every morning in its bright-orange hue. It gave me something to hide behind when the world got too much. I hoped with all my heart that it concealed how tired and confused I was.

Yet I have to say, as hard as it all was, and as desperate as I some-times felt, I never, *ever* wished for a different life. I never lost sight of the fact that I *was* free. Never did I ever wish I was back in my cage – because no matter how challenging it was, I had *chosen* to do it. I didn't *have* to do any of these things that I found so hard, whether going to the shops or walking down the street: I *chose* to do them. That made the world of difference. I was not being imposed upon, for the first time in my life. And with that in mind, I was able to weather even the most ferocious storms.

Even though I was not able to fill my days with social events as I'd once hoped, I still relished the lack of a regimented schedule. I could choose to do what I wanted, when I wanted. For a long while, I simply slept. It was as if all the years of stress and anxiety had finally caught up with me so I crashed out. To be free to sleep as much as I wanted was a liberty; in the cult I'd always had to rise bright and early and do everything to schedule. Now, I could let myself recuperate without any punishment falling on my head. That was blissful.

I loved listening to music, too. I'd regularly turn the TV to the music channel, in so doing discovering upbeat artists like Katy Perry, whose music, especially her song 'Roar', really resonated with me. I'd never heard anything like it before.

Weirdly, though, I struggled to understand song lyrics. I couldn't follow them. If I found a transcript of the lyrics and read them, *then* I could understand, but there seemed to be a disconnect between my ears and my brain. I didn't know why – was it because no demands had ever been made on me to engage with what I was listening to? It was peculiar, but it didn't stop my enjoyment. I felt like any other young person with that TV on, listening to the latest hits.

I also adored the freedom finally to watch the *Harry Potter* and

Lord of the Rings films I had missed. It was one of the first things I did once I was home from the hospital and it was so fantastic. When the eighth Potter film drew to its close, with Voldemort defeated, I felt such a kinship with Harry. I may not have had a Hagrid, but I had made my own magic nonetheless.

Perhaps one of the very best things about being free, however, was the slow process of losing my unperson status. Yvonne applied for a certified copy of my birth certificate for me, which was the first step in so many other official applications – opening a bank account, for example, or being named as a resident of an address. Each small step, each form I filled in, was a stepping stone to becoming a *person*.

The only thing I disliked about all that was that the name on my birth certificate was Prem Maopinduzi Davies. This dulled the excitement of receiving my first-ever letter, for example, because the sight of that ugly name made me cringe. I longed to change it formally, but was told I couldn't yet. I was desperate for the day when I could jettison that hateful label and embrace my *true* identity.

Nonetheless, it was still quite a moment to hold my birth certificate in my hand, whatever name was on it. The shadow-child was not quite so shadowy any more. I was born in St James's Hospital in Balham, I read. I was definitively female, despite everything I'd been told about my gender growing up.

My mother was Sian Davies.

My father was a straight black line; the box had been left blank.

There was one element in particular on the birth certificate that snagged my interest. My Welsh-born mother had falsely given 'Manchester' as her place of birth. I believed she'd done that because she'd been brainwashed by AB to cut her family out of her life. I thought that she *really* didn't want her mum to find out she'd had a daughter, so she'd lied. It made me feel so sad to see it.

The more I thought about it, though, the more that lie on the official record gave me hope. For if my granny, Ceri, *had* ever investigated – and I had no idea whether she had or not – if she had somehow stumbled on this documentation, she would not have thought that this Sian was her daughter. So she could never have known I was her grandchild. Perhaps that was why she'd never come looking for me? It made sense to me, now. For even if she'd tracked me down, Sian's false trail would have led her astray.

I felt a quickening in my heart. Now that I was Out, once I felt ready, I would be able to let Ceri know all about me, false trail or not. We would finally get to have that family reunion I'd fantasized about for so long. A rare smile lit up my lips. I couldn't wait to meet her.

53

'Look at me, Rosie,' Yvonne's voice encouraged. 'Look up, look up.'

But I much preferred staring at the floor; I didn't want to look in her eyes or hold her gaze. So I kept my head dropped to my chest and all she saw of me as we talked in her office was the very top of my head.

I really struggled with making eye contact when I first came Out. It was something I'd avoided in the cult anyway, but I think I found it hard to look at Yvonne in particular because she was a person of authority in my life. I didn't want to see her judging me. I was petrified of those who had any perceived power over me, even though I knew Yvonne to be a warm and lovely person. I remained terrified of being controlled or disciplined by others. Therefore, I found it hard to trust her.

I was also very scared of what other people might think of me. I hated groups or crowds; I felt uncomfortable even talking to more than one person at a time, in case people ignored me, isolated me or ganged up on me, as used to happen in the cult. I was frightened of saying the wrong thing and then being criticized in front of others. This made it very hard to engage with people, because I felt everyone – whether in authority or not – was assessing me. So it was easier by far not to look up, no matter how much Yvonne urged me to.

While I was not yet ready to look at her, I did, however, feel comfortable hanging out in the Palm Cove offices. No one ever talked freaky nonsense there and Yvonne was nothing but sympathetic and supportive. That made me feel able to talk to her about what it was really like in the cult – about the fact that it had been no life, merely existence. That was partly why I was finding it so hard to be on the Outside, I mused to myself, because it *was* life, with all the colour, intensity, happiness and heartache that could offer. Painful though it was, it was better by far than the dreary, dishcloth-coloured destiny I'd had before.

Somewhat to my surprise, I found I was no longer writing now I was Out. There were a number of reasons, I think, primary among them being that I finally had someone Outside to talk to in Yvonne. Why communicate on paper when I could tell it to her? There was also so much going on that I had neither the time nor the headspace to be able to craft sentences in the way I once had. I didn't even keep my diary, which I guess was another type of freedom. I wasn't tied down to any day or date, even in my own head. Instead, I was free-falling through time.

But though I got on OK with Yvonne and Gerard, I found it difficult to talk to other people. It was another frustration: all my life I had longed for friends, but now I was free to make them, I felt unable. When I chatted with someone in the protected environment Yvonne had created for me – for I really only spoke to her and Gerard, the comrades, the doctors, police and charity staff in those first few weeks – I felt this strange combination of being thrilled to be paid some attention, yet at the same time overwhelmed by it. I felt a desperate need to preserve my privacy because the cult members, who were the only people I'd known before, had made such a habit of disrespecting my personal space. I was somehow still on that yoyo string: wanting to reach out to others, yet scurrying back the moment I grew close.

Not long after we escaped, psychologists from the Helen Bamber Foundation (HBF) came to speak with us. HBF is a specialist charity with extensive experience of working with those who have survived extreme psychological, physical or sexual violence. The psychologists were there to help us, but while I spoke to them as much as I could, I found it very hard and was extremely slow to engage. I remember my mind sort of 'freezing' and going blank. I had never spoken my deepest thoughts to anyone before, so even trying to do it was strange.

Nor was it just speaking in person I struggled with. Now I was Out, I could finally use the secret mobile phone that Josie had bought me while we were still in the cult. But when Yvonne rang me, I couldn't work out at first how to hold it or where to speak.

'I can't hear you,' Yvonne used to say patiently, even though I was shouting, 'Hello? Hello?' at the top of my voice at her. It was another thing I found hard.

Perhaps the hardest thing of all, though, was when that protected environment started to expand and I began to come into contact with the other residents of Palm Cove. In the cult, I'd always gazed longingly out of the window when I'd seen Josie talking to the neighbours, wishing I could do the same. But now I had the freedom to join in those conversations I felt overshadowed by Josie's confidence. The neighbours seemed to gravitate towards her and I felt they ignored me because she was shining so brightly.

It was a huge shock to find that I was nowhere near as outgoing as I'd thought I'd be. For years I'd enviously watched young people making friends and I'd always imagined I'd be like them *if* I had the chance: brash and lively, larking about. But it just wasn't me. I thought, at that time, that it was a failing. I felt so awkward and self-conscious; I simply had no social skills. Having never had the chance to interact with people (except those for whom I could do nothing right) I had little idea of *how* to forge friendships or show the best side of myself. Being quiet, I didn't have the ability to draw their attention either.

It made me feel sad and resentful. It felt like Josie had loads of friends and I had nobody – *still*, nobody. It wasn't her fault – she just had a different personality to me, as well as so much more experience of these things – but neither did she try to help me engage. Perhaps she was so used to me being in the shadows that she didn't appreciate that I'd have liked to be more involved in those friendships now I was free.

Or perhaps there was something else going on. Because, even though I was theoretically free, the many disabilities that were my legacy from the cult meant I was still as tied to the comrades as I'd always been. I could not leave the house without them. In more ways than one, it felt as if our unit of house-elves had simply been lifted out of the Collective and placed in Leeds. Though I was grateful not to suffer AB's Vampire Puking, restrictive guidelines and physical violence any more, in almost every other way my life was exactly the same.

And in Bala's absence, Josie stepped up to become our leader. It was Josie who now decided who should go shopping and what we should buy; what we should do as a trio and when; Josie who became the lynchpin in all the decisions. She walked at the head of our crocodile when we went Out, and it was to Josie that Aisha and I both gave the emergency funds the charity arranged for us as individuals. Yvonne expressed concern at this, but we reassured her that Josie had always handled the housekeeping money; this was the way it had always been – though of course the money had never before been mine. Yet I was more than happy to hand it over; I had so much else to think about, money was the last thing on my mind.

I was aware that it felt as if history was repeating itself, however. It felt uncomfortable, but at the same time I knew I couldn't function on my own, so I relied on Josie massively. Yet that overshadowing I felt when we spoke to others kept coming up in other elements of our lives. When I needed help to do things, she would take over and do it for me, rather than showing me what to do. In some ways it was comforting for me to be mothered like that, especially because I was finding the outside world so overwhelming, but I also felt controlled by her. It felt to me as if she did not want me to become independent.

When she did things for me, even if it came from a place of kindness, it left me feeling useless, for I had not achieved anything for myself and was thus no further forward when I next faced the same dilemma. Yet I found it impossible to untangle myself from our tight-knit trio. When I tried to keep things to myself, a conversation I'd had or similar, Josie would get upset if it later came out that I'd done it and not told her. All three of us were still expected to update the others on everything going on in our lives: we were not supposed to have a conversation with anyone else, no matter how personal or confidential, without later sharing it with the group. The way we communicated, finishing each other's sentences, was still as secure as ever.

I think my subconscious rang a warning bell before the rest of my brain woke up. I started having lots of nightmares about Josie calling AB and telling him where we were, and him and Chanda then moving into the Palm Cove flat. Consequently, when I was sitting with Josie in the office one day in November, I said intently, 'I want to get a restraining order to ensure that Bala and Chanda can't find us.' They were still free, living in the flat back in London, and I was terrified my nightmare was going to come true.

The strangest thing happened. Josie fixed her blue eyes on me and spoke in a voice I hadn't heard for several years: it was the voice she spoke with when she was under Bala's spell. I could feel Hyde coming up, and sure enough . . .

'No,' she exclaimed in horror, 'you can't do that to AB!'

I thought you were on my side . . . But all along I'd known that wasn't really true.

'What about Chanda?' I asked quickly, playing the old card that had always worked before. 'We don't want her involved.'

I was hoping Josie would agree, but she was not in the mood. She looked suspicious about what I'd said, and I felt a creeping anxiety slide up my spine: I had still never spoken to her about how I *really* felt about AB. I let the matter drop, but I was worried all the same.

On 20 November, I decided to make a dramatic statement to show how much I was trying to break away from my life before. With purpose, I gripped a razorblade in my hand. Yet instead of pressing it to my breasts, this time I cleared a bald path all along the side of my skull. I'd decided to shave my head – completely. It felt like a rebirth: the beginning of a new era.

I was not sorry to see the strands of dark hair fall to the floor. Though *I* had been rescued, my hair seemed beyond hope. As it had been for so many years in the cult, it was thin and unhealthy and I could do nothing with it. I was glad to get rid of it. By the time it grew back, I was determined to be a different person.

So I was as bald as a baby when I heard the news the following day. It was somehow apt that my moment of transformation was mirrored by one my father made. He had been a god, a leader, a laughable fantasist . . . Now, he officially added a new role to his roster: suspect.

On 21 November 2013, he and Chanda were arrested.

54

'This is an extraordinary case,' Detective Inspector Kevin Hyland of Scotland Yard commented to the media immediately after the arrests, speaking amid the glare of camera lights and flashbulbs. 'We have had cases where people have been held for up to ten years previously, but three decades is unseen before in the United Kingdom . . . We've never seen anything of this magnitude before.'

We suddenly found that our story was headline news. DI Hyland explained that the police had delayed the arrests until the facts had been established, but now they had enough information to justify their move. AB and his wife had been arrested by the Human Trafficking Unit as part of an investigation into slavery and domestic servitude; I had told the police how Josie and Aisha had been treated as slaves. There was still a lot the police didn't know, however, as none of us had yet given a formal statement.

Though part of me was glad to hear the news, it was also frightening, especially for Josie and Aisha. With AB arrested by the fascist state, they wondered: would JACKIE now make his move? They were almost frenzied about it. It felt scary being alone in the flat and we asked Yvonne and Gerard to move in with us, but this they couldn't do. With the story having caused such a storm in the media, however, we were very exposed. The police were trying to get a reporting embargo put in place by the courts, but in the meantime any journalist – or, in Josie and Aisha's view, any agent of JACKIE – could come looking for us. It wasn't safe.

Yvonne came up with a solution. Generously, she invited the three of us to stay at her and Gerard's house while the police secured the embargo. I wouldn't have minded being doorstepped by the media: I wanted to tell everybody what had happened to me, having been silenced for so long. But at the same time I was more than

341

happy to go because it was the first time I'd ever stayed at somebody else's house. It was like going on holiday!

Yvonne and Gerard didn't live in Leeds but in a small village with spectacular views of the countryside. Their home was like a country cottage, painted inside in soothing tones of coffee and cream. I was thrilled to be there; amazed by all the mod cons. Their kitchen was filled with good-quality appliances that *never* blew up! Perhaps because of that, Yvonne and Gerard didn't seem scared of electricity in the least – not like I was.

On the day of the arrest, and for the next week or so, Yvonne and Gerard took time off work so they could stay with us 24/7. Spending more time in their company, I was excited to observe the way they could look up almost anything on the internet on their smartphones. In the cult, I used to like reading the dictionary, but to have that same encyclopaedic knowledge at the touch of a button was simply *amazing*.

On the day we arrived, we sat and watched the news in the living room. 'We've established that all three women were held in this situation for at least thirty years,' DI Hyland said.

I shifted uncomfortably in my seat. I felt as though Josie, Aisha and I were being lumped together, our experiences assumed to be the same, when, although they *had* been treated badly, the two of them had originally joined the cult by choice. It felt as though what had happened to me was being brushed under the carpet, which had always been what happened in the Collective: my individual experience was not deemed to be valid.

Over the days that followed, more stories came out in the press. I learned that, when I was fifteen, someone had contacted the police about me, having spotted that I never went to school. The police apparently passed the complaint to social services, but they'd said they weren't prepared to take action. I felt so disappointed: why had *nobody* followed it up? I realized, too, how clever AB had been in telling me never to look out of the window when I was young; had people known there was a kid in the house, they might have known something wasn't right and called social services sooner. A fifteen-year-old probably wasn't as high a priority as a younger child.

Aneeta Prem of the Freedom Charity, who had helped organize our rescue, commented to the press: 'I don't believe the neighbours knew anything about it at all. It was just an ordinary house in an ordinary street.'

The media coverage also informed us that the police were now seizing evidence from that house. Boxes and bags of paperwork, diaries and notes were being carried out and painstakingly sorted through; I read that they'd taken 2,500 items in 52 bags! I was glad they were being so thorough, though I squirmed at the idea of them reading any notes of mine.

Josie, on the other hand, was angry and upset when she heard the officers had seized evidence. Perhaps it was because she knew that whatever was in there would get Bala into trouble. I had no such feelings of concern; I felt only a sense of vindication.

It was at this time, too, that I let go of the final barrier that had been holding me back from talking to the police in full myself: my fears for Roddy. In the end, it was actually the police who enabled me to have one final interaction with him. Initially, they had said that it was not a good idea to contact him, as he might be needed as a witness in the case, but ultimately it was agreed that an officer would pass a letter from me to him. The policewoman asked him if he wanted to reply, then wrote down what he said and sent it on to me.

How I treasured that note. He said thanks for the letter, and that I should make sure I stayed strong and calm when the case went to court. He promised he would always be my friend and wished me the very best for the future. He signed it off with: 'Roddy, your old pal.' I loved it so much that I slept with it under my pillow for quite a while. It was the release I needed to feel free to speak out; I could also see the police were reasonable and that my fears for Roddy had been unfounded. It was an important development because it had been so essential to me to protect him because of my deep feelings for him.

As time passed, though, I drifted apart from my Ringdove. I think I had so much to learn in the real world that I didn't have much chance for fantasies any more. Helped by Yvonne, I began to put things into perspective and in time I could see that my 'love' for him was more a means of survival than anything else. In some ways, I will always love him, because he truly did save me, but I appreciate, now, that you can't love someone unless you know them. And I hardly knew him. From my secret-reading of things like *Romeo and*

Juliet, I'd thought it was standard behaviour to ask him to run away with me just after we met, but modern people – real people – don't think like that. It was rather disappointing to learn that the love affairs I'd read about weren't reflective of real life.

As my understanding of relationships was entirely predicated on books, it was a steep learning curve for me to try to understand that living people did things differently. And while it's easy to understand something in theory, it is quite another to put that into practice.

In due course, Yvonne also talked to me about sexual relationships and how they work: what's customary, what's abusive and how things should be. Her theories seemed to suggest that Roddy had been exploiting me for sexual gratification: I didn't want to hear that at first. He had been my boyfriend! We were in a loving relationship!

But now I can see why people might think that. I honestly don't know what his motive was or why he acted as he did. What I can say is that, at that time, he was the best thing that had ever happened to me. I remain grateful to him for saving my life by giving me something to hold on to and to live for. Whether he was in it for himself or not, he gave me more than he took.

While we were staying at Yvonne and Gerard's, there came an afternoon when the police came to see us. They asked the three of us if we'd be prepared to give a formal statement, submitting to interview at the local police station to tell them everything that had gone on.

'I need more time to think about it,' Aisha replied hesitantly. Josie concurred.

The police turned to me and asked the same question. I could feel Josie's eyes boring into me but I paid her no heed. I imagined Bala's face, full of anger, hatred and betrayal, and thought of all the terrible things he had put me through. *This is my chance*, I thought. *For too long my voice has been silenced.*

So I turned to the officers and in a loud, affirmative voice I said, 'Yes.'

55

My first formal police interview took place on 26 November 2013.
I dressed with extra care that morning, winding a scarf around my
shaven head. As she helped me choose my clothes, Josie was cold and
cross. She was not happy at all that I was going to give evidence
against AB, spilling the secrets of the closed Collective.

In the days since I'd agreed to help the police, I'd spoken openly
to Yvonne and Gerard – in front of Josie – about how I really felt
about AB. Ever since I had been freed from my fears for Roddy,
there was no longer any need not to speak the full truth. Yet Josie
was taken aback by my words; understandably, as I'd always been
careful to conceal my authentic feelings about AB. As it was only
once we were living with Yvonne and Gerard that I'd spoken out,
however, Josie now became convinced that they'd brainwashed me.

It was a sign, I think, of how she really viewed me. Though I was
thirty years old, she still saw me as a silly little girl who had no sense.
That was partly why she cossetted me so much, telling me it was too
dangerous to lift the kettle or that I was too weak to chop carrots.
'Don't touch that, it's eeee!' she would say in alarm, echoing my
own word for electricity, if I came too close to something electrical.
Given my long-held fear of it, I was quick to obey her warnings.

But just because I was scared of electricity, and had been made
disabled in how to live Outside, it did not mean I did not have my
own mind. It riled me that she was so dismissive of my views. I was
proud of my ability to devise my own opinions. I wasn't a blank slate
that anyone could write on. I'd never have escaped from the cult if
that had been the case.

Josie was also put out because my family – my *real* family – had been
in touch after all the press coverage. Sian's cousin Eleri, whose disem-
bodied voice I had once heard shouting from a telephone in the wake of
my mother's death, had been informed that her cousin had had a

daughter. Apparently, she was keen to arrange a family reunion to meet me when the time was right. I was over the moon about it. But Josie saw my desire to connect with my family as a betrayal of the Collective.

She tried her hardest to dissuade me. That morning, before I left for the police station, she took me to one side.

'If you betray AB and the Collective like this,' she hissed at me, 'and if you want contact with your cousin in London, then we will have to go our separate ways.'

Now it was my turn to be taken aback. Up until that point I'd still thought she cared enough about me to respect my decisions, even if she couldn't agree with them.

Her words had no effect. I can only assume she thought I was so reliant on her that the idea of being without her would force me to rethink, but it didn't. Unlike when I was trapped in the cult, I had other options now. I had other people to help me. Not for a moment did I think of withdrawing my agreement to give evidence or of shunning my relatives. I was no longer prepared to be told that I couldn't speak out or that I had to hide away to please her.

'We'll have to take that chance,' I said to her gently.

I realized, sadly, that my going ahead was likely to prove the beginning of the end of my friendship with Josie. That split was not on my part, not at all – I knew she had saved my life in getting me out and when she was Jekyll I completely adored her – but I appreciated that, for her, my speaking to the police would be a cardinal sin. She would never be able to forgive this. In her eyes, if I went to the police station today, I would be no better than a fascist agent.

But I didn't care. I couldn't care. In fact, I took a perverse pleasure in it. For I had never been a part of the cult, except under duress. They were not my tribe and I didn't owe them any loyalty. To be able to give a statement to the police made me feel more empowered than I ever had in my life.

Yvonne had said she would drive me to the police station. Leaving Josie behind, her eyes still boring into me, I slipped into the front seat and together we drove off.

It was a very anxious journey. Before we'd left, Josie had warned me: 'You'll have an accident on the way; JACKIE will make something horrible happen. You're never going to get there safely . . .' I think it made both Yvonne and me a bit jumpy.

'I'll tell you what,' Yvonne said in the end, 'we'll put the radio on.'

As she turned the dial, I wondered what we would hear. Josie or Aisha, I was sure, would be primed to hear news of a devastating earthquake or tsunami: a dramatic global disaster caused by JACKIE to dissuade me from my path. But instead of a newsreader's solemn tones, the rhythmic drumbeat of one of my favourite songs was just beginning and a female voice soared beautifully over it.

It was Katy Perry's 'Roar'.

The song is about female empowerment: speaking out, speaking up, after being abused and held down and silenced. It's about breaking through barriers and having confidence in your own voice to roar as loud as you can to correct injustice. There could not have been a more perfect song to encourage me that what I was doing was right. I felt as if the universe was telling me: look, your voice is free now and you too must roar.

'Let's sing!' Yvonne suggested.

And so the two of us hollered at the tops of our voices – all the way there.

Leigh, the blonde policewoman who had been with us on the day of our rescue, was going to interview me, together with a male colleague. I threw my arms around all the police officers I met once we arrived at the station. I'd been trying to work out how you greeted people Outside – it wasn't something I'd ever had to learn – and Aisha hugged people a lot so I followed her lead. I was, in fact, delighted that this was the way people did things; having been denied hugs for so many years, I craved physical affection. So it was with enormous enthusiasm that I caught the officers in my arms and squeezed them all, smiling broadly. I wanted to come across to people as warm and approachable, and in this way my arms could say what I had previously struggled to articulate.

After the greetings were concluded, Leigh ushered me into an interview room, where I would be videoed giving my statement. I felt a stab of nerves. It was very isolating, going it alone, despite my brave words to Josie that morning. I felt so disappointed – and betrayed – that the comrades did not feel able to stand beside me. Yet I knew Yvonne and Gerard, at least, supported my actions, and I also thought that my grandmother, Ceri, would want me to do this – for my mum and for so many others whose lives had been blighted by the Dark Lord. I had to speak out on behalf of those who were no longer with us, as well as for myself. So when Leigh asked me if I was ready, I determinedly nodded my head.

I didn't cry as I told her everything that had happened; given the length of my captivity, this was a process that took several days. If anything, in fact, I was more likely to laugh because the nervous giggle that had always been with me now rose up inside me like an old enemy to twist my true distress into peals of unhappy joy. When things were stressful, or when I felt embarrassed about what I had to say, my voice tried to make things funny. It was as if I knew my anxiety might destroy me if I didn't get a handle on it.

The police seemed to understand, however. They were very good and sympathetic. Some of what they asked was intrusive; I felt awkward, for example, when they questioned me about Roddy or my personal life. I didn't like having to admit that I'd self-harmed or had suicidal thoughts, either, but I knew it was necessary as part of the process.

On the whole, and for a large section of the interviews, I rather detached from what I was saying. I found it was the only way I could get through it. It became, in the end, as if I was just telling a story: *this is not what happened to* me. I disassociated so that I didn't have to feel all those emotions again, pulling down a shield between me and what had happened: a sheet of window glass I actually wanted for once. It was a strange feeling, but it was the only way I could complete what I had started.

Leigh was wonderful. She became like a kind of big sister in a way, guiding me through everything. Though my interview was recorded, there was also a paper statement I had to sign. When Leigh pushed it towards me across the table, I felt overwhelmed.

There it is: that is my life. That was *my life.*

To see it written down *by somebody else*, when I had always thought the story would stay in the house and die with me, was such a powerful moment.

I only hoped that other people would believe me – the police and the prosecutors and the jury . . . For without Aisha and Josie being willing to speak out, mine was a lone voice. I felt like Frodo ranged against Sauron and, despite my bravery, it seemed impossible that I alone could bring down the Dark Lord.

56

'What you have done,' Josie said after I'd made my statement, 'is as good as an own goal.'

She said no jury would ever listen to me – once they realized the context in which everything had happened.

'In war situations,' she said confidently, 'children are often kept indoors to keep them safe.'

In her mind, because this too was a 'war situation' – the Collective versus the fascist state – Bala would surely walk it and the charges would be thrown out.

I almost laughed, but stopped myself. It was funny, though: I was concerned people would not believe my story because it was so outlandish; Josie, on the other hand, seemed to feel they would believe it so much that they would clear AB of any wrongdoing!

More than amusement, though, I felt sorry for her. It was as if everything we had gone through together over the past few years had never happened. She had gone back on everything: all the small steps we'd taken to get to the point of defying Bala's guidelines had been retraced to ground zero. It was a surprise to realize how deluded she really was.

I should have known better, though, really – the Black Rider in her was too powerful. I had always known, in my heart of hearts, that she worshipped AB too much ever to change. But I had hoped she might have found a different way to live now we'd got Out. That wasn't the case. Instead, she tried her hardest to stop me from continuing with the police case against AB, even after my statement was recorded, telling me over and over that Comrade Bala had brought me up, so how could I be so ungrateful as to betray him?

Nine days after Bala was arrested, the police finally secured their media embargo and it became safe for the three of us to return to Palm Cove. It was a very different trio that returned, however, now

I had made my decision to help the police. I felt Josie became grumpy and unfriendly. She used to stare and glare at me and took every available opportunity to sing the praises of the Dark Lord, which annoyed me greatly. When my support worker urged me to keep at least *some* of my money for myself, and I did, Josie refused to cook a nice dinner for us all, blaming me for not contributing. When I said after watching the news what a relief it was not to have to listen to AB rant about it any more, she always responded with a nasty retort or simply a deathly silence pregnant with poisonous hate.

Unsurprisingly, I wanted to spend less and less time in her company and consequently I spent more and more time in the offices of the Palm Cove Society, hanging out with the support workers or Yvonne and Gerard. (I had gone there so often by now with the comrades that it was easy for me to navigate the short route alone.) As the weeks drew on, I went there so often that I was hardly in the flat at all.

To my delight, I found I could learn much more from the Outsiders than Josie had ever shown me. It was Yvonne and Gerard who had a quiet word with me to say that, actually, people didn't greet everyone they met with a hug. With some people, of course, it was fine, but I needed to learn where the line was. Though it was very friendly to hug everybody, the other person also had to want it – and not everybody did. I nodded, understanding; the last thing I wanted was to make anybody feel uncomfortable. Yvonne and Gerard taught me to look for body-language cues and encouraged me to say a simple 'hello' instead, or to shake hands if the other person proffered theirs. I learned it was inappropriate to hug the policemen when I met them, and that it was wrong to grab hold of people generally.

They also helped me when it came to interacting with the other residents of Palm Cove. As I was divided from Josie a bit more now, I had a few of my own conversations with them. One day, one of them commented on what a lovely coat I had.

Hurriedly, I slid it from my shoulders and held it out to them: 'Do you want it?' I asked, eager to please.

I think my actions were motivated by my own experiences – in the cult, I had liked Outsiders' things so much but no one had ever offered me anything nice. I felt that if somebody liked something I had, I wanted to give it to them because I didn't want anyone else to feel the way I had.

Yvonne and Gerard spoke to me about it. 'You don't need to offer your things in that circumstance,' they explained, 'they were just saying you had a nice coat. It's a compliment. You can just say, "Thank you."'

I only hoped I had picked up enough from them not to embarrass myself as a momentous day approached. On 19 December 2013, I was scheduled to meet my family for the very first time.

As I stood in front of the mirror in the flat, I slid a long blonde curly wig on to my bald head and apprehensively turned this way and that, examining my reflection. The hairpiece was like something Beyoncé might wear; I hoped for a little of her sassy confidence on this very important day. I re-checked my make-up, pleased with the deep-orange glow that graced my skin, and fiddled with the wig again.

The beauty of this magical long fake hair was that I could always swing it in front of my face if I felt uncomfortable. I'd started doing that already, ever since I'd bought it; I found I could look up at Yvonne now – as long as the wig shielded me from view.

It was a very odd feeling to know I was going to be *seen* at last by my blood relatives. I didn't know quite how I would feel beneath their scrutiny. As always, I was worried they would judge me. That was why the wig was an absolute must; I also wanted to look glamorous and make a good impression.

At the appointed hour, I climbed into Yvonne and Gerard's car; they had offered to drive me to the reunion. We were meeting at a hotel in Bradford, where we were going to have tea and sandwiches. I was scheduled to meet Sian's cousin, Eleri, and her brother, but Ceri had not been mentioned; I assumed she was too elderly to make the long trip from Wales. Though I was disappointed not to meet my granny today, I still hoped I would get to meet her soon so that I could play out – for real at last – my long-held fantasy of our emotional reunion.

When we arrived, Yvonne escorted me into the hotel lobby while Gerard waited in the car. I carefully adjusted the wig on my head and walked my slow walk as we went together to find my family. My emotions were strangely stilted. It was exactly the same situation as on my first night of freedom: I had imagined meeting my family so many times already that it felt as if I'd done this a hundred times before.

There was no tingle of excitement or a rising anticipation. Instead, I was rather like a weary commuter, going through the motions.

A woman rose to greet me. Short and in her sixties, she seemed warm and motherly, if a little anxious. Yet even that anxiety was welcome in a way, for with both pain and pleasure it reminded me of Sian. The bald man beside her had the same kind manner that Eleri exuded.

Despite that kind aura, I felt shy as I lumbered towards them. I didn't know what I should do – to hug or not to hug? – so I let Eleri lead the way.

She chose to reach out a hand and held mine. There was a moment of connection that meant more than simply skin on skin. Though I'd known both my parents, I had never known them as *family*. But Eleri was family. Her blood was my blood. That was something very special.

'Hello,' she said, and her voice had the tiniest lilt of a Welsh accent, just as it had done in my dreams.

We all sat down and I nervously twitched the blonde wig in front of my face. Eleri asked me questions and I responded eagerly, but I was too anxious to talk in much more depth beyond the answers I gave. I didn't have the confidence to ask questions myself, so it was hard for us to build up a rapport, nor could I manage a fluid back-and-forth exchange. Just to be sat there with them was miraculous to me. Everything was stunning, in every sense of that word: the hotel setting, and the range of sandwiches that a smartly dressed waiter brought for us, and the fact I was sitting there with my family at all . . . I struggled to get my head around it.

As we sat there chatting, I screwed up all my courage to make a statement: 'I've always wanted to meet my grandmother.'

Saying such a thing would have got me beaten in the cult. I'd expected my words to be more warmly received in this environment, but disconcertingly only a short silence followed. Eleri slowly put down her plate.

'I'm very sorry to have to tell you,' she began, speaking so sensitively to me, 'that Aunty Ceri passed away eight years ago.'

No . . . No!

I felt the loss so deep inside me I didn't know where I ended and the pain began. It was as if my heart was being torn out. My granny and I had been going to meet – I'd dreamed of it for so long and in such detail.

'My long-lost granddaughter! How long I have waited for you!'

'Yes, Gran, me too!'

My long wait was finally over. But no grandmotherly arms embraced me; no older woman with my mother's eyes looked me up and down with love. Bala's father had died as well by now, so this news meant I had no grandparents left at all. I would never know love like I'd imagined. I would never visit my mother's grave with my granny; I would never live with her in Wales in a home that was built on happiness and not hate. Everything I'd dreamed of was nothing but fantasy, as fake as the synthetic blonde hair upon my head.

'When did she die?' I asked, the words like rocks in my mouth.

'The twenty-ninth of April, 2005,' Eleri replied.

It was three days before I had tried to escape on 2 May. If I'd made it out of the cult to my original schedule – the date I'd had in mind before Josie had reported me for packing – I might just have had a chance to meet her; to let her know she had a granddaughter at least.

But Ceri had died without ever knowing of my existence. That made me feel so sad. It seemed from what Eleri said that she'd often wondered whether she had a grandchild; I think it was wishful thinking. She'd been lonely, from the sounds of things: first she'd lost her husband to suicide and then Sian to the cult, and then she had nobody. But I'd been there all along and we could have had each other. The thought of that was just unbearable: beyond any words I have.

I tried my best not to show how upset I was. Because I'd been beaten for crying in the cult, I was well practised at that at least. I'd always repressed my tears in front of the others because I'd never wanted AB to know he was getting to me. So, even now, despite my pain, no liquid pooled in my eyes.

Eleri had brought some photographs of her to show me. In a grainy black-and-white image stood a tall, slim, handsome woman. She wore a stylish patterned dress, black leather gloves and a pale hat. In her hands, she carried a glamorous clutch. Sian stood with her – they were posed outside a church at a family wedding – wearing a long, white, halter-necked dress that showed off her shoulders, a broad-brimmed hat perched jauntily on her head. Despite my agony, I was glad to see them. For I too loved fashion and I could see from this image that this was something that ran in our family. That made me feel connected to them.

Eleri told me what they had both been like as people and I listened with all the rapt attention of a child at storytime. Ceri was lovely, she said, a classy lady who loved to wear fur coats and smart clothes. Sian was very giving: generous and fun. Eleri said that when they were young women she and Sian had used to go clubbing together; Sian had always loved to dress up in the latest fashions and had always looked beautifully turned out. Eleri revealed that it had broken her heart when she saw how unkempt Sian looked at the time of her death; Eleri had identified her body. She told me how Sian had changed after she met AB. That lovely, giving person had completely disappeared.

'I know Sian was nasty to you,' Eleri later said, 'but that wasn't the Sian I knew. She was a nice, kind person, which is what Balakrishnan focused in on.'

I almost felt my loss all over again to hear her words – to know for sure that my mother had been a different woman entirely to the one that I had known. I had been right in thinking those flashes of her that I'd seen when she was sick were the *real* Sian.

If only she hadn't met him, I thought, tautologically. *If only she had met somebody better.* But in that instance I would never have been born. I hated what had happened to her, but what had happened led to me. One could not be divorced from the other.

I wasn't allowed to discuss the circumstances of Sian's death with Eleri; the police were reopening the investigation into my mother's demise so they'd told me not to talk about it. But that didn't matter. I much preferred to picture her in her life as a young person anyway – before Bala had got to her; before she'd plunged those three storeys and lay in that pool of black blood. Eleri brought her back to life for me with her memories and that was the way I wanted to remember her.

The sandwiches were eaten; the tea had been drunk. At the end of our reunion Eleri and I stood up and then, to my delight, we had a great big hug. It was very special indeed. I remember thinking, *If only my mum could have been here to see this!*

Eleri said she would keep in touch. I hugged her brother too and then I bade them both farewell.

As I walked back to Yvonne and Gerard's car, I found I couldn't stop thinking about my poor dead granny. I'd been so certain she and I would meet *one day* . . . It was one of the dreams that had kept me going in the cult. I hadn't wanted her to die alone.

As the car sped me away, thoughts went round and round my head. *If it hadn't been for the cult keeping me captive, I'd have seen my grandmother. If I'd got away in 2005, I might have made it out in time.* I thought of where we were headed now: back to the Palm Cove flat, where Josie and Aisha would be bustling about with their irritatingly familiar routines. I felt a rush of rage run through me. *If it hadn't been for them, I'd have met my granny years ago! They kept me chained as well! They are as much to blame! They have deprived me of my family!*

It was a cut-off point: a breaking away. It was something I couldn't come back from.

I cleared my throat to gain Yvonne's attention. I think she knew from the set of my face that I had come to a decision.

'I can't go back and live with them,' I declared. 'I don't want to be with them, I *can't* be with them any more.'

Come what may, I was finally breaking free of *all* my chains.

57

To their credit, Yvonne and Gerard immediately acknowledged that I had to be moved. Now I was thinking of Josie and Aisha as perpetrators and not friends, it wasn't right for me to stay with them. But the problem we all had was: where could I go? I didn't have the life skills to be able to live alone. There was still so much I didn't know how to do.

Yvonne, Gerard and social services tried to find some adult foster care for me, but my case, as a thirty-year-old who wasn't physically or mentally disabled but who nevertheless needed support, was rare if not unprecedented, and there was nowhere for me to go. I knew where I wanted to live: with Yvonne and Gerard.

To my eternal gratitude, they said they would be willing to take me, but the decision had to go before a panel – the police and social services and the support workers and so on. For me to move in with them apparently crossed some kind of professional boundary, so everything had to be above board.

While we waited for formal approval, I had no choice but to return to Josie and Aisha until it was sorted out. I agreed to do it as long as it was temporary. I couldn't bear to be with them at that time. When I returned from the family reunion, full of grief about my grandmother as well as the novelty of having relatives at last, I found I couldn't stop talking about my family, the stories spilling out of me despite the company I kept. Though I told her everything, Josie just didn't get how I felt.

'Stop talking about your family all the time!' she would snap, her words an echo of AB's rules. When I tried to tell her how devastated I was that my granny had died without ever knowing I existed, she seemed unable or unwilling to understand.

It drove me out of the flat even more. When I wasn't in the Palm Cove office, I spent time with our neighbours instead. Two months on from our escape, I really felt I was making strides in making friends. I now had the confidence to let myself out of the front door to walk to the next-door apartment block to visit the Palm Cove residents living there; the charity had three blocks of flats all close together and I made lots of friends with the other people also being helped.

I adored the simple fact of being able to open and close my front door at will and go where I wanted. I'd nip next door to watch TV with this person or that person. Sometimes, I even visited them when it was dark! I could so clearly remember *longing* to go Out at night when we'd lived below Peregrine McConaughey: now I too got to have my own Oin. That was really special to me.

One night the people upstairs had a problem – I think they put something metal in the microwave and it went *boom*. I was able to go up to see them and say, 'Are you all right?' That was a real moment for me, to have the freedom to do that, to help my neighbours when something went wrong.

Special, too, was being able to accept a social invitation if someone asked me to visit their flat. Back in the launderette in London, Bala had always curtailed such offers. But now, if I ran into another resident in the office and they said, 'Come over to my place!' I could go! That felt so good. It felt grown-up.

'Rosie,' some of them started saying, as our friendships deepened in that winter of 2013, 'can you lend me a bit of money?'

I was happy to. I wanted to help people as much as I could. In the cult, everybody had said no to me all the time; now I was Out, I didn't want to be the kind of person who was hard and said no to others. I trusted that they were only asking me because they genuinely needed my help, and I was happy to give it. First I gave them £1, then £2, then £5 . . . Whatever they needed, I wanted to be there for them. If they said they had no money, I would say: 'Have mine.'

'I'll pay you back,' they promised.

It was a long while before I noticed that they never did.

I think my attitude towards them was another rejection of AB in a way. He had always warned me about Outsiders: they were fascist agents, not to be trusted. But AB spoke nonsense! So my heart was always open. I wanted to believe the best of everybody; to flip AB's paranoid teachings on their head. And because *I* would never take advantage of someone, I did not believe anyone else would act that way either. My friends were my friends.

In January 2014, I turned thirty-one. Yvonne and Gerard wanted to take me out to celebrate, but unfortunately I had a terrible cold and was too poorly to go. However, I was well enough to accept when they invited me to stay at their house for the weekend at the end of the month.

While I was there, on 31 January, an email came through to say that the panel had approved my moving to Yvonne and Gerard's. I was so excited. It couldn't have come soon enough, for my relationship with Josie was going from bad to worse. The fact that she seemed unable to acknowledge that what had happened in the house was wrong was too much for me to cope with. We were having arguments all the time.

When I took a step back from the situation, I felt in my heart that none of this was really her fault – she had been brainwashed, after all. That meant she didn't deserve my wrath, so I felt bad about my behaviour. Despite my being able to appreciate that, however, she had become impossible for me to live with.

It was Gerard who broke the news to Josie and Aisha that I was moving out, when we went back to the flat to pick up my things. Aisha seemed happy for me and glad that I had an opportunity to move on, but Josie appeared bereft.

'You don't understand the closeness between us!' she told Gerard. 'It's like losing my daughter!'

Despite her words about me being her 'daughter', she showed no motherly love as I left. She gave me filthy looks and though she didn't say much, she emanated anger, disgust and a sense of betrayal. She acted about Yvonne and Gerard the same way she had about Peregrine and Roddy, as though she believed them to be evil fascist agents taking me away from the Collective (with the corollary that I was a stupid, brainwashed, retarded little girl who had been duped by them).

It was in the car on the way to Yvonne and Gerard's that Yvonne revealed what was, perhaps, the real reason Josie wanted me to stay with her.

'Josie wants to go back to Bala,' she informed me.

'What?' I exclaimed. Though I'd known, from her behaviour, that this was coming, I didn't think she'd be so open about it.

'Bala has done nothing wrong!' she'd told Yvonne. 'And yet he's been deprived of his home and so much more!'

I remember thinking when I heard that: *But you lot deprived me of everything – and that's all right?*

When I realized what Josie wanted to do, I knew why she was so desperate for me to stay. I think she wanted me to go back to Bala with her – to keep her company. She'd been fond of saying, in the cult, how much my friendship helped her, so I think she must have been thinking, *When I go back, how will I survive without Rosie?* Because nobody else was kind to her.

As Gerard drove me away from the comrades who had been with me every day of my life, I felt glad to be moving on. Life should be about change. Nothing stays the same for ever, nor would anyone really want it to; I knew that from experience. As I settled into my seat for the journey, I looked forward to my new life *apart*. I was sure that this was change for the better. I'd so often felt sad since my escape, but I imagined all that would disappear when I moved in with what I already thought of as my new family. I couldn't wait for my new life to begin.

58

I have to admit, I was shocked when the move didn't magically solve all my problems. In storybooks, such as *Harry Potter*, when abused kids leave their horrible homes and move in with a kind foster family, they feel happy at once. It was a disappointment to learn that my anxiety did not vanish.

In many ways, I felt caged again. Since the family reunion, when I'd first asked to leave, I'd made all those friends in the neighbouring flats, but now I didn't live in Leeds any more I couldn't come and go as I'd learned to. I completely lost that community I'd been beginning to build up. Living in the unfamiliar village that I didn't yet know how to navigate, I was a prisoner once more: able to go to the garden alone, but no more than that. Though Yvonne and Gerard gave me personal space in a way I'd never had before, I almost felt *too* isolated.

I missed the comrades, too. Josie rang first thing every morning and again at night, but it was not the same as living in each other's pockets. I did very well without them for the first couple of weeks, just as one might on a holiday, but then I began to hanker for them. After that, I used to go and visit them and that was a good compromise: we could be friends on my terms, but I also had my own life away from them.

To my annoyance, Josie spent a lot of our time together badmouthing Yvonne and Gerard. Hearing her 'reports' didn't make me feel any differently towards them, but it made me concerned about what else she might be 'reporting'. Because Yvonne and Gerard were my authority figures, I became petrified that, behind my back, Josie was reporting me to them, telling them bad things about me as she always used to with AB. So could I trust them when I was alone with them in the house – or might they be about to turn on me? Such worries made me scared, so that I still struggled to hold

Yvonne's gaze, even though she was now my main carer and I had been out of the cult for more than three months. That's how deeply scarred I was inside when it came to building relationships.

The only friendship I had that seemed free of mistrust at that time was with Aisha. To my relief, and somewhat to my surprise, she now agreed that she would give a statement to the police to support my case. She did it only to help me, not herself, and we both kept it secret from Josie, though I believe she later found out. In some ways, Aisha was even braver than I was in giving evidence because she still believed in JACKIE. So she believed that when the Malaysian Airlines flight disappeared that spring with 239 people on board, it came about because she had betrayed AB.

Yet despite that extreme psychological pressure, unlike Josie Aisha seemed able to free herself from the clutches of the cult. Perhaps she had never properly believed in AB's divinity, not like the others; perhaps she had always just been scared she'd be deported, but now she had the right to remain. If she was afraid of JACKIE, and I'm sure on many days she was, she seemed determined to live a free life regardless. Later that year, she too moved out and got her own flat in some sheltered accommodation.

Her new home has a lunch club and things like that and it seems to suit her very well. I'm pleased to say that Aisha has apologized to me for the way she treated me in the cult – even though she was the least worst offender. We haven't discussed it a lot, though; I get the feeling she doesn't like to think about it, which I put down to shame and embarrassment and I can understand that. If she now rejects everything Bala taught, and owns up to that in her mind, that means she's wasted forty years of her life following a madman. In a situation like that, perhaps it's best not to think too much.

Once I moved into Yvonne and Gerard's, it was a shock to me to learn that *I* now had to think when it came to making everyday decisions. Though I'd had an inkling of it, I had not been aware of just how much Josie had cosseted me in the past few months. To give her the benefit of the doubt, though, it's also possible that I just wasn't ready to learn. Now, however, I had no choice but to, as Yvonne and Gerard – with patience and kindness – were determined that I would gain the knowledge to be able to live independently.

So when Yvonne prepared a platter of food for us as we watched

TV or spread a range of sandwiches before us, no longer could I get away with not having to make a choice.

'You choose for me,' I would wheedle. '*Please.*'

'I'm not choosing,' she would say. 'What would you like to eat?'

'I don't know,' I'd say, anxiety winding up inside me like a siren. 'People have always just given me what I have to have . . .'

'Well, I'm not doing that. Please choose whatever you would like. This is part of being an adult: *you* make decisions.'

I really struggled with it, even a simple binary choice, such as did I want a ham or a cheese sandwich? I think it was because I'd never been allowed to voice an opinion by AB. If I did – and it was contrary to his – he would shout abuse at me, insult me or physically assault me. It left me fearful of giving an honest opinion to others, even on such an innocuous subject. I did not want to be mocked or punished for making the wrong choice. To be offered a choice at all was so rare, too, that I didn't want to mess it up in case I didn't get the chance again. And the food at Yvonne's – and in the restaurants they took me to – was so new to me that I was scared of choosing something I didn't like. I'd never tasted most of the things spread out before me. How did I know what I wanted when I'd never tried it before? How would I cope with the agonizing social embarrassment if I chose something I did not like?

Yvonne was incredibly patient with me, yet she was also insistent that I must learn, no matter how long it took me to make a decision. She'd stand there in silence, not rushing me or directing me to one choice or the other, just allowing me the peace and quiet to come to a conclusion on my own. She always made a point of giving me choice at mealtimes, whether it was the main course, drink or dessert – or all three – so it was something I had to practise every day. Even so, it took me months to master it.

I think from the very start of my moving in, she and Gerard shared an aim to try to rehabilitate me into society so that I could integrate and learn the skills and social graces I needed to survive in the outside world alone. They did it very naturally, on a day-to-day basis, and they understood I could only work at my own pace. We spent a lot of time just talking – talking about relationships, as Yvonne helped me to understand about love and sex, and about how friendships should be. I also did lots of reading on the subject, as that remained my favourite method of learning; after my experiences with Bala's untruths, I didn't like learning solely from what someone said to me, as I thought of that as 'their opinion'. But a book written by a specialist with expert knowledge, who could authoritatively explain their position in a convincing way, seemed more reassuring. Most of all, I listened to my heart and only took knowledge on board if it also felt right to me.

One of the things I learned was taking a balanced view about people. Though I'd long despised Bala's blinkered viewpoints, I came to appreciate that my devoted 'love' for Roddy and Peregrine – where I'd denounced their detractors and had been unable to see any wrong in my beloveds at all – was just as skewed. I realized that there was good and bad in everybody, even those we love. Even those we hate will have positive aspects to them. That was an important lesson to learn.

It wasn't long before I had a chance to put my new understanding of people into practice. Though Yvonne, Gerard and I were the only people living in the house, they had a large family and almost every weekend one group of relatives or another would come by or a grandchild's birthday party would be hosted at their home. It was very, very sociable – and I felt very, very uncomfortable.

I was partly handicapped because the police had told me I had to keep my identity secret. I could tell no one that I was the girl rescued from the London cult that had been all over the papers last year. So I couldn't explain to people why I found it so difficult to interact with them, which made me even more self-conscious in case people thought me strange. When the living room was full of individuals, all chattering away, I felt as if I was an alien who had crash-landed on a different planet. Everybody was so loud and talkative; it actually made me dislike them simply because the noise alone made me feel awful.

Sometimes, the people visiting the house would try to engage me in conversation. I tried really hard to respond, not least because another of Yvonne and Gerard's lessons was that it wasn't usual to sit and stare at people: one should try to join in. But how could I participate when the conversation centred on where people had been on holiday or what they'd studied at school or even on the games they'd once played as children? I was back to climbing upwards, without any handholds or footholds. I had no connecting point with them: I'd never been on holiday or gone to school or played or had any friends at all . . . I could not contribute, no matter how much I wanted to. I was left with a sort of 'goldfish bowl' feeling because I couldn't relate to those around me and nor could they to me.

I also found it difficult to follow what people said – not just in person, on TV too. If I had a lot of repetition or if, for example, I read a book and *then* saw the movie adaptation, I was fine, but I struggled otherwise. I couldn't remember people's faces nor follow the dialogue; I guess I'd never had to before. It was disorientating.

The other strange thing about adjusting to life with Yvonne and Gerard was meeting their grandchildren. It reminded me, painfully, of my own grandmother and the fact that the two of us had never had a chance to form our own relationship. Every time I heard the children call Yvonne 'Granny', it was like a knife through my heart. Sometimes I had to excuse myself to the loo just so that I could have a good cry. I never spoke to anyone about it because it was too pain-ful to articulate.

In addition, I was used to being the only 'child' in my world, so I found it hard to know what to do with these small people. When they cried, which they did remarkably often, I was flummoxed. I didn't know what I was supposed to say or do. In the cult, such behaviour was denigrated as 'infantile disorder'. When Yvonne swept them up into a cuddle and wiped their eyes, I was a little sur-prised at first.

And, I have to say, also a little jealous.

It was hard for me to see that kind of comfort being so freely given. It wasn't just the grandchildren, but also other children I saw Outside. They ran and played and laughed. They were cuddled and lifted and loved. They had no idea of how beautifully lucky they all were.

Because I had never had any of that. Living with a family at last, I think I became even more aware of the childhood that had been stolen from me; of *all* that had been stolen from me. I'd missed out on all personal relationships – no parents, siblings, cousins, boy-friends, best friends or work colleagues. At thirty-one years old, I'd been deprived of having a family of my own, given no chance to find a husband or have my own children. When I saw the grandkids at Yvonne and Gerard's, I felt regretful, resentful, jealous and even a little grief-stricken for what I had lost and could never regain. If my baby had been born, they would have been four years old by now.

Yvonne and Gerard seemed aware of my sense of loss – one beautiful day, they took me shopping as a belated birthday treat and said we would buy something for each decade of my life. We went to the Disney store and they bought me a doll to represent 0–10; to a music shop to buy CDs for 11–20; to a clothes store to buy earrings and a smart fur coat for 21–30. Each time we stepped across the threshold of the shop on our way inside, we said we were stepping back in time.

It was such a magical gesture and I was truly grateful. But we didn't live in the world of Harry Potter, as much as I might wish to. There was no such thing as magic. What I'd lost, I could never find. Time in our lives marches in only one direction. I could do nothing but march along with it as best I could, taking step after slow, lumbering step.

59

In March 2014, Yvonne and Gerard generously gave me an iPod. For the first time, I had access to the internet – and the wonders of social media.

Much as it has done for society at large, it revolutionized my world.

It worked for me on so many levels. It meant I could make friends without revealing my full identity; I could make friends who I already knew shared my interests, be it the Labour Party, spirituality, tolerance, philosophy or psychology, which gave us an immediate starting point to build on; and, best of all, it meant I could communicate through my favourite medium: writing.

It was striking, how much more confident I was with the written word. Of course, that had been my only way of expressing myself in the cult. To *speak* to people rendered me mute and I found it difficult to listen to their responses, but to exchange written messages on social media felt as natural to me as breathing. It was wonderful to find that I wasn't completely unable to communicate, I'd just had to find a way that worked for me.

The downside was that you couldn't be sure who was on the other end and what their intentions might be, so I was always very careful in what I shared. Ultimately, I trusted my intuition, and if the other person felt at all dodgy, they were gone. But I also made some great friends and it built up my confidence massively to connect with like-minded individuals. I spent hours 'chatting' to them and setting the world to rights. Much further down the line, I even met some of them in person; they have since become trusted buddies who help and support me a great deal.

I think I coped quite well with using the new technology, especially given I'd never even had access to a computer in the cult. One of the support workers at Palm Cove gave me some lessons on basic computer skills and Yvonne showed me how to work the Apple devices. I mastered the different applications very quickly and learned how to play my music from a docking station. The only thing I struggled with was reading on a small screen because of my poor eyes, so Yvonne and Gerard generously gave me an iPad, too, which had a much larger screen. I used to google all the time and look up whatever I liked, learning about all sorts of new things.

All this helped me to gain more confidence offline too. Finally I was able to meet Yvonne's eyes when I spoke to her. We discussed my mask of make-up and I found I was ready to let it go at last. I stopped using the deep, orange colour that I'd always worn in the cult and had liked to hide behind. I chose a dark foundation instead that gave my face a more sun-kissed glow.

By this time, my shaven hair had grown back. Naturally, it was a very dark brown and I disliked it immensely, feeling as if it was Bala's stamp on me. I wanted to embrace a different identity, so I dyed it blonde. I was so happy looking in the mirror: inside, I felt like a different person and now I looked it on the outside, too.

My welfare payments started coming through now so Yvonne and Gerard suggested that we go shopping for some new clothes. I had grown out of many of the items I'd taken with me from the cult; now I was no longer dying from undiagnosed diabetes, the weight I'd lost had come back on so my tiny clothes no longer fitted me. I agreed to go with them to a place called Marks and Spencer.

I felt very worried about it; a headache came on and gripped me before we'd even looked for a single thing. I didn't know how to shop for clothes; Josie had always bought what I needed. I didn't even know what size I was.

In the end, I plucked items that caught my eye from the rails and shoved them into the trolley. In pain from my head, I tried to do it as quickly as possible, so everything from a size 8 to a size 18 went in.

'What size are you, Rosie?' Yvonne asked when she noticed this.

'Oh, it'll fit, it'll fit!' I declared, not knowing what answer to give.

'Why don't we try them on?' she suggested. 'The changing room is just over there.'

But I had never used a changing room in my life. What did it involve? Would Yvonne want to come in with me? The idea of taking off my clothes in public, possibly in front of her, was abhorrent. I didn't want to let her think I was OK with such things.

'No!' I said testily. 'I will not try them on.'

It took time for me to understand the protocol of shopping. Now, unless I'm buying something online, I always try things on. Though I found it embarrassing at first, I love clothes shopping now . . . just like my mum used to do.

Back at home, my education continued. I thought I knew how to cook, because I'd helped the comrades in the kitchen for years, but my knowledge proved very limited. I was used to following whatever instruction Josie gave me and hadn't had to do it all on my own before, so I struggled with timings and so on; I couldn't actually make a meal from scratch. Yvonne now showed me how to cook simple dishes such as spaghetti Bolognese and shepherd's pie.

Getting over my fear of electricity was a huge part of my domestic education. Having observed Yvonne and Gerard using their appliances, my fears had been considerably allayed as there seemed to be no sparks or shocks. But my memories of seeing the comrades getting shocked were traumatic and, to be honest, I still don't feel entirely comfortable around electrical appliances. Nevertheless, I mastered it enough to be able to learn how to use the microwave, kettle, cooker, washing machine and tumble dryer. I'd used the latter at the launderette, but never in a domestic setting, and I soon got to grips with them all.

Yvonne and Gerard praised me non-stop for all I was learning; they were impressed, I think, at how quickly I grasped things. I was simultaneously thrilled and clumsily self-conscious to hear their kind words. In the cult, I had yearned for praise and was never given it, so to receive it now felt awkward, though I did savour it secretly.

I was learning so quickly that Yvonne and Gerard decided I was ready for the next challenge. In April 2014, I faced my biggest test yet: learning to navigate the Outside world.

'OK, Rosie,' Yvonne said as the three of us walked along the village high street. 'Can you see where the kerb disappears here on to the road?'

I nodded.

'That's where you have to stop in order to cross. You look over your right shoulder and your left shoulder and once the road is clear, you go.'

We practised it over and over, just walking round the village centre and stopping, looking, listening, crossing. At one point, when they were letting me lead the decision of when to go, I looked and saw a white van driving along the road. The direction in which it was currently travelling would not take it into our path, so I started to step out.

I felt Gerard's hand on my shoulder stop me dead.

'No, look!' he exclaimed. 'The indicator!'

The white van turned into our road, one of its sidelights blinking orange, and zoomed past us at speed, the driver papping his hooter several times. 'Didn't you see me?' he shouted out of the window in annoyance.

'What's an indicator?' I asked.

When they explained it was one of those orange lights at the side of a vehicle, and that the side on which it was flashing indicated where the car wanted to go, I was taken aback. I had seen indicators before, of course, but no one had ever told me they *meant* something. For all I'd known, they were disco lights flashing in time with the driver's music. It was just one more code that I had to crack; traffic lights and pelican crossings were another mystery.

'If the green man is flashing,' Yvonne explained, 'you have to stand and wait because the lights are about to change and you may not have enough time to cross the road.'

Other people would be crossing beside us, racing across, so sometimes I got confused. 'Can we go?' I'd ask.

'No,' Yvonne would insist. 'Wait for the static green man. It doesn't matter what anyone else is doing, you wait until it's safe to cross.'

She drummed it into me, again and again, until I understood.

Once I'd mastered stopping, looking and listening, Yvonne started trying to educate me in navigation. The first thing we had to overcome was my need to look straight ahead down my tunnel vision. If someone was with me, I could happily wander down a street with no idea where I was going or what I'd just passed because my eyes were simply not trained to take anything in. But of course I had to learn how to do it because the whole point was that I would one day be walking down the street alone.

'You've got to look,' said Yvonne. 'Move your head. Look at things as you're going. *That's* the way you remember where you are.'

They started taking me on the bus and teaching me where to get off for their house.

'As you're approaching the traffic lights,' Gerard explained, 'you'll pass this first bus stop, which isn't the one we want. But once you pass it, ring the bell and stand up because you'll be getting off at the next one.'

We did it several times, the two of them leaving it up to me to press the bell at the right moment, but to my frustration I kept missing it. I found it hard to see the traffic lights or the bus stop somehow; or, weirdly, any other landmarks they tried to suggest, such as a church steeple or a big bushy tree. There was only one thing that worked.

'Give me words to look for,' I suggested. And *that* was the Eureka moment: the instant Gerard said I needed to press the bell when we passed the Co-op, I could read the shop sign and know when to do it. After that, navigating became easy – I'd look for a Phillips garage or a Matalan or whatever the nearest worded landmark was and then I knew exactly what to do and when to do it.

The village in which Yvonne and Gerard lived was quite some distance from the Palm Cove offices, especially by public transport. Yet I was keen to learn how to do the commute because, once I'd mastered that, I would be able to go and see my friends by myself and have much more independence. (Yvonne and Gerard kindly drove me to visit them, but it wasn't the same as being able to get there under my own steam.) They taught me in stages: how to walk to the bus stop and catch the first bus to the station; then how to get a bus or train into Leeds city centre; and then a final bus to Palm Cove. They made sure I knew how to pay and taught me all about money. They accompanied me a couple of times and told me exactly what to do – and then I did it on my own!

Funnily enough, the first time I went alone was 2 May 2014: the ninth anniversary of my first escape attempt. It was daunting and I was terrified, but I so wanted to learn that I was determined not to let my anxiety win. I stayed focused at all times and kept my wits about me. The personal pride I felt when I walked, alone, into the offices having come all that way by myself was extraordinary: a real sense of achievement. It was a very special day for me. I felt amazing!

The liberty I gained once I was confident enough to go out and about was wonderful, for no longer was I stuck inside, without the ability to get Out on my own. In fact, 'Out' became just 'out' now: another part of my world, rather than a completely different country I didn't have the documents to enter. It also meant I was able to develop much more of a social life. I was very happy living at Yvonne and Gerard's then: it was the best of all worlds.

The friends I saw the most at that time were still Josie and Aisha; I hadn't yet spread my wings very wide. I would see them regularly, perhaps a couple of times a week. I wanted to encourage them to try new things too, such as going to the pub. We went that summer of 2014. I looked around me in awe to find myself in such a place. I'd read about pubs in books, bastions of bonhomie, and it was extraordinary to be there, propping up the bar with a drink in my hand. I found I still didn't like the taste of alcohol – it was rather like medicine, I thought – but to have a glass of water in such a nice, social environment was a pleasant thing; as long as it didn't get too noisy. Then it was too much.

The best evening drink of all, however, came that same summer. Back when I'd lived in the house in Brixton, I'd spent many evenings with my face pressed jealously to the window as the neighbours drank a sun-downer in their sunlit gardens. I'd longed to be able to do the same: to sit with a cool drink outside as a pleasant breeze caressed my skin. I'd never thought such a thing would ever happen to me.

But that summer Josie and I took a drink to Burley Park one evening. We sat on a bench and gazed dreamily at the sky: it was pink and red and gold at sunset. I opened the caramel milkshake I'd brought with me and raised it to my lips.

The liquid was very sugary, but the sweetness I tasted had nothing to do with that.

60

On 30 July 2014, Yvonne and Gerard sat me down to share some news about the continuing police investigation against AB. More victims, they told me, had now come forward.

Leanne and Cindy had been resurrected from the dead.

Their allegations against AB were shocking and yet, somehow, also not. They told the police that AB had subjected them to years of rape and sexual assault. It was surprising only because of Bala's puritanical approach to sex.

Leanne and Cindy said the abuse had started after Chanda had fallen ill and gone to hospital back in 1980. Bala had started wearing aftershave and took to rubbing his unshaven chin on the women's faces, kissing them roughly. Then he began making allusions to animal sexual activity – bulls covering the females, for example – that he found described in magazine articles. It wasn't long before he progressed to what was termed 'full sexual degradation'.

His first sexual assault on Cindy was her first sexual contact with a man, she said; he'd slipped into her room at night and removed her clothes. She was too scared and shocked to fight back at first as he pressed his body against hers and started kissing her and touching her breasts. But when she tried to resist his advances, he punched her in the stomach until she doubled over in pain. Then he forced her to give him oral sex, telling her to swallow his semen and 'drink the elixir of life'. After that first time he regularly made her do it, for the next twelve years, until she finally found the courage to leave.

He raped both her and Leanne, all the while sleeping with Sian as well, and apparently used to make them all queue up outside his room. When he raped them, he said he was 'purifying them' to 'scrub them clean of the bourgeois culture' in the outside world. He wanted total power over them: he even made Leanne lick his anus. Leanne and Cindy said they were cowed into submission by his violence and psychological abuse: they stayed in the Collective too frightened to leave yet hating to stay. Cindy remembered him beating her so hard in the head that she lost her hearing and blood poured out of her ear; to this day, she said, she still suffered from hearing loss in both her ears because of his beatings.

Though I had personally seen no sign of the sexual abuse while they lived with me – beyond, of course, their obvious symptoms of anxiety and distress – their account of how he had treated them was so typical of his behaviour that I accepted their claims without question. In my opinion, it wasn't about sex for him, but dominance over others. He had never cared about such things as consent and respect for others; he had always termed such things 'fascist individualism'. I think he truly believed, as leader of the Collective, that he had a divine right over their minds and bodies: he saw them as his property, just as he had always done with me.

I did wonder if he had raped Sian too. Was I a product of such a violent, non-consensual act? I cannot know for sure, of course, but what I can say is that, at the time I knew her, in Sian's view everything AB did was right. It's an interesting question: if you're brainwashed, do you actually have the mental capacity to consent? I believe she was a willing participant, but perhaps it was rape and she dressed it up as love. In his own, sick way, I think AB did love my mother: 'She's a beautiful woman who I am 3,000 per cent with,' he had once declared. But it was a very unhealthy relationship, with her doing all the giving and he the eternal taker. I will never really know the truth about how I came to be. That's just something I have to live with.

Rather than shock, what I felt when I heard the news was an enormous sense of relief. Though Aisha supported what I was saying, she wasn't saying AB had hurt *her*: up until this point I had been the only one pointing the finger to say I had been harmed by him. Now, Leanne and Cindy had joined me on the frontline.

Up until then, too, I thought I was the only one who'd had an issue with the cult; after all, Josie thought it so wonderful she wanted to go back! Although my intuition, and the Outsiders I'd met, had told me I was right to hate what had gone on, a tiny bit of me had still wondered whether I was just pampered, as I'd always been told, and perhaps what had happened wasn't *so* bad. But with Leanne and Cindy coming forward to say they too had been abused – and they complained about the same psychological and physical torture I did – I felt more confident in my complaints and in my ultimate rejection of the cult.

In the wake of the revelations, I did sometimes feel upset to think about how many lives my father had ruined. I almost felt responsible for it; guilty my dad did so many bad things. I wished I could make things better for those he had hurt. I guessed the only way I could was to continue on the path I was already walking: trying to hold him to account.

Part of that process included writing a victim impact statement to be considered by the prosecutors as they decided whether or not to press charges. It was my chance to report at last, having been reported on all my life, but I felt a strange mix of emotions, not all of them positive, as I put pen to paper to describe the impact of AB's actions. I found it empowering on the one hand, but it was also sobering, upsetting and sad to think back over all the years. I imagined AB listening to it being read out, but I thought all he'd do was laugh at me and shake his head, thinking cruelly to himself, 'What an ungrateful cunt!'

In September 2014, I was assessed by a forensic psychologist from the National Crime Agency, as well as, in due course, several other doctors. Their reports would form part of the court case – *if* the case went ahead.

The most wonderful news came out of these tests: I had an IQ of 120. To my astonishment, this put me in the rank just below 'genius': I was graded as having 'very superior intelligence'. Given I'd been told for years what an idiot I was and that I was mentally retarded, it felt absolutely incredible to know that was definitively not the case. Yet another weak excuse of AB's to justify my captivity fell by the wayside in an instant.

The NCA also diagnosed me as suffering from chronic Post-Traumatic Stress Disorder. It was helpful to have a label to explain my ongoing anxiety and why I found large groups so painful to be part of. Because of my condition, I needed lots of peace and quiet to unwind.

The assessments ultimately threw up another legacy from my time in the cult, of which I had previously been unaware. The doctors told me I had both visual and auditory processing issues. It meant I couldn't process information quickly, or at a speed that most 'normal' people would. (I don't like the word 'normal' as to me it suggests people are mass-produced, when we are in fact all unique individuals, beautiful in our diversity.) This condition was why I couldn't hear song lyrics and immediately understand them; why I couldn't recall faces and dialogue on TV; why I found it physically painful to be in noisy environments. It basically meant my brain had been affected by my upbringing, leaving me with a legacy that made life much more challenging. Stimulus would go into my brain, but I struggled to process the information and make sense of it; it may also have affected my memory.

When I heard the diagnosis, it made total sense to me and I was glad to have an answer to the eternal question of why I found things in the outside world so difficult. I also felt extremely angry towards AB. He had done this to me. He had been given the gift of a baby daughter and he had trashed my life chances as uncaringly as he might crush a sheet of blank paper. He'd balled me up and thrown me in the bin and I felt rage rising in my stomach as I realized just how much he had disabled me. How I *hated* him in that moment!

It made me all the more determined to see justice done. In the final months of 2014, I finally learned the decision of the Crown Prosecution Service when it came to pressing charges. AB would go forward to trial and face charges of rape, indecent assault, ABH, child cruelty and false imprisonment.

Chanda would go free. All charges against her were now dropped.

I was shocked when I found out: in my opinion, she had made me feel wretched in the house. But I understood why they couldn't find anything to charge her with: Chanda's treatment of me was silent, ghosting me or giving me what I called her basilisk stares. She didn't pinch me or slap me or take my food away. She'd nonetheless done enough to emotionally hurt me, but not enough to have a charge laid against her.

As for what she and AB had done to Aisha and Josie, treating them as slaves, at that time there was no Modern Slavery Act to be cited against the Dark Lord Monsters; the law only came into being in 2015. If we'd been rescued today, charges of slavery may well have been brought, but back then they couldn't be. Josie and Aisha, of course, had made no complaint either.

Though I was very pleased AB would now go on trial, in many

ways it felt unfair to me that it was *only* him in the dock. Though he'd led the cult, I believed that it couldn't have been the way it was without the rest of them supporting, watching and reporting. It was not just Bala: it was a collective thing. They *all* helped it happen and I wasn't sure it was right that Bala was taking the blame for everything.

But Chanda could not be charged and I didn't want Josie or Aisha to get in trouble, so that was the end of that. Josie had saved my life and it did not feel right to bring up the past after all she'd done for me at the end. She too was a victim, even though she would not agree with that.

Josie did not take kindly to the news of AB being charged. When we three house-elves met up now, convening at Aisha's new flat, she would glower at the two of us as we had fun. She said we shouldn't enjoy ourselves while the fascist state was attacking AB. She would spend the whole visit sighing. From that point onwards, I really didn't feel she was much of a friend.

I felt pity for her that she was still as trapped as ever. Around this same time, though, I realized *I* was trapped too – but, this time, my only captor was myself.

I kept thinking about something I'd read during my secret-reading, which had stuck with me through the years. It was a quote from Nelson Mandela. 'As I walked out the door toward the gate that would lead to my freedom,' he had said, 'I knew if I didn't leave my bitterness and hatred behind, I'd still be in prison.'

As I'd slowly discovered all my many disabilities upon leaving the cult, I'd become angrier and angrier with AB for making me this way. But I now realized that the only victim of such feelings was myself. If I allowed myself to dwell on the negative, to be fuelled by feelings of hate and anger, it could take over my whole life. Where was the joy in that, when I had waited so long to live a free and happy life?

In the cult, I had battled to defeat my desire to hate my captors: now, I needed to do the same again. So I rationalized it.

It doesn't help me in any way to be angry.

It doesn't make a jot of difference to AB either.

It is wasted energy that could be channelled into living a more positive life.

If I keep feeling angry and hateful towards him, I realized in the end, *he still has the control.*

I thought of what I'd learned about people: that everyone has both good and bad aspects. My father wasn't an evil Dark Lord, even though he had done evil things. He wasn't a god or a demon: he was just a man. Who knew how I would have behaved if I'd been surrounded by worshippers telling me all I did was right? I can't say with absolute certainty that it wouldn't have gone to my head. What he did was wrong, but he was also a product of his circumstances. Let he who is without blame throw the first stone . . . At the end of the day, we all live in glass houses.

I did more reading around these ideas of forgiveness and positive thinking; I remembered all I'd read in the cult about Buddhism, Hinduism and Christianity. Though I did not follow any one religion, I was spiritual and I believed strongly in their messages of love and forgiveness, kindness and compassion. Despite what Bala had tried to teach me, I knew I always had.

What, I wondered in the end, *would Dumbledore do?*

And, with that thought in mind, I decided to forgive my father.

61

I felt cleansed by my decision. It seemed only fitting that as the new year began, a baptism of a different kind had also finally come.

On 20 January 2015, I legally changed my name by deed poll.

I had longed to do it ever since I'd escaped. I'd not wanted to do anything official, such as register to vote or sign up to college, until I could formally use my new identity. At long last, that day had now come. In my life, I'd been Prem and Preethi, Bryony and Claretta, and latterly Rosie Davies. Now I signed them all away with a stroke of a black-inked pen.

'I absolutely and entirely renounce, relinquish and abandon the use of my said former name of Prem Maopinduzi Davies,' ran the formal documentation, 'and assume, adopt and determine to take and use from the date hereof the names of Katherine Roseanne Francesca Morgan-Davies.'

Prem was dead. Long live Katy.

It was one of the proudest moments of my life so far. I chose Katherine as my first name for a number of reasons, not least because I'd discovered that my great-aunt and great-great-grandmother on my mother's side were called that. The 'Morgan' in my surname comes from my mum's family too; it had been Ceri's surname before she married. Finally: a name that suited my Celtic heritage and unputdownable spirit.

From that very first day, I loved being able to give my name in any official capacity; now I looked at my letters with pride, rather than cringing with disgust. I felt like my real life could finally begin. I registered to vote and immediately afterwards joined the Labour Party, which had long been a dream of mine. From my secret-reading, a longtime hero of mine had been Lord Longford, one of the Party's longest-serving politicians; I dreamt of becoming a social reformer like him, changing negative attitudes to people and making sure everyone was treated with love and had the necessary support. I hoped joining the Labour Party would enable me to follow that path. I was full of enthusiasm from the very first, volunteering to help canvass during the upcoming general election; much later, I was even elected as the BAME (Black, Asian and Minority Ethnic) officer for my local branch.

By this time, I was spending most of my days in Leeds, getting the bus and train every morning from Yvonne and Gerard's. Really, it didn't make much sense for me to be living so far away. By now, I could cook, clean, cross the road, shop and travel. I was independent at last: I was ready for the next step. In April 2015, aged thirty-two, after just fourteen months of 'training' with my foster parents, I moved out to a place of my own.

I absolutely loved it. What was brilliant was that I essentially moved into the 'halfway house' I had hoped for in the cult: I moved back into a Palm Cove property, this time sharing a six-bedroomed flat with five other women whom I did not know beforehand. They came variously from Ethiopia, Eritrea and Vietnam and could hardly speak a word of English. I saw them very little as I was always out!

I regularly took buses all over West Yorkshire – just for the sheer pleasure of travelling. I used to put my earphones in and listen to music, at first to calm me as it was initially intimidating, but later just for fun. I got a smartphone, too, which meant I always had Google Maps to fall back on if I ever got stuck, so really there was nothing to fear.

My 'bussing about', as I called it, was essential to help me get a feel for where everything was in my new hometown. I used to go to the top of the bus and sit at the front and then ride the whole length of the journey, from the first stop to the last, on any particular service. It helped me to plot a mental map of Leeds so that I didn't panic or feel scared if I missed my bus stop. I realized there was nothing to be afraid of in getting lost – on the contrary, to discover new places was an adventure.

Yvonne and Gerard also asked one of the support workers to show me how to use the trains to go even further afield. Now *that* was exciting! All my old dreams of becoming a train driver came back to me. I just loved it. I went all over: York, Manchester, Sheffield, Nottingham . . . My new confidence even enabled me to help others. When new residents arrived at Palm Cove and were unsure how to get to places, I would step in.

'Oh, you don't know how to get to York? I'll take you!'

'Huddersfield, you say? Come with me, I'll see you right.'

When I wasn't out on one of my bussing or train trips, or at a Labour meeting or event, any free time was spent on the campaign trail, where I made many wonderful pals. With the general election less than a month away, there was much to do.

I used to 'run the board', which meant I was in charge of the teams who would go out knocking on the doors, assigning them the addresses they had to visit. Though I didn't do the actual door-knocking, which I'd still have felt awkward about, it was an immensely empowering experience. All the people working with me, such as my psychotherapist, said how much I changed when I joined Labour and how much more confident I became.

I felt so much more self-possessed that, these days, when my friends at Palm Cove asked me for more money, I politely said no. I realized I was being taken for a ride and decided not to give them any more cash; I didn't like to be unkind, but it was bad for both of us if I said yes all the time. It was disappointing to find out that, sometimes, not everyone could be trusted.

The only downside to moving back into Palm Cove was that Josie was still staying there; she lived in the flat directly opposite mine. She used to stand and stare at me through the window when I was home; I found it unnerving. I was already on edge about her because, before I'd moved back, I'd discovered she was helping Bala with his defence. She'd been walking me to the train station after a visit one day when her mobile had rung unexpectedly: I had heard a male voice speaking before she quickly told him to ring back later as she was otherwise occupied. When I'd asked her who was calling, she went all cagey and said, 'Just a friend, that's all.'

But Josie had no male friends. I became terrified she was communicating with AB directly and had arranged for him to be waiting at the train station, either to kidnap me or to push me into the path of an oncoming train. She knew where I lived; she knew the route I was taking . . . That was a very anxious journey as I kept expecting AB to pop up at any moment. When I mentioned all this to Yvonne once I was safely home, she told me Josie had made contact with

Bala's lawyer. I was relieved it was not Bala himself, but felt betrayed she would do such a thing behind my back, even though it was hardly surprising.

But it put me in a difficult position – made worse by our now being neighbours. I didn't resent her talking to the lawyer, as she had the right to do what she believed to be correct, but neither did I want her to pass back information about me to AB and Chanda. I felt intimidated by her standing at the window; it felt like she was spying. I mentioned it to the police and they sent her a letter to warn her that she would be arrested if she tried to intimidate me, but nonetheless I still felt anxious.

In the end, it was one of my new friends from the Labour Party who really helped me. He was an elderly gentleman who smoked a pipe and had a moustache and glasses. I thought him very jolly indeed, and he listened intently as I told him how intimidated I felt by her.

'You know what you need to do?' he said bluntly. 'Cut the crap out of your life!'

I took his advice. After that, I scaled down my meetings with Josie and in time stopped seeing her altogether. Now, I only saw her when we chanced upon each other outside. I felt sad it had come to that, but it was better for us both. We were still friendly when we saw each other; we used to hug and then part ways.

Yet even those few occurrences happened less and less as time went on – because I had places to be. In late April 2015, a few weeks after moving back to Palm Cove, I started college, studying creative writing.

I attended a college for adults, which was great; I'd initially thought I might be one of the only adult learners, because of my past, but that wasn't the case at all. My teacher was a smiley Russian woman called Leonora. When I struggled with something, I did not feel criticized or stupid, but supported.

I absolutely loved it – especially when we got to do poetry. I was complimented on my vocabulary – all those years of reading the dictionary finally coming into their own! – but found it difficult when asked to describe things. Perhaps that's to do with my information-processing problems: I can't transform the input of the sight of something into the output of a description. I'd had such a limited range of things to see when I was growing up that maybe I emerged from the cult unable to articulate difference. I still don't know, and it's something I struggle with today, though it's no longer as bad as it was.

It was a bit of a battle making friends at college at first. It was frustrating not being able to reveal my full identity; I couldn't say, for example, why I didn't have any qualifications. That was hard, but I got by. I was so excited to be there that I think I gave off a positive vibe and everyone was nice. They seemed to look beyond the fact that I still felt tongue-tied in large groups; I couldn't seem to become that outgoing girl I'd always dreamed of being, no matter how much more confident I now felt inside. In time, I made some amazing pals.

A few weeks after I started at college came one of the defining days of my life. On 7 May 2015, I voted in my first-ever election.

How can I put into words the meaning of that moment? Everything about it, from walking into the polling station and giving my proper name, to the agency of marking my vote on the ballot paper, was imbued with empowerment. I remembered how I used to seethe when I saw the Collective filling in the Census form without my name on it; how upset I was to be eighteen and unable to vote. Knowing how much Bala would hate me voting made me feel even gladder to do it – but really this day had nothing to do with him. He chose to absent himself from the democratic process: I participated. Voting in an election is about having your voice heard and I was ready to roar from the rooftops.

My hand trembled as the people at the desk passed me the forms. I turned and secreted myself in the wooden booth, picking up the little pencil to vote. As I did so, tears began pouring down my face so that I could hardly see. With a smile that was like the sunshine after rain, I proudly marked a cross.

And as I voted, I remember thinking, *I am no longer an Unperson. My vote counts. I am a valued member of society, not just a nameless, faceless entity who doesn't exist.*

It was the moment I truly ceased to be a shadow-woman and stepped into the light.

62

In September 2015, I enrolled on formal courses in English and maths at the same college I'd been attending since April. It was the first rung on a ladder I'd decided I wanted to climb: to become a train driver, I needed to obtain good passes in English and maths GCSE. For the next few years I had to complete foundation courses in those subjects, but I was now working towards taking my national examinations, with a view to getting a job as a driver in the distant future. *How wonderful it will be*, I thought, *to drive those lovely trains!*

That same autumn, I learned something about myself which made me feel more joyful still. I'd recently joined Amnesty International and after one of their meetings, a group of us went to the pub and started chatting. At some point, one of the guys at my table asked us all: 'If there was a choice between mercy and justice, which would you choose?'

'Mercy, of course,' I replied.

'That shows something about your personality,' he commented.

I was intrigued – psychology had long been a favourite subject of mine – and he said to look up the Myers-Briggs test online. I did it the very next day and received the personality type INFP: Introverted, iNtuitive, Feeling and Perceiving.

It was a breakthrough moment. Ever since I'd escaped from Dark Tower, I'd despised myself for being so quiet and reflective: not the bolshie, chatty woman I'd imagined I'd be once free. After doing the test, I realized that was simply not who I was: I was an introvert, not an extrovert. I could now appreciate that there were plenty of other people besides me who didn't like to be the loud one in a group or who disliked socializing in gaggles: it didn't mean I was strange, it was just the way I was. That knowledge enabled me to feel a lot more comfortable with who I was and to embrace my personality type, rather than denigrate it.

In fact, there was an awful lot to be proud of in being an INFP. I learned that it is the peacekeeping personality type; it is also known for being unconventional and rebellious, with very strong values. Blake at stellarmaze.com wrote: 'No one can make [an INFP] budge off their moral certainty . . . Nothing can make them change their deep conviction about what they feel is right. You can beat the living shit out of them and they will cry and weep. You can pour on heaps of emotional abuse and psychological torture and they will go to pieces. And then they will reassemble themselves and carry on as if nothing happened . . . You cannot make an INFP believe anything which they don't inherently believe.'

When I read that, the description fit like a glove. That's how I'd lived my whole life; how I'd resisted the dark message of Dark Tower. For me, when something doesn't feel right, it doesn't feel right, and I'm not going to be told it *is* right when I think differently. It also made sense about my always trusting my intuition.

Once I understood myself better, I found it much easier to make friends. I can chatter away to close buddies now, but I will never be the one holding forth in a group – and that's OK. For me, it works much better to have a few intimate friends than a mass of acquaintances. To those friends, I can show my heart. The window glass melts away and I can reach out and connect. The Myers-Briggs test showed me we all have our strengths and weaknesses. The most important thing is to learn to be happy with who you are.

It was an essential message for me to grasp and it came at just the right time. For that autumn, I faced a daunting experience that even people who had not been caged for thirty years might struggle to surmount. In November 2015, I had to face my father in court.

The trial of Aravindan Balakrishnan began, I believe, on 12 November 2015. AB sat impassively in the dock as he heard he faced a total of sixteen charges, all of which he denied. The newspapers reported he had thinning grey hair and thick glasses; he was now seventy-five years old.

The prosecuting barrister began by setting the scene: 'From being a collective agitating for the rights of the proletariat, the group had become the cult of Aravindan Balakrishnan,' explained Rosina Cottage QC.

To my relief, I wasn't called in the first week of evidence: instead, Leanne and Cindy had their chance to tell their stories. I was very pleased they did it that way round, as I still feared no jury would believe the outlandishness of my experiences, and there was so much to explain – the way we were kept in line by AB's alleged power over life and death; his divinity; his violence; JACKIE and Overt . . . I thought it would take me a thousand years to explain it all.

But with the former cult members going before me that at least gave the jury some context to my story, for theirs was the world into which I was born. I could only hope it might make my own evidence that little bit more believable.

I was petrified that AB was going to win this final battle. With him and Chanda and Josie all ranged against me, I had little hope of being believed. By my own evidence I was a writer and dreamer who had spent much of my life in the cult with my head in my cloud-filled cocoon; surely his lawyer would argue my allegations were the stuff of fantasy? Leanne and Cindy had left decades before I'd escaped, so their evidence would be of no help for the later years of my incarceration. I feared AB would use his frighteningly impressive skills of manipulation to whitewash everything so that, even if Leanne and Cindy secured convictions for the crimes against them, what had happened to me would be deemed OK.

As I was a witness, I was kept away from the proceedings. I would only go to court when it was time to say my piece. I think someone else may have been following them, though – and I guess that person didn't like what they heard. On the evening of 15 November 2015, a few days before I was due to take the stand, I was accosted by Josie as I walked to Aisha's flat.

Something seemed wrong. For an instant, as she loomed up out of the darkness, I imagined she might be about to take a knife to me, to shut me up for good. I swallowed my fear and managed to speak: 'Are you all right?'

She grabbed my arm, crying and trembling.

'No,' Josie sobbed, her voice shaking and distressed. 'I'm not OK. I'm so upset about AB.' She took a deep breath. 'Please, can't you find it in your heart to forgive him? I know you are extremely angry, but can't you put that aside? AB will be going to prison like this!'

I spoke to her gently. 'It is the court that decides that, not me,'

I said. 'I have already forgiven him, but I have to go through with this process. I promise I will only tell the truth. Then it's up to the court to decide.'

I gave her a hug. 'I'm sure everything will be all right,' I said, and then I walked away.

I meant what I said: I had forgiven him. In giving evidence against him, I wasn't looking for revenge or punishment: I simply wanted an acknowledgement of the facts. I wanted a conviction because that would be proof that what he had done to me was wrong. I'd been told all my life that the way I was treated was right and good and *I* was in the wrong for questioning it. I just wanted the record to be set straight.

My first day in court was 19 November 2015. I went down to London for it. I was due to give evidence via videolink, so I would not be in the courtroom itself – which meant I wouldn't be in the same room as AB. I was pleased about that; I felt creeped out by the idea of even being in the same room as him again, worried in case he tried anything, even as seemingly innocuous as a belch, to make me feel uncomfortable and powerless. I didn't want him even to breathe the same air as me: that was too close for comfort. I didn't quite trust that AB would not be able to find some way of manipulating me or of making me feel guilty about allegedly 'betraying' him. Better by far to do the videolink, which felt comfortable for me, more like a one-to-one conversation than giving evidence in court.

Knowing I would be seen onscreen, however, I dressed carefully: a black-and-gold tunic, black tights and high-heeled boots, which I'd recently managed to master walking in. I bought a new coat especially for the occasion, a grey cashmere one with a fur collar from Marks and Spencer. I wanted to look proper for the jury, but I also wanted Bala to see how well I was doing. I wanted him to see I was dressing in a way he would not approve of; for the same reason, I took particular pleasure in styling my *blonde* hair that morning too.

As I walked into Southwark Crown Court, my heels clicking with that *boom boom boom* of businesswomen that I'd always loved, it did feel as if I was about to face a final showdown. Yet it wasn't on the scale of Harry versus Voldemort or Frodo ranged against Sauron, though I took courage from their victories. Those books had taught me that no matter how big a monster is, you can defeat them – but AB wasn't a monster to me, not any more. In fact, he seemed very much diminished.

Yvonne accompanied me to court. With a final hug just down the corridor from the evidence room, she left me alone with the court usher. I don't remember feeling anything in particular as she walked away: I was just eager to get this done.

It's funny how the most bland environments can be the setting for the most important moments in a life. The usher and the court intermediary, Tina, soon escorted me into a smallish room with a number of easy chairs. I sat with Tina on the sofa opposite the screen and we waited for proceedings to begin.

As we did so, I hoped desperately that my mind wouldn't freeze. I hoped that I wouldn't laugh my nervous laugh. But Yvonne had told me beforehand that the jury had been briefed about that: 'If you need to laugh, you can,' she'd said. It had been explained to them that if I giggled it didn't mean I was happy or that I wasn't taking it seriously: it was actually a sign of distress. That was a relief, at least. Because I had a feeling I was going to feel hugely embarrassed over the next few days, in discussing all the nonsense that had gone on in the cult and how I had been forced to believe in it. I didn't know quite what I was going to be asked. The day before I went to London, one of my best friends told me that if ever it got on top of me during giving evidence, I should think of a special image in my mind: of clouds blowing away to reveal the stars. I could only hope that beautiful image of a natural Enlightenment would be enough to see me through.

I really didn't know anything about the process. I hadn't realized that the prosecution would outline my case to the jury beforehand, but that's exactly what they did. I thought I'd have to stand there and try to explain everything coherently from scratch, which would have been impossible with such a case as mine, but instead they set the scene and the questions to me only came afterwards.

'[Katy Morgan-Davies],' declared Rosina Cottage QC, 'was bullied, beaten and separated from the world. She never went to school, played with a friend, saw a doctor or dentist. She barely left the house. She was hidden from the outside world. [Told she had no parents, she developed a feeling] of being a non-person that she carried through her life until she left the Collective.'

She told them how Sian was not allowed to cuddle or breastfeed me because I was 'Collective property'; how I never even knew for sure she was my mum until after Sian had died.

'If any of them were to go against [AB] they would die,' Cottage went on, 'and even if they were to have a bad thought about him they would die, fall ill or something bad would befall. Everything was controlled by him. He said he had magical powers and was going to overthrow all governments and become leader of the world. He said he had a mind-control machine that monitored all their thoughts.'

As she drew to a close, I realized I would soon be called upon to give my evidence. I took a deep breath. Fears flitted through my head – *would I laugh? Would I remember enough? Would I freeze? Would I say the right things?* – but I just remember thinking in the end: *I have to give it my all.*

After all that worry, it turned out to be easy. The question-and-answer format was so simple; and I didn't need to worry about remembering everything because it soon became clear that my childhood diaries formed a massive part of the prosecution's case. I hadn't seen them since the day I'd left them behind when I escaped, but since then the police and barristers had gone through them all with a fine-tooth comb – specific entries were annotated, bright-pink Post-it notes stuck to the relevant pages to make them easy to cite. I didn't have to wrack my brains to dredge up memories because it was all there, written in my childish handwriting: all I had to do was explain each entry.

'Comrade Bala disciplined Comrade Prem – talking in bed,' was one such entry from 1990, when I was seven. 'He gave her 21 beats. He said 17 more to come.'

'Comrade Bala said if Comrade Prem carries on talking rubbish . . . he will give her 25 beats.'

'Comrade Bala made Comrade Prem go down on her knees. He said how can she criticise others if you don't criticise yourself.'

'Comrade Bala told Comrade Prem *not* to look out of windows. If she does, Death Row dogs . . . will think that Comrade Prem is very keen to go with them and will take her with them . . . Comrade Bala said if Comrade Prem insists on looking out of windows . . . he would not take her out any more.'

'Comrade Bala will hate and hit Comrade Prem if she thinks about herself.'

'Comrade Bala said ugly dirty whites will kill Comrade Prem if she violates Comrade Bala's Guidelines.'

'Comrade Prem should never go anywhere by herself . . .'

There were years and years and years of this. Project Prem, ironically, turned out to be a saving grace. Had AB not been so arrogant about his supposedly superlative child-rearing innovation, insisting on religiously recording my abusive upbringing, all this evidence would simply not exist. It would only have been in my memory, and who would have believed me then? But it was here before the jury in blue Biro and red pen – in my writing, Sian's writing and AB's.

'This child,' AB had been fond of saying, 'will be my worst enemy.'

It was ironic, in a way, that this was the one prediction he did get right.

The use of the diaries felt like karma. I'd been forced to write much of them, bullied and humiliated into recording my alleged 'crimes' against the Collective, but now they had ended up as evidence against AB. That was an incredibly empowering experience, the way everything had been turned on its head.

Yvonne later said I spoke very eloquently. I did giggle a bit when I was particularly embarrassed or uncomfortable, but once I got into it I found I could do it without laughing. In fact, it was sobering to hear everything I'd endured over so many years. On the whole, though, I felt few emotions. I just tried to get through it all as best I could.

After the prosecution had finished with me, it was the turn of the defence. I watched AB's lawyer on the screen apprehensively as he prepared to question me. Neither he nor Rosina Cottage wore their wigs and gowns, so that at least was not intimidating. But that didn't mean he was going to give me an easy ride.

He too went through the diaries. He was trying to make me feel bad. He'd pick out, for example, those entries in which I'd recorded Bala going to the Science Museum. 'He brought you back a microscope and a snakey, which you describe as "very lovely",' he would say, showing me the entry. He made a point of picking out those few occasions where I'd been taken out of the house and then quizzed me about my enthusiastic notes; about my delight at the rare, precious treat.

'You wrote that, didn't you?' he'd say.

'Yes,' I'd have to reply. I started worrying: *how is anybody going to believe me that Bala was abusive? Because all these nice things happened too, will the jury think I'm just making up stories or blowing things out of proportion?* I felt panic rising within me and tried to concentrate hard on that image of the clouds blowing away to reveal the stars. I found it helped immensely.

'Didn't you like that?' the lawyer went on. 'He took you out on educational trips, didn't he? He bought you things?'

I took a deep breath. 'Yes, that's true,' I said. 'All those things are true. He did do all that.' I stared directly at the screen. 'But that *didn't* give him the right to beat me up and keep me in the cage.'

I felt like the lawyer buckled after that; he didn't seem to have an answer for it. His cross-examination was nowhere near as difficult as I'd expected and I was proud of the way I held my ground.

After four days of testimony, my part in the trial was over. But my ordeal had only just begun. Unlike in the cult, Bala was receiving a *fair* trial – so when the prosecution rested, the defence could plead their case. He would get a chance to give his side of the story.

What was he going to say?

63

Bala was the only defence witness. Back at home in Leeds, I turned the possibilities of his defence over in my mind. Would he say I was a fantasist? Would he say I was mad? How would he talk his way out of this?

As it turned out, he did what one should always do in the witness box: he told the truth.

The truth, that is, according to AB.

'JACKIE is an electronic satellite warfare machine built by the Communist Party of China and the People's Liberation Army,' he said in his evidence. 'It has got unbelievable control. It can pull your head out from your body.'

'Do you really expect people to believe that?' asked his lawyer wryly.

AB glowered at him. 'You want to be very careful because I could set JACKIE on you now and you could get seriously hurt!'

I imagine the barrister may have given a smile; the papers described him as seeming 'exasperated'.

'I'll take my chances,' he said. And a laugh ran round the court.

When I heard what Bala had done, that he had corroborated it all, I literally jumped for joy. If he'd been smart about it, he could have denied certain parts of the story, which would have made him sound sensible, but the way he did it, he just made it clear that he was off his rocker. My personal opinion is that he must have been desperate by the time the case came to court and perhaps thought he might be able to scare people, the same way he tried to scare us in the cult.

Yvonne, who watched his evidence, said he came across as blasé. He knew exactly what he was doing when he'd locked me up and hurt the comrades, but he thought it was OK to treat people in that way. I was a stupid child whom he had to protect from the rest of the world in case I came to some dreadful harm, so he was doing it in my best interests. That's the 'defence' he was going for – but the more he spoke, the more bizarre it seemed.

I think, from experience, that he believed his own rhetoric. I think he does believe in JACKIE. I can't know if he always did; was it, at one point, a conscious method to control us? Who knows? But I think he still believes he is going to take over the world. I think he believes he controls the world already. He told the jury that a challenge to his leadership resulted in the Challenger space shuttle disaster in 1986 and that JACKIE killed Malaysian Prime Minister Abdul Razak. He also claimed responsibility for the election of Jeremy Corbyn as Labour leader. God only knows what he was thinking.

On 4 December 2015, I was tidying up my flat in Palm Cove, having just come home from my maths class, when my phone beeped with a text from Yvonne. It contained just two words:

Found guilty.

It was an overwhelming feeling to read them. Despite all that had happened in court, I still hadn't trusted that things would go my way, so the feeling of vindication was extraordinary. To know I'd been believed by the jury was quite wonderful.

I felt sad for my father too, though. Although he had not yet been sentenced, I felt as if I was putting him in a cage, and that didn't feel right. The only thing that felt right was finally to have confirmation that what had happened to me – and Leanne and Cindy – was wrong. That was very special indeed.

Two days later, I buzzed on the door of the flat opposite mine. Genuinely concerned about how Josie would be taking the verdict, I wanted to check she was OK. I carried round a handful of clothes that I'd grown out of and knew she liked, hoping they might cheer her up.

'Hello, stranger!' I said in a jolly voice when she answered the buzzer.

'Is that Rosie?' she grunted. (I hadn't told her about my deed-poll change.)

'Yes,' I replied.

'OK. Come in,' she said huffily.

I could tell from her tone of voice that it wasn't going to be a pleasant meeting – and I was right. Yet I was shocked by what I saw when I walked into her flat. Her voice, her face ... everything about her was like someone possessed. She had *turned*. During the trial she had spent time with AB again and it was almost as if she had been reprogrammed. She was completely hostile towards me: the Josie she'd been in the worst days of the cult. One hundred per cent Hyde; I couldn't see Jekyll in her eyes at all. It was horrendous and pitifully sad to watch.

'Beloved Comrade Bala has asked me to pass on a message from him,' she told me, a certain glee glazing her words.

'Oh yes?' I said.

'He hates you more than anything else in the world.'

She watched my face eagerly as she spoke; I can only assume she was hoping to see me flinch. Once upon a time, back in the cult, I would have done, being so afraid to lose the little freedom I had. My defiant nonchalance now left her seeming shocked.

Coolly, I replied, 'It's his prerogative to feel like that, but it doesn't affect me either way. I don't need or want his approval.'

Josie was so angry that she was unable to speak coherently. She'd given a TV interview in the wake of AB's conviction, denouncing it as a miscarriage of justice, and in it she had said she loved me.

'Don't be deceived by those words,' she told me now. 'My love for you does not preclude me from "struggling" with you if I believe you are doing wrong!'

She spoke to me as she had done when I was a child, as though she was stuck in a time-warp: she the adult and I the baby; she the prison warden and I the prisoner. She actually believed that she was so important to me that her disapproval would ruffle me – but I went to visit her not to beg her friendship, but because I felt sorry for her, brainwashed as she was; and also because I cared. Though I had respected her position when it came to the trial, she seemed unable to do the same for me, even though I was almost thirty-three years old and I knew my own mind. I didn't need anyone to 'struggle' with me. I had struggled quite enough.

'Bala warned me to be careful about you,' she hissed. 'He said you are a nasty manipulative bitch!'

She hurled the words at me, clearly hoping for them to hurt, but they didn't – I just felt sorrier for her, and her master, than ever. She rejected the clothes I offered her.

'I don't want anything more to do with you!' she declared.

I respected her wishes. 'That's entirely up to you,' I replied. I strode to the door with my head held high.

She slammed it behind me and the sound was a full stop: a punctuation point that marked the end of everything between us.

It didn't escape my notice that while I could walk away, she was now the one who was blocked behind the door. The prison warden had become the prisoner – but the tragedy was, she could not even see it.

On 29 January 2016, AB returned to Southwark Crown Court to be sentenced for his crimes. He had been assessed by doctors in the intervening weeks and found to have a 'narcissistic personality disorder' and a 'grandiose' sense of his own self-importance. When I read that in the papers, I thought, *I knew it all along!*

Judge Deborah Taylor handed down the sentence. In her remarks, she said: 'These are grave and serious crimes conducted over a long period of time and you have shown no remorse whatsoever. You were ruthless in your exploitation of [your victims].

'Your daughter was an experiment, deprived of love and affection – you lied to her that she was an orphan, you never formally acknowledged that she was your daughter until the trial. Your treatment of her from her birth to [adulthood] was a catalogue of mental and physical abuse. You decided to treat her as a project, not a person. You claimed to do it for her to protect her from the outside world, but you created a cruel environment. You kept Katherine Morgan-Davies under your control; she had been born into the regime and had been unable to escape from it, as she was unable to leave the house on her own.'

After her remarks, for all AB's crimes – for the rapes and the assaults, the child cruelty and the false imprisonment – she sentenced him to twenty-three years in jail.

Bala did not react as the judge gave her verdict, but Josie shouted from the public gallery, 'This is political persecution!'; a view Chanda echoed in her own press statements. On the steps outside, as she stood beside Chanda, Josie wore a T-shirt that read in big black letters: 'AB framed by the fascist state.' I felt very sad when I saw that.

I felt sad, too, when I heard the sentence. Gerard was of the opinion that AB should have got thirty years, the same as I served in my cage, but I felt it was too long as it was. 'If there was a choice between mercy and justice, which would you choose?' my friend had asked me. And, for me, it's mercy every time.

Bala put me in a cage, but now I've done the same to him, and that feels wrong; it feels like petty revenge, which I don't believe in. I wanted him convicted, for that message to be sent, but I do feel uncomfortable with the punishment of prison. I guess it's because I know exactly how it feels.

I wonder, too, if it is really the right place for him. Perhaps he would stand more chance of rehabilitation in a mental hospital.

The day he was sentenced, I gave a televised interview to ITN. After all my 'TV interviews' in Wembley, it felt most peculiar finally to be doing one for real. It reminded me of those bad old days – and of how far I'd come.

I showed my face to the camera. I gave my beautiful real name. With complete certainty, I chose to waive my anonymity. For why would I want to stay in the shadows, when I had already been a shadow-woman all my life? I'd been anonymous for thirty-three years already; a single second longer felt too long. I wanted to stand up and be counted; to reclaim my identity; to use my voice to help make the world a better place, as much as I could.

'He took my freedom,' I told the reporter. 'He deprived me of family, childhood, friends, love, affection, a sense of belonging, a sense of home . . . but I forgive him for what happened. After all, life is a journey, isn't it?'

And not all those who wander are lost.

Epilogue

On 12 May 2016 – eleven years and ten days after I made my first bid for freedom – I moved out of my Palm Cove flat and into an apartment of my very own. It's a modern, one-bedroomed flat that I've furnished with a claret velvet sofa and beech-wood tables and chairs. I was so proud of myself that day, that I had learned enough over the past few years to enable me to live independently. To be self-sufficient is the best feeling in the world.

I plan, in time, to display photographs of my mum and granny, but they're not up just yet. I have stayed in touch with my mother's family, though: Eleri and I speak once a week.

In August 2016, we went together to Tregaron, Wales, to take a trip down memory lane. This was where my mother had grown up; where Granny had lived until she died. Eleri took me to see Ceri's old house. If things had been different, it might have been my home.

We also went to visit my mother's grave. After Sian died, Ceri took her back to Wales and buried her with her father; when Ceri had passed on in 2005, she'd joined them in the same plot. So now all my family lie beneath a shiny black marble slab in a churchyard by a chapel, their names picked out in gold leaf.

I took yellow flowers for Sian, as bright as the sunshine that beamed down upon us that day. But, inside, I felt completely cold. I've found that's another legacy of the cult: I often feel quite dead inside. I think my emotions were manipulated so much that I don't allow myself to feel things now, even though I'm free, because I'm still scared I might get hurt. The mind games Bala played after Roddy was banished have left me unable to enjoy things: I don't look forward to upcoming events, and when they happen, I don't believe they're real. I'm still scarred by the idea nice things might be taken away from me, so I disconnect to protect myself.

But it's not all the time. I am healing slowly and though it's difficult at times, the happiness is gaining, bit by bit. When the people closest to my heart hug me, I don't feel cold: I feel *love*. My cousin Eleri told me about *cwtch*, the Welsh word for cuddle. A *cwtch* is more than just an embrace: it's a hug that takes away all pain, a hug that expresses love and acceptance, a hug that feels like a shelter in a storm. *Cwtch* is now my favourite word, as well as my favourite thing to do. When I'm hugging my family – Eleri; Yvonne and Gerard, who are the parents I never had; and all the lovely new friends I've made – I feel as if nothing can ever hurt me again. That's the power of *cwtch*.

One of the friends I embrace is someone I once called Comrade Aisha. We try to see each other once a week and it is always a pleasure to visit. Aisha was always fair and just; I believe the horrid things she did in the cult she did only because she was scared. She has coped really well since we escaped; in 2016, she even got her teeth fixed. I was so happy for her: she looked great, and it was such a huge signpost to show how much she had moved on from the madness of the cult. We spend our Christmases together now, having roast dinners and prawn cocktails; last year, I made my own Christmas cake, with all the marzipan and icing. It tasted pretty good!

Together, Aisha and I took part in a documentary about our experiences that aired on the BBC in January 2017. The film-maker interviewed lots of different people, including our former neighbours. One of them was the man who had given me such pleasure when he built his wall. He cried on film as he talked about me. He said he had not known what was going on behind my window.

I felt incredibly touched when I saw that, and sorry he felt so bad. I don't think he should feel upset or guilty: he bears no responsibility at all. There was no way anyone outside could have known what was happening to me: the cult were so secretive and so good at manipulating people that I'm amazed anyone noticed me at all. The fact that he remembered me, the fact that another neighbour even called to report my not attending school, are miracles given the lengths AB went to to try to keep me hidden. Nor do I blame those in authority for not looking out for me. I don't know why the police or social services didn't fully investigate when flags were raised. All I can think is that we kept moving house, so they never got to catch up.

What troubles me more is *why* it happened in the first place. It's too easy to say AB was evil or that it was an 'evil spell': these are childish concepts, more suited to a storybook than to real life. Nor was it Communism, as I'd concluded while in the cult: I've since met people who call themselves Communists who are not like that at all. It *always* troubled me because I knew – and loved – these people as individuals. When I was cooking with Josie or hugging Oh or even having a trip to a museum with AB, these were pleasurable activities with people I could genuinely see had good hearts. Yet when they got together, something about the group dynamic sparked a conflagration that turned these pleasant individuals into a many-headed monster. I have never got to the bottom of it, but I still want to understand. One day, I might study psychology, perhaps even do a degree in it, and maybe that will shed some light.

Josie did not take part in the documentary. After the trial, she moved out of Palm Cove and returned to London. I read in a newspaper that she's moved back in with Chanda, but I don't know if that's true. She tries her hardest to prove herself to them, campaigning on AB's behalf against the 'miscarriage of justice'. She says he has been imprisoned on false charges – essentially, that I'm lying, when she knows *everything* I have said is true. Still, she treats me as a child, portraying me as a pawn in the Metropolitan Police's plans to bring about AB's downfall. She feels no remorse for what happened to me; she believes I was kept in my cage for better things: that I was being kept safe until the Overt arrived and Bala ruled the world.

Her campaign is annoying, and laughable, and tragic. No matter what evidence is shown to her, and there is plenty, she just can't get past the mindset that she holds. My main emotions towards her now are pity and compassion.

I do wonder what she will do when AB, inevitably, dies. He is nearly seventy-eight years old now and – despite what he always preached – he will not live for ever. He used to say only bad people died, so will Josie think less of him then? I think that's optimistic. She'll probably say that the fascist state are lying and he is still alive; or that he'll one day be resurrected; or – most likely of all – that my 'crimes' killed him.

When the day comes, I don't think it will bother me, one way or the other. Before he passes on, I would like him to acknowledge the harm he did to me and apologize for it – for his sake as much as mine – but I don't hold out much hope of that happening. I can't see prison rehabilitating him; I wouldn't be surprised if he was trying to create another cult in there. I still feel uncomfortable about him being in prison; after spending thirty years in captivity myself, I can hardly wish that on anyone else, not even my worst enemy. I just wish he had listened to my requests for freedom and none of this had happened. But at the same time I am glad to know that the law deems what he did a crime.

He still doesn't think so, though. And with people like Josie hanging around him who uphold his narcissism, I doubt he will ever change his view about what's happened. He will never be forced to ask questions of himself so long as he has the comfort of people telling him he did everything right.

Unlike him, I have to face up, on a daily basis, to the reality of what he did. To this day, I walk slowly and cautiously, not trusting my body to take me where I need to go because it does not have the full capacity to do it. It's frustrating not to be able to run for a bus; to be anxious all the time in case I trip and fall. Sometimes I feel I need a stick to lean on, but that seems like something only elderly people would do, so I put on a brave face.

I remain very scared about what people think of me, too, which can sometimes make the window glass feel like it's still there, though it happens a lot less than it used to. I'm often afraid of saying the wrong thing, so I struggle with social anxiety. I find I'm waiting for others to mock or reject me. To this day I am terrified of the sound of angry shouting; it makes me feel faint with fear. I still jump at any loud, sudden movement, my instincts reacting to the way AB used to dart across the room to smash me in the face. And even though I've got a small selection of close friends now, I rarely cry in front of them because old habits die hard. To be beaten from birth for my tears has meant it's been difficult to let those emotions come back: they are so deeply suppressed that I have struggled to find a way to release them.

My information processing also continues to be a problem. I'd like to get a job, but I can't right now because people expect you to do everything fast, and I am unable. I don't work at the speed that others do: it's beyond my brain to keep up. To my dismay, I've also discovered that I won't be able to become a train driver because of my diabetes: they don't employ drivers with the condition just in case they lose control. I was devastated when I found that out; I still get tears in my eyes sometimes at the station when I hear the announcements and see the trains pulling out. *My God*, I always think, *how I would just love to do that, to go all over the place driving those trains.*

But despite my ongoing challenges, I hold no grudges. The only person affected by that would be me. Thirty years of my life were stolen by Bala and I'm not going to let what happened eat up any more of it. Life is too short: I don't want to spend it angry and hateful. I don't want to waste it in that way.

My favourite quotation is 'We are all walking each other home' by Ram Dass. We all need care and kindness and acceptance for who we are. I can't stand harsh, condemning, judgemental attitudes to other people. I despise the way we have a tendency to focus on the wrong things people do and pillory them for it, rather than focusing on their achievements. It reminds me of how the cult worked: no matter how devoted a member was, if they made a 'mistake' in Bala or Chanda's eyes, that would be all that would be remembered about them and everything else they did would be negated. It makes me profoundly sad to see anyone treated like that. I am passionate about everyone having a second chance, no matter who they are or what they are meant to have done. Everyone deserves the chance to be loved and accepted, and live their lives free of bullying and persecution. Rather than judging and condemning others, we need to love them – to help them become the best versions of themselves.

That applies to AB too. If my father could bring himself to acknowledge what he has done, I would be open to a relationship with him, as long as it was on equal terms. If he could bring himself to admit what he did was harmful, then we could begin to move forward. He is my only close blood relative left alive and that means something to me, although I've learned since escaping that water can often be thicker than blood. Perhaps a reunion is a goal for us to work towards – but the first step towards that has to come from him.

In August 2017, I traced the familiar route to college to pick up my exam results. I was still doing foundation courses in maths, but that summer I had sat my first major national examination in GCSE

English. As I walked my slow walk, I told myself, *You can always do it again.* I was convinced I had failed.

My bespectacled teacher, Gill, met me there. I thought from her reassuring manner I must have done OK, but nothing prepared me for the shock of opening that envelope to see the results.

I had received a 9 grade: the highest possible.

That felt like a real achievement. I was so proud of it, and it made me feel a lot more confident than I was before. To have done that makes me think: *Maybe I can do more things!* I feel excited about all that the future has to offer. I messaged Yvonne to let her know and she replied: 'Fantastic news! Well done, you star!'

It was still so refreshing to hear a simple 'Well done' and not a chastisement for self-love, nor a claim that AB must take the credit. This was something *I* had done, not him.

Yet the achievement also made me think: *what might have been . . . ?* If I'd taken my GCSEs when I was sixteen instead of thirty-four, what might I be doing now? What might I have achieved in the world if I'd lived a less unusual life?

But there is no use crying about what has been lost: you just have to make the best of what you have. Life is a journey and everybody has different experiences. I don't think it's right to indulge in feeling sorry for myself because everybody has their own cage in a way. Those who seemingly have everything going for them may suffer from depression; others are blocked by bad relationships or bad bosses or ill health . . . So many things can happen in a life. We all have our own unique journey. I believe that everything happens for a reason.

So I'd like to use my experiences to help people, as best I can. Maybe some good can come of them then. I'm passionate about helping others: I don't want anyone else to feel as isolated or mis-understood as I did all the time. I'd like, perhaps, to do some public speaking to spread my message far and wide. I'm strongly against censorship – because of the years of censorship in the cult, where not only my voice but my very self was silenced. In addition, I am an active advocate for civil liberties and freedom of expression. I'm still inspired by Lord Longford and aspire to bring about social reform. There are lots of wrongs in the world that need addressing; too many people living in their own Dark Towers. I'd like to give my voice to that and say loudly: 'Don't treat people badly.'

For that has been the only disappointment about escaping; the only thing that has not lived up to my expectations about the outside world. I thought when I left the cult that I was leaving behind the nastiness that people do to one another; I'd hoped out here that everybody would be nice and kind and behave properly towards their fellow men. To discover that people are just as unkind – albeit in a different way – has been bitter. It really upsets me. I remember I read a review of a horror novel in the Collective once: it said that however sinister the characters in the story were, nothing was more horrible than human nature. It hurts to realize that reviewer was right; it pains me to see people hating each other. There's nothing I despise more than bullying. Whenever I witness it, I want to protect the person under attack.

And I try to. I try every day. I try to be kind to everybody. I try always to take a balanced view. It's small steps, but I know from experience that small steps can sometimes lead to very big journeys.

In some ways, I'm even grateful for the unique outlook my life has given me. I hear people complaining every day about the most immaterial things – they want a better car or phone or house or job – but I am just glad to be alive. Those who have a lot going for them don't seem able to appreciate the tiny details of a happy life, but I do. To have your own front-door key; to be able to open a window; to be able to step out into a nice breeze; to talk to those you'd like to: these are the things I treasure, which most people take for granted, which make me grateful and thankful for my life.

I find freedom has infiltrated every aspect of it. I feel so comfortable in my own skin now that I rarely even apply foundation any more. I wear sleeveless tops and dresses, and skirts without tights. I love to sunbathe in the summer and now have a lovely, natural sun-kissed glow. My hair is also thick and healthy. I love colouring it and trying out different looks. The ability to *change*, where before I was always static, is one I continue to cherish.

No longer do I struggle to make a choice. When it comes to choosing a meal in a restaurant now, I always select something new because I like to try different things and there are so many options that I haven't yet savoured. It doesn't matter if I don't like it – because I can always have something different next time.

My desire to try new things reaches well beyond restaurants. I want to learn to swim – and drive. I don't know if my processing issues will be a problem with the latter, but I'm going to give it a go. How funny it would be if I ended up riding a motorcycle, like that man I loved to watch in Wembley!

I also want to travel. I haven't yet got a passport, but it's in the pipeline. On my bucket list are Ireland, Italy, Austria and America. My ultimate dream is to feed hummingbirds in the United States. I've seen it on YouTube videos and I think it would be heavenly if I could do that. I'm excited about making new memories.

On the night I got my exam results, a group of us went to the pub to celebrate. Gill made a short speech and said how proud she was of me – and everyone applauded! To hear that sound ringing in my ears and know it was in honour of my achievement was so special to me. From that little girl who was being held captive to *this* . . . But in a weird way, I didn't really think of Prem. I don't feel like her any more: I feel like a different person. Perhaps I'm like a snake, shedding skins. I have left Prem far behind me now.

The pub was a venue that I held very dear. For Gill ran a regular poetry night there and earlier that year I had stood on the stage and read the poems I'd written in the Collective aloud to the gathered audience. That had given me a fantastic feeling, because I'd once been certain those words would die with me, but now they were winging their way into the world. It was a feeling beyond any words.

Though I enjoyed the open mic nights, and would still like to write in the future, I'm not writing much poetry at present. I'm too happy, I think! It was my miracle medicine but now I have been cured. Yet reading and writing still mean the world to me. I'm well aware that if I hadn't been literate, my life would have been very different. Without my secret-reading, I'd never have seen the light. Without my writing, I'd never have stayed sane. A lot of people have asked me how I managed to survive, and the answer is reading, writing and imagining. Without all that, I'd still be in the cage.

The fact that I'm not still feels like a miracle. I have no favourite memory or day of being free because every day is marvellous: I am just so happy not to be where I was. Every hour of my day holds a treasure. Sometimes, I still stare at my front door from the inside and remember what it was like when I was unable to open it. These days, I keep my precious door key looped on a keyring that is graced with a four-leaf clover. I know, every time I use it, that I am lucky indeed.

On warm days, I stand at the window and relish being able to open it at will. I love those sunny days because my eyes don't hurt half as much as they used to, in fact they hardly hurt at all and now I can often go out into the bright light without having to wear sunglasses. My flat doesn't have a garden, but there are grounds, and the knowledge that I can step out into them at any time, whenever I please, is the best feeling in the world.

Walk with me now, as I open that door and step out into the sunshine. I stand on the green grass and look up into the sky. There's a bird above our heads, soaring through the iridescent morning. Its wings are wide and many-feathered. It knows exactly what to do.

So do I. I shake my own wings back from my shoulders. *See how they shine* . . . It took me time to grow them back, but they keep me airborne now, wherever I choose to go. I hover on my tiptoes. I stare up at the sky. I leap and I shimmy . . . and I fly.

Out beyond ideas
of wrongdoing and rightdoing,
there is a field.
I'll meet you there.

Jelaluddin Rumi, 13th century

ABOUT THE AUTHOR

Katy Morgan-Davies now lives and studies in Leeds. Every day, in every small way, she relishes her freedom. She hopes that in sharing her story she will inspire others to speak out about the oppression they suffer. Her ambition for the future is to help people, and to stop anyone from feeling as sad and lonely as she did for so many years.